Communications
in Computer and Information Science ￼ 2001

Rationale

The CCIS series is devoted to the publication of proceedings of computer science conferences. Its aim is to efficiently disseminate original research results in informatics in printed and electronic form. While the focus is on publication of peer-reviewed full papers presenting mature work, inclusion of reviewed short papers reporting on work in progress is welcome, too. Besides globally relevant meetings with internationally representative program committees guaranteeing a strict peer-reviewing and paper selection process, conferences run by societies or of high regional or national relevance are also considered for publication.

Topics

The topical scope of CCIS spans the entire spectrum of informatics ranging from foundational topics in the theory of computing to information and communications science and technology and a broad variety of interdisciplinary application fields.

Information for Volume Editors and Authors

Publication in CCIS is free of charge. No royalties are paid, however, we offer registered conference participants temporary free access to the online version of the conference proceedings on SpringerLink (http://link.springer.com) by means of an http referrer from the conference website and/or a number of complimentary printed copies, as specified in the official acceptance email of the event.

CCIS proceedings can be published in time for distribution at conferences or as post-proceedings, and delivered in the form of printed books and/or electronically as USBs and/or e-content licenses for accessing proceedings at SpringerLink. Furthermore, CCIS proceedings are included in the CCIS electronic book series hosted in the SpringerLink digital library at http://link.springer.com/bookseries/7899. Conferences publishing in CCIS are allowed to use Online Conference Service (OCS) for managing the whole proceedings lifecycle (from submission and reviewing to preparing for publication) free of charge.

Publication process

The language of publication is exclusively English. Authors publishing in CCIS have to sign the Springer CCIS copyright transfer form, however, they are free to use their material published in CCIS for substantially changed, more elaborate subsequent publications elsewhere. For the preparation of the camera-ready papers/files, authors have to strictly adhere to the Springer CCIS Authors' Instructions and are strongly encouraged to use the CCIS LaTeX style files or templates.

Abstracting/Indexing

CCIS is abstracted/indexed in DBLP, Google Scholar, EI-Compendex, Mathematical Reviews, SCImago, Scopus. CCIS volumes are also submitted for the inclusion in ISI Proceedings.

How to start

To start the evaluation of your proposal for inclusion in the CCIS series, please send an e-mail to ccis@springer.com.

Nur Haryani Zakaria · Nur Suhaili Mansor ·
Husniza Husni · Fathey Mohammed
Editors

Computing and Informatics

9th International Conference, ICOCI 2023
Kuala Lumpur, Malaysia, September 13–14, 2023
Revised Selected Papers, Part I

 Springer

Editors
Nur Haryani Zakaria 🆔
Universiti Utara Malaysia
Sintok, Malaysia

Nur Suhaili Mansor 🆔
Universiti Utara Malaysia
Sintok, Malaysia

Husniza Husni 🆔
Universiti Utara Malaysia
Sintok, Malaysia

Fathey Mohammed 🆔
Sunway University
Selangor, Malaysia

ISSN 1865-0929   ISSN 1865-0937 (electronic)
Communications in Computer and Information Science
ISBN 978-981-99-9588-2   ISBN 978-981-99-9589-9 (eBook)
https://doi.org/10.1007/978-981-99-9589-9

This Springer imprint is published by the registered company Springer Nature Singapore Pte Ltd.
The registered company address is: 152 Beach Road, #21-01/04 Gateway East, Singapore 189721, Singapore

Paper in this product is recyclable.

Preface

This year's International Conference on Computing and Informatics (ICOCI 2023) conference proceedings, centered around the theme "Nurturing an inclusive digital society for a sustainable nation," reflect the ever-evolving intersection of technology and society. The exploration of how we can harness digital innovation to foster sustainability, unity, and growth underscores our shared commitment to shaping a better digital landscape for our nations and the world.

The dedication and enthusiasm demonstrated by contributors from various countries highlight the significance of the addressed topics. Congratulations and appreciation are extended to all authors and presenters for their valuable contributions to this intellectual discourse.

As these proceedings find their place in our esteemed publication venues, they mark the continuation of the journey of knowledge dissemination. The enriched understanding and insights contained within these works pave the way for future research and innovations, contributing to a positive ripple effect that extends beyond the confines of this conference and into our societies.

The sub-themes of this year's conference proceedings are Digital Entrepreneurship and Innovation, Digital Healthcare and Well-Being, Digital Media and Information Literacy, Education Transformation through Technology, Ensuring Cybersecurity and Privacy, Harnessing Technology for Sustainable Development, and Navigating AI Development and Deployment. All these sub-themes serve as focal points for the exploration of diverse facets within the digital landscape.

This comprehensive exploration reflects the global perspective embedded in our discussions, showcasing the collaborative effort of minds from various corners of the world. The rich diversity of ideas and experiences brought forward by our contributors enriches the depth of understanding in each sub-theme.

We received a total of 134 paper submissions, a testament to the widespread interest and engagement in the topics under consideration. Through a rigorous double-blind review process, each paper was meticulously evaluated by at least 3 reviewers. Out of the submissions, 55 papers were selected for inclusion in these proceedings, representing the highest standards of academic rigor and relevance.

We sincerely hope that the knowledge shared within the pages of these conference proceedings serves as a robust foundation for future advancements and positive change in our ever-evolving digital societies. May the insights contained herein inspire further exploration, innovation, and collaboration, leading us towards a more inclusive, sustainable, and digitally connected future.

Warm regards,

Nur Haryani Zakaria

ICOCI 2023 Committee

Patron

Mohd. Foad Sakdan   Universiti Utara Malaysia

Advisor

Osman Ghazali   Universiti Utara Malaysia

Conference Chair

Norliza Katuk   Universiti Utara Malaysia

Vice-chair

Nur Azzah Abu Bakar   Universiti Utara Malaysia

Treasurer

Aniza Mohamed Din   Universiti Utara Malaysia

Secretary

Alawiyah Abd Wahab   Universiti Utara Malaysia

Finance and Sponsorship

Mazni Omar   Universiti Utara Malaysia
Norliza Katuk   Universiti Utara Malaysia

Secretariat

Alawiyah Abd Wahab	Universiti Utara Malaysia
Nur Azzah Abu Bakar	Universiti Utara Malaysia

Logistics and Accommodation

Suwannit Chareen Chit Sop Chit	Universiti Utara Malaysia

Paperwork and Proceedings

Nur Haryani Zakaria	Universiti Utara Malaysia
Husniza Husni	Universiti Utara Malaysia
Fathey Mohammed	Sunway University, Malaysia
Nur Suhaili Mansor	Universiti Utara Malaysia

Promotion and Publicity

Syamsul Bahrin Zaibon	Universiti Utara Malaysia
Azizi Abas	Universiti Utara Malaysia

International Technical Committee

Mario Jose Divan Koller	Intel, Argentina
Bakr Ahmed Taha	Universiti Kebangsaan Malaysia, Malaysia
Fateh Seghir	University Ferhat Abbas Setif 1, Algeria
Boubakeur Annane	University Ferhat Abbas Setif 1, Algeria
Adel Alti	University Ferhat Abbas Setif 1, Algeria
Shahzad Qaiser	Flextronics International (Flex), Austria
Safaet Hossain	City University, Bangladesh
Yong Wu	Institute of Applied Physics and Computational Mathematics, China
Lo Man Fung	University of Hong Kong, China
Sunil Kumar	Amity University, Noida, India
G. S. Pradeep Ghantasala	Chitkara University, India
Chetna	Chitkara University, India
Sanjoy Kumar Debnath	Chitkara University, India
Ankit Bansal	Chitkara University, India

Nazeer Unnisa Qurishi	Muffakham Jah College of Engineering and Technology, India
Ali M. Abdulshahed	Misurata University, India
Pooja Gupta	Parul University, India
Prateek Agrawal	Lovely Professional University, India
Gulfam Ahamad	Baba Ghulam Shah Badshah University, India
Prashant Johri	Galgotias University, India
M. A. Ansari	Gautam Buddha University, India
Swagata Dey	Bhairab Ganguly College, India
Venkatesh Gauri Shankar	Manipal University Jaipur, India
Bali Devi	Manipal University Jaipur, India
Vikas Kamra	Krishna Institute of Engineering and Technology, India
Lalit Kumar	Galgotias University, India
R. Raja Subramanian	Kalasalingam Academy of Research and Education, India
Shrddha Sagar	Galgotias University, India
Vikram Kumar	Indian Institute of Information Technology Una, India
Susama Bagchi	Chitkara University, India
P. Sardar Maran	Sathyabama Institute of Science and Technology, India
Amit Kumar Mishra	Jain University, India
Ade Novia Maulana	Islamic State University of Sulthan Thaha Saifuddin Jambi, Indonesia
Apri Siswanto	Universitas Islam Riau, Indonesia
Abdullah	Universitas Islam Indragiri, Indonesia
Tito Sugiharto	Universitas Kuningan, Indonesia
Rio Andriyat Krisdiawan	Universitas Kuningan, Indonesia
Erlan Darmawan	Universitas Kuningan, Indonesia
Evizal Abdul Kadir	Universitas Islam Riau, Indonesia
Yeffry Handoko Putra	Universitas Komputer Indonesia, Indonesia
Waleed Khalid Al-Hadban	Charmo University, Iraq
Athraa Jasim Mohammed	University of Technology, Iraq
Suhaib Kh. Hamed	Universiti Kebangsaan Malaysia, Malaysia
Mohammed Rashad Baker	Kirkuk University, Iraq
Firas Mahmood Mustafa Zakho	Duhok Polytechnic University, Iraq
Khalid Shaker	University of Anbar, Iraq
Arwa Alqudsi Ramadi	Universiti Kebangsaan Malaysia, Malaysia
Hussein K. Almulla	University of Anbar, Iraq
Roberto Vergallo	University of Salento, Italy
Mohd Nor Akmal Khalid	Japan Advanced Institute of Science and Technology, Japan

Mustafa Ali Abuzaraida	Misurata University, Libya
Bhagyashree S. R.	ATME College of Engineering, Libya
Mohd Hasbullah Omar	Universiti Utara Malaysia, Malaysia
Rubijesmin Abdul Latif	Universiti Tenaga Nasional, Malaysia
Mohd Helmy Abd Wahab	Universiti Tun Hussein Onn Malaysia, Malaysia
Husna Sarirah Husin	Universiti Kuala Lumpur Malaysian Institute of Information Technology, Malaysia
Aida Zamnah Zainal Abidin	Asia Pacific University of Technology & Innovation, Malaysia
Mohammed Gamal Alsamman	Universiti Utara Malaysia, Malaysia
Quah Wei Boon	Ministry of Higher Education, Malaysia
Ihsan Ali	University of Malaya, Malaysia
Abdulrazak Yahya Saleh	Universiti Malaysia Sarawak, Malaysia
Rajina R. Mohamed	Universiti Tenaga Nasional, Malaysia
Dalilah Binti Abdullah	Universiti Kuala Lumpur, Malaysia
Shahrinaz Ismail	Albukhary International University, Malaysia
Ruhaya Ab. Aziz	Universiti Tun Hussain Onn Malaysia, Malaysia
Syahrul Fahmy	University College TATI, Malaysia
Nooraida Samsudin	University College TATI, Malaysia
Norhafizah Ismail	Politeknik Mersing, Malaysia
Noormadinah Allias	Tunku Abdul Rahman University of Management and Technology, Malaysia
Zainab Attar Bashi	International Islamic University Malaysia, Malaysia
Ashikin Ali	Universiti Tun Hussein Onn Malaysia, Malaysia
Roziyani Setik	Universiti Selangor, Malaysia
Siti Fairuz Nurr Sadikan	Universiti Teknologi MARA, Malaysia
Safyzan Salim	Universiti Kuala Lumpur British Malaysian Institute, Malaysia
Marwan Nafea	University of Nottingham Malaysia, Malaysia
Irny Suzila Ishak	Universiti Selangor, Malaysia
Abdul Majid Soomro	Universiti Tun Hussein Onn Malaysia, Malaysia
Nor Masharah Husain	Universiti Pendidikan Sultan Idris, Malaysia
Nur Intan Raihana Ruhaiyem	Universiti Sains Malaysia, Malaysia
Nik Zulkarnaen Khidzir	Universiti Malaysia Kelantan, Malaysia
Nadilah Mohd Ralim	Universiti Kuala Lumpur, Malaysia
Kavikumar Jacob	Universiti Tun Hussein Onn Malaysia, Malaysia
Fawad Salam Khan	Universiti Tun Hussein Onn Malaysia, Malaysia
Muhammad Abdulrazaaq Thanoon	Universiti Kebangsaan Malaysia, Malaysia
Mohammad Jassim Mohammad	Universiti Kebangsaan Malaysia, Malaysia
Muazam Ali	Universiti Tun Hussein Onn Malaysia, Malaysia

Khairol Amali Ahmad	Universiti Pertahanan Malaysia, Malaysia
Juliana Aida Abu Bakar	Universiti Utara Malaysia, Malaysia
Mohd Nizam Omar	Universiti Utara Malaysia, Malaysia
Waqas Ahmed	Universiti Kuala Lumpur, Malaysia
Shakiroh Khamis	Universiti Utara Malaysia, Malaysia
Habiba Akter	Universiti Kuala Lumpur, Malaysia
Noris Mohd Norowi	Universiti Putra Malaysia, Malaysia
Siti Munirah Mohd	Universiti Sains Islam Malaysia, Malaysia
Sulaiman Mahzan	Universiti Teknologi MARA, Malaysia
Shahidatul Arfah Baharudin	Universiti Kuala Lumpur, Malaysia
Pantea Keikhosrokiani	Universiti Sains Malaysia, Malaysia
Renugah Rengasamy	Social Institute of Malaysia, Malaysia
Khalid Hussain	Albukhary International University, Malaysia
Massudi Mahmuddin	Unversiti Utara Malaysia, Malaysia
Mahmood Abdullah Bazel	Unversiti Utara Malaysia, Malaysia
Masitah Ghazali	Malaysia-Japan International Institute of Technology, Malaysia
Norhanisha Yusof	Politeknik Balik Pulau, Malaysia
Saiful Bakhtiar Osman	PNB Commercial Sdn. Berhad, Malaysia
Azliza Mohd Ali	Universiti Teknologi MARA, Malaysia
Norhasyimatul Naquiah Ghazali	Universiti Utara Malaysia, Malaysia
Yusmadi Yah Jusoh	Universiti Utara Malaysia, Malaysia
Jasni Ahmad	Universiti Utara Malaysia, Malaysia
Azlin Nordin	International Islamic University Malaysia, Malaysia
Abdullah Al-Sakkaf	Universiti Utara Malaysia, Malaysia
Kamsiah Mohamed	Universiti Selangor, Malaysia
Mudiana Mokhsin	Universiti Teknologi MARA, Malaysia
Suhaimi Abd-Latif	Otago Polytechnic, New Zealand
Sani Salisu	Federal University Dutse, Nigeria
Ijaz Ahmad	Majan University College, Oman
Ghaith Abdulsattar Al-Kubaisi	University of Technology and Applied Sciences, Oman
Qamar Ul Islam	Dhofar University, Oman
Abdulrazak F. Shahatha Al-Mashhadani	Sohar University, Oman
Muhammad Kashif Shaikh	Sir Syed University of Engineering and Technology, Pakistan
Mir Jamal Ud Din	Abbottabad University of Science & Technology, Pakistan
Najia Saher	Islamia University Bahawalpur, Pakistan
Tasneem Mohammad Ameen Duridi	Palestine Technical University, Palestine

Krzysztof Marian Tomiczek	Silesian University of Technology, Poland
Abdullah Hussein Al-Ghushami	Community College of Qatar, Qatar
Abayomi Abdultaofeek	Mangosuthu University of Technology, South Africa
Fathima Musfira Ameer	South Eastern University of Sri Lanka, Sri Lanka
Mohammed Ahmed Taiye	Linnaeus University, Sweden
Sasalak Tongkaw	Songkhla Rajabhat University, Thailand
Abdulfattah Esmail Hasan Abdullah Ba Alawi	Ataturk University, Turkey
Mehmet Nergiz	Dicle University, Turkey
Huseyin First	Dicle University, Turkey
Ismail Rakip Karas	Karabuk University, Turkey
Mehmet Sirac Ozerdem	Dicle University, Turkey
Evi Indriasari Mansor	Abu Dhabi School of Management, UAE
Hamzah Alaidaros	Al-Ahgaff University, Yemen
Munya Saleh Ba Matraf	Hadhramout University, Yemen
Abdullah Almogahed	Taiz University, Yemen
Abdulaziz Yahya Yahya Al-Nahari	UNITAR International University, Malaysia
Ridhima Rani	Chitkara University, India
Hani Mizhir Magid	Al Furat Al Awsat Technical University, Iraq
Rohaida Romli	Universiti Utara Malaysia, Malaysia
Shaymah Akram Yasear	Al-Qasim Green University, Iraq
Mohd Hafizul Afifi Abdullah	Universiti Teknologi Petronas, Malaysia

Contents – Part I

Digital Media and Information Literacy

Navigating AI Development and Deployment

Harnessing Technology for Sustainable Development

Contents – Part II

Education Transformation Through Technology

Digital Entrepreneurship and Innovation

Ensuring Cybersecurity and Privacy

Key Issues in Cybersecurity Implementation in Government Agencies: A Case Study in Jakarta Smart City

R. G. Guntur Alam[1(✉)], Huda Ibrahim[2] ⓘ, and Ismail Rakip Karas[3] ⓘ

[1] Sistem Informasi, Fakultas Teknik, Universitas Muhammadiyah Bengkulu, Bengkulu, Indonesia
`rggunturalam@umb.ac.id`
[2] School of Computing, Universiti Utara Malaysia, 06010 Sintok, Kedah, Malaysia
[3] Computer Engineering Department, Demir Celik Campus, 78050 Karabuk, Turkey

Abstract. Information Security Governance has become one of the main focus areas of government management because of its importance in protecting the overall information assets of government organizations. The Cybersecurity Governance Framework that is applied in the government environment should ideally follow the flow of government management and bureaucracy. Government management and bureaucracy directives are usually interpreted, disseminated, and implemented through a series of policies related to cybersecurity. Policies should ideally be implemented from the policy-making level to the operational level, where they are eventually being implemented. Implementing cybersecurity will involve many stakeholders which are regulated by rules and regulations. This study reports on follow-up and interviews of key actors/informants in Jakarta Smart City (JSC). Initial experience shows that the implementation of cyber security in JSC must follow the flow of the prevailing government bureaucracy. Three factors were involved in implementing bureaucracy-based cybersecurity: Legal Fundamental for Cybersecurity Management, Security Management, and Cybersecurity Stakeholders.

Keywords: Information Security · Security management · Security Framework · Security Bureaucracy

1 Introduction

At the beginning of the twenty-first century, cyber-based threats added a new dimension to understanding security threats from the previous century. Advances in information and communication technology (ICT), especially those based on the internet, have led almost everyone to utilize and use it in various ways. This implies that both governmental and non-governmental entities possess the capability to pose threats to network disruption, as attributing actions in cyberspace to specific perpetrators be-comes challenging, especially when actions occurring in one location can have worldwide consequences [1].

N. H. Zakaria et al. (Eds.): ICOCI 2023, CCIS 2001, pp. 3–16, 2024.
https://doi.org/10.1007/978-981-99-9589-9_1

The advent of a wave of information and communication technology transformation is a viable choice for providing excellent service to city people [2]. Techno-logical developments have driven expansion in the provision of innovative offerings by individuals and groups to ensure the growth of smart cities. In general, Information Technology is changing our daily life and trans-forming the city into a smart and sustainable way to make the economy, environment, quality of life, control, and express the city more efficient and effective.

The operation and implementation of a smart city relies heavily on cloud computing that provides storage and delivering all information. Cloud computing is not only a source of information but also a place to store data and a place for users to connect; simultaneously, a huge security risk is unavoidable [3].

According to [4] cybersecurity in smart cities is determined by three actors: people, process, and technology as below:

1. People - refer to people with a smart vision and a relationship with smart cities as users, policymakers, planners, and service providers.
2. Process - about value systems and behavioral guidelines that support the implementation of cybersecurity in smart cities, including multi-stakeholder partnerships, regulations, and policies that are in line with local wisdom from the local area.
3. Technology - focuses on cybersecurity technology infrastructure, includes cloud computing infrastructure, internet of things (IoT), machine to machine (M2M), and various application services provided by smart cities.

In general, all national cyber security policies aim to defend cyberspace from enemies while at the same time developing cyber resilience. However, the topography of cyber threats, the socio-political situation, security trends, traditions, and different levels of cyber awareness have led to significant differences in the cybersecurity tactics of different countries [5]. Although in general the goal of cyber security in various countries is the same to protect the cyber world from adversaries, many cyber security implementations experience different problems, fail to fulfill their objectives, and are not implemented properly, especially in developing countries [6]. [7] identify that regulatory factors, policy and legal issues, organizational structure, Cooperation, and local wisdom values cause the failure of cybersecurity implementation. Therefore, this study will explore in-depth the cybersecurity challenges in smart cities and the fac-tors involved. This study uses Actor-Network Theory [8] as a theoretical lens to explore phenomena in actor collaboration in networks involving humans and non-humans. The actor-network theory (ANT) is reviewed in the following section.

2 Theory Review

Actor-Network Theory (ANT) is an interdisciplinary theory spanning social science and technology created in the 1980s by Callon and Latour to analyze and understand numerous sorts of events [9]. According to [10], ANT is defined by three main principles: general symmetry (researchers are dedicated to treating hu-mans and non-humans equally), agnosticism (not siding with humans or non-humans), and free association (not separating humans and non-humans). As a result, ANT researchers must consider both human and non-human agents, analyze them from the same perspective, and treat them equally [11]. The moment of translation from the ANT viewpoint is frequently employed as a theoretical lens in information system studies [13]. ANT views humans and non-humans (such as data storage, concepts, papers, technology, or anything similar) as actors [9]. The purpose of the ANT deliberation on non-human actors is to study the potential and constraints of non-human actors' engagement in certain situations [14].

Technology cannot be separated from its social aspect therefore, the use of ANT is crucial in exploring the phenomenon of cybersecurity networks in Smart cities because smart cities involve information technology and social elements simultaneously as a heterogeneous socio-technical system [12].

3 Research Method

This research uses an interpretive case study based on ANT elements to explore in-depth the cybersecurity challenges in the smart city of Jakarta and the factors involved. Interpretive case studies are qualitative research that can be descriptive, interpretive, or evaluative used as an examination of certain phenomena, such as programs, events, processes, institutions, or social groups [20].

The philosophy of critical realism frames this research. Critical realism must go below the surface to understand and explain why things happen the way they are and speculate about the structures and mechanisms that underpin observed social events [15]. This research is a type of study that looks back at social phenomena, asks questions about their reality, and finds new sets of answers. The concern behind this research is to find out how the situation, obstacles, challenges, and elements in cyber security aspects in Jakarta Smart City (JSC). Many factors or actors are involved, potentially from elements of people, technology, processes, policies, finance, and many more.

A case study approach was used to collect data for this study, and an informal and semi-structured interview style was used. This method is adaptable as it allows the researcher to ask additional questions during and after the interview [21]. The main objective of this interview is to identify human and non-human elements in implementing cyber security in smart cities in Indonesia. The unit of analysis in this research is the network actor who implements cyber security in JSC. In analyzing the data, this study uses the concept of template analysis, which requires the researcher to create a list of codes (templates) that represent the themes identified in the textual data [22].

4 ANT Based Framework

ANT is rich in concepts and elements to support Information System research in under-standing the evaluation or planning of new IS projects based on a network of various human and non-human actors. Based on the elements of ANT, this study presents the framework for achieving the objectives of this research (see Fig. 1).

The framework developed based on ANT translation moments that represent interac-tions between actors. It focuses more on mutual determination between actors when they communicate. The translation involves a process of change that follows four moments, namely (a) problematization, (b) intervention, (c) enrolment, and (d) mobilization. Problematization requires the identification of actors and the establishment of OPP. Problematization involves i) identifying the issue or problem, ii) recognizing various actors through punctualized actors, iii) identifying the interests and roles of each actor, iv) determining the OPP, and v) identifying potential obstacles towards achieving the OPP.

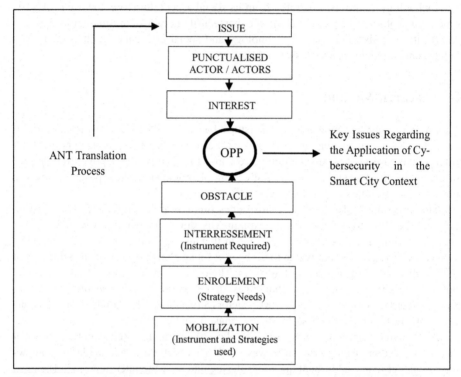

Fig. 1. Framework utilizing Actor-Network Theory for the examination of cybersecurity implementation network within JSC.

The following translation is the moment of interressment, to convince other actors to accept the role given by the main actor through the creation of an interressment mechanism. The next moment is enrolment, about determining a series of strategies as an actor-focused effort to define and connect various roles that allow other actors to accept the role assigned by the main actor. Mobilization is the last stage of translation, which includes the use of various methods by the focal actor to ensure that representatives or spokespersons of all actors act following the agreement and do not betray the proponent's interests.

5 Punctualization in Actor Networks

Before analyzing the following section regarding the inhibiting and supporting fac-tors for the cybersecurity implementation by the four translational moments, it is necessary to describe the network actors in the cybersecurity implementation in JSC. Therefore, this section will begin with the punctualization of opening each black box actor or punctualized actor by enlarging each black box and explaining its contents. The concept of punctualization allows the conversion of the entire network to a single point [16].

This concept helps reduce the complexity of the actor-network or enlarge it for deeper and more detailed investigations [19]. This research follows the main actors in the network of cybersecurity actors: the Director of JSC, The Special Capital Region (DKI) Jakarta Province Communication Informatics and Statistics Agency, and the Operational Executing Unit. The concept of punctualization presents the reasons and details for selecting actors in the following sections.

5.1 The Punctualized Actor of the Director of Jakarta Smart City

The Director of Jakarta Smart City performs the JSC system's planning, and manage-ment, as regulated in DKI Jakarta Governor Regulation Number 280 of 2014. Therefore, the Director of the JSC has sufficient authority to establish and develop the JSC. In 2020, through the Decree of the Governor of DKI Jakarta Number 17 of 2020, JSC was des-ignated as a technical implementing unit that implements the Financial Management Pattern of Regional Public Service Agencies (BULD). With the change of status to BLUD, JSC has more flexibility in managing finances without relying on the Regional Revenue and Expenditure Budget (APBD) and has the authority to establish partnerships to serve interests. Since turning into a BLUD, the initiator of JSC is the Director of JSC. Therefore, the Director of JSC can be identified as the main actor in this project.

As the main actor, the JSC director is responsible for coordinating all the actors in JSC. The first responsibility is to lead and coordinate the executors of tasks under him. Regarding cybersecurity, the JSC director leads the entire task force to work closely together to ensure that all Jakarta's data and information technology infrastructure is secure. Second, to coordinate and establish Cooperation with other parties from gov-ernment and private institutions to smooth JSC management. Third, report and account for all tasks at JSC. The Director of JSC is fully aware that to achieve good cybersecu-rity management. It is necessary to comply with applicable standards, regulations, and rules. Standardization, Regulation, and Rules can be categorized into non-human actors (processes). Rules and regulations become the foundation for focal actors to mobilize other actors, such as people and technology.

In short, the focal actor must associate with other actors, namely processes, people, and technology, to motivate or compel the relevant actors to enroll in the cybersecurity implementation actor-network. The JSC director can be defined as the main actor in the actor-network. The process is used as the basis and rule to mobilize the people in managing the technology to implement cyber security in JSC.

5.2 The Punctualized Actor of the DKI Jakarta Province Communication, Informatics, and Statistics Agency

The DKI Jakarta Province Communication, Informatics, and Statistics Agency is the agency that regulates matters of communication, informatics, statistics, and coding. In carrying out its duties, this institution is led by a head of service who is under and responsible to the governor through the regional secretary (DKI Jakarta governor regulation No. 265/2016). The functions of this institution include:

a. Prepare strategic plans, work plans, and budgets for the DKI Jakarta Provincial Communication Information and Statistics agency.
b. Develop and formulate communication, informatics, statistics, and coding policies.
c. Develop norms, standards, procedures, and criteria in communication, informatics, statistics, and coding.
d. Provide technical guidance, supervision, monitoring, evaluation, and reporting on all activities, communications, informatics, statistics, and coding.

The agency has five areas, three secretarial divisions, and four technical service units. One of the technical service units is JSC (DKI Jakarta Governor Regulation No. 265/2016). In carrying out his duties, the director of JSC must comply with the regulations and policies that have been set and be responsible to the DKI Jakarta Provincial Communication Information and Statistics agency. In the eyes of the focal actor (director of JSC), the DKI Jakarta Provincial Communication Information and Statistics Agency is seen as a potential actor in cyber security implementation, therefore it is registered in the main actor-network. When this actor is zoomed in, it is seen that the agency has a role as a policymaker, coordinator of cyber security implementation, and governance. However, cybersecurity implementation at JSC is entirely the responsibility of the JSC director.

At this point, it can be concluded that this network of actors consists of: (1) the DKI Jakarta Provincial Communication Information and Statistics Agency, which plays a role in formulating rules, regulations, and standards for the successful implementation of cyber security, (2) Rules, regulations, and standards that is a non-human actor who becomes the reference for the focus actor (JSC director) in carrying out his duties.

5.3 The Punctualized Actor of the Operational Executing Unit

In carrying out his activities, the main actor (JSC director) cannot do all the work alone. The Director of JSC needs people who can assist him in carrying out his work. Based on DKI Jakarta Government Regulation Number 280 of 2014, the director of JSC was assisted by:

a. Administration Subdivision
b. Planning, Research and Development Implementing Unit
c. Operational implementing unit
d. Functional position subgroup

Of the four sections above, those directly related to cybersecurity are the operational implementing unit. The duties of the Operational Implementing Unit according to DKI Jakarta Government Regulation Number 280 of 2014 related to cyber security, include:

a. Develop standards and operational procedures for the implementation of JSC's information technology facilities and infrastructure.
b. Prepare plans for procurement and maintenance of JSC informatics facilities and infrastructure.
c. Carry out the process of providing, maintaining, and maintaining JSC's information technology infrastructure and facilities.
d. Monitor and evaluate the availability of the feasibility and readiness of JSC information technology infrastructure and facilities.
e. Implement JSC information technology management
f. Manage the JSC system/application and its infrastructure.
g. Collect, process, present, develop, and report data and information related to JSC.

From the explanation above, it is concluded that this network of actors consists of: (1) Operational Implementing Unit whose task is to assist the main actors in planning, implementing, and reporting for the successful implementation of cyber security, (2) rules, regulations, and standards which are non-humans actors become the foundation of this actor-network to work, and (3) technology that is the work object of this actor-network. The details of each punctualized actor are summarized in Table 1.

Table 1. Overview of the punctualized actor in cybersecurity implementation

Puctualized Actor	Actors	Interest	Obstacle
Director of JSC	Element of Process, People, Technology	- Negotiate, motivate, coordinate and then work with other punctulized actors - Initiation, implementation, monitoring and evaluation of cybersecurity	- Flexibility in budgets and collaboration - Freedom of governance for smart city development
The DKI Jakarta Province Communication, Informatics and Statistics Agency	Element of Process	- Prepare rules, regulations, and standards for the successful implementation of cybersecurity - Leadership in cybersecurity implementation	Must be assisted by other units to carry out the functions assigned by the governor
The Operational Executing Unit	People, Technology	- Implementing cyber security for public services in Jakarta Smart City - Improve cybersecurity in public services	Work according to the rules, regulations, and direction of the leadership

6   Setting Up Obligatory Passage Points

Obligatory Passage Point (OPP) refers to motivating actors to accept tasks and functions by focused actors who show interest and explain how the functions and tasks can help achieve their interests. However, in carrying out their duties, functions, and personal interests, all actors must overcome a series of obstacles [18]. Different actors have to deal with different problems. In the cyber security actor-network, all the main actors have their interests and constraints. The details of the punctualized actors in the network shown in Table 1 can be illustrated with the following OOP diagram (see Fig. 2).

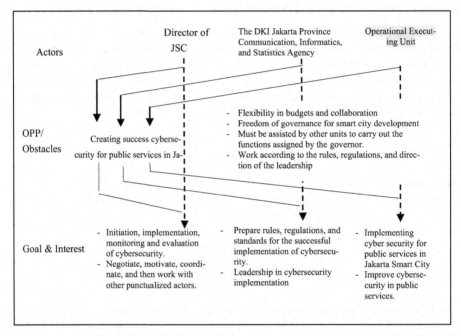

Fig. 2. The OPP of Actor-Network of cybersecurity in JSC

Figure 2 shows, first, the actor-network contains three main actors as previously described, (i) Director of JSC, (ii) The DKI Jakarta Provincial Communication Information and Statistics Agency, and (iii) Operational Executing Unit. Second, from the point of view of the focus actor, OPP is to create cybersecurity public services in JSC. Third, in achieving OPP, all actors will have their own interests. The JSC Director will carry out his functions in initiating, implementing, monitoring, and evaluating cybersecurity. The DKI Jakarta Provincial Communication Information and Statistics Agency will control cyber security in Jakarta, and the Operational Implementation Unit can improve cyber security in public services in Jakarta. Fourth, achieving this OPP will not be easy because each actor must overcome obstacles. The DKI Jakarta Provincial Communication Information and Statistics Agency cannot implement cybersecurity alone, so it involves other units to implement it. The Operational Implementing Unit cannot freely carry out its duties. It must comply with the leadership's, rules, regulations, and direction. Finally, if all the actors can overcome the obstacles, they will benefit as determined, and the actor-network mission will be complete. This OPP cannot perfectly unite all actors in the translation process, which results in the actor network's mission not being fully completed. The imperfections in completing the mission of the actor-network will be analyzed to find the factors that support and hinder the completion of the mission of the actor-network.

7   Interessement Moment

In the problematization process, the actors involved agreed to be included in the network. In practice, it is not guaranteed that they are all consistent in the network of actors, some of whom may think they are not worthy of joining because of their identity. Therefore, it takes a second moment, namely interrressement. Several tools were used to establish a balance of power that favored each actor in overcoming obstacles to passing the OPP. Referring to the network of cyber security actors at JSC, the instruments needed for the moment of interest are standardizations, Standard Operating Procedures, Laws and regulations, policies, and leader instructions.

Standardization is an instrument needed by non-human actors, especially in electronic systems for public services. It acts as a liaison between the focus actor and other actors and helps the focus actor in coercing and controlling other actors to perform the required activities in the actor network. Standard Operating Procedures are necessary tools for human and non-human actors, especially in software and hardware maintenance. If the network actor does not have this device, there is no good communication between the security system, hardware, and users. In other words, this device can help non-human actors to have a universal language to interact or communicate in the actor-network.

Laws and regulations are other significant instruments needed by a network of actors. Laws and regulations are the main handle of the focus actor (JSC Director) to lock all human actors in position. Like laws and regulations, policies are another crucial instrument a network of actors needs. Policies are very effective to use in imposing the interests of various actors in the network. Lead instruction is another tool used to conduct the interessement of several actors in the network.

8   Enrollment Moment

Enrollment is the third moment of translation, which refers to a set of strategies as actor-focused efforts to define and link various roles that allow other actors to be enrolled. This process relates to the transforming or moving intangible things such as ideas, concepts, and plans into something tangible in the real world [17]. The analysis of enrollment moments in this study is summarized in Table 2.

Table 2. Enrollment process summary

	Enrollment Moment			
	Process Aspect	People Aspect	Technology Aspect	Governance Aspect
ISSUE	A need for legal basic of cyber security development	People is the weakest link in the context of cybersecurity	Rapid technology is accompanied by increased risk of cybercrime interest	Regional Leaders determine information security governance
ACTORS	- Director of JSC - The DKI Jakarta Province Communication, Informatics, and Statistics Agency	- Director of JSC - The DKI Jakarta Province Communication, Informatics, and Statistics Agency - Operational Executing	- Director of JSC - The DKI Jakarta Province Communication, Informatics, and Statistics Agency - Operational Executing	- Director of JSC - The DKI Jakarta Province Communication, Informatics, and Statistics Agency
INTEREST	Align all actors' interests in procuring cybersecurity needs at JSC	- Maintaining the stability of the actor network	Negotiate with actors regarding security optimization	Providing cybersecurity governance solutions
OPP	Availability of legal basis for procurement of cyber security development needs	Creating a stable actors-network in aligning the interests of each actor	Availability of security devices in accordance to technological developments	Availability of references for the cybersecurity governance
OBSTACLES	- Cybersecurity management must refer to applicable laws and regulations - Cybersecurity in smart cities is still not considered a priority	Awareness Ego Sectoral Leadership Commitment Knowledge Habit and Behaviour	Limited budget for Procurement of security devices Security technology devices have not embraced cyber security by design	National cyber security governance master plan has not been developed
INTERESMENT MECHANISM	Instrument Used: - Presidential Regulation Number 95 of 2018 - Ministerial Regulation Number 4 of 2016	Instrument Used: Standardization Law and regulations Policy SOP Leader Instructions	Instrument Used: Standardization Law and regulations Policy SOP Leader Instructions	Instrument Used: Standardization Law and regulations Policy SOP Leader Instructions
ENROLLMENT MECHANISHM	Strategy Taken: -Conduct a study to establish the legal basis for the procurement of cyber security development needs -Include security in procurement as needed	Strategy Taken: Digital literacy - Applying the consequences of laws and regulations - Update knowledge regularly - Socialize the risk security - Automated periodic password changes	Strategy Taken: Conduct Proof of concept (POC) to negotiate with actors in the network to provide an understanding of how a security technology product can be used optimally	Strategy Taken: Provide own team to ensure the system built is safe and in accordance with the rules

9 Mobilization Moment

Mobilization includes the use of various methods by the focal actor to ensure that representatives or spokespersons of all actors' act under the agreement and do not betray the interests of the proponent. The following section describes the existence of several actors that remained stable during the mobilization of the JSC cybersecurity network.

9.1 Legal Fundamental of Cybersecurity Actor Network

To keep all actors aligned for a certain period on the interests of actor focus, controlling all activities of human and non-human actors is necessary. Control can only be carried out based on existing laws and regulations or other considerations that do not conflict with the rules. In the network of actors at JSC, the main actors have the freedom to determine policies in security governance. This policy setting aims to define in detail the policies used to control the implementation of security, from defining security requirements, implementing security to measuring security maturity. In deriving policies, the focused actor (director of JSC) should consider the purpose of establishing the JSC to align the policies made with the objectives of the JSC.

9.2 Security Policy Control

To mobilize the network, the main actors must comply with the central government's rules, regulations, and compliance requirements. The rules and regulations the central government set are usually general. To be implemented following the objectives of the JSC, the main actors must reduce these rules to policies that are directly related to security. Security policy control is under guard by the fundamentals of security management in a policy framework. Security standards and policies generated from general laws and regulations are part of the security framework, whereas security requirements are formed from compliance requirements. It can be concluded that security policy control is a security framework that includes security policies, security standards, and security requirements.

9.3 Security Implementation Control

Security implementation involves three components, namely people, technology, and process. Human resource managers and policymakers are part of the people. Policies, protocols, and guidelines that create a protective environment for safeguarding systems and data are process. While technology consists of hardware and software to protect systems and data from external and internal threats. Security implementation control in the people aspect, as explained in the enrollment moment is the main actor, focuses on overcoming problems related to awareness, sectoral ego, knowledge, leadership commitment, and the behavior of actors in the network. From the technological aspect, controlling the implementation of security is focused on improving network security. Efforts that have been made to improve security are improving the quality of the firewall from layer three to layer seven. In addition, the use of other technology devices using the latest version. In the process aspect, the main actor link to the activities carried out by the government in general. The process aspect includes all policies, protocols, standards, SOPs, and guidelines that create a protective environment to ensure the security of systems, technology, and data.

9.4 Evaluation and Measurement of Security Maturity

Security maturity evaluation and measurement are used to assess the overall security program and specific security domains. At JSC, the evaluation and measurement of security maturity begin with an audit of the system use. The audit was conducted on governance, end-to-end, and data storage aspects. The audit is carried out in two stages, internal audit by the JSC team and validation by external audit, invited auditors, or consultants. The results of this audit become an obligation to be corrected or become input for future security improvements. BSSN measured security maturity or national external security audit. This measurement is carried out in the partnership contract to measure mal protection and administration of electronic certificates. In addition, a government agency's information security governance system must be evaluated with the KAMI index (Information Security Index). The KAMI index is an application to evaluate the maturity level and completeness of the application of SNI ISO/IEC 27001:2009.

9.5 Collaboration and Cooperation

Collaboration and cooperation with other parties are needed to anticipate cyberattacks and respond quickly to cybersecurity incidents. Collaboration and cooperation carried out by JSC with BSSN, Other Units in Local Government Environments, Academics and Universities, and Security Professionals. Because the function of JSC is to provide services for all circles and agencies, JSC must collaborate on security matters with other units within the Regional Government. Together with academics and universities, cooperation is built to strengthen governance. University academics and experts will assist the JSC team in technical guidance related to cybersecurity governance. To deal with specific security incidents, the JSC team requires professional assistance when the incident occurs. Therefore, JSC is also working closely with security professionals. With BSSN, JSC cooperates concerning the use of electronic certificates.

10 Conclusion

This study has identified three sets of interrelated factors that are key to the implementation of cybersecurity in Jakarta Smart City, namely (1) Cyber Security Stakeholders, (2) Legal Fundamental for Cyber Security Management, and (3) Security Management. From the punctualized actors, two stakeholders related to cyber security were identified. These stakeholders are the DKI Jakarta Provincial Communication Information and Statistics Agency and the Director of JSC with the Operational executing Unit (Smart city management). The DKI Jakarta Provincial Communication Information and Statistics Agency is interested in preparing rules, regulations, and standards to implement cybersecurity successfully.

Through enrollment moments and mobilization moments, other stakeholders are identified. First BSSN, in terms of measuring security maturity or external security audits at the national level and the use of electronic certificates. Second, academics from various universities provide technical guidance related to cybersecurity governance. Third, security professionals in handle certain incidents that the smart city team has never handled. Fourth, co-operate with private companies to realize effective cybersecurity and protect smart cities from cyber-attacks most of the technology infrastructure is owned and operated by private companies.

The second factor identified is the Legal Fundamental for Cybersecurity Management. The implementation of cyber security must have a clear legal foundation. At the moment of interessement, two legal instruments were identified as guidelines for policy-makers in managing cyber security. These instruments are international security standards and laws. At the moment of mobilization, the JSC director reduced the general laws and regulations into policies at the technical level. In carrying out the derivation, the policies made by the director of JSC must be in line with the objectives of the JSC. Therefore, the purpose of the smart city has also been identified as the basis of cybersecurity management.

The third factor is security management. Security management controls three aspects: security policy control, security implementation control, and security audit and evaluation. Security Policy Controls are built into a security framework including security policies, standards, and requirements. Meanwhile, Security Implementation Control includes people, technology, and processes integrated into the implementation framework. Internal and external audits carry out evaluation and security audits at JSC. The JSC team takes up the internal audit, while the external audit invites an auditor or consultant to validate the results of the internal audit result.

Acknowledgement. We greatly appreciate the support from agencies like Universiti Utara Malaysia and University Muhammadiyah Bengkulu, as well as organizations like Cyber Security Malaysia (CSM) and Jakarta Smart City (JSC). Their cooperation was crucial for the success of our study.

References

1. Cavelty, M.D., Wenger A.: Cyber security between socio-technological uncertainty and political fragmentation. In: Cyber Security Politics, pp. 1–14. Routledge (2022)
2. Wu, J., Guo, S., Huang, H., Liu, W., Xiang, Y.: Information and communications technologies for sustainable development goals: state-of-the-art, needs and perspectives. IEEE Commun. Surv. Tutorials **20**(3), 2389–2406 (2018)
3. Zurita, G., Pino, J.A., Baloian N.: Supporting smart community decision making for self-governance with multiple views.In: García-Chamizo, J., Fortino, G., Ochoa, S. (eds.) Ubiquitous Computing and Ambient Intelligence. Sensing, Processing, and Using Environmental Information. UCAmI 2015. Lecture Notes in Computer Science(), vol. 9454, pp. 134-143. Springer, Cham (2015). https://doi.org/10.1007/978-3-319-26401-1_13
4. Piro, G., Cianci, I., Grieco, L.A., Boggia, G., Camarda, P.: Information centric services in smart cities. J. Syst. Softw. **88**(1), 169–188 (2014)

5. Nautinyal, L., Malik, P., Agarwal, A.: Cybersecurity system: an essential pillar of smart cities, 25–50 (2018)
6. Sen, R.: Challenges to cybersecurity: current State of affairs. Commun. Assoc. Inf. Syst. (2018)
7. Kabanda, S., Tanner, M., Kent, C.: Exploring SME cybersecurity practices in developing countries. J. Organ. Comput. Electron. Commer. **28**(3), 269–282 (2018)
8. Anindra, F., Warnars, H.S.H.L., Min, D. M.: Smart city implementation modelling in Indonesia with integration platform approach. In: 2018 International Conference on Information Management and Technology (ICIMTech), pp. 1–9. IEEE (2018)
9. Callon, M., Latour, B.: Unscrewing the big leviathan: how actors macro-structure reality and how sociologists help them to do so. Adv. Soc. Theor. Method.: Toward Integr. Micro Macro Sociol. (1981)
10. Cressman, D.: A brief overview of actor-network theory: punctualisation, heterogeneous engineering & translation. Published online (2009)
11. Callon, M.: The Sociology of an actor-network: the case of the electric vehicle. In: Callon, M., Law, J., Rip, A. (eds.) Mapping the Dynamics of Science and Technology, pp. 19–34. Palgrave Macmillan, London (1986). https://doi.org/10.1007/978-1-349-07408-2_2
12. Effah, J.: Mobilizing culture for e-business in developing countries: an actor network theory account. Electron. J. Inf. Syst. Dev. Ctries **52**(1), 1–18 (2012)
13. Ruikar, S., Chang, P.C.: Achieving network stability through convergence--case study of an e-government project using actor network theory. In: In 2012 45th Hawaii International Conference on System Sciences, pp. 2593–2602. IEEE (2012)
14. Müller, M., Schurr, C.: Assemblage thinking and actor-network theory: conjunctions, disjunctions, cross-fertilisations. Trans. Inst. Br. Geogr. **41**(3), 217–229 (2016)
15. Sarker, S., Sidorova, A.: Understanding business process change failure: an actor-network perspective. J. Manag. Inf. Syst. **23**(1), 51–86 (2006)
16. Law, J.: Notes on the theory of the actor network ordering, strategy and heterogeneity. Syst. Pract. **5**, 379–393 (1992)
17. Law, J., Callon, M.: The life and death of an aircraft: a network analysis of technical change. Shap. Technol. Build. Soc.: Stud. Sociotech. Change, 21–52 (1992)
18. Czarniawska, B.: Remembering while forgetting: the role of automorphism in city management in Warsaw. Public Adm. Rev. **62**(2), 163–173 (2002)
19. Callon, M.: Techno-economic networks and irreversibility. Sociol. Rev. **38**(1), 132–161 (1990)
20. Monteiro, E.: Monsters: from systems to actor-networks. Planet Internet (1999)
21. Baxter, P., Jack, S.: The qualitative report qualitative case study methodology: study design and implementation for novice researchers. Qual. Rep. **13**(2), 544–559 (2008)
22. King, N.: 21——using templates in the thematic analysis of text——. Essent. Guide Qual. Meth. Organ. Res., 256. (2004)

Large Scale Web Crawling and Distributed Search Engines: Techniques, Challenges, Current Trends, and Future Prospects

Asadullah Al Galib[✉] [ID], Md Humaion Kabir Mehedi, Ehsanur Rahman Rhythm,
and Annajiat Alim Rasel

Department of Computer Science and Engineering, BRAC University, Dhaka, Bangladesh
{asadullah.al.galib,humaion.kabir.mehedi,
ehsanur.rahman.rhyth}@g.bracu.ac.bd

Abstract. The heart of any substantial search engine is a crawler. A crawler is a program that collects web pages by following links from one web page to the next. Due to our complete dependence on search engines for finding information and insights into every aspect of human endeavors, from finding cat videos to the deep mysteries of the universe, we tend to overlook the enormous complexities of today's search engines powered by the web crawlers to index and aggregate everything found on the internet. The sheer scale and technological innovation that enabled the vast body of knowledge on the internet to be indexed and easily accessible upon queries is constantly evolving. In this paper, we look at the current state of the massive apparatus of crawling the internet, specifically focusing on deep web crawling, given the explosion of information behind an interface that cannot be extracted from raw text. We also explore distributed search engines and the way forward for finding information in the age of large language models like ChatGPT or Bard. Our primary goal is to explore the junction of large-scale web crawling and search engines in an integrative approach to identify the emerging challenges and scopes in massive data where recent advancements in AI upend traditional means of information retrieval. Finally, we present the design of a new asynchronous crawler that can extract information from any domain into a structured format.

Keywords: Web Crawling · Crawler · Distributed Systems · Search Engines · Deep Web Crawling · Large Language Models · Asynchronous Crawler

1 Introduction

The technology behind web crawling has come a long way since Google was first introduced in the late 1990s. According to the original PageRank paper [1], Google employed a distributed web crawler architecture to download content from hundreds of millions of web pages. Since then, the technology behind web crawlers has grown ever more complex to accommodate billions of existing websites [2].

N. H. Zakaria et al. (Eds.): ICOCI 2023, CCIS 2001, pp. 17–29, 2024.
https://doi.org/10.1007/978-981-99-9589-9_2

Even though crawling and related technologies have gone through tremendous innovations in the past decade, the ever-expanding and fluid nature of the internet means crawling tools and techniques need to stay on top of the current trends of the web to collect and aggregate information. Due to the explosion of various web technologies, most of the data on the internet now sits behind various search forms that can only be accessed using search queries. This adds another layer of complexity for the crawlers. Along with the current technological advancements in the field of large-scale web crawling, we also focus on deep web crawling, where crawlers need to interact with various web forms to access information. We explore and analyze research materials with a primary focus on old and new crawling techniques capable of withstanding the ever-growing data space. Distributed crawling techniques built on open-source tools show great promise for a future of decentralized indexing of vast amounts of data.

We look at the current status of distributed search engines and the challenges it faces in the era of big data. To consider the disruptive AI conversational agents like ChatGPT and Bard and to understand their implications on how people search for information on the web, we explore how these agents can upend the status quo of current search engines. Finally, we are proposing a new asynchronous web crawling technique that can be employed by small to medium organizations for domain-agnostic crawling needs that require data to be extracted from web pages with similar content architectures and stored in specific formats.

The *Introduction* describes the motivation and overall targets of the paper. In the *Related Work* section, we will explore previous survey works related to web crawling techniques and various architectures of distributed search engines. In the next section, *Crawling*, we will take a detailed look at various current crawling techniques and different scaling issues that crawlers need to deal with. In the *Distributed Search Engine* section, we will go through various architectural challenges and prospects of distributed search engines. In the section, *AI Conversational Agents*, we will discuss the implications of ChatGPT and other conversational AI agents for the domain of search engines and how we acquire information from the web. The section, *Domain-Agnostic Asynchronous Crawler,* proposes a new asynchronous crawler suitable for crawling sites of any domain, all of which share a common architecture. Finally, we will conclude with the utility and prospects of crawling in the age of AI and generated content.

2   Related Work

A comprehensive study of deep web crawling techniques is explained in [3]. The authors also highlight the lack of standards and evaluation metrics to measure the performance of deep web crawlers against some common datasets. They provide a framework to compare different deep web crawling algorithms and features to infer entry points for various user interfaces and search panels to initiate crawling. A systematic literature review of over 1488 articles on web crawling is conducted in [4]. Various crawling techniques such as universal, topical, and hidden or deep web crawlers are described here. The authors highlight the challenges of large-scale web crawling an [5] d a set of policies that web crawlers should adhere to so that servers do not get overwhelmed by the parallel requests of different crawlers. Paper [6] discusses efficiently crawling board sites and how they perform against traditional graph crawling techniques. The authors introduce a type of preferential crawler, Board Forum Crawling, designed explicitly for crawling forum sites efficiently. Traditional breadth-first crawling for forum sites struggles with spider-trap due to duplicate pages and noisy links for various user actions. In their preferential or topical crawler, authors describe a structured approach to crawling all the post pages on a forum site. The authors of [7] describe the challenges and learnings of a high-performance web crawler, Mercator, that is distributed, scalable, and extensible. In, the authors propose a distributed search engine based on a cooperative model, where local search engines reduce the update interval time as compared to a centralized search engine. Each local search engine maintains a local index by accessing files locally. A Hadoop-based distributed search engine is proposed in [4]. Due to the ever evolving and constantly growing internet size, a distributed search engine is proposed to reduce query time. Hadoop consists of two dimensions, the storage dimension and the processing dimension. The proposed system uses Hadoop Distributed File System or HDFS for storage, and for indexing and processing users' requests, MapReduce is used. This personalized distributed search engine presents an end-to-end model where crawling, extracting, indexing, and fetching results for users' queries are implemented in Hadoop. A detailed explanation of various crawlers as well as a comparison among crawlers in terms of applicability, usability, and scalability, can be found in [2].

3 Crawling

The essential components of a web crawler are - a list of URLs to start crawling from, an aggregator that collects web pages using the URLs from the initial list, and a parser that parses the content of web pages and adds new URLs in the initial list. The crawler keeps repeating this process until the crawling list is empty or some other thresholds are achieved [4]. In this section, we will focus on the recent advancements in the crawling field along with the challenges that arise as the size of the data grows.

3.1 Types of Crawlers

Based on the scope and type of information collected during crawling, crawlers can be divided into multiple categories, such as universal crawlers, topical crawlers, forum crawlers, and hidden or deep web crawlers [4].

As the internet grows rapidly, the vast majority of the world's accumulated information can be found hidden behind millions of databases that are only accessible through search panels or forms. To collect data from these hidden parts of the internet, a new type of crawler has emerged, called hidden or deep web crawlers. These crawlers need to generate queries for the search interfaces to acquire information buried in various databases and storage systems.

For the indexed data to be useful, it needs to stay updated as time passes. Instead of visiting new web pages, Incremental crawlers update existing and already crawled sites and remove various redundancies to increase storage efficiencies [8]. Running multiple instances of the crawler in a distributed architecture to minimize traffic load and scale horizontally is a required attribute of modern web crawlers [1].

3.2 Techniques

This section will explore emerging technologies and approaches for distributed and hidden web crawlers.

In a stand-alone crawler module, also known as centralized crawling, a single instance performs all required steps of crawling. While this approach is easy to implement and maintain, given the sheer scale of data, this approach is only suitable for simple use cases [9].

In a distributed system, each crawler instance is a complete crawling module equipped with the necessary tools to perform the end-to-end crawling task. Depending on how these individual modules are managed and run, distributed crawling can be divided into master-worker and peer-to-peer crawling. Distributed crawling is slightly different from parallel crawling. In parallel crawling, individual crawler instances reside in the same LAN, whereas crawler instances in the distributed architecture are scattered across different geographical locations [9].

The hybrid crawling architecture tries to combine the simplicity of centralized crawling with the scalability of distributed crawling. In this approach, URL queue management is centralized, and content fetching from the URLs is distributed across many instances [9].

In the master-worker mode of distributed crawling, a master node performs an orchestrator's job, where crawling tasks are managed and assigned to worker nodes to perform the actual crawling tasks. The master node manages the global URL list of pages to visit and assigns URLs to each crawler instance [10]. The master node can perform load balancing to avoid overwhelming crawler instances.

In a peer-to-peer architecture, crawler instances independently discover and visit web pages without a master node. Some disadvantages of this approach include - a lack of load balancing where one crawler may be downloading a huge number of pages, whereas other crawlers may not have a sufficient number of URLs to crawl data from.

3.3 Distributed Crawling Architectures

Some recent implementations of distributed crawling use various open-source crawling frameworks and combine those with the power of cloud services to build robust and scalable systems. Some of these approaches are described below:

Scrapy and Redis: Scrapy is an open-source crawling and scraping framework. Redis is an efficient, in-memory, and key-value data store that is used to manage the message queues used to assign tasks to crawler instances. The Scrapy-Redis distributed component can be used to crawl sites with semi-structured information efficiently [10, 11].

Container Clustering: This approach uses a docker container cluster that hosts the crawler instances. Kubernetes is used to orchestrate the clusters of distributed containers. Apache Kafka is used as the communication medium for the crawling instances [10].

Apache Nutch: Apache Nutch is an open-source, powerful, highly scalable, and configurable web crawler that can be customized in various ways to handle all sorts of web pages found on the internet. It uses Hadoop for data processing [12].

Apache Spark: Apache Spark is a highly scalable data processing framework that can quickly process large datasets. The ability of Spark to orchestrate data processing on extremely large datasets [13] makes it a good candidate for large-scale crawling. Based on the master-worker architecture, a distributed crawling system can be designed using Spark. A control node manages child crawling nodes, distributes crawling tasks to nodes, and keeps the crawled information up-to-date to prevent redundant crawling by child nodes [14].

A regular focused crawler can be enhanced by introducing a language model component in the architecture so that the crawler only processes sites containing actionable information for a given domain [4]. First, the machine learning classifier determines the site's category, and then a language model is used on the site's content to rank its usability for the task at hand [4].

3.4 Common Crawl

Common Crawl is an initiative where monthly crawled data is made accessible for the public to conduct research and analytical tasks. It publishes the crawled data using Amazon S3 [15]. Data from the March-April, 2023 archive contains around 3 billion web pages from 34 million domains [16]. Common Crawl uses Apache Nutch to run its web crawler in a distributed system and MapReduce to find potential crawling targets from the collected data [15]. Datasets crawled by Common Crawl have been used for training the GPT-3 large language model [17].

3.5 Challenges and Prospects

As the size of the internet keeps growing and web technologies are transforming rapidly, web crawlers at the heart of information gathering must adapt to new challenges. Some of the challenges facing modern web crawlers include -

Scale and Resource Utilization: As the number of web pages is increasing rapidly, crawlers, with finite resources, need to balance visiting new and relevant web pages and updating the index for existing crawled pages.

Hidden Web Crawling: As more and more websites adopt dynamic and user-friendly content that relies heavily on client-side scripting, it presents a new challenge for traditional crawlers that follow hyperlinks and fetch the content from those links. Identifying search panels and interfaces that can be used to crawl the deep web is a major challenge in deep web crawling.

Lack of Standards: Due to the lack of standards and agreed-upon policies, servers containing the web pages that are being crawled are at the mercy of the crawlers. Web crawlers can ignore the robots.txt file, which tells crawlers which pages to crawl and which to avoid. Aggressive crawling on a server can lead to poor performance for the real users of that particular server.

Ethical considerations: As more and more people are available online for most of their waking hours, as they upload and post information on various social media sites, online users' privacy and data protection are of major concern. It is now possible to deanonymize people using sophisticated crawling techniques even if their real identity is hidden behind some authentication protocols [18]. As crawling tools get more efficient and competent in discovering data in the deep web, users' privacy and, in some cases, their safety due to their political or social activism can be threatened using mass surveillance tools powered by large-scale invasive crawling.

Despite these major challenges, many optimization techniques can be applied to increase the efficiency of the crawlers. To identify more effective search panels or user interfaces for deep web crawling, advanced machine learning models can be applied to infer the usability of search interfaces or forms. In deep web crawling, AI can generate better queries to extract more data with few queries. Emerging cloud services could be used to make distributed crawling more efficient and cost-effective. To counter the unfair use of personal data and protect people's privacy, there should be proper regulations to prevent both private and public sectors from aggressive and indiscriminate crawling without respecting Robots Exclusion Protocols.

4   Distributed Search Engine

In a centralized search engine architecture, every component of the search engine is controlled by a central server. The search engine providers control the indexes of the web as well as the ranking algorithms that present users with the most relevant results per their algorithms. The concept of distributed or peer-to-peer search engines has emerged to democratize the web and create a community-built search engine [19].

4.1   Architectures

In a distributed or decentralized search engine, no single node controls the different components of the search engine. When using a search engine, users are primarily concerned about three things - the quality of the ranking of search results, low latency response, and a considerable amount of web pages being available in the index which powers the search results [20]. For distributed search engines to be useful in the real world, these constraints must be met in an efficient, scalable, and cost-effective way.

A P2P system, such as Gnutella, provides a simple keyword search mechanism that broadcasts the users' search queries over the entire overlay network. This approach is quite slow, even with a limited document size. To solve this issue, Distributed hash Table or DHT is introduced to store document links against some IDs [21].

YaCy (https://yacy.net/) implements a peer-to-peer distributed search engine where individual nodes participate in crawling and updating DHT.

4.2   Open-Source Search Engines

While the most popular search engines like Google, Bing, or Baidu are commercial projects, some powerful open-source indexing and search engine frameworks are used extensively to build search applications.

Apache Lucene: Lucene is a high-performance indexing and search engine library. Many websites use Lucene to implement their internal search engines. It indexes text documents and then, upon query, generates ranked search results from the indexed content [22]. For the data structure, Lucene uses an inverted index. To provide the auto-complete feature, Lucene uses an n-gram tokenizer.

Elasticsearch: Elasticsearch is another open-source distributed analytics and search engine built on Lucene [23]. It provides REST APIs to index and search relevant documents using highly configurable and advanced queries. Due to its distributed architecture using clustering of nodes, Elasticsearch can scale horizontally and rebalance indexes as necessary. It uses JSON as its document storage type [23].

4.3   Challenges and Prospects

Even though the idea of an open and censor-free web is very promising, there are major technical and practical challenges while running a highly scalable, distributed, and fault-tolerant search engine at the internet scale. Current implementations of P2P text-based searching using DHT works efficiently for a fraction of the actual size of the web. Two main issues regarding decentralized search engines are available storage on individual nodes considering the ever-expanding nature of the internet, and constraints on network bandwidth used during full-text searching on a P2P network [21]. Another challenge is reducing search queries' response time, given that multiple nodes with indexed data need to be queried before a result can be sent to the users. Since no central server controls the addition of new nodes, some adversarial entities can manipulate the crawled index and ranking of search results [19].

Recent advancements in blockchain technologies can be used to optimize different aspects of a distributed search engine, such as crawling, indexing, and storage [19]. Extensive research is also needed to prevent attacks on the P2P system from adversarial players.

5   AI Conversational Agents

The emergence of ChatGPT has taken the internet by storm. Since it was published in November 2022, ChatGPT has become one of the most popular sites on the web in just a couple of months [24].

ChatGPT is based on GPT-3, a large language model [17] trained on petabytes of data to produce human-like text.

5.1   Challenges to Traditional Search Engines

People have been using ChatGPT to generate text and as an interactive search engine to find information. While search engines return a list of web pages, these AI conversational agents provide information in a way that humans are more comfortable with. We need to keep in mind that the purpose of search engines is to parse users' queries, find relevant pages or documents, and finally rank the search results to provide high-quality responses that are beneficial to the users. Large language models generate a sequence of words with a starting prompt. Moreover, the models cannot access the most recent data since their training and cannot provide all sources that played a role in generating certain content.

The appeal of these conversational agents in finding information on the web stems from the fact that search engines cannot combine information from multiple sources and then aggregate it to produce a coherent and factually correct answer. Whereas these agents answer questions like another human expert would [25].

Due to the lack of reference materials for generated content, it is more difficult to ascertain the authenticity of generated content by these models.

5.2 Societal and Ethical Impacts

The world is already plagued by propaganda and disinformation abundant on social media sites. Since these models are trained on human-generated text in the first place, they may have inherent biases due to the training datasets. Producing disinformation will be much easier with human-like text and will exacerbate the already fragile social and political divides worldwide. Any task that is about generating text on a given topic now needs to be re-examined and re-evaluated. Various professional roles in the domain of content generation, whether article writers or programmers, will be transformed significantly. Prompt engineering, in other words, providing the correct starting sequence of words to generate the best possible output, will be a key skill in the coming days. Exams and evaluation criteria of all sorts need to be rethought in light of the ubiquity of these language models.

5.3 Future Prospects

A key area of research that needs to take place is to retain the sources of information generated by the language models and provide them as references to the users. Since people will be using these AI agents to find information on the web, further improvements can be introduced to incorporate recent events in the generated content and references. Much more attention should be given to de-bias the training datasets and shielding the models from being tricked into generating harmful and dangerous content.

6 Domain-Agnostic Asynchronous Crawler

Traditional crawling approaches fetch raw page data and index them for future use during users' searching queries. Based on the existence and relevance of keywords in the crawled documents, search results are generated by ranking a list of URLs to present high-scoring documents on top. But what if the target of crawling is to generate structured data from unstructured raw content, sourced not only from a handful of similar sites rather each site will have a completely different architecture. Some commercial large-scale crawling tools, such as DiffBot (https://www.diffbot.com/), can crawl sites of the same content type but with different architectures.

To create an open-source crawling engine that can handle a multitude of sites, all having different content types and architectures, we have designed a domain-agnostic asynchronous crawler. Given some basic extraction rules, this crawler can fetch raw content and produce structured data from sites of any domain.

6.1 Architecture

Here we will describe the architecture of the asynchronous crawler in detail. The crawler is written entirely in Python. For parsing HTML content, we have used beautifulsoup4. Asynchronous API calls have been implemented using asyncio and aiohttp. We have used Amazon DynamoDB as our storage service. Communications with AWS services from the crawler are performed through the boto3 library.

The crawler has four major components: Orchestrator, BaseCrawler, SiteHandler, and Utility. Asynchronous crawling is implemented at four different levels, namely at the root level, site level, page level, and item level. Item is any entity that has attributes describing some properties of that entity, e.g. when crawling an e-commerce site, item is the product in that site.

Orchestrator: Orchestrator is the starting point of the crawling engine. First is the list of seed URLs, which describes the starting point for every site that needs crawling. After loading the seed URLs, the orchestrator dynamically imports site handlers from the

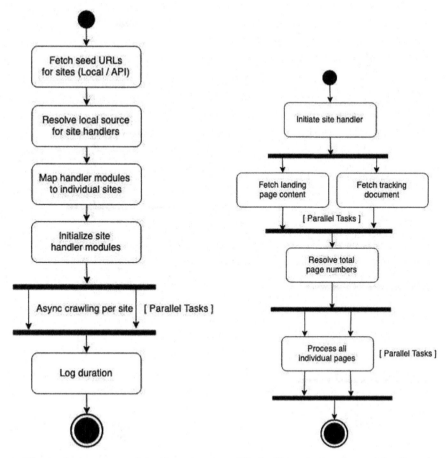

Fig. 1. Orchestrator activity diagram.   **Fig. 2.** Singe site handler activity diagram.

local directory. Each site has a handler associated with it. Each handler is imported as a separate module and mapped to the corresponding site. Finally, the orchestrator creates separate asynchronous crawling tasks for each site and initiates them all at once (see Fig. 1). Once all the crawling tasks have finished, the orchestrator logs the total duration and exits the program.

BaseCrawler: BaseCrawler is the root class that defines the structure of every SiteHandler. The starting point of every site crawler is the asynchronous "crawl" method. Here, the handler gets initialized first and then site-specific pagination is extracted. Since each site will have its own way of handling pagination, SiteHandler instances implement a method that returns pagination counts depending on the site. For each page, the site crawler creates an asynchronous task and initiates them all at once (see Fig. 2). Inside each page handler, all the items that are available on that page are extracted first. The page handler then creates an asynchronous task for each item and initiates them all at once (see Fig. 3). Each item handler initializes the item depending on the site. Then all the required information is collected asynchronous (see Fig. 4). Finally, the item is

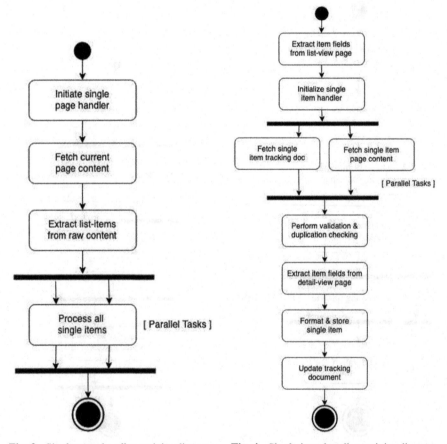

Fig. 3. Single page handler activity diagram.   **Fig. 4.** Single item handler activity diagram.

stored on Amazon DynamoDB. Once all the items on a page are processed, each page handler returns to the site handler. Similarly, once all the pages in a site are processed, each site handler returns to the orchestrator.

SiteHandler: For every site in the seed URL list, there is a corresponding SiteHandler module created to provide site-specific functionalities such as extracting pagination count, extracting items from the list-view page, and extracting item attributes from the details-view page. Each SiteHandler contains two components - item schema for items in this site and implementation of abstract methods from BaseCrawler. No matter how structurally different a site is, as long as it has a list-view and details-view page structure, the custom crawler can crawl those sites.

Utility: This module contains all the utility functions and services, such as the base model for all custom item models, methods to fetch and upload documents to DynamoDB, functions to process raw page content, and generic functions for asynchronous I/O.

6.2 Experiment

We ran the crawler in two modes - once in synchronous mode and the other in asynchronous mode in a single thread using asynchronous I/O. At first, we used two seed URLs. Each URL was from a popular e-commerce site. One of the sites had 167 pages and the other had 33 pages. For the synchronous version of the crawling, it took around 382 min to complete the crawling of all 200 pages with dozens of items on each page. Whereas for the asynchronous crawler, the elapsed time was 79 min. Initially, both the seed URLs and site handlers are stored locally with the Orchestrator engine. This approach soon becomes untenable as the number of sites grows to hundreds or even thousands. After applying a modified version of the asynchronous crawler to dozens of bidding sites, we observed that initiating the crawler for a large number of sites often produced unusual asynchronous errors, which were difficult to analyze and debug. We also noticed the need for an extensible, generic item model to support diverse sites and their items. The crawler got stuck multiple times for items that included supplementary documents in various formats in the details pages. The duplication resolver struggled for individual items with the same titles hosted on multiple sites. For some sites, determining the last crawled items was difficult using only the published date as the sites updated their interfaces and layouts.

6.3 Usage, Scopes, and Limitations

This asynchronous crawler can crawl data from sites of any domain containing data in a list-view and details-view structure. Using the custom SiteHandler instances, the same asynchronous crawler can create documents of different schemas without needing to change anything in the base crawler module.

For small and medium crawling tasks that require structured datasets generation from sites of a particular domain, this asynchronous crawler can set up a custom SiteHandler and generate structured datasets within hours rather than days.

There are some limitations of the current version of the crawler that we plan to improve in future versions. The crawler does not keep extensive log records for API calls and crawling errors. Instead of manually checking and running the crawler for failed sites or items, a better approach would be to include an auto-healing mechanism where the crawler uses exponential backoff to retry crawling problematic sites before raising an alarm. The current version of the crawler does not include any mechanism to handle rate-limiting from servers. We would also like to include a mechanism to fetch content from dynamically loaded web pages requiring client-side scripting interaction with the site.

7 Conclusion

This paper describes techniques for large-scale crawling that are currently being used in various crawling applications. We have explored different distributed crawling architectures and the challenges and future directions of large-scale crawling in the age of big data. Then, we looked at the current status of distributed or peer-to-peer search engines as well as some open-source versions such as Apache Lucene and Elasticsearch. We also highlighted the scope of improvement for distributed searching. With the ubiquity of large language models, users have started to use these models for collecting information from the web. We explored the impact of these models on traditional search engines. Finally, we described the proposed domain-agnostic asynchronous crawler in detail and showed the performance improvement of a simple single-threaded asynchronous crawler over its synchronous version by crawling 200 pages from two popular e-commerce sites. Crawling will always be a part of our web experience. Without crawling, we cannot find the right content in the ocean of raw data. To overcome the upcoming challenges due to the vastness of the internet, crawlers need to invent new ways of aggregating information constantly.

References

1. Brin, S., Page, L.: The anatomy of a large-scale hypertextual web search engine. Comput. Netw. ISDN Syst. **30**, 107–117 (1998). https://doi.org/10.1016/S0169-7552(98)00110-X
2. Armstrong, M.: Number of websites. https://www.statista.com/chart/19058/number-of-web sites-online. Accessed 13 Aug 2023
3. Hernández, I., Rivero, C.R., Ruiz, D.: Deep Web crawling: a survey. World Wide Web **22**, 1577–1610 (2019)
4. Rattan, D., Bhatia, R., Kumar, M.: A survey of web crawlers for information retrieval. WIREs Data Min. Knowl. Discov. **7**, e1218 (2017). https://doi.org/10.1002/widm.1218
5. Sato, N., Uehara, M., Sakai, Y., Mori, H.: Distributed information retrieval by using cooperative meta search engines. In: Proceedings 21st International Conference on Distributed Computing Systems Workshops, pp. 345–350 (2001)
6. Guo, Y., Li, K., Zhang, G., Zhang, K.: Board forum crawling: a web crawling method for web forum. In: IEEE/WIC/ACM International Conference on Web Intelligence (WI 2006 Main Conference Proceedings) (WI'06), pp. 745–748 (2006)
7. Heydon, A., Najork, M.: High-Performance Web Crawling. Springer, Cham (2002)
8. How Google Search organizes information

9. Koloveas, P., Chantzios, T., Tryfonopoulos, C., Skiadopoulos, S.: A crawler architecture for harvesting the clear, social, and dark web for IoT-related cyber-threat intelligence. In: IEEE World Congress on Services (SERVICES), pp. 3–8 (2019)
10. Ren, X., Wang, H., Dai, D.: A summary of research on web data acquisition methods based on distributed crawler. In: IEEE 6th International Conference on Computer and Communications (ICCC), pp. 1682–1688 (2020)
11. Yin, F., He, X., Zhixin, L.: Research on scrapy-based distributed crawler system for crawling semi-structure information at high speed. In: IEEE 4th International Conference on Computer and Communications (ICCC), pp. 1356–1359 (2018)
12. Apache Nutch Homepage. https://nutch.apache.org. Accessed 13 Aug 2023
13. Apache Spark Homepage. https://spark.apache.org. Accessed 13 Aug 2023
14. Liu, F., Xin, W.: Implementation of distributed crawler system based on spark for massive data mining. In: 5th International Conference on Computer and Communication Systems (ICCCS), pp. 482–485 (2020)
15. Common Crawl Homepage. https://commoncrawl.org. Accessed 13 Aug 2023
16. Common Crawl. https://commoncrawl.org/2023/04/mar-apr-2023-crawl-archive-now-ava ilable. Accessed 13 Aug 2023
17. Brown, T.B., et al.: Language models are few-shot learners. In: Advances in Neural Information Processing Systems, vol. 33, pp. 1877–1901 (2020)
18. Gold, Z., Mark, L.: Robots welcome: ethical and legal considerations for web crawling and scraping. Wash. JL Tech. Arts **13**, 275 (2017)
19. Knowledge Coin. https://rorur.com/kcoin2.pdf. Accessed 13 Aug 2023
20. Cambazoglu, B.B., Varol, E., Kayaaslan, E., Aykanat, C., Baeza-Yates, R.: Query forwarding in geographically distributed search engines. In: SIGIR 2010 Proceedings of the 33rd International ACM SIGIR Conference on Research and Development in Information Retrieval, pp. 90–97 (2010).https://doi.org/10.1145/1835449.1835467
21. Li, J., Loo, B.T., Hellerstein, J.M., Kaashoek, M.F., Karger, D.R., Morris, R.: On the feasibility of peer-to-peer web indexing and search. In: International Workshop on Peer-to-Peer Systems, pp. 207–215 (2003)
22. Apache Lucene Homepage. https://lucene.apache.org. Accessed 13 Aug 2023
23. Elasticsearch Homepage. https://www.elastic.co/what-is/elasticsearch. Accessed 13 Aug 2023
24. Introducing ChatGPT. https://openai.com/blog/chatgpt. Accessed 13 Aug 2023
25. Language Model and Search Engine. https://www.technologyreview.com/2021/05/14/102 4918/language-models-gpt3-search-engine-google. Accessed 13 Aug 2023

Data Archiving Model on Cloud for Video Surveillance Systems with Integrity Check

Norliza Katuk[1] , Mohd Hasbullah Omar[2](✉) , Muhammad Syafiq Mohd Pozi[1] ,
and Ekaterina Chzhan[3]

[1] School of Computing, Universiti Utara Malaysia, UUM, 06010 Sintok, Kedah, Malaysia
[2] Data Management and Software Solution Research Lab, School of Computing,
Universiti Utara Malaysia, Sintok, Malaysia
mhomar@uum.edu.my
[3] Siberian Federal University, 660041 Krasnoyarsk, Russia

Abstract. Video data has grown significantly as a result of the expanding usage
of high-resolution cameras and longer retention periods, necessitating effective
archiving solutions, such as video surveillance systems, that make data easy to
retrieve and maintain data integrity. These systems are relied upon by businesses
and private users to protect their assets and guarantee that video recordings are
properly archived for later use. In order to solve the issues of data storage, integrity,
and retrieval in surveillance systems, this study proposes a data archiving model
with an integrity check for video surveillance systems saved on the cloud. The
suggested model has four parts: system architecture, data archiving method, data
integrity check, and data schema. These components enable metadata production, effective cloud storage, AI-based human identification, and data security.
The model's critical elements are developed, tested, and evaluated in this study to
guarantee its dependability and efficiency when managing video surveillance data.
Coding the archiving module, testing the software with a pertinent dataset, and creating the integrity check module are all included in the scope. The integrity check
module's performance was tested by comparing compromised and uncompromised data to see how well the model could distinguish between real data and data
that had been tampered with. The findings imply that the suggested methodology
successfully addresses the problems associated with archiving video surveillance
data, improving security, resource management, and data protection. Additionally,
it promotes the creation of reliable, tamper-resistant surveillance systems, creating
a more dependable digital video surveillance landscape.

Keywords: Data archiving · data retrieval · integrity · security · surveillance
systems

1 Introduction

Any surveillance system that involves recording and storing video data must include data
archiving. In order to increase the security of their houses, buildings, and possessions,
businesses and domestic users rely on surveillance systems [1], thus it is crucial to make

© The Author(s), under exclusive license to Springer Nature Singapore Pte Ltd. 2024
N. H. Zakaria et al. (Eds.): ICOCI 2023, CCIS 2001, pp. 30–43, 2024.
https://doi.org/10.1007/978-981-99-9589-9_3

sure that video recordings are properly preserved and maintained for future use. For video recording and archiving in security systems that use IP cameras or independent devices that link to analogue cameras, network and digital video recorders are two typical technologies. Both devices have the ability to record and save video data and can be set to retain recordings for a predetermined time. Recent years have seen a rise in the popularity of internet-connected home video surveillance systems that enable users to remotely monitor their homes and properties from anywhere in the world [2]. These systems often archive video recordings using cloud-based storage, giving users a quick and safe means to store and access data [3]. The majority of the time, security system video records are maintained for 30 to 90 days [4]. During an incident or security breach, organizations and users can review footage without using up unnecessary storage space. Any surveillance system must have practical data archiving to guarantee that priceless video recordings are saved for later use and to help increase the security of structures, residences, and assets.

For businesses that rely on surveillance systems for building security, video data storage presents a significant difficulty. The data generated by these systems has greatly increased, necessitating a large amount of storage space, due to the growing usage of high-resolution cameras and prolonged retention periods. However, many organizations have trouble devising effective solutions to store this data, and the absence of useful data archiving can have a number of negative effects. Finding specific pieces of information in the archive is one of the major issues of preserving big amounts of video data [5]. Without efficient search capabilities, finding specific evidence might take time and be irritating [6]. Finding and retrieving pertinent information is made more difficult by the fact that video data is frequently saved in several formats and resolutions [7]. The absence of effective methods for data archiving is a further problem. For storing and managing video data, many organizations still use antiquated and ineffective methods like physical cassettes or hard drives. Data loss, corruption, and restricted scalability may result [8]. As a result, businesses need to spend money on cutting-edge data archiving solutions built to manage the unique needs of video data. The difficulties of data archiving and storage in surveillance systems call for serious thought and preparation. Organizations can increase security and incident response by using effective archiving systems that enable quick data retrieval and are made to handle the special characteristics of video data.

In order to assure secure and convenient retrieval of recorded data, efficient and effective models can be developed to handle the issues of data archiving for video surveillance systems. This work suggests a model that, by providing a technique for extracting particular chunks of data from the archive, addresses the problems associated with data archiving for video surveillance systems. The three main components of the suggested model are: identifying people in the video; creating metadata for a particular frame; and storing the metadata in the cloud. The first step entails identifying humans in the video material using a method based on artificial intelligence. Advanced algorithms that recognize human faces and other traits can be used to accomplish it. Once the humans have been located, the model generates metadata for that particular frame, including the date, time, and other pertinent information. Then, for convenient access and analysis, this metadata is kept in the cloud. Integrity checks of the data stored in the cloud are performed using a hash function that is embedded in the second component of the model. It guarantees that data is safe from alteration or corruption and that access and analysis may be done in a secure manner. It is essential in deepfake films, which may be used to edit video to fabricate scenarios [9]. The integrity of the footage is protected by utilizing a hash function to detect any data manipulation or alteration. Additionally, it ensures that the data can be securely accessed and analyzed without being altered or corrupted. The approach is anticipated to assist organizations by enhancing data retrieval abilities and archiving processes, which will lead to increased security and better incident reaction times.

2 Related Studies

A substantial amount of research has been done recently to improve the administration and effectiveness of surveillance systems, with a focus on video data analytics in particular. Real-time object detection, tracking, and activity recognition are now possible because to the development of cutting-edge technologies like deep learning, computer vision, and edge computing. This development has significantly increased the overall effectiveness and usefulness of surveillance systems. However, there is a dearth of research on the critical component of surveillance systems—archiving and retrieving the data. For efficiently maintaining and gaining access to huge volumes of video data, effective archiving and retrieval procedures are crucial [10]. Given the current state of growing data breaches and cyber threats, it may be difficult to ensure data integrity, security, and privacy when storing and retrieving video surveillance data due to this study gap. As a result, there is an urgent need for more research and the creation of fresh strategies to deal with the problems related to the storage and retrieval of surveillance data [11]. Closing the gap would result in more thorough and reliable monitoring systems that may better meet the needs of many stakeholders, including private companies and law enforcement authorities.

A methodology for protecting the confidentiality and integrity of high-end video data stored in the cloud was put forth by Megala and Swarnalatha [12]. The system incorporates a number of methods, including video summarization and homomorphic encryption, to safeguard private material while permitting authorized users to view and operate with it. The proposed approach is designed to be flexible, scalable, and applicable to various video surveillance scenarios. However, the main limitation of this study lies in its primary focus on privacy preservation. While it does address integrity concerns to an extent, it does not provide a solution for data integrity checks, which could leave some gaps in the overall security of video surveillance data stored in the cloud. Another study by [13] presented a video surveillance system that leverages cloud computing for data storage and processing. The proposed system addresses multiple issues, such as single points of failure and data storage limitations, by distributing the video data across multiple cloud servers. Additionally, it aims to improve the efficiency and cost-effectiveness of video surveillance systems. However, the study's central gap is its lack of focus on data integrity checks. While the system addresses several other aspects of video surveillance, it does not explicitly look at the mechanisms to ensure that the archived data has not been tampered with or compromised, which could be a significant limitation in real-world applications.

Concerns regarding the lack of a data integrity check while obtaining archived video data are raised by the research gaps in present surveillance systems, particularly in archiving and retrieval. When accessing the data for legal or investigative purposes, data integrity is essential to guaranteeing that surveillance film is correct, dependable, and undamaged [14]. The utility of stored video data could be jeopardized if this component is not prioritized since it could be subject to tampering, corruption, or unauthorized access. Furthermore, the reliability of the surveillance system itself may be harmed by the lack of a reliable data integrity check mechanism in the retrieval process. Therefore, it is crucial to design and implement efficient methods for confirming the legitimacy and dependability of retrieved archival video data. To guarantee data integrity during the retrieval process, methods including digital signatures, hashing algorithms, and blockchain-based systems might be used. Moreover, addressing this limitation can lead to more secure, reliable, and efficient surveillance systems capable of handling the ever-growing volume of daily video data. By incorporating data integrity checks into the archiving and retrieval process [15], surveillance systems can better serve the needs of various stakeholders, including law enforcement agencies, businesses, and individuals, who rely on accurate and trustworthy video data for decision-making, investigations, and security management. Ultimately, focusing on data integrity in the archiving and retrieval process will help create a more dependable and resilient foundation [16] for video surveillance systems in the future.

Hash functions have become the most common method for ensuring data integrity [17], particularly in digital files. Their usage extends to various applications, including the integrity checks of archived surveillance systems. By generating unique hash values for each file, these functions enable the detection of even minor alterations, ensuring the authenticity and reliability of the stored data. As surveillance footage is often critical in various situations, such as legal proceedings or security investigations, hash functions for data integrity checks have become increasingly essential to maintain the credibility and accuracy of archived information. For example, [18] introduced a lightweight hashing method for verifying the integrity of video files of vehicle black box systems. The method ensures the authenticity and reliability of the video data without compromising system performance. It consists of four main steps (1) key frame extraction, (2) feature extraction, (3) hash generation, and (4) hash storage and verification. It provided a practical solution for verifying the integrity of video files in-vehicle black box systems, where resources are often limited.

3   The Proposed Model

This study proposed a model to enhance the efficiency and effectiveness of the data archiving model for video surveillance systems on the cloud. The research model includes four critical components designed to enhance the performance of the data archiving model, (1) a system architecture, (2) a data archiving algorithm, (3) a data integrity check, and (4) data schema.

First, the system architecture for video archiving surveillance systems on the cloud explains the structure of the proposed model that includes devices, front-end and back-end applications, communication channels, storage solutions, and system modules. It demonstrates the basic need for a system architecture to ensure critical surveillance data is stored securely and efficiently accessible when needed. The second component of the data archiving model focuses on the archiving algorithm, which performs several critical tasks to ensure that only relevant data are stored in the cloud. The algorithm reads the video feed, identifies humans, captures the scene, cuts and stores it in a new image file, creates metadata about the individual, and stores it along with the image file, with an index table created to enable quick and easy retrieval of the archived data. By incorporating integrity checks using hash functions, which produce a distinct digital fingerprint, or hash value, for each data file, the third component addresses the security issue and ensures that the highest levels of data security and reliability are maintained. Last but not least, the data schema is a crucial part of the data archiving architecture for cloud-based video surveillance systems. It outlines the metadata and other pertinent information, as well as the structure of the stored data. The efficiency and efficacy of the surveillance system are increased when the archived data is readily available and retrievable for authorized users thanks to a well-designed data structure.

Modern video surveillance operations require a system architecture for video archiving of surveillance equipment on the cloud. Different devices, front-end and back-end applications, communication routes, storage options, and system modules must all be supported by the architecture. The gadgets often consist of cameras, sensors, and other monitoring tools that record and provide data to the system, including video. The incoming data must be captured, processed, and sent to the back end for archiving by the front-end application. The back-end program is in charge of archiving the data in the cloud and giving authorized users access to search and retrieval capability. The data transmission requires channels across a virtual private network (VPN) between the devices, the back end, and the cloud. Data preservation and retrieval solutions are essential for system modules including person detection, scene cropping, indexing, and metadata development. Critical surveillance data may be saved safely and made easily accessible when needed with the aid of a well-designed system architecture for video archiving surveillance systems on the cloud. The system architecture for video archiving of surveillance systems in the cloud is shown in Fig. 1.

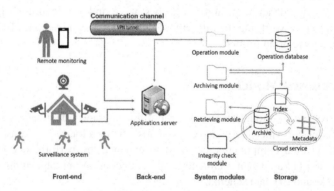

Fig. 1. System architecture for cloud-based video archiving of surveillance systems

The archiving algorithm is the main emphasis of the second part of the data archiving paradigm for cloud-based video surveillance systems. In order to make sure that only pertinent data is kept in the cloud, the algorithm completes a number of critical tasks. The system first scans the video feed to find any humans that may be there. The remaining non-human objects are subsequently discarded, ensuring that only pertinent information is kept. The algorithm then records the original file name, time, and frame number for each detected human. It then captures the scene containing the human, cuts and stores it in a new image file, and stores it in the cloud. The system then adds metadata, such as information on the person's movements and physical traits, to a new image file about the human. Finally, the metadata is stored along with the image file, and an index table is created to enable quick and easy retrieval of the archived data. By implementing this archiving algorithm, the data archiving model can efficiently store and manage large volumes of video data while ensuring that only relevant data is archived. As a result, it reduces storage costs since only relevant data is stored. Algorithm 1 describes the process of data archiving.

Algorithm 1 Data archiving algorithm for video surveillance systems on the cloud.

1. Start reading the video feed.
2. Identify if there are any humans present in the video.
3. If no humans are present, go back to Step 1 and continue reading the video.
4. If humans are present, capture the original file name, time, and frame number.
5. Discard any objects that are not human.
6. For each human identified, capture the scene containing the human.
7. Cut the scene and store it in a new image file.
8. Store the new image file in the cloud.
9. Create metadata for the new image file containing information about the humans in the scene, such as physical characteristics and movements.
10. Store the metadata along with the image file.
11. Calculate hash values for the metadata and image file.
12. Store the hash values, metadata, and image file.
13. Create an index table for the metadata to retrieve the archived data easily.
14. Go back to Step 1 and continue reading the video until there is no more video to be processed.

The third component addresses the security issue, a significant concern when storing sensitive surveillance data on the cloud. The integrity check ensures that the data archived on the cloud is free from tampering or corruption. Algorithms are used to accomplish this, ensuring the data's accuracy, dependability, and security throughout the archiving process. The integrity check [19] of data preserved in the cloud relies heavily on hash algorithms. Each data file is given a distinct digital fingerprint, or hash value, by these routines [20], which is then compared to the original hash value to confirm the integrity of the file. Since hash algorithms can identify even the slightest data changes, any tampering or corruption will be rapidly discovered. This method gives organizations a highly effective and efficient means to check the accuracy of preserved data, allowing them to uphold the highest standards of data security and dependability. By implementing hash functions into the data archiving strategy, organizations may guarantee that their crucial surveillance data is accurate and safe while enabling quick and easy retrieval.

Algorithm 2 Data integrity checking using a hash function.

---
1. Retrieve the information and picture data for each image file kept in the cloud.
2. Utilizing a hash function to determine the image data's hash value.
3. Verify that the hash value generated matches the hash value recorded in the metadata.
4. The data is still intact if the hash values line up. Transfer to the following file.
5. If the hash values are different, the data has been tampered with or corrupted. Notify the system administrator and place the file in quarantine.
6. Repeat steps 1-5 for all cloud-stored image files.

The data structure, which includes tables to store the information produced by the algorithm, is the fourth component. For example, a table is needed to store information about the video feeds, like the original file name, time, and frame number. Next, a table is needed to store information about the humans in the video, like their physical characteristics, movements, and scene. Next, the metadata requires a separate table to capture information about the new image file, including about the humans in the scene. This table would also include fields for storing the hash values of both the metadata and the image file. Finally, an index table is necessary to retrieve the archived data quickly, with a searchable database of the archived data. Each table in the data schema would have a primary key field to identify each record uniquely. Additionally, there would be foreign key relationships between the tables to ensure that data is appropriately linked and can be accessed and analysed meaningfully.

Tables 1, 2, 3 and 4 list the four tables that make up the proposed data schema: Video_Feed, Human_Identification, Metadata, and Index_Table. The original file name, frame number, and time of the video feed are all stored in the Video_Feed table. The Human_Identification database keeps track of details about the people in the video, such as their appearance, how they move, and the scene in which they are present. The new image file's metadata, including details about the people in the scene and the hash values of the metadata and image file, are stored in the metadata table. The Index_Table, which offers a searchable database of the saved data and enables simple retrieval, is the final component.

Table 1. Video_Feed.

Column Name	Data Type	Description
Video_Feed_ID	INT	Primary key field to uniquely identify video record
Date	DATETIME	The video feed's date of capture
Time	DATETIME	The time the video was captured
Frame_Number	INT	The frame number of the video

Table 2. Human_Identification.

Column Name	Data Type	Description
Human_ID	INT	Primary key field to uniquely identify each human
Video_Feed_ID	INT	Foreign key relationship to Video_Feed table
Frame_Number	INT	The frame where human was detected
Image_File	IMAGE	The image containing the human
Hash_Value	VARCHAR	The frame image's hash value

Table 3. Metadata.

Column Name	Data Type	Description
Metadata_ID	INT	Primary key field to uniquely identify metadata
Human_ID	INT	Foreign key relationship to Human_Identification table
Hash_Value	VARCHAR	The frame image's hash value

Table 4. Index_Table.

Column Name	Data Type	Description
Index_ID	INT	Primary key field to uniquely identify index
Metadata_ID	INT	Foreign key relationship to Metadata table
Hash_Value	VARCHAR	The frame image's hash value

An entity-relationship diagram (ERD) was created to represent the data schema as in Fig. 2. The Video_Feed table has a one-to-many relationship with the Human_Identification table, indicating that each video feed can have multiple human identification records associated with it. The Human_Identification table has a one-to-many relationship with the Metadata table, indicating that each human identification record can have multiple associated metadata records. Finally, the Metadata table has a one-to-many relationship with the Index_Table table, indicating that each metadata record can have multiple associated index table entries. This diagram provides a visual representation of the data schema and its relationships, which is essential for understanding the data structure and how the various components of the system interact.

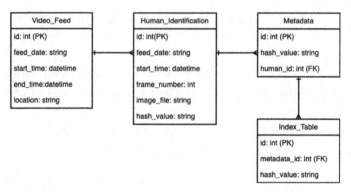

Fig. 2. The entity-relationship diagram for the data schema.

4 Evaluation and Results

This paper presents preliminary and pilot studies to evaluate the proposed model for video surveillance data archiving on the cloud with integrity checks. The section focuses on developing and testing essential components of the model, ensuring its reliability and effectiveness in handling video surveillance data. The scope of the work presented in this paper includes coding the archiving module, testing the program using a relevant dataset, and developing the integrity check module. A critical experiment assessed the integrity check module's performance by comparing compromised and non-compromised data. This experimental approach helped determine the model's ability to differentiate between authentic and tampered data and maintain the integrity of stored footage. The work aims to create a robust and reliable solution for securely archiving and verifying video surveillance data in the cloud, ultimately enhancing the effectiveness of such systems in crime prevention and investigation.

4.1 Coding of the Archiving Module

The development of a Python-based software utilizing IDLE shell 3.9.6 and OpenCV is covered in this section, with an emphasis on the archiving and integrity check modules. The application was developed and tested on an Intel Core i7-1165G7 processor from the 11th generation, running at 2.80 GHz with 16.0 GB of RAM and a 64-bit version of Microsoft Windows. The application uses Drop-box for archive storage and keeps surveillance data there as well. The integrity check module ensures that the video files are unaltered and uncompromised by confirming the validity and accuracy of the data that has been stored. Together, these modules offer a solid response for preserving the integrity and security of video surveillance data stored in the cloud, meeting the rising need for trustworthy and readily available material.

To find and follow people in a video, a Python script uses the OpenCV library and the Histogram of Oriented Gradients (HOG) descriptor for the archiving module. The script imports necessary libraries, including NumPy, OpenCV, and hashlib, then initialises the HOG descriptor and sets the default human detector. Next, it initialises a window and opens a video file to capture frames. The script retrieves the video's frames per second (FPS), frame count, and duration and writes this metadata to a text file. It also defines a function, 'hash_file', which computes the SHA-1 hash of a given file. The main loop iterates through each video frame, resizing and converting it to grayscale for faster detection. Finally, the script uses the HOG descriptor to detect humans in the frame, returning bounding boxes and weights. Detected humans are outlined with green rectangles, and each frame is saved to the 'output' folder with a unique filename. The script also generates an SHA-1 hash for each saved frame and appends this information and the frame number to the metadata text file. The loop continues until the video ends. Then, the script releases the video capture and closes any open windows and the metadata file.

4.2 Dataset

The program's effectiveness was evaluated using a CCTV video feed sourced from YouTube (https://www.youtube.com/watch?v=uQXaOX-_1kQ), a platform owned by Google LLC. The video, created by Swann Outdoor Security Camera, serves as a sample of CCTV footage review. The footage has 30 frames per second (FPS), totalling 1800 in 60 s. The program successfully analysed the feed, detecting the human presence in 843 frames. This test demonstrates the program's ability to efficiently process and analyse video data, providing valuable insights into human activity within the footage. Figure 3 shows an example of an image file generated from the sampled video. The human presence was marked in green boxes. In addition, for every frame containing a human, a separate image file was generated and recorded in the Human_Identification table, as shown in Fig. 4.

Fig. 3. An image file containing humans (marked in green boxes) was generated from frame number 229 of the video feed dataset. (Color figure online)

4.3 Integrity Check Module

The integrity check module, a crucial component of the data archiving model for video surveillance systems, can be seamlessly embedded with the retrieval module. Although

Num.	Feed Date	Feed Time	Frame Num.	SHA-1
1	28042023	1300	5	c7143e79adf3a7b046f91b47ce636e130bd26a14
2	28042023	1300	6	a5ca908c812f184b2f15e02224f6c46d40787920
3	28042023	1300	7	eb4f35100ad579651b58cfdaaab187b45e0d7270
4	28042023	1300	7	d8556893bbaef5a688a01df780e32da2710cdf40
5	28042023	1300	8	02514ccb24ff109f8c1b5a5872bbe00139686045
6	28042023	1300	8	38f8604bc4caa66d2d9fd20d2298f1b03e621c94
7	28042023	1300	9	5ed90524470461a866d8baf1e6fb0078f7762d73
8	28042023	1300	10	264506c72d978787b3e329c5ef5a25df3c68ab38
9	28042023	1300	11	3b6577274fb8c1e600b76abba2e809af0eb42dcf
10	28042023	1300	11	4efb46e75239481d7428b5c1b6b6f0eca48a0266
11	28042023	1300	11	7d4c61dab0484597906b3ade0d5e96d75c7b816c
12	28042023	1300	12	97482a06933eeccad3951a0f97810a2df6994340
13	28042023	1300	12	d7ba7da49d4f19757a7bbe389eb8f1957ec0af30
14	28042023	1300	12	b7ecb002eaf567a5b14d85d6e8239cbd0fad0770
15	28042023	1300	13	f93c45028a538454895c590facbed655aeb85393
16	28042023	1300	13	afe0a8efcbfca3aed8ec9b8c8f16b3515409d671
17	28042023	1300	13	e134b33366a2103bd95006a62c94dd6ae2da9885
18	28042023	1300	14	e72c84248ffa353015171a6250c69a22228339ab
19	28042023	1300	14	56bba9f4b22e5cda29f1a3c7c1092154bd8c39ed
20	28042023	1300	14	c291187f40f42318d85a16bd9ce98b00c8e8998b
21	28042023	1300	15	4fbb8904c01c61f05c62c61c1e1a19901954fa48
22	28042023	1300	15	027312a459b678fe5fb7d5087c26ab2a46970652
23	28042023	1300	15	466c48dc0a6da3b064f1db42ebbd309922941835
24	28042023	1300	16	9bbf06a33691a70bf138f693befb99fb3e9675ed
25	28042023	1300	16	8d1126281343b2480bfd25450032a2e586647c0f
26	28042023	1300	16	e0ce2387ab8994baf6f55bc5d35d43db25634429
27	28042023	1300	17	1fb4fcc4a3989785f8971640d8d43108dee6757e
28	28042023	1300	17	8f5aa912ef3bdd1601588cbede8ccf2b134ab5e4

Fig. 4. The data in the table for the humans' identification with a hash value.

the retrieval module is beyond the scope of this paper, as it could involve data mining and machine learning techniques, integrating the integrity check module with it ensures a robust system for data verification. The process of the integrity check module consists of several steps. First, the hash value is calculated using SHA-1 for the given image files, representing the selected frame of the video footage. Next, the stored hash value in the Human_Identification table, calculated during the archiving process, is retrieved. These two hash values are then compared to determine the integrity of the data. If the hash values match, the data is confirmed intact, ensuring the system's reliability. However, if the hash values do not match, the data has likely been corrupted or tampered with. When combined with the retrieval module, this process fortifies the security and trustworthiness of video surveillance systems, paving the way for a more secure digital landscape. Figure 5 shows the function for calculating the hash value using SHA-1.

```
def hash_file(filename):
    h = hashlib.sha1()
    with open(filename,'rb') as file:
        chunk = 0
        while chunk != b'':
            chunk = file.read(1024)
            h.update(chunk)
    return h.hexdigest()
```

Fig. 5. The function for calculating hash value using SHA-1.

The first image file containing humans generated by the algorithm of the archiving model was used as a sample to test the integrity check module. The file's name is 1–5.jpg, in which 1 represents the first image file generated from the footage, and 5 represents the number of frame sequences. The module calculated the hash value (i.e., SHA-1) of the 1–5.jpg file stored in the client cloud storage and compared it with the value stored in the metadata table generated during the archiving process. A non-compromised file will return the same hash value. The same image file was edited regarding the brightness using photo editing software and renamed 1-5v1.jpg. Then the hash value for the file was calculated. A compromised file will return a different hash value. The screen for the test is shown in Fig. 6.

```
Integrity check of the non-compromised image file
The        hash        value       for        output/1-5.jpg      is
c7143e79adf3a7b046f91b47ce636e130bd26a14


File Edit Format View Help
1-5.jpg c7143e79adf3a7b046f91b47ce636e130bd26a14


Integrity check of the compromised image file (brightness edited)
The        Hash        value       for        output/1-5v1.jpg     is
f277ede67d2d6e1495cbe2d7574c3a260ac35cc2
```

Fig. 6. Integrity checked of the original and compromised files.

4.4 Discussion

The proposed model for data archiving for video surveillance systems has potential contributions in addressing the challenges of data storage, retrieval, and integrity in the context of security systems. In order to speed up retrieval and make it simpler to locate pertinent information in the video archive, the model first provides an efficient and effective method for extracting specific information from the footage, identifying people in the video, and generating metadata for the particular frame. Second, the model's integration of a hash function for integrity checks and use of cloud storage makes sure that the data is secure and shielded from tampering or corruption. Last but not least, it makes managing and analyzing the data over a longer time span easier, which is crucial when data needs to be maintained for lengthy periods of time.

For organizations that rely on video surveillance systems for security, the implications of this paradigm are important. It provides a more effective way to manage data and retrieve pertinent information, enhancing security overall and response times. Advanced algorithms and cloud storage can also reduce costs and improve scalability, making it simpler for businesses to expand their security systems as necessary. In conclusion, the suggested model presents a promising strategy for resolving issues with data preservation for video surveillance systems. It has the potential to revolutionize how businesses handle and analyze security data, resulting in better outcomes and increased community and individual safety.

5   Conclusion

A data archiving model with an integrity check for cloud-based video surveillance systems was developed in this study, and it has been shown that the two tested modules—the archiving module and the data integrity check module—are both effective. By addressing the issues with data storage and resource limitations, the archiving module offers a practical and scalable option for storing video surveillance data on the cloud. The data integrity check module, however, used hash algorithms (specifically, SHA-1) to guarantee the integrity of image files containing people during storage and retrieval.

Researchers could investigate the application of machine learning approaches for automatically detecting unauthorized changes in the cloud environment or explore the development of more effective and reliable hash algorithms specifically customized for different video material types. Additionally, integrating the archiving and data integrity check modules into existing surveillance systems hosted on the cloud could be examined, ensuring seamless adoption of these techniques into real-world applications. Continuously refining and advancing cloud-based data archiving models with integrated integrity checks for video surveillance systems will provide a more secure and reliable digital landscape.

Acknowledgments. The authors thank the Ministry of Higher Education Malaysia for funding this study under the Fundamental Research Grant Scheme (Ref: FRGS/1/2019/ICT02/UUM/02/2, UUM S/O Code: 14358), and Research and Innovation Management Centre, Universiti Utara Malaysia for the administration of this study. The content of this article is solely the responsibility of the authors and does not necessarily represent the official views of MoHE, Malaysia. The authors would also like to extend their gratitude to the Data Management & Software Solution Research Lab, School of Computing, Universiti Utara Malaysia for their generous support in sponsoring the publication of this article.

References

1. Goud, K, N., K, S.: Enhanced security for smart door using biometrics and OTP. In: Gunjan, V.K., Zurada, J.M. (eds.) Modern Approaches in Machine Learning & Cognitive Science: A Walkthrough. Studies in Computational Intelligence, vol. 1027, pp. 517–526. Springer, Cham (2022). https://doi.org/10.1007/978-3-030-96634-8_47

2. Kalbo, N., Mirsky, Y., Shabtai, A., Elovici, Y.: The security of IP-based video surveillance systems. Sensors (Switzerland) **20**, 1–27 (2020). https://doi.org/10.3390/s20174806

3. Elharrouss, O., Noor, A., Somaya, A.-M.: A review of video surveillance systems. J. Vis. Commun. Image Represent. **77**, 103116 (2021). https://doi.org/10.1016/j.jvcir.2021.103116

4. Danewid, A., Andersson, P.: Long term storage in a surveillance environment (2019)

5. Muhammad, K., Hussain, T., Del Ser, J., Ding, W., Gandomi, A.H., De Albuquerque, V.H.C.: Efficient video summarization for smart surveillance systems. In: IEEE Symposium Series on Computational Intelligence (SSCI), pp. 672–677 IEEE (2022)

6. Wang, Y., Wang, Y., Dai, Y., Jiang, C., Huang, Q.: Intelligent video surveillance platform based on FFmpeg and Yolov5. In: Proceedings of the 4th ACM International Conference on Multimedia in Asia, pp. 1–3 (2022). https://doi.org/10.1145/3551626.3564972

7. Chui, K.T., Vasant, P., Ryan, W.L.: Chui, K.T., Vasant, P., Liu, R.W.: Smart city is a safe city: information and communication technology–enhanced urban space monitoring and surveillance systems: the promise and limitations. In: Smart cities: Issues and challenges, pp. 111–124 (2019)
8. Usha Rani, J., Raviraj, P.: Real-time human detection for intelligent video surveillance: an empirical research and in-depth review of its applications. SN Comput. Sci. **4**, 258 (2023)
9. Khan, P.W., Byun, Y.C., Park, N.: A data verification system for CCTV surveillance cameras using blockchain technology in smart cities. Electronics **9**, 484 (2020). https://doi.org/10.3390/electronics9030484
10. Müller, H., Nicolas, M., David, B., Antoine, G.: A review of content-based image retrieval systems in medical applications—clinical benefits and future directions. Int. J. Med. Inform. **73**, 1–23 (2004)
11. Šerić, L., Ivanda, A., Bugarić, M., Braović, M.: Semantic conceptual framework for environmental monitoring and surveillance—a case study on forest fire video monitoring and surveillance. Electron **11** (2022). https://doi.org/10.3390/electronics11020275
12. Megala, G., Swarnalatha, P.: Efficient high-end video data privacy preservation with integrity verification in cloud storage. Comput. Electr. Eng. **102**, 108226 (2022). https://doi.org/10.1016/j.compeleceng.2022.108226
13. Rodríguez-Silva, D.A., Adkinson-Orellana, L., Gonz'lez-Castaño, F.J., Armiño-Franco, I., Gonz'lez-Martínez, D.: Video surveillance based on cloud storage. IEEE Fifth International Conference on Cloud Computing, pp. 991–992 (2012)
14. Halfawy, M.R., Jantira, H.: Automated defect detection in sewer closed circuit television images using histograms of oriented gradients and support vector machine. Autom. Constr. **38**, 1–13 (2014)
15. Kavya, V., Sumathi, R., Shwetha, A. N.: A survey on data auditing approaches to preserve privacy and data integrity in cloud computing. In: Karrupusamy, P., Chen, Joy, Shi, Yong (eds.) Sustainable Communication Networks and Application. Lecture Notes on Data Engineering and Communications Technologies, vol. 39, pp. 108–118. Springer, Cham (2020). https://doi.org/10.1007/978-3-030-34515-0_12
16. Zafar, F., et al.: A survey of cloud computing data integrity schemes: design challenges, taxonomy and future trends. Comput. Secur. **65**, 29–49 (2017)
17. Sivathanu, G., Wright, C.P., Zadok, E.: Ensuring data integrity in storage: Techniques and applications. In: StorageSS'05 - Proceedings of the 2005 ACM Workshop on Storage Security and Survivability, pp. 26–36 (2005). https://doi.org/10.1145/1103780.1103784
18. Choi, D., Chung, C.Y., Seyha, T., Young, J.: Factors affecting organizations' resistance to the adoption of blockchain technology in supply networks. Sustainability **12**, 1–37 (2020). https://doi.org/10.3390/su12218882
19. Rene, C.I., Katuk, N., Osman, B.: A survey of cryptographic algorithms for lightweight authentication schemes in the internet of things environment. In: International Conference of Computer and Informatics Engineering (IC2IE), pp. 179–185 (2022)
20. Mohamed, N.N., Yussoff, Y.M., Saleh, M.A., Hashim, H.: Hybrid cryptographic approach for internet of things applications: a review. J. Inf. Commun. Technol. **19**, 279–319 (2020). https://doi.org/10.32890/jict2020.19.3.1

Blockchain-Based Supply Chain for a Sustainable Digital Society: Security Challenges and Proposed Approach

Norshakinah Md Nasir[1(✉)] , Khuzairi Mohd Zaini[2] , Suhaidi Hassan[2] ,
and Noradila Nordin[3]

[1] Politeknik Sultan Abdul Halim Mua'dzam Shah, Bandar Darulaman,
06000 Jitra, Kedah, Malaysia
shakinah@polimas.edu.my
[2] InterNetWorks Research Laboratory, School of Computing, Universiti Utara Malaysia,
06000 Sintok, Kedah, Malaysia
[3] School of Games and Creative Technology, University for the Creative Arts,
Farnham GU9 7DS, England, UK

Abstract. Blockchain technology is a distributed digital ledger in a decentralized network that offers immutability, security, and transparency in various applications among digital societies. The consensus mechanism is the defining technology behind the security and performance of the Blockchain system. Under the Industrial Revolution 4.0, blockchain has been considered for integration into supply chain business as an innovative solution to tackle the challenges of traceability, transparency, lack of trust, and data counterfeiting in digital supply chain management. A private permissioned Blockchain is the most suitable type of Blockchain for Supply Chain Management (SCM) as it promises better performance with high throughput and low latency. However, private Blockchains that use the Byzantine Fault Tolerance (BFT) consensus mechanism have low-security capabilities and are more vulnerable to cyber-attacks triggered by malicious nodes. In this paper, we outline the research challenges from the security aspect towards the integration of Blockchain with SCM. Then we design an approach for a private Blockchain-based Supply Chain with security capabilities by proposing an enhancement consensus model to the BFT consensus mechanism for identifying and terminating malicious nodes in the consensus process. The performance of the proposed approach will be validated experimentally and compared against Practical Byzantine Fault Tolerance (PBFT). The proposed approach is expected to prevent security attacks on the consensus mechanism, thereby improving the security and performance of the Blockchain system.

Keywords: Byzantine Fault Tolerance · Consensus Algorithm · Supply Chain

1 Introduction

The digital communications revolution has led to the support of all types of information interchange using online transactions. Those technologies made the process of business transactions more efficient and secure in a variety of ways. Businesses engaged in the

N. H. Zakaria et al. (Eds.): ICOCI 2023, CCIS 2001, pp. 44–57, 2024.
https://doi.org/10.1007/978-981-99-9589-9_4

supply chain process are a significant component common to the trade and industrial sectors. Since digital commerce has grown rapidly, there has never been more of a demand for better-enhanced product transparency and source-to-store traceability to understand the provenance of the supply chain products. However, traditional approaches such as centralized databases are no longer appropriate for modern Supply Chain Management (SCM) as they carry the risk of being triggered by increased identity fraud, privacy concerns, and the rising data breach [43]. While digital communication has influenced production and business organizations, they have not yet succeeded in effectively digitizing supply chain transactions. Security concerns and the difficulty of aligning information flows among the multiple parties involved in supply chain transactions have prevented attempts to digitalize supply chain trade [11]. Maintaining data privacy and security in the digital supply chain is critical as private information changes rapidly worldwide. Data transmission in such digital networks is possible to be threatened with various cyber-attacks. Protecting the system from such attacks requires a secure architecture that guarantees the safety of data transferred and stored in the system. Therefore, leveraging modern technology is an innovative solution to better regulate supply chain flows [29] and tackle security, traceability, and transparency issues in digital SCM.

Blockchain technology is a new innovative technology under the fourth industrial revolution (Industry 4.0) that is being considered for integration into SCM. The first application of blockchain as the technology underlying Bitcoin cryptocurrencies [30]. The potential use of Blockchain to assist businesses with effective SCM has already been widely studied in academic literature and business players. Blockchain becomes more secure than conventional centralized business models because transactions and ledgers are encrypted. Thus, it possesses the potential to improve the trustworthiness, security, transparency, and traceability of data shared throughout a business network [17]. A permissioned Blockchain with a private network is the most appropriate Blockchain model for the supply chain because it is designed specifically for private transactions and allows for faster transaction processing time in real-time [13, 45]. However, private Blockchain has lower security than public Blockchain [20]. Since private and permissioned Blockchains are governed by a central authority with limited consensus-achieving nodes, the systems become more centralized and more vulnerable to malicious nodes and traditional hacking attacks [9]. The current consensus algorithm used by private blockchain provides a possible attack strategy because the correct consensus can be reached only when less than one-third of the malicious nodes are present [8].

In this paper, we undertake an effort in describing and addressing this challenge. We present a comprehensive discussion on the latest progress and challenges, especially from the security aspect of integrating Blockchain technology with SCM. As an additional contribution, this study then presents an approach to prevent the security attack by proposing a consensus model of an enhancement Byzantine Fault Tolerance (BFT) consensus mechanism. This proposed consensus model is expected to weaken the overall influence of malicious nodes, reduce the probability of malicious behavior, and further improve the security and performance of private Blockchain-based supply chains.

2 Blockchain Technology

Blockchain is an append-only Distributed Ledger Technology offering immutability, privacy, security, and transparency in a decentralized network. It represents a paradigm shift in the way business partners trust each other by enabling more effective and secure data sharing [31]. Blockchain is a digital way to store data from a collection of digital rules specified, approved, and performed digitally by all node participants [10]. The digital data stored in the blockchain comes in blocks that are cryptographically chained together in chronological order to make the data immutable and can never be changed again. Blockchain integrates a set of tools consisting of the hash function, timestamp, and Merkle tree technologies used to improve time series and data credit approval; using consensus algorithm and peer-to-peer (P2P) technology to execute collective database maintenance; and cryptography algorithm used to protect user privacy [31]. Blockchain technology distributes recorded data across computer networks, eliminating the possibility of a single point of failure [18].

Blockchain operates with a decentralized P2P network model in which there is no single node, and nodes do not need to trust each other. Untrusted nodes in networks can engage with each other in a verifiable way without the requirement for a reliable centralized authority to function. Since each participant in a Blockchain network depends on the technology that follows predetermined rules, there is no need for an external or internal authority to meet consensus. The transactions among peers will be verified using consensus algorithms. In conjunction with the cryptographic protocols, the consensus algorithm will ensure that the network is secure and guarantee data are true and accurate. Blockchain networks can be differentiated by two dimensions: public or private, defining who is permitted to participate and permissioned or permissionless, defining how participants obtain accessibility to the network [18]. Public and private blockchain is different in the context of the degree of accessibility, where a public network allows anyone to join and perform a transaction without any approval from a third party. Meanwhile, just a restricted number of members can access and monitor the transactions as trusted parties in a private Blockchain.

The innovation of Blockchain technology is to develop data structures that feature built-in security qualities. Security in Blockchain technology is triggered by the creative usage of integrating technologies which are the cryptography hashing function and the consensus mechanism, and by being distributed in P2P and decentralization networks [18]. Blockchain's consensus mechanisms can be regarded as its pillar component since they enforce consistency and trustworthiness, creating tamper-proof and immutable features [34]. An excellent consensus mechanism can ensure the security and fault tolerance of Blockchain systems [52]. The security and performance standard of the Blockchain system will be impacted directly by the selection of the consensus mechanism.

2.1 Fundamentals of Consensus Mechanism in Blockchain

A consensus mechanism is a protocol used to make sure that all the users joining the Blockchain platform are adhering to the established rules, and it elevates the Blockchain to a secure, reliable, and trustless solution for digital transactions [5]. The consensus algorithm is applied to determine how the validation network's nodes reach an agreement to append a new block to the blockchain without a need for a central authority, and that there is no double-spending. The groundwork for the consensus algorithm was established in the 1970s by Lamport [24] and Schneider [42] in their effort to create algorithms that were tolerant of a particular kind of faults [46].

There are several representative methods of consensus mechanisms recently with performance and scalability trade-offs [39] including Proof of Work (PoW), Proof of Stake (PoS), and Practical Byzantine Fault Tolerance (PBFT). Consensus mechanisms generally can be categorized into two main categories that are proof-based and voting-based. The proof-based consensus algorithm is used frequently on public Blockchains, while the voting-based consensus algorithm is generally employed in private blockchain [33]. A proof-based consensus mechanism necessitates nodes that join the network to prove they are more efficient in undertaking the task of adding blocks than the others. The node that delivers adequate proof of work will be granted permission to add a new block to the chain and rewarded [33]. PoW is the most extensively employed proof-based consensus protocol in Blockchain digital cryptocurrency.

Meanwhile, in voting-based consensus algorithms, nodes directly select the block they believe is legitimate instead of choosing a leader or competing for power over transaction orders [3]. A voting-based consensus needs results exchanged among network nodes before deciding to confirm a new block or transaction [33]. Figure 1 presented illustratively an overview of transactions and consensus processes in the Blockchain system [35].

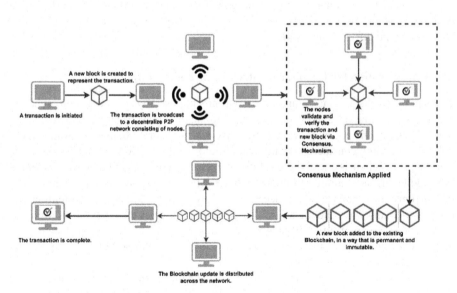

Fig. 1. Overview of the Blockchain processes [35].

In Blockchain-based SCM, secure and faster consensus mechanisms are essential for enhancing and automating business logistics between various stakeholders. However, most of the existent consensus mechanisms of typical blockchain still face many difficulties that affect the technology, such as high computational power, low transactional throughput, and transaction latency. Several consensus mechanisms such as PoW and PoS have been presented considering the requirements of secure digital transactions. This has led SCM applications to face challenges in maintaining consistency and scalability. Moreover, the consensus mechanism for private Blockchain must be able to deal with the Byzantine General Problem (BGP) where the possibility of malicious nodes' existence in the Blockchain network deliberately weakens the consensus process [25].

2.2 Supply Chain Management (SCM)

SCM plays an important role as the backbone of modern business and an indicator of organizational performance in achieving success, efficiency, and responsiveness, especially for financial benefits and sustainability [51]. Some of the essential aspects that affect the efficiency of the SCM ecosystem are enhanced data visibility, improved product traceability, and effective data sharing amongst various stakeholders. Data accuracy and strategic business processes are essential to all stakeholders in a supply chain system. SCM networks frequently experience exponential growth, necessitating fast communication between many stakeholders. As found by several studies, current supply chain systems are experiencing several problems such as the inefficiency of information sharing, transparency for the stakeholders, the lack of trust in the collaborative system [2, 16], and the difficulty to track the provenance of the products [51]. The problem of security against data tampering by unauthorized individuals [36] and counterfeiting at different product levels also arise and can have negative consequences for consumers, businesses, and governments [44].

2.3 Consideration for Enabling of Blockchain-Based Supply Chain

To adapt to the challenging competitive environment posed by an increasingly dynamic and demanding market, a modern customized application must be implemented to better regulate supply chain flow [29]. In accordance with Industry 4.0, new innovative technologies are being considered for integration into the digital SCM as a trusted service solution. Blockchain is one of these solutions and is gaining momentum in various industries and enterprises, aiming to integrate heterogeneous systems, manage commercial transactions, and enhance asset traceability. Blockchain technology is revolutionizing business in many ways and the use of Blockchain in SCM has the potential to eliminate inefficiencies common in traditional management models [6]. It is projected that the transparency and trustworthiness of traceability information in SCM to be increased by utilizing Blockchain technology.

Since business operations are conducted based on information, the information needs to be more accurate and quickly received. Blockchain is ideal for distributing information because it stores real-time, shareable, and entirely transparent data on an immutable ledger. Moreover, Blockchain efficiently simplifies recording transactions and tracking assets in a business network. On a Blockchain network, almost anything of value could be transacted and tracked, minimizing the risk, and cutting costs for all parties involved [19]. Considering its major strengths, Blockchain technology emerges as an outstanding alternative to be integrated with industrial facilities since it covers the whole industrial cycle [37].

3 Challenges of Blockchain-Enabled in Supply Chain

Although Blockchain technology has a revolutionary impact in different sectors, there are some potential issues and challenges before its widespread use in the supply chain [21]. Blockchain technology is still very much in the early stages of development, particularly in terms of supply chain traceability [2]. Scalability is also a growing challenge due to the ineffectiveness of the available conventional consensus methods in addressing scalability issues and the inability to offer the required transaction throughput and latency. Their level of security and operational effectiveness still falls well short of the actual requirements of the industries [48]. In addition, the unavailability of any specifically designed consensus algorithms to tackle supply chain issues has made the process of integrating Blockchain into SCM a significant challenge [40].

When implementing a private Blockchain for SCM, the main technological issue is to reach a consensus more efficiently and correctly without sacrificing the system's security. However, private permissioned blockchain is less secure and more vulnerable to traditional hacking attacks. This is according to the concept of the Blockchain design where the lesser nodes there are on a Blockchain, the simpler it is for malicious actors to collaborate [47]. The most recommended solution refers to improving the consensus protocol [12, 23], which is accountable for preserving the integrity and security of the Blockchain system entirely where each node joining in the network achieves a particular agreement. This consideration has triggered significant research from academia and industry on practical distributed consensus algorithms that are efficient, scalable, secure, trustworthy, and suitable for adaptation within the supply chain applications [23]. However, it is challenging to design a consensus algorithm due to the numerous contrasting interests involved in reaching an agreement. To devise a strategy for reaching a consensus in private blockchain, there is a need to provide an efficient consensus mechanism that meets the desired qualities of security, decentralization, and scalability.

3.1 Security Vulnerabilities in Blockchain

While Blockchain technology has its security capabilities and provides a tamper-proof ledger of transactions, cyber-criminals are constantly inventing new strategies for illegally breaking into Blockchain technology. Consequently, applications that are built using blockchain still hold the possibility for security issues and are vulnerable to a wide range of cyberattacks that could endanger the system operation [1, 28]. Various types of attacks are possible over the Blockchain network where the attack mostly originated from malicious nodes involved in reaching consensus, known as The Byzantine General's Problem (BGP) [25].

The BGP is the possibility of malicious nodes' existence in the Blockchain network that deliberately weakens the consensus process [25]. The previously designed consensus mechanism assumes that the probabilistic behavior of nodes in the Blockchain network is well-meant. In contentious environments, nodes may engage in malicious behavior that results in Byzantine faults or digress from the standard protocol. The BGP is one of the main theories applied in creating a Blockchain technology which outlines the difficulties to reach a consensus when there is mutual distrust between users of decentralized systems [25]. The security of the Blockchain system depends on the extent of the security and resilience of the consensus model being applied. A security vulnerability at this layer can be particularly serious since it affects all Blockchain applications as a whole [38].

3.2 Malicious Nodes and Security Attacks in Blockchain

The attacks over the Blockchain network mostly originated from the existence of malicious nodes involved in the process of reaching consensus [48]. Some nodes may act maliciously against the common goal and possibly launch security attacks on the Blockchain system. Those with malicious intentions have successfully carried out several hacks and frauds over the years by manipulating known vulnerabilities in Blockchain technology [18]. This is due to the lack of complete consensus among the nodes, which creates certain functional constraints and trade-offs between the performance and security of the system [2]. Malicious nodes are the nodes that illegally breach the trusted consensus protocol and interfere with transaction records, causing the security and efficiency of the Blockchain system to be endangered [48].

As shown in Fig. 2, the highlighted attack vectors by malicious nodes can result in a severe impact on the applications that are based on the Blockchain network. Those possible attacks can be divided according to vectors in Blockchain architecture. The security attacks including the Denial of Service (Dos), Eclipse attack, Sybil attack, and routing attack are attempts to attack the Blockchain network as a whole [14, 41]. Meanwhile, the attacks like Double spending attack, 51% attack, and Finney attack are among the security attacks specifically over the transaction verification mechanism in Blockchain [14], which revealed serious weaknesses in the consensus protocol that made these attacks possible [41].

Creating a precise categorizer in a Byzantine Blockchain network is complicated due to the imbalance between legitimate and malicious nodes' behavior [53]. Therefore, it is important to analyze such cyber-attacks to identify weaknesses in consensus mechanisms that could result in attacks targeting digital transactions. Further, to propose a

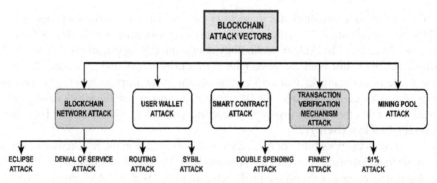

Fig. 2. Blockchain attack vectors.

preventive solution to these attacks to enhance security in private Blockchain supply chain systems while maintaining their performance. From the preliminary analysis that has been carried out, this study found that there is a research gap related to developing an appropriate consensus algorithm for equivalence security and performance which is essential to addressing challenges in supply chain business applications based on Blockchain technology.

4   Challenges of Blockchain-Enabled in Supply Chain

Several current works on Blockchain-based supply chain and consensus algorithms, as well as some earlier studies, contributed as the motivation for our work. This section includes a succinct overview of some related existing works.

4.1   Blockchain-Based Supply Chain System

The employment of Blockchain technology in the supply chain has drawn the interest of academia and industry to enhance product safety and traceability, increase trust, and secure data sharing while lessening costs at the same time. An alternative approach has been proposed in [2] by integrating Blockchain with IoT elements to build trust throughout the supply chain system. Their results show that data sharing can be simplified, and the latency, storage, and computational requirements can be reduced. Hu et al. [15] proposed a trust framework for the organic agricultural supply chain (OASC) leveraging the immutability of blockchain in conjunction with the edge computing paradigm. The trust framework proposed by this work aims to support tamper-proof records to make OASCs more authentic, transparent, and trustworthy. Blockchain has also attracted widespread interest in the food supply chain industry. Walmart [32] is a commercial venture that leverages Blockchain technology to digitally transform the supply chain process to bring transparency to a decentralized food supply chain ecosystem.

The original blockchain established by Satoshi Nakamoto [30] is entirely public and had 100% distributed control. However, this design is not suitable for all possible ledger applications due to the differing degrees of control required by different applications. Moreover, traditional public Blockchain applications experience low throughput and high latency due to the massive commitment of computational power caused by the complexity of the consensus process. Due to security concerns, the importance of data privacy, and competitiveness concerns among participants, the supply-chain Blockchains would need to be permissioned with central access controlled and limited to authorized participants [22, 47]. This is one of the factors why IBM contributed to the implementation of the private permissioned blockchain in the enterprise known as the Linux Foundation's Hyperledger Project [22]. A private permissioned Blockchain restricts public access to the Blockchain network to participants who have received permission from predetermined administrators, therefore, these Blockchains are only partially decentralized [47]. Therefore, private permissioned Blockchain is the most suitable type of Blockchain network for supply chain because it is designed specifically for private transactions and has high real-time transaction speed [45]. Corda, Hyperledger, and Quorum are among the prominent permissioned blockchain around nowadays.

4.2 Consensus Mechanisms for Private Blockchain

It has been discovered that SCM based on Blockchains has the possibility to enhance the effectiveness of information sharing across the supply chain. However, due to the inefficient and incomplete consensus mechanism, it is impractical to directly integrate Blockchain in SCM for efficiency [40]. Litke et al. [27] discussed the feasibility of SCM and outlined a number of decentralized consensus techniques that can be applied in SCM-based applications. They concluded that even if there are existing consensus approaches, there remains a demand for consensus mechanisms that can handle a diverse range of use cases and applications for different supply chains domain. Since private and permissioned Blockchains are governed by a central authority with limited consensus-achieving nodes, the systems become more centralized, less secure, and more vulnerable to malicious nodes and traditional hacking attacks [9, 20]. Likewise, private permissioned Blockchains face the critical problem of finding a balance between security and consensus efficiency that needs to be addressed immediately [53]. Most protocols for achieving consensus in private and permissioned Blockchain systems are based on BFT and BGP solving [46]. However, the BFT consensus algorithm is vulnerable to malicious nodes because BFT can tolerate even with up to one-third of failure nodes and the correct consensus can still be reached [8]. Although there are a limited number of recognized participants in private and permissioned Blockchains, it is impossible to determine between trustworthy and malicious nodes with absolute confidence. Recent consensus approaches proposed for the consensus process under BFT focus on improving performance and scalability and addressing the problem of centralization in a private Blockchain. Among the most common consensus mechanisms under the BFT are PBFT and Federated Byzantine Fault Tolerance (FBFT).

PBFT [7] is a low-complexity consensus algorithm with high practicability in distributed systems. PBFT requires every consensus to be performed in the same sequence on every copy among known participants that can tolerate up to a third of the participant's failure [52]. The main benefit of PBFT is that it consumes less electricity due to lower processing complexity and higher throughput. However, PBFT is developed for systems with a few nodes [46] and does not prioritize security or enhance the handling of malicious nodes [50]. The PBFT consensus algorithm and its variations are susceptible to numerous attacks directed toward the primary node and cannot identify and remove faulty nodes in the blockchain system [26].

FBFT is designed to solve the large-scale communication challenge by implying that nodes interchange messages only with trusted nodes [49]. While FBFT has several advantages such as high throughput, network scalability, and low transaction costs, the FBFT has the unique capability to blend known and unknown participants, which could increase the risks to financial trustworthiness. Moreover, FBFT suffers from security flaws due to faulty or malicious nodes [4]. How to reach a balance between scalability, security, and decentralization remains a challenge that needs to be immediately resolved within private and permissioned Blockchains [53].

5   The Proposed Approach

Selecting an effective way to identify and terminate malicious entities on a private per-missioned Blockchain network is important to offer complete security on the Blockchain network. Several researchers have taken steps to tackle the issues; the most recommended solution refers to improving the consensus protocol [12, 23]. However, reaching a bal-ance between security and performance remains a challenge that needs to be immediately resolved within private Blockchains [53]. In this essence, this research aims to reduce the most prominent problem in the consensus process which is the existence of mali-cious nodes that can cause cyber-attacks over private Blockchain-based SCM. In order to reduce the number of malicious nodes, this study proposes an approach by designing an enhanced consensus model for the consensus process to improve the security and performance of private Blockchain-based supply chain systems compared to existing mechanisms. The proposed approach was formulated with a critical review of the earlier employed consensus mechanisms based on the BFT consensus mechanism.

5.1   The System Model and Consensus Schemes

Figure 3 shows the proposed system model of the consensus mechanism in a private Blockchain-based SCM. The consensus process in current consensus mechanisms of a private and permissioned Blockchain consists of two main phases that are the selection of the consensus nodes (1. Consensus Nodes Selection Scheme) and the achievement of the consensus on the verification of the block (2. Consensus Achievement Scheme) [22]. This study proposes new schemes for the consensus mechanism to improve the security and performance in a private Blockchain-based supply chain system compared to existing schemes. The proposed consensus model comprises two schemes: the identification of malicious nodes and the termination of malicious nodes.

The first scheme is initiating the malicious node identification based on the node's behavior. During the consensus process, the consensus node is monitored by the primary node to obtain reputation information based on the behavior of the node to be analyzed. The behavioral-based analysis depends on validating actions and reputation the node issues in network transactions. When the primary node detects that the node's reputation dropped under a specified threshold, the malicious node is identified, and the consensus process will be stopped. The consensus process will enter the second scheme, the voting-based termination module for malicious node termination. All network nodes will vote for the identified malicious nodes for termination from the consensus process. When the votes are more than half of the nodes, the malicious node will be terminated, and the consensus process will be continued. When the consensus is achieved, the transaction will be verified, the block will be added to the Blockchain ledger, and the transaction is complete.

The proposed schemes will be designed based on the BFT consensus mechanism in a private and permissioned Blockchain architectural environment which is based on the Hyperledger Fabric Blockchain framework. Network Simulator 3 (NS-3) is selected in this proposed research plan to emulate the actual Blockchain network scenarios. The simulation and evaluation of this research will be strictly conducted within the private

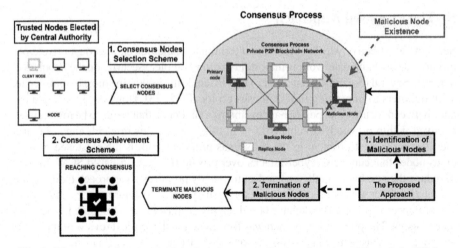

Fig. 3. The proposed system model of consensus mechanism for private Blockchain SCM.

and permissioned Blockchain environment. Specifically, a private Blockchain environment and consensus mechanism will be created with malicious node identification and termination schemes using NS-3. Finally, the performance evaluation results of the proposed schemes will be analyzed and compared with the previous studies to support and prove its effectiveness. The success factor of this proposed model is the correctness of achieving consensus with better security and improvement of performance in private blockchain.

6 Conclusion

Research on blockchain and its application in SCM is extensive, and many challenges will be ahead. This study undertakes an effort to present a comprehensive discussion on the latest progress and challenges, especially from the security aspect towards integrating Blockchain technology with SCM. We first present an overview of Blockchain technology, and the surfaced issues encountered in the SCM which led to considerations for the Blockchain technology integration into SCM. In particular, this study outlines the research challenges from the security aspect that arise in Blockchain-based SCM. As an additional contribution, this study then presents an approach to prevent security attacks by proposing a consensus model of an enhancement to the BFT consensus mechanism for identifying and terminating malicious nodes in the consensus process. In contrast to previous related studies, we also outline the importance of using appropriate network models and consensus methods towards delivering reliable and efficient Blockchain-based SCM. We conclude that to increase security while maintaining a Blockchain-based SCM's performance standard, comprehensive research must be carried out to identify such security problems and formulate solutions. Blockchain technology will potentially ensure efficiency and transparency, enhancing financial performance and the entire SCM. We hope our discussion and the proposed approach here will open up opportunities for the researchers to create new ideas and approaches for a secure Blockchain-based Supply Chain for a sustainable digital society.

Acknowledgments. This research is supported by the Ministry of Higher Education (MoHE) of Malaysia through the Fundamental Research Grant Scheme (FRGS/1/2020/ICT11/UUM/02/1).

References

1. Al-Farsi, S., Rathore, M.M., Bakiras, S.: Security of blockchain-based supply chain management systems: challenges and opportunities. Appl. Sci. **11**(12), 5585 (2021)
2. Al-Rakhami, M.S., Al-Mashari, M.: A blockchain-based trust model for internet of things supply chain management. Sensors **21**(5), 1759 (2021)
3. Altarawneh, A.: Liveness analysis, modeling, and simulation of blockchain consensus algorithms' ability to tolerate malicious miners. Ph.D. thesis, University of Tennessee at Chattanooga (2021)
4. Bains, P.: Blockchain consensus mechanism: a primer for supervision. International Monetary Fund (2022)
5. Baliga, A.: Understanding blockchain consensus models. Persistent **4**(1), 14 (2017)
6. Borah, M.D., Naik, V.B., Patgiri, R., Bhargav, A., Phukan, B., Basani, S.G.M.: Supply chain management in agriculture using blockchain and IoT. In: Kim, S., Deka, G.C. (eds.) Advanced applications of blockchain technology. SBD, vol. 60, pp. 227–242. Springer, Singapore (2020). https://doi.org/10.1007/978-981-13-8775-3_11
7. Castro, M., Liskov, B.: Practical byzantine fault tolerance and proactive recovery. ACM Trans. Comput. Syst. (TOCS) **20**(4), 398–461 (2002)
8. Castro, M., Liskov, B., et al.: Practical byzantine fault tolerance. In: OsDI, vol. 99, pp. 173–186 (1999)
9. Cryptopedia: The blockchain trilemma: fast, secure, and scalable networks. gemini.com. https://www.gemini.com/cryptopedia/blockchain-trilemma-decentralization-scalability-definition. Accessed 08 Oct 2022
10. Fu, H., Zhao, C., Cheng, C., Ma, H.: Blockchain-based agri-food supply chain management: case study in China. Int. Food Agribus. Manage. Rev. **23**(5), 667–679 (2020). https://doi.org/10.22434/ifamr2019.0152
11. Ganne, E.: Can blockchain revolutionize international trade? World Trade Organization, Geneva (2018)
12. Geroni, D.: Blockchain Scalability Problem – Why is it Difficult to Scale Blockchain. https://101blockchains.com/blockchain-scalability-challenges/. Accessed 30Sept 2021
13. Gupta, M.: Blockchain for Dummies, 3rd IBM Limited Edition. Wiley, Hoboken (2020)
14. Hassija, V., Zeadally, S., Jain, I., Tahiliani, A., Chamola, V., Gupta, S.: Framework for determining the suitability of blockchain: criteria and issues to consider. Trans. Emerg. Telecommun. Technol. **32**(10), e4334 (2021). https://doi.org/10.1002/ett.4334
15. Hu, S., Huang, S., Huang, J., Su, J.: Blockchain and edge computing technology enabling organic agricultural supply chain: a framework solution to trust crisis. Comput. Ind. Eng. **153**, 107079 (2021). https://doi.org/10.1016/j.cie.2020.107079
16. Hua, A.V., Notland, J.S.: Blockchain enabled trust & transparency in supply chains. Norwegian University of Science and Technology (2016)
17. IBM: Benefits of Blockchain (2022). https://www.ibm.com/topics/benefits-of-blockchain
18. IBM: What is blockchain security? (2022). https://www.ibm.com/topics/blockchain-security

56 N. Md Nasir et al.

19. IBM: What is blockchain technology? https://www.ibm.com/my-en/topics/what-is-blockc hain. Accessed 30 Dec 2021
20. Iredale, G.: Introduction to Permissioned Blockchains. https://101blockchains.com/permis sioned-blockchain/. Accessed 02 June 2019
21. Jabbar, S., Lloyd, H., Hammoudeh, M., Adebisi, B., Raza, U.: Blockchain-enabled supply chain: analysis, challenges, and future directions. Multimedia Syst. **27**(4), 787–806 (2021)
22. Jaeger, L.G.: Public versus private: what to know before getting started with blockchain (2018). https://www.ibm.com/blogs/blockchain/2018/public-versus-private-what-to-know-before-getting-started-with-blockchain/
23. Khan, D., Jung, L.T., Hashmani, M.A.: Systematic literature review of challenges in blockchain scalability. Appl. Sci. **11**(20), 9372 (2021)
24. Lamport, L.: Time, clocks, and the ordering of events in a distributed system. Commun. ACM **21**, 558–565 (1978)
25. Lamport, L., Shostak, R., Pease, M.: The byzantine generals problem. ACM Trans. Program. Lang. Syst. (TOPLAS) **4**(3), 382–401 (1982). https://doi.org/10.1145/357172.357176
26. Lei, K., Zhang, Q., Xu, L., Qi, Z.: Reputation-based byzantine fault-tolerance for consortium blockchain. In: 2018 IEEE 24th International Conference on Parallel and Distributed Systems (ICPADS), pp. 604–611 (2018). https://doi.org/10.1109/PADSW.2018.8644933
27. Litke, A., Anagnostopoulos, D., Varvarigou, T.: Blockchains for supply chain management: architectural elements and challenges towards a global scale deployment. Logistics **3**(1), 5 (2019)
28. Maskey, S.R.: Reputation-based miner node selection in blockchain-based vehicular networks. Ph.D. thesis, University of Nevada, Reno (2021)
29. Meidute-Kavaliauskiene, I., Yıldız, B., Çiğdem, Ş, Činčikaitė, R.: An integrated impact of blockchain on supply chain applications. Logistics **5**(2), 33 (2021)
30. Nakamoto, S.: Bitcoin: A peer-to-peer electronic cash system. Decentralized Business Review, p. 21260 (2008)
31. Nasir, N.M., Hassan, S., Zaini, K.M., Nordin, N.: Blockchain trust impact in agribusiness supply chain: a survey, challenges, and directions. In: 2022 IEEE Region 10 Symposium (TENSYMP), pp. 1–6 (2022). https://doi.org/10.1109/TENSYMP54529.2022.9864418
32. Nation, J.: Walmart tests food safety with blockchain traceability. Abgerufen unter (10.09. 2018) (2017). https://www.ethnews.com/walmart-testsfood-safety-with-blockchaintraceabi lity
33. Nguyen, G.T., Kim, K.: A survey about consensus algorithms used in blockchain. J. Inf. Process. Syst. **14**(1), 101–128 (2018)
34. Oyinloye, D.P., Teh, J.S., Jamil, N., Alawida, M.: Blockchain consensus: an overview of alternative protocols. Symmetry **13**(8), 1363 (2021)
35. Puthal, D., Malik, N., Mohanty, S.P., Kougianos, E., Das, G.: Everything you wanted to know about the blockchain: its promise, components, processes, and problems. IEEE Consum. Electron. Mag. **7**(4), 6–14 (2018)
36. Rana, S.K., et al.: Blockchain-based model to improve the performance of the next-generation digital supply chain. Sustainability **13**(18), 10008 (2021)
37. Rosa Righi, Rd., Alberti, A.M., Singh, M. (eds.): Blockchain Technology for Industry 4.0. BT, Springer, Singapore (2020). https://doi.org/10.1007/978-981-15-1137-0
38. Roßbach, P.: Security in blockchain applications. Technical report, 2018-03-13 (2018)
39. Rouhani, S.: Data trust framework using blockchain and smart contracts. Ph.D. thesis, University of Saskatchewan (2021)
40. Sarfaraz, A., Chakrabortty, R., L Essam, D.: RPoC: an efficient and scalable consensus algorithm for SCM applications (2021)
41. Sayeed, S., Marco-Gisbert, H.: Assessing blockchain consensus and security mechanisms against the 51% attack. Appl. Sci. **9**(9), 1788 (2019)

42. Schneider, F.B.: Implementing fault-tolerant services using the state machine approach: a tutorial. ACM Comput. Surv. (CSUR) **22**(4), 299–319 (1990)
43. Sharma, S., Kumar, A., Bhushan, M., Goyal, N., Iyer, S.S.: Is blockchain technology secure to work on? In: Blockchain and AI Technology in the Industrial Internet of Things, pp. 66–80. IGI Global (2021)
44. Shashiraja: How to Leverage Technology for Traceability and Anti-counterfeiting? – Data For Decisions. https://dford.co.in/how-to-leverage-technology-for-traceability-and-anti-cou nterfeiting/. Accessed 23 Jun 2022
45. Surjandari, I., Yusuf, H., Laoh, E., Maulida, R.: Designing a permissioned blockchain network for the halal industry using hyperledger fabric with multiple channels and the raft consensus mechanism. J. Big Data **8**(1), 1–16 (2021)
46. Tomić, N.Z.: A review of consensus protocols in permissioned blockchains. J. Comput. Sci. Res. **3**(2), 32–39 (2021)
47. Wegrzyn, K.E., Wang, E.: Types of blockchain: public, private, or something in between (2021). https://www.foley.com/en/insights/publications/2021/08/types-of-blockc hain-public-private-between
48. Yang, F., Zhou, W., Wu, Q., Long, R., Xiong, N.N., Zhou, M.: Delegated proof of stake with downgrade: a secure and efficient blockchain consensus algorithm with downgrade mechanism. IEEE Access **7**, 118541–118555 (2019)
49. Yoo, J., Jung, Y., Shin, D., Bae, M., Jee, E.: Formal modeling and verification of a federated byzantine agreement algorithm for blockchain platforms. In: 2019 IEEE International Workshop on Blockchain Oriented Software Engineering (IWBOSE), pp. 11–21. IEEE (2019)
50. Yu, X., Qin, J., Chen, P.: Gpbft: A practical byzantine fault-tolerant consensus algorithm based on dual administrator short group signatures. Secur. Commun. Netw. **2022**, 1–11 (2022)
51. Zhang, J.: Deploying blockchain technology in the supply chain. In: Computer Security Threats, p. 57. IntechOpen, London (2019)
52. Zhang, S., Lee, J.H.: Analysis of the main consensus protocols of blockchain. ICT Exp. **6**(2), 93–97 (2020). https://doi.org/10.1016/j.icte.2019.08.001
53. Zhang, X., Xue, M., Miao, X.: A consensus algorithm based on risk assessment model for permissioned blockchain. Wirel. Commun. Mob. Comput. **2022**, 1–21 (2022)

An Exploratory Study of Automated Anti-phishing System

Mochamad Azkal Azkiya Aziz[1](✉) [iD], Basheer Riskhan[1] [iD], Nur Haryani Zakaria[2] [iD], and Mohamad Nazim Jambli[3] [iD]

[1] Albukhary International University, 05200 Alor Setar, Kedah, Malaysia
moch.azkal21@gmail.com, b.riskhan@aiu.edu.my
[2] Data Management & Software Solution Research Lab, School of Computing, Universiti Utara Malaysia, 06010 Sintok, Kedah, Malaysia
[3] Faculty of Computer Science and Information Technology, University Malaysia Sarawak, Kota Samarahan, Sarawak, Malaysia

Abstract. Phishing attacks have emerged as a major problem in the digital world due to a rising trend in their frequency. While various approaches have been developed to detect and prevent phishing attacks, a definitive solution to the problem has yet to be discovered. This study discusses automated anti-phishing systems while analyzing and comparing various anti-phishing strategies using exploratory research. Traditional, machine learning, and deep learning-based anti-phishing systems are discussed in the article. The study highlights the use of Artificial Intelligence (AI) based systems, particularly utilizing methods such as Convolutional Neural Networks, Support Vector Machines, and Recurrent Neural Networks. These AI-based approaches dominate the current trend in the field. This study could potentially be helpful for researchers who wish to delve deeper into the topic of automated phishing detection and prevention systems with a comprehensive review. It is advised to carry out further research to investigate the strengths and limitations of different methods and algorithms used in automated anti-phishing systems to understand their performance and effectiveness better.

Keywords: Phishing · Anti-phishing · Machine Learning · Deep Learning

1 Introduction

As computer technology advances, the entire aspect of human life becomes increasingly dependent on it. The Internet has played a significant role in shaping the world today, connecting people from all corners of the globe and enabling new forms of communication and collaboration. It has become essential resource for healthcare, education, and businesses organizations, allowing people to access information and services from anywhere in the world. A report shows that 50% of the world's population is active internet users, with 4.59 billion active on social media alone [1].

The Internet has also profoundly impacted how we conduct business, enabling the growth of e-commerce and online marketplaces and allowing multi-national organizations to expand their reach and connect with customers and partners in new ways. It has

N. H. Zakaria et al. (Eds.): ICOCI 2023, CCIS 2001, pp. 58–69, 2024.
https://doi.org/10.1007/978-981-99-9589-9_5

also revolutionized the healthcare industry, enabling telemedicine, remote consultation, and online education for healthcare professionals, providing better healthcare access for many people, especially in remote or underserved areas. However, as the reliance on technology and the Internet increases, so does the risk of security threats. Cyber-criminals are constantly developing new methods to exploit vulnerabilities in networks and systems, and the internet has become a breeding ground for cybercrime, including phishing attacks, malware, and other forms of cyber-attacks. Therefore, it is crucial now more than ever to be vigilant and to take steps to protect our cyberspace from these threats.

One of the most prevalent threats facing internet users today is phishing attacks, which are criminal activities that aim to retrieve personal information through social engineering and other advanced techniques. Phishing attacks typically involve using fake websites, emails, or other forms of communication to trick victims into revealing sensitive information such as credit card numbers or login credentials. According to a report by the Anti Phishing Working Group (APWG), the number of observed phishing attacks in 2022 reached a record high of 1,097,811 cases, with a 47% increase in threats on social media specifically [2]. This indicates that strategies used by the attackers are becoming more sophisticated in their methods, while victims may not be sufficiently equipped to defend themselves.

In order to combat the threat of phishing attacks, various approaches have been developed. These approaches can incorporate both social engineering prevention and technical prevention methods. The method of social engineering prevention is centered on educating and creating awareness among the cyberspace users about the potential dangers of phishing attacks, as well as how to identify and avoid them. This can include providing information on how to recognize and report phishing attempts, as well as training organizational workers on how to spot and report suspicious activity.

The other method, known as technical prevention, revolves around using technology to recognize and prevent phishing attacks before they even begin to cause any damage. Automated phishing detection and prevention systems are among the most successful technical prevention methods. These automated solutions detect and block phishing attempts in real time by utilizing modern algorithms and technologies that include machine learning, natural language processing, and threat intelligence. These systems can recognize and flag suspicious activity and take appropriate action to prevent it from reaching the intended targets of the attackers by continually monitoring and analyzing network traffic and email interactions. Some systems also include features such as browser extensions or APIs that can be integrated with other security systems to provide additional protection. They can also provide detailed reports and analytics on phishing attempts, helping organizations understand the threat's nature and scope and allowing them to make more informed decisions about protecting their networks and assets. In conclusion, automated anti-phishing systems provide a critical layer of protection for internet users by continuously monitoring and analyzing network traffic and user communications, and these systems are capable of identifying and flagging suspicious activity and take appropriate action to prevent it from reaching the intended targets of the attackers.

As the advancements in internet technology progresses, so does the sophistication of phishing attacks that malicious actors carry out. These attacks pose a growing threat to individuals and organizations; as they evolve, they become progressively more challenging to detect and employ diverse approaches. In order to effectively counter phishing threats, the development of automated anti-phishing systems must keep pace with the advancements in current technologies. Therefore, it becomes crucial to identify the effectiveness and efficiency of advanced automated anti-phishing. This study aims to identify common methods for automated phishing detection and prevention and comprehensively review the related literature. In order to do this, two research questions were constructed to drive the study, which are; (1) what are the available automated methods for detecting and preventing phishing, and (2) how efficient are these common detection and prevention methods.

The research aims to investigate the use of automated detection and prevention systems in combating phishing attacks. It will thoroughly review existing literature and studies in the field, including scientific papers, articles, and reports. The objective of the review is to understand the various technologies and algorithms used in these systems and evaluate their effectiveness in detecting and preventing phishing attacks. The research will also identify current systems' limitations and challenges and determine areas for future research. It is important to note that the research is limited to a literature review and does not involve primary research or experimentation. The information available in the literature may be influenced by the current state of research on the subject and may affect the scope of the research.

This research is significant as it addresses the growing need for effective solutions to combat the increasing progression of phishing attacks. The research findings can contribute to the community by identifying suitable anti-phishing systems and providing insights to the limitations and challenges faced by current systems. It can also serve as a reference for future studies in the field and benefit other researchers who are interested in the topic. The significance of the research lies in its support to the development of methods for countering phishing attempts and provides information on their challenges and limitations. Additionally, it contributes to the body of information regarding the development of automated systems that can successfully detect and stop phishing attacks. This article is organized as follows; the next section will discuss the literature review, the methodology, the results and findings will be presented, and a discussion and conclusion.

2   Literature Review

2.1   Phishing Attack

Phishing is a malicious cybercrime that employs social engineering techniques to fool victims and steal their personal information and credentials. It is considered a significant threat in the cyber world, as highlighted by [3]. The history of phishing began in 1996 when an attack on internet provider AOL was conducted using social engineering techniques to acquire users' billing information by pretending to be an authority [4]. From that point onwards, phishing has become a common cyber threat that is recognized by many. Research studies have shown that it is a major factor in 90% of data breaches [5]. Phishing attacks often start with emails that frighten the targets into responding right away. This often involves the act of clicking on a link or opening an attachment, which are actions that can lead to malware being installed on the target's computer, personal information being stolen, or the target being directed to a fraudulent website designed to steal sensitive information.

Phishing attacks have become more sophisticated, and cybercriminals constantly invent new methods to evade detection and steal sensitive information. As technology develops, so do the tactics used by phishers. They can now target other platforms such as social networks, blogs, forums, mobile apps, messaging platforms, and emails [6, 7]. With the rise of phishing, it's becoming more and more crucial for individuals and organizations to be vigilant and take measures to protect themselves from phishing attacks. This includes educating themselves about the different types of phishing attacks, how to recognize them, and implementing security measures such as firewalls, antivirus software, and intrusion detection systems.

2.2 Automated Anti-phishing System

Phishing is a prevalent form of cybercrime that involves tricking victims into revealing personal information and credentials using social engineering tactics. A study conducted by [7] found that most research indicates that phishing through URLs and fake websites is the main technique attackers use. Innovative solutions have been proposed to reduce the chances of victims falling for phishing attempts, such as using browser extensions and warning systems before the victim proceeds to a malicious URL. However, despite these proposed security tools, the human factor is still the primary key in successful phishing attempts [8].

Various solutions to encountering phishing attacks are described in [3]. The first is awareness and education for the victim, and the second is using blacklisting to block suspected phishing sites, but this solution is not always effective. The third solution is using machine learning and deep learning approaches, which can be effective but require high knowledge and expertise. Despite the various proposed solutions, there is still no definite answer and decisive solution to encountering the challenges of phishing attacks.

Machine learning approaches have become increasingly popular for the automated detection of phishing websites, as it can be treated as a simple binary classification problem, where the goal is to classify a website as either legitimate or phishing. In order train a machine learning model for a learning-based detection system, data must be related to phishing and legitimate website classes [9]. The scale of the datasets, however, presents a considerable challenge when using machine learning approaches to detect potentially dangerous URLs. This problem can be tedious and computationally resource-consuming [10]. To overcome this challenge, one possible solution is to use feature selection techniques, which can help reduce the complexity of the dataset.

Another method for automated anti-phishing systems involves the use of deep learning. Recent progress in the field of deep learning has indicated that employing deep neural networks to categorize phishing websites could potentially yield better results compared to the more traditional machine learning algorithms [11]. Research carried out by [12] uncovered that a majority of studies released from 2019 to 2020 favors deep learning, which frequently produced better performance outcomes. Nonetheless, there are certain limitations when delving into the realm of the deep learning method, including lengthy training periods, the need for large datasets, and the heavy consumption of computing resources.

According to [13] and [14], deep learning is a subset of machine learning based on artificial neural networks. The neural network architecture is designed to learn features automatically and adaptively from the data, which allows it to classify new data samples even when the data is not labeled. Deep learning is therefore particularly helpful for finding patterns in unstructured data, notably text and images. Overall, deep learning-based anti-phishing systems have the potential to outperform traditional machine learning-based solutions in terms of its effectiveness. However, using deep learning requires large amounts of data and significant computing resources, which can be a limitation. Despite these limitations, many researchers predict that deep learning-based anti-phishing systems will become increasingly prevalent as technology advances.

3 Methodology

3.1 Research Approach

This study's research approach focuses on analyzing the common methods used to detect and prevent phishing attacks using qualitative research methods. The data for this research will be acquired from current secondary sources. This means that the researcher will collect information from existing sources such as scientific papers, articles, and reports rather than gathering new data using primary research methods such as surveys or experiments. This approach is useful for deeply understanding this field's current state and identifying areas where further research is needed.

3.2 Research Design

The research design is divided into literature selection and data analysis. The literature selection process will involve identifying relevant literature and studies on automated detection and prevention systems against phishing attacks. This is done by searching academic databases, online journals, and technical reports. Once the relevant literatures have been identified, a thorough review was conducted, focusing on the methods and technologies used in automated detection and prevention systems, as well as their effectiveness in detecting and preventing phishing attacks. The limitations and challenges of current systems and identifying areas where further research is needed were also conducted.

The research design is adapted based on the systematic literature review proposed by [15, 16]. The methodology of the research can be explained in the following Table 1:

Table 1. Research Design

Research Phase	Description
Phase 1	• Baselining the research questions • Creating data source of the research • Determine inclusion and exclusion criteria • Literature and study selection
Phase 2	• Conducting review • Data extraction and analysis

During the first phase of the research, the research question was clearly stated, and the foundation for the study was established. In addition, the data sources and criteria for selecting literature were found. This included using inclusion and exclusion criteria to identify and extract relevant literature for the study [17]. The inclusion criteria refer to the characteristics the literature must possess to be included in the study. In contrast, the exclusion criteria refer to characteristics that eliminate the literature from being included in the study [18]. Together, these criteria helped to ensure that only the most relevant and useful literature was used in the research (Table 2).

Table 2. Literature Criteria

Criteria List	Details
Electronic Database and Search Engine	• ProQuest (www.proquest.com) • Google Scholar (scholar.google.com) • arXiv (arxiv.org) • Research Gate (researchgate.net) • Springer (link.springer.com) • IEEE (ieeexplore.ieee.org) • ScienceDirect (sciencedirect.com) • Semantic Scholar (semanticscholar.org)
Searched Item	• Journal • Conference • Book • Statistic Report
Language	English
Publication Period	Year 2017–2023
Inclusion Criteria	• Article that includes information related to phishing attacks or anti-phishing attacks • Article that provides information of automated anti-phishing prevention and detection technique • Article that provides information of the evaluation of the automated anti-phishing prevention and detection technique

(*continued*)

Table 2. (*continued*)

Criteria List	Details
Exclusion Criteria	• Article that does not cover the automated anti-phishing prevention and detection technique • Article that does not relevant and highlight the research question

The systematic review of existing literature followed a structured process involving searches across multiple databases. This search utilized specific keywords and phrases closely tied to the subject matter of the study. The inclusion criteria were applied to select the literature, which included studies published from 2017 to 2022 and primarily focused on anti-phishing and machine learning or deep learning. Additionally, exclusion criteria were applied to remove studies that were unrelated to the topic or not presented in English. As a result, a total of 22 papers underwent further analysis and review. The breakdown of these sources, including the journals and conferences in which the studies were published, is detailed in Table 3. This table serves to offer a comprehensive view of source distribution and aids in the identification of potential trends or patterns within the literature.

Table 3. Final Search Results

No.	Source	Count
1	ProQuest	4
2	arXiv	1
3	Research Gate	6
4	Springer	4
5	IEEE	5
6	ScienceDirect	1
7	Semantic Scholar	1
Total		22

4   Results and Findings

4.1   Common Automated Phishing Detection and Prevention System

The methods used for automated anti-phishing were investigated using qualitative research techniques as the main component of the research methodology. In contrast to primary research techniques like surveys or experiments intended to generate new data, the study's data extraction depended on current secondary sources, which means that information already present from sources like academic papers, articles, and reports was acquired. This methodology provided insightful information, giving a thorough overview of the situation at the time and highlighting certain areas that called for further investigation.

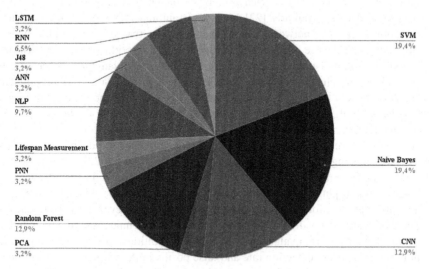

Fig. 1. Common Automated Phishing Detection and Prevention System.

The literature highlights that the use artificial intelligence (AI) based anti-phishing systems is becoming increasingly important as phishing attacks evolve and become more sophisticated. These AI-based systems have the advantage of being able to identify new and unknown threats, which is a major challenge for traditional detection methods. Figure 1 depicts the types of models or algorithms that are found across the literature. It also reveals that the use of Support Vector Machine (SVM) and naïve Bayes models, both of which are machine learning-based models, are the most common within the literature, followed by deep learning-based algorithm the Convolutional Neural Network (CNN). [19] points out that AI-based systems are better equipped to handle this challenge as they can adapt and learn to identify new and unforeseen threats. To address this challenge, researchers are exploring various approaches for improving the efficiency and accuracy of AI-based anti-phishing systems. For instance, combining multiple machine learning and deep learning models has been shown to enhance the performance of these systems.

Lifespan measurements is proposed to be used in conjunction with machine learning models to increase the detection rate and reduce false positive detections for malware and phishing-related content [20]. It is worth noting that despite the potential benefits of AI-based anti-phishing systems, these systems have limitations. For example, they require a large amount of data to train the models, and they can be vulnerable to adversarial attacks that exploit their weaknesses. Further research is needed to address these limitations and continue improving these systems' performance.

4.2 Various Methods of Implementing Anti-phishing Systems

According to the second objective of the research, this section examines the various methods of implementing anti-phishing systems and presents a brief evaluation of their results. [21] make use of both random forest and naive bayes machine learning algorithms and deep learning-based methods such as convolutional neural networks and long-short term memory networks. Similarly, [22] discusses an automated anti-phishing system that uses convolutional neural networks and recurrent neural networks. Other studies such as [23–30] emphasize the use of multiple machine learning algorithms including decision tree-based algorithms, support vector machines, and natural language processing to classify and identify phishing content in emails and URLs of websites. [30] proposed an anti-phishing system that leverages deep learning to classify the phishing content, and machine learning algorithms to identify phishing content based on the homographs of the website domain name.

These studies' results suggest that using machine learning and deep learning algorithms is a promising approach for anti-phishing systems. Of the 22 studies reviewed, only one proposed a non-machine and deep learning-based method. The advantage of using AI-based anti-phishing systems is the ability to identify new and unknown threats, a significant challenge for traditional detection methods. However, the performance of these methods varies depending on the specific models and techniques used. Some studies have found that deep learning algorithms outperform traditional machine learning methods in terms of malware detection rate and false positive rate, while others have found that a combination of machine learning and deep learning methods is more effective.

As a result, the use of a combination of machine learning and deep learning has become widely adopted in the development of anti-phishing systems. It is important to note that the results of these studies may vary depending on the specific dataset and evaluation metrics used. Furthermore, the constantly evolving nature of phishing attacks requires the development of new and innovative anti-phishing systems that can adapt to changing threats. As a result, further research is needed to improve anti-phishing systems' performance and accuracy.

5 Discussion and Conclusion

The results show that the automated anti-phishing system described in this research may be divided into three major groups depending on the models used: heuristic-based, machine learning, and deep learning. Heuristic-based systems, often known as traditional anti-phishing solutions, apply established standards and heuristics to detect and label potential phishing attempts. These systems include techniques such as keyword-based filtering, in which both emails and URLs are scanned for certain terms that may indicate a phishing effort [31]. These heuristic algorithms, as discussed in [32], can successfully categorize URLs based on specified properties. They may, however, fail in circumstances when a rule or heuristic for a certain attribute is missing.

One of the major disadvantages of heuristic-based systems is that they can easily be bypassed by attackers who use variations of keywords or different languages to evade detection. Additionally, these systems may generate many false positives, where legitimate emails or URLs are incorrectly flagged as phishing attempts. Despite these limitations, heuristic-based systems can still have high accuracy levels. However, it is important to keep in mind that they may not be able to analyze a spam feature that has been recently added.

In conclusion, while heuristic-based systems have been used as a traditional anti-phishing approach, they have certain limitations that attackers can bypass. Literature suggests that while they can have high accuracy, they may not be able to analyze recently added spam features. Therefore, it is important to consider other approaches, such as machine learning or deep learning methods, to improve the overall effectiveness of anti-phishing systems.

Overall, the literature suggests that machine learning and deep learning algorithms are highly effective approaches for anti-phishing systems. As per the research done by [33], it is observed that most researchers prefer using supervised machine learning algorithms when building email-related phishing detection models. These algorithms, such as support vector machines and naive Bayes, are preferred over unsupervised algorithms like principal component analysis because they are more suited for phishing detection as they could learn from labeled data and generalize to unseen data. Moreover, [34, 35] also found that machine learning, data mining, neural networks, and deep learning are the most used techniques for detecting computer crimes, such as in phishing cases.

Deep learning, specifically deep neural networks (DNN) and hybrid deep learning models are the best-performing algorithms for anti-phishing systems. These models can automatically find the representations and features required for classification from raw data and can provide better accuracy by training on larger datasets. Studies have also shown that deep learning algorithms do not require feature selection algorithms, as they are able to handle large amounts of high-dimensional data. Integrating natural language processing (NLP) with deep learning has also effectively detected email-related phishing. As deep-learning algorithms can analyze the text elements of emails/URLs and NLP can be used to extract features from the text, this integration can lead to better accuracy in email-related phishing detection models.

Machine learning has also been proposed as an effective way to detect email-related phishing attacks promptly. Machine learning-based phishing detection techniques can identify and predict advanced attacks by analyzing large datasets. For example, machine learning can build a phishing detection model based on profiles, where data, time, geolocation, and relation graphs are analyzed. Then, incoming emails are compared to the profile, and alerts are raised for email-related phishing attacks in case of deviation. Studies have shown that machine learning-based techniques used by modern email security platforms can detect around 98% of advanced phishing attacks. [29] found that the random forest algorithm performed the best with an accuracy of 99.2%, and [28] showed that the support vector machine with a radial basis function kernel performed the best with an accuracy of 98.9%.

Acknowledgement. This research was supported by the Ministry of Higher Education (MoHE) through the Fundamental Research Grant Scheme (Ref: FRGS/1/2020/ICT03/UUM/02/1). The content of this article is solely the responsibility of the authors and does not necessarily represent the official views of MoHE, Malaysia. The authors would also like to extend their gratitude to the Data Management & Software Solution Research Lab, School of Computing, Universiti Utara Malaysia for their generous support in sponsoring the publication of this article (S/O Code:14839).

References

1. Statista. https://www.statista.com/statistics/278414/number-of-worldwide-social-network-users. Accessed 20 Dec 2022
2. Anti-Phishing Working Group (APWG) Legacy Reports. https://docs.apwg.org/reports/apwg_trends_report_q2_2022.pdf. Accessed 22 Dec 2022
3. Benavides, E., Fuertes, W., Sanchez, S., Sanchez, M.: Classification of phishing attack solutions by employing deep learning techniques: a systematic literature review. In: Rocha, Á., Pereira, R.P. (eds.) Developments and Advances in Defense and Security. SIST, vol. 152, pp. 51–64. Springer, Singapore (2020). https://doi.org/10.1007/978-981-13-9155-2_5
4. Cui, Q., et al.: Tracking phishing attacks over time. In: Proceedings of the 26th International Conference on World Wide Web (2017)
5. Retruster. Phishing Statistics and Email Fraud Statistics. Retruster (2019). https://retruster.com/blog/2019-phishing-and-email-fraud-statistics.html
6. Basit, A., Zafar, M., Liu, X., et al.: A comprehensive survey of AI-enabled phishing attacks detection techniques. Telecomm. Syst. **76**, 139–154 (2021). https://doi.org/10.1007/s11235-020-00733-2
7. Xia, P., et al.: Characterizing cryptocurrency exchange scams. Comput. Sec. **98**, 101993 (2020)
8. Das, S.: All about phishing exploring user research through a systematic literature review (2019)
9. Ferreira, M.: Malicious URL detection using machine learning algorithms. In: Proceedings of the Digital Privacy Security Conference, pp. 114–122. Springer (2019)
10. Sahoo, D., Liu, C., Hoi, S.C.: Malicious URL detection using machine learning: a survey. arXiv preprint arXiv:1701.07179
11. Vrbančič, G., Fister, I., Jr., Podgorelec, V.: Swarm intelligence approaches for parameter setting of deep learning neural network: case study on phishing websites classification, pp. 1–8. https://doi.org/10.1145/3227609.3227655
12. Catal, C., Giray, G., Tekinerdogan, B., Kumar, S., Shukla, S.: Applications of deep learning for phishing detection: a systematic literature review. Knowl. Inf. Syst. **64**(6), 1457–1500 (2022). https://doi.org/10.1007/s10115-022-01672-x
13. Shrestha, A., Mahmood, A.: Review of deep learning algorithms and architectures. IEEE Access **7**, 53040–53065 (2019). https://doi.org/10.1109/ACCESS.2019.2912200
14. LeCun, Y., Bengio, Y., Hinton, G.: Deep learning. Nature **521**, 436–444 (2015). https://doi.org/10.1038/nature14539
15. Arshad, A., Rehman, A.U., Javaid, S., Ali, T.M., Sheikh, J.A., Azeem, M.A.: Systematic literature review on phishing and anti-phishing techniques. Pakistan J. Eng. Technol. **04**(01), 163–168 (2021)
16. Jayatilleke, S., Lai, R.: A systematic review of requirements change management. Inf. Softw. Technol. **93**, 163–185 (2018). https://doi.org/10.1016/j.infsof.2017.09.004
17. Khan, A.A., Keung, J., Niazi, M., Hussain, S., Ahmad, A.: Systematic literature review and empirical investigation. Inf. Softw. Technol. (2017). https://doi.org/10.1016/j.infsof.2017.03.006
18. Kitchenham, B., et al.: Systematic literature reviews in software engineering - a systematic literature review. Inf. Softw. Technol. **51**(1), 7–15 (2009). https://doi.org/10.1016/j.infsof.2008.09.009
19. Al-Khater, W.A., Al-Maadeed, S., Ahmed, A.A., Sadiq, A.S., Khan, M.K.: Comprehensive review of cybercrime detection techniques. IEEE Access **8**, 137293–137311 (2020). https://doi.org/10.1109/ACCESS.2020.3011259

20. Cilleruelo, C., Enrique-Larriba, L., De-Marcos, L., Martinez-Herráiz, J.J.: Malware detection inside app stores based on lifespan measurements. IEEE Access **9**, 119967–119976 (2021). https://doi.org/10.1109/ACCESS.2021.3107903
21. Hijji, M., Alam, G.: A multivocal literature review on growing social engineering based cyber-attacks/threats during the COVID-19 pandemic: challenges and prospective solutions. IEEE Access **8**, 1 (2020). https://doi.org/10.1109/ACCESS.2020.3048839
22. Alazab, M.: Automated malware detection in mobile app stores based on robust feature generation. Electronics **9**(3), 435 (2020). https://doi.org/10.3390/electronics9030435
23. Churi, T., Sawardekar, P., Pardeshi, A., Vartak, P.: A secured methodology for anti-phishing. In: 2017 International Conference on Innovations in Information, Embedded and Communication Systems (ICIIECS), pp. 1–4. IEEE (2017)
24. Salloum, S., Gaber, T., Vadera, S., Shaalan, K.: Phishing email detection using natural language processing techniques: a literature survey. Procedia Comput. Sci. **189**, 19–28 (2021). https://doi.org/10.1016/j.procs.2021.05.077
25. Vadariya, A., Jadav, N.K.: A survey on phishing URL detection using artificial intelligence. In: Gunjan, V.K., Zurada, J.M. (eds.) Proceedings of International Conference on Recent Trends in Machine Learning, IoT, Smart Cities and Applications. AISC, vol. 1245, pp. 9–20. Springer, Singapore (2021). https://doi.org/10.1007/978-981-15-7234-0_2
26. Mukherjee, A., Agrawal, N., Gupta, S.: A survey on automatic phishing email detection using natural language processing techniques. Int. Res. J. Eng. Technol. **6**(11), 1881–1886 (2019)
27. Kumar, A., Chatterjee, J.M., Díaz, V.G.: A novel hybrid approach of SVM combined with NLP and probabilistic neural network for email phishing. Int. J. Electr. Comput. Eng. **10**(1), 486 (2020)
28. Alshingiti, Z., Alaqel, R., Al-Muhtadi, J., Haq, Q.E., Saleem, K., Faheem, M.H.: A deep learning-based phishing detection system using CNN, LSTM, and LSTM-CNN. Electronics **12**(1), 232 (2023). https://doi.org/10.3390/electronics12010232
29. Spaulding, J., Mohaisen, A.: Defending internet of things against malicious domain names using D-FENS. In: IEEE/ACM Symposium on Edge Computing (SEC), pp. 387–392 (2018). https://doi.org/10.1109/SEC.2018.00051
30. Sarker, I.H., Kayes, A.S.M., Badsha, S., Alqahtani, H., Watters, P., Ng, A.: Cybersecurity data science: an overview from machine learning perspective. J. Big Data **7**(1), 1–19 (2020). https://doi.org/10.1186/s40537-020-00318-5
31. Ahmad, H., Erdodi, L.: Overview of phishing landscape and homographs in Arabic domain names. Secur. Priv. **4**(4), 1–14 (2021). https://doi.org/10.1002/spy2.159
32. Feitosa, E.L., Silva, C.M.R.D., Garcia, V.C.: Heuristic-based strategy for phishing prediction: a survey of URL-based approach. Comput. Secur. **88**, 101613 (2019)
33. Glăvan, D., Răcuciu, C., Moinescu, R., Eftimie, S.: Detection of phishing attacks using the anti-phishing framework. Sci. Bull. "Mircea Cel Batran" Naval Acad. **23**(1), 208–212, 208A (2020). https://doi.org/10.21279/1454-864X-20-I1-028
34. Atlam, H.F., Oluwatimilehin, O.: Business email compromise phishing detection based on machine learning: a systematic literature review. Electronics **12**(1), 42 (2023). https://doi.org/10.3390/electronics12010042
35. Chipa, I.H., Gamboa-Cruzado, J., Jimmy, R.V.: Mobile applications for cyber-crime prevention: a comprehensive systematic review. Int. J. Adv. Comput. Sci. Appl. **13**(10), (2022). https://doi.org/10.14569/IJACSA.2022.0131010

Remote Public Data Auditing to Secure Cloud Storage

Muhammad Farooq and Osman Ghazali[✉]

School of Computing, University Utara Malaysia, 06010 Sintok, Kedah, Malaysia
osman@uum.edu.my

Abstract. Cloud computing is a pay-as-you-go business model that offers elastic remote data storage, and computing resources have become necessary due to the emergence of big data. After data outsourcing to the cloud, cloud users lose control over data and are always concerned about data privacy and security in adopting the cloud service model. So, to ensure remote data integrity, a trusted auditor can make auditing tasks according to the users' request, which is helpful to release auditing overheads on a user device and meaningfully improve the scalability of cloud services. Although numerous data auditing techniques have been designed with TPA so far, these techniques need to improve on data security and efficiency issues. First, these techniques cannot authenticate block indices, so the server can produce valid proof without an original data block to pass the audit process. Second, existing approaches do not include position fields, so the server can replace the tampered data block with a healthy one to pass the audit phase. To overcome these issues, this paper introduces a new public data authentication scheme, ERPDA. The proposed technique incorporated a newly designed Merkle Tree (MT) based structure, Sequence and Position-based Tree (SPT) that minimises computation complexity to find nodes in data audit and avoid data replacement attacks. The experimental outputs showed that our suggested technique is effective with the comparative data auditing techniques in computation overheads, and the security is proved under the random model.

Keywords: Cloud Computing · Third-party Auditing · Proof of Data Possession

1 Introduction

With the quick expansion in the cloud architecture, the size of digital streaming data presents a rampant progress inclination [1–3]. The researchers reported an average of around 5200GB of data for each person in 2020 [4]. Nevertheless, the data storage capacity of tenants is so restricted that they cannot maintain such a massive amount of data. Thus, huge data storage is a significant issue, particularly for energy-restricted devices. Auspiciously, Cloud Service Providers (CSPs) give a possible solution to address problems managing and maintaining massive data storage. By agreeing to cloud storage as a service, the tenants should outsource their data to remote storage servers, thus minimising local storage and computation overheads [5, 6]. Due to these appealing characteristics, an

N. H. Zakaria et al. (Eds.): ICOCI 2023, CCIS 2001, pp. 70–79, 2024.
https://doi.org/10.1007/978-981-99-9589-9_6

immensely increasing number of tenants opt to use cloud storage services. Cisco reported that there were 3.6 billion Internet clients at the start of 2020; 55% incorporated cloud data storage [7].

In data storage services, the administration of remotely stored data is entirely sep-arated from its possession [8, 9]. Thus, tenants could lose direct control over uploaded data, and consequently be unable to achieve any processes over remotely stored files [10]. In other words, CSP can perform all procedures on the client's data uploaded to the storage servers. However, the storage server is unreliable and might not reasonably carry out these procedures according to the client's instructions. As a result, even though storage as a service has enormous benefits, it unavoidably experiences a lot of challeng-ing issues [11], for example, integrity, confidentiality, the privacy of the outsourced data files, etc. If these issues, specifically data integrity, are not appropriately resolved, it can significantly prevent clients from adopting and using cloud infrastructure [12].

Several studies have presented a solution to confirm the accessibility and verify the correctness of outsourced tenants' files [13–15]. Nevertheless, these techniques still face different issues that must be resolved solidly. First, these techniques cannot authenticate block indices; thus, CSP can produce valid proof without having an actual data block to pass the audit process. Second, existing approaches do not include position fields; consequently, CSP can replace the tampered data block with a healthy one to validate proof in the audit phase. Third, most previous techniques are based on the proof of data possession approach, whose computational overheads increase almost linearly with the sizes of uploaded data files [8]. Last, even though some past techniques simultaneously verify data integrity and confidentiality, the feasibility and universality are restricted and need to be implemented in extensive data outsourcing.

The above discussion shows that some issues with state-of-the-art techniques still need to be addressed. As a result, the primary concern of this research work is to develop a new scheme to resolve the abovementioned issues concurrently. We introduce a new data structure based on the Merkle Tree, named Sequence and Position-based Tree (SPT), that minimises computation complexity to find nodes in data audit and avoid data replacement attacks. As a result, this paper's primary contributions are described below. The remaining part of this paper can be described below: the literature on current data auditing methods is presented in Sect. 2. The design of the suggested protocol is presented in Sect. 3. Section 4 defines the analysis and performance of the proposed scheme. Sections 5 and 6 describes the conclusion and future research works.

2 Literature Review

Juels and Kaliske [16] presented the first evidence of the data retrievability technique. The sentinel (block masking) approach was used to hide the value in the standard data block so that the server cannot differentiate hashed data blocks. The users may down-load and confirm the accuracy of data simultaneously. They use symmetric encryption methodology to secure user data, which imposes little computation overhead. However, it is limited to the number of requested blocks as the pre-processed Message Authen-tication Codes (MACs) are used in the audit phase. Also, these schemes support static data and cannot support public audits.

Erway et al. [17] determine the dynamic data behaviour using a ranked skip list to validate remote user data integrity. They introduced a dynamic PDP (DPDP) technique by extending the PDP approach to provide verifiable update operations for remote data storage. Their technique requires only 415 KB of proof size. They also defined how to implement their technique in a version control scenario. This scheme involves O(*logn*) computation overhead while dynamic data update operations impose 30 ms computation time for 1 GB data file. This innovative mechanism shares many integrities verification paths during the data process, significantly increasing communication overhead.

Wang et al. [18] introduced a sequence-enforced MHT data structure to verify block authenticator and suggest a proficient dynamic data scheme. They use the bilinear aggregate signature mechanism's property for supporting multiple auditing tasks concurrently. However, they do not include the position field while creating the block, so their proposed structure is susceptible to data replacement attacks. A public data auditing technique that uses identity-based combined signatures is suggested by [19]. The user permits the Third-party Auditor (TPA) to perform an audit job to release the computation overhead using users' identities.

Anju et al. [13] developed a data integrity verification scheme named PVMS to authenticate the remotely stored sensitive data about the patient. The TPA is involved in the authentication to perform audit procedures for their clients' commands. The standard MT [20] has been adopted to verify data block tags to authenticate data accuracy. Nevertheless, the authenticator creation procedure acquires huge computational overheads, and the suggested method performs like a linear search in the audit process. For eight bits of data nodes, it needs to search all the nodes to find the exact location of the requested node from the tree in the audit phase. Furthermore, their suggested method is unable to prevent data replacement attacks.

An integrity auditing method based on an attribute approach was proposed in [14], known as DAFA. The users secure their data using the RSA cryptographic and MD5 hashing mechanisms before data is uploaded to the remote servers. The TPA is incorporated to delegate audit processes to release the burden on user devices. Nevertheless, the proposed protocol involves high computation complexity for making file and node authenticators. The signature size is much larger, requiring extra communication overheads, and the client must also pay for additional storage capacity. Moreover, it does not authenticate indices and is vulnerable to replacement attacks.

An efficient data integrity protocol based on a homomorphic mechanism for securing remote data was developed by Alsudani et al. [15]. They handed over the computational tasks involved in audit phases to the main controlling server named AS, which triggered the audit tasks according to users' commands. The suggested scheme is proficient by introducing an extra AS server; however, the integrity confirmation approach needs to be addressed, which is considered the main apprehension of tenants due to the cloud infrastructure being a semi-honest service model. It also does not verify block indices and is susceptible to data replacement attacks.

3   Development of the Proposed Scheme

The BLS [21] short signature approach, ECC [22] encryption with Diffie hardness supposition [23], and MT [20] data structure. Table 1 presents all the notations used in the proposed scheme for easy understanding.

Table 1. Symbols used in the proposed technique.

Symbols	Description	Symbols	Description
S_{key}	Secret key	r	Rank information
P_{key}	Public key	v	Version number
$file_{chunks}$	Data file chunks	c	Challenge set
$random_n^{chunk}$	Random number for a chunk	x	Data block
s_n	Serial number	ξ	Vector number
ς	Date node	δ	Signature
$File$	Data file	$hashing$	Hash function
φ	Signature set	$auxiliary_{path}$	Auxiliary path of a node

3.1   System Model

The proposed technique authenticates the correctness of the outsourced data, which helps maintain the trust between the tenant and CSP. Three parties are involved in the proposed technique (see Fig. 1). 1) Tenant or data owner required to upload data to cloud storage. 2) CSP offers a scalable storage server and services on a pay-as-you-go model. 3) TPA

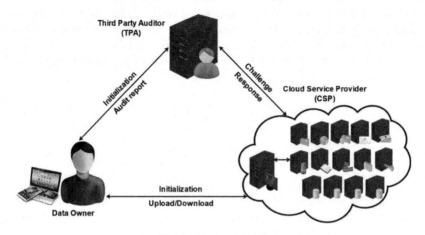

Fig. 1. System Model.

is responsible for performing the audit activities on tenants' commands and generating audit reports.

The solid arrows are denoted data flow and audit procedures of the proposed system, labelled with the respective process. The tenant generates the system parameters and public and private keys, files, and blocks' authenticators. Then, share the tree structure, public, and metadata with CSP and tags with the TPA. The auditor computes the audit request for CSP to check the data correctness, and the server computes the proof for requested blocks. After getting proof, TPA creates an audit report on whether the data is accurate.

3.2 System Development

The subsequent algorithms are involved in constructing the suggested protocol:

The tenant executes the tree functions in phase one, such as 1) system parameters generator; this method is used to initialise the system's security parameters to compute public and private key pair (p_k, s_k). . 2) Generate node authenticators; this method divides the file into chunks, encrypts these chunks, and includes position parameters as 0 or 1 where 0, 1 denotes the left and right side of the node in each sibling node of the tree. This position field helps to find the exact location of the node and avoid replacement attacks in case of incidentally or accidental data tempering by CSP. The server cannot replace this temper node with a healthy one to pass the audit phase. 3) Generate tag; all the blocks are arranged with respective authenticators to create internal and external tree nodes with left-to-right sequence order to create the root tree node treated as file tag f_t. This tag will be used as integrity evidence to authenticate the correctness of the remote data file in auditing procedures. Then, the tenant transfers all blocks and metadata to the CSP and files with block authenticators on the TPA.

In the second phase, TPA and CSP perform the audit jobs according to the tenants' commands; this phase also includes three methods. Like, 1) Generate audit request; TPA computes the audit request by randomly generating the sample data blocks $random_n{}^{chunks}$ from the given data blocks set and shares this request with the cloud to verify the correctness of requested blocks $ch = \{ch_1, ch_2, ch_3, \ldots, ch_n\}$. . 2) Generate data possession proof; after receiving a data auditing request from the TPA, the server generates the proof of data authentication. If the server cannot find the requested data node from the tree, it generates the failure report and sends it to the TPA; otherwise, compute the following proof.

$$\varsigma_{[s_n]} = \sum\nolimits_{[s_n]=l_1}^{l_m} x_{[s_n]}\left(\xi_{[s_n]}\right) \tag{1}$$

$$\delta_{[s_n]} = \prod\nolimits_{[s_n]=l_1}^{l_m} \delta_{[s_n]}^{(\xi_{[s_n]})} \tag{2}$$

and transfers an arbitrary number $\varsigma_{[s_n]}$ and $\delta_{[s_n]}$ block information to TPA; where s_n is a serial number of the node. 3) Proof verification; TPA authenticates the proof received from the CSP. If the proof is verified, the TPA generates the success report; otherwise, the failure report sends it to the tenant.

3.3 The Design Process of EPT

To reduce the computation complexity for searching nodes from the tree, we improve the current MT structure [13, 14, 18] to address the problems mentioned in the literature section. We adopted the left-to-right sequence order to quickly search the location of the nodes from the tree, which minimizes the computation complexity. We also include position parameters as 0 or 1, where 0, 1 denotes the left and right position of the node in each sibling node of the tree. Consequently, the auxiliary information in the newly created EPT structure differs from the structures defined in [13, 14, 18]. Thus, we can generate the nodes with the equation $x_i = h(h(x_i) \| x_i.p)$, where $h(x_i)$, and $x_i.p$ denotes the hash value and position of the given node. The internal nodes can be computed as $x_A = h(x_1 \| x_2 \| x_A.p)$, and the root node can be computed as $x_r = h(x_E \| x_F)$, we can notice that there is no position field in the root node. Figure 2 shows the 8 bits data block structure in EPT.

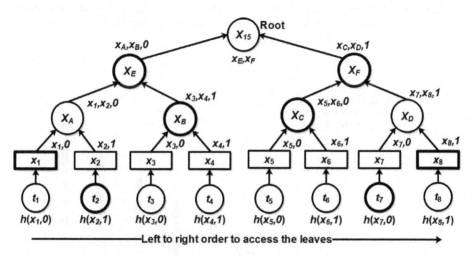

Fig. 2. EPT Structure.

4 Experiment and Discussion

To verify the proficiency of the proposed technique, we have developed a testbed environment using the PBC 5.14 [24] library, SSL 1.0 [25], BLS short signature method [21], and ECC [22] as 80bits of security level in C language. The testbed was run on a 2.2GHz CPU and 2GB RAM under Ubuntu 20.04 OS and used 10KB to 100KB of data files with 10 iterators.

In the initialization process, the current data auditing techniques [13, 14] acquire huge computational complexity on the tenant, which is not practically implemented specifically for resourced-restricted devices. As shown in Fig. 3, our technique reduces computation overheads compared to the existing techniques to generate the blocks and file authenticators. The experiments show that our technique is proficient and ensures privacy without compromising the security level of the cryptographic approach.

The time complexity of every entity is different because TPA only acquires the time to compute the audit request, verify the response message received from the CSP, and generate the audit report for a tenant. The time at CSP only occurs for generating the root value to create a proof of data the TPA requests. The tenant randomly chooses 460 nodes to authenticate the correctness of remotely stored data for 1% of data tempering to achieve 99% probability. Due to adopting a standard MT structure, the current techniques [13, 14] have acquired extra computational costs in the data auditing procedures than the proposed scheme.

In the challenge-request phase, the computational overhead of the existing techniques [13, 14] to find requested nodes is high $O(n)$, and linearly increase with the number of nodes because they do not utilized the sequence and position information to find the exact location of the node quickly. Due to the use of different indices fields, the EPT structure minimizes the computational cost from $O(n)$ to $O(logn)$ to search requested nodes as $(2n - 1)$ from the tree. Figure 4 shows the computational cost concerning the requested block in the challenge-response phase.

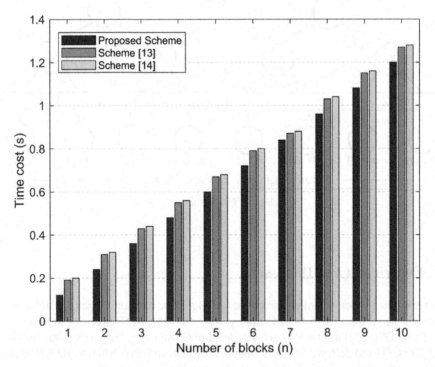

Fig. 3. Computation Complexity of all Operations.

The evaluation presents that our suggested scheme is more proficient and imposes minimum computation overheads.

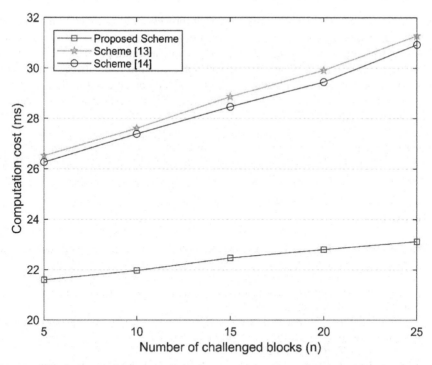

Fig. 4. Computation Complexity Concerning Number of Requested Blocks.

5 Conclusion

The proposed technique presents a public auditing mechanism based on the EPT structure to authenticate the correctness of uploaded files. The new construction of the EPT structure helps to minimise the time complexity of searching the requested nodes from the tree in the audit phase. The indices fields confirm the accuracy of uploaded tenants' files, which is very helpful to ensure that the CSP does not create a response other than the requested data blocks. The position field supports the prevention of replacement attacks because the position of requested blocks can be traced with this field. The proposed mechanism also supports performing an unrestricted number of queries to ensure data correctness. Additionally, it acquires and reduces the computational cost from $O(n)$ to $O(logn)$, with the newly designed EPT structure for a tenant, TPA, and cloud servers. The experimental evaluation shows that our proposed technique is secure and effective in computation and communicational overheads and does not linearly increase concerning data blocks. Therefore, our proposed scheme can be deployed in big data streaming of wireless networks and IoT environments.

6 Future Research Directions

We further plan to enhance the security mechanism at CSP so that tenants or TPAs cannot wrongly propagate that their data is not accurate to claim some compensation from CSP. On the other hand, CSP must perform dynamic data procedures before changing the altered data with a healthy block to pass the audit process or avoid sending the success message. Hence, a dispute will occur between the tenant and CSP, so it is important to trace which party is deceiving the other. Thus, data auditing protocol must address this problem to prevent non-repudiation attacks that create mistrust between tenants and CSPs, and the cloud can lose clients. In addition, an authorisation procedure does not exist between TPA and the cloud, which puts the audit as a service at risk and causes denial-of-service attacks.

Acknowledgements. This research was supported by the Ministry of Higher Education (MoHE) of Malaysia through Fundamental Research Grant Scheme (FRGS/1/2018/ICT04/UUM/02/17).

References

1. Yang, C., Zhao, F., Tao, X., Wang, Y.: Publicly verifiable outsourced data migration scheme supporting efficient integrity checking. J. Netw. Comput. Appl. **192**, 103184 (2021)
2. Chen, Z., et al.: The potential of nighttime light remote sensing data to evaluate the development of digital economy: a case study of China at the city level. Comput. Environ. Urban Syst.. Environ. Urban Syst. **92**, 101749 (2022)
3. Li, X., Liu, H., Wang, W., Zheng, Y., Lv, H., Lv, Z.: Big data analysis of the internet of things in the digital twins of smart city based on deep learning. Futur. Gener. Comput. Syst.. Gener. Comput. Syst. **128**, 167–177 (2022)
4. Wang, T., Zhou, J., Chen, X., Wang, G., Liu, A., Liu, Y.: A three-layer privacy-preserving cloud storage scheme based on computational intelligence in fog computing. IEEE Trans. Emerging Top. Comput. Intell. **2**(1), 3–12 (2018)
5. Xue, K., Chen, W., Li, W., Hong, J., Hong, P.: Combining data owner-side and cloud-side access control for encrypted cloud storage. IEEE Trans. Inf. Forensics Secur.Secur. **13**(8), 2062–2074 (2018)
6. Yang, R., Yu, F.R., Si, P., Yang, Z., Zhang, Y.: Integrated blockchain and edge computing systems: a survey, some research issues and challenges. IEEE Commun. Surv. Tutorials **21**(2), 1508–1532 (2019)
7. Yang, C., Tao, X., Zhao, F., Wang, Y.: Secure data transfer and deletion from counting bloom filter in cloud computing. Chin. J. Electron. **29**(2), 273–280 (2020)
8. Yang, C., Liu, Y., Zhao, F., Zhang, S.: Provable data deletion from efficient data integrity auditing and insertion in cloud storage. Comput. Stand. Interfaces **82**, 103629 (2022)
9. Koo, D., Hur, J.: Privacy-preserving deduplication of encrypted data with dynamic ownership management in fog computing. Futur. Gener. Comput. Syst.. Gener. **78**, 739–752 (2018)
10. El Kafhali, S., El Mir, I., Hanini, M.: Security threats, defence mechanisms, challenges, and future directions in cloud computing. Archives Comput. Methods Eng. **29**(1), 223–246 (2022)
11. Ahmad, W., Rasool, A., Javed, A.R., Baker, T., Jalil, Z.: Cyber security in IoT-based cloud computing: a comprehensive survey. Electronics **11**(1), 16 (2022)
12. Han, H., Fei, S., Yan, Z., Zhou, X.: A survey on blockchain-based integrity auditing for cloud data. Digital Communications and Networks (2022)
13. Anju, S.S., Sravani, B., Madala, S.R.: Publicly verifiable vibrant digital medical information systems. J. Phys. Conf. Ser. 2021, vol. 2089, no. 1: IOP Publishing, p. 012074
14. Dhansukhbhai, P.T., Dwivedi, P.: Data auditing and privacy preserving in cloud using fuzzy RSA algorithm. Research Journal of Engineering Technology and Medical Sciences (ISSN: 2582–6212), vol. 4, no. 03 (2021)

15. Alsudani, M.Q., Fakhruldeen, H.F., Al-Asady, H.A.-J., Jabbar, F.I.: Storage and encryption file authentication for cloud-based data retrieval. Bull. Electr. Eng. Inform. **11**(2), 1110–1116 (2022)
16. Juels, A., Kaliski Jr, B.S.: PORs: proofs of retrievability for large files. Presented at the Proceedings of the 14th ACM Conference on Computer and Communications Security (2007)
17. Erway, C., Küpçü, A., Papamanthou, C., Tamassia, R.: Dynamic provable data possession. Presented at the Proceedings of the 16th ACM Conference on Computer and Communications security, Chicago, Illinois, USA (2009)
18. Wang, Q., Wang, C., Ren, K., Lou, W., Li, J.: Enabling public auditability and data dynamics for storage security in cloud computing. IEEE Trans. Parallel Distrib. Syst. **22**(5), 847–859 (2011)
19. Tan, S., Jia, Y.: NaEPASC: a novel and efficient public auditing scheme for cloud data. J. Zhejiang Univ. Sci. C **15**(9), 794–804 (2015)
20. Merkle, R.C.: Protocols for public key cryptosystems. Presented at the IEEE Symposium on Security and Privacy (1980)
21. Boneh, D., Gentry, C., Lynn, B., Shacham, H.: Aggregate and verifiably encrypted signatures from bilinear maps. Presented at the International Conference on the Theory and Applications of Cryptographic Techniques (2003)
22. Hankerson, D., Menezes, A.J., Vanstone, S.: Guide to elliptic curve cryptography. Springer Science & Business Media (2006)
23. Boneh, D.: The decision Diffie-Hellman problem. Presented at the International Algorithmic Number Theory Symposium (1998)
24. Lynn, B.: The Pairing-based Cryptography Library (PBC). https://crypto.stanford.edu/pbc/download.html. Accessed 20 Jan 2023
25. O. Team. OpenSSL Project. https://www.openssl.org/docs/manmaster/man7/crypto.html. Accessed 20 Jan 2023

A Systematic Literature Review of Ransomware Detection Methods and Tools for Mitigating Potential Attacks

Mujeeb ur Rehman[1]($\boxtimes$) (ID), Rehan Akbar[1] (ID), Mazni Omar[2], and Abdul Rehman Gilal[3]

[1] Computer and Information Sciences Department, Universiti Teknologi PETRONAS, Seri Iskandar, Malaysia
mujeeb_22007910@utp.edu.my
[2] School of Computing, Universiti Utara Malaysia, 06010 Sintok, Malaysia
[3] School of Computing, University of Portsmouth, Portsmouth, UK

Abstract. In today's world, cybersecurity is critical in the field of information technology. With the rise of cyber-attacks, including ransomware attacks, protecting user data has become a top priority. Despite the various strategies employed by governments and companies to counteract cybercrime, ransomware continues to be a major concern. Therefore, there is a need to detect and obfuscate viruses in a better way. This immutable impact on the target is what recognizes ransomware attacks from traditional malware. Ransomware attacks are expected to become more problematic in the future. Attackers might use new encryption methods or obfuscation techniques to make ransomware detection and analysis a difficult job. To protect against such attacks, organizations and users employ various tools, guidelines, security guards, and best practices. However, despite these efforts, cyber-attacks have increased exponentially in recent years. Among the most devastating of these attacks is ransomware, which can encrypt user files or lock their devices' interfaces, rendering them unusable. This research paper provides a valuable resource for researchers, practitioners, and policymakers seeking to enhance their understanding of ransomware detection and mitigation. It also examines defense tactics, such as system backups and network breakdowns, which can help mitigate the impact of an attack. Finally, the paper considers upcoming challenges in the field of cybersecurity and the importance of staying vigilant in protecting against cyber threats.

Keywords: Cyberattack · Cybersecurity · Ransomware detection · Ransomware mitigation

1 Introduction

The Internet is currently the fastest-growing infrastructure, and modern technologies are transforming human activities. However, the widespread use of technology has resulted in increased cybercrime and the vulnerability of personal information [1]. The term "ransomware" originated from the word "ransom" and "malware," and it has become a

© The Author(s), under exclusive license to Springer Nature Singapore Pte Ltd. 2024
N. H. Zakaria et al. (Eds.): ICOCI 2023, CCIS 2001, pp. 80–95, 2024.
https://doi.org/10.1007/978-981-99-9589-9_7

significant contributor to the surge in cyberattacks as it can generate profits for attackers. In the past, hackers had difficulties profiting from their attacks, but this is no longer the case. Cybercriminals are increasingly using ransomware attacks where they gain access to a victim's data, encrypt it, and demand payment [2].

Ransomware is a type of virus that can prevent users from accessing their computer system. It frequently spreads through malicious websites that take advantage of flaws in hardware and software. Some of the most common ransomware viruses include CryptoLocker, Petya, Bad Rabbit, Ryuk and Maze [3]. These viruses primarily target document storage files, such as MS office, PDF, and CSV files, and use strong encryption to make them virtually inaccessible without a specific decryption key. Once infected, the attacker demands payment from the victim and provides instructions on how to retrieve the encrypted files. If the ransom is paid, the attacker will post a message on the computer screen with information on how to retrieve the files, thus ending the attack. This technique is known as cryptovirology [4].

Ransomware, which can appear as Crypto or Locker variations, is a highly hazardous and complex form of malware. Targeting and seizing control of crucial infrastructure and computer systems is its main goal. These assaults are generally carried out for financial gain, either directly by requesting ransom payments in exchange for decryption keys or indirectly. Researchers have thoroughly examined scholarly literature on the inner workings of ransomware, including its particular assault patterns and tactics, in the hunt for viable solutions [5, 6]. These effects can include data loss as a consequence of file encryption, significant costs for incident response and other security-related issues, and, in the worst cases, even fatalities as a result of unanticipated failures of vital medical equipment [7, 8].

Prior systematic reviews in academic literature have mostly focused on the effects of ransomware within specialized industries, such as healthcare, while ignoring the larger fact that ransomware assaults are prevalent across multiple areas. This study aims to fill this specific vacuum by providing a thorough analysis of the complete ransomware attack lifecycle and an understanding of its unique characteristics. This thorough study is meant to act as a basis for future research projects in this area. The report also explores current approaches for the detection and prevention of ransomware, offering a comprehensive evaluation of their relative benefits and drawbacks. Additionally, the article provides details on a variety of preventive techniques that may be used to reduce the risk associated with malicious activities.

1.1 Prior Research

Computer networks may be vulnerable to attacks that compromise the system or its users by taking advantage of connection or network flaws. These assaults may be roughly divided into two categories: active and passive, with each using a variety of strategies and ways to illegally obtain data, identities, or financial assets. While passive attacks only observe or eavesdrop on network activity without doing any harm, active attacks are intentional attempts to manipulate or harm the network [9].

Joseph L. Popp is known as the "father of ransomware" for creating the first ransomware virus in 1989. This set the stage for modern ransomware threats, which can be spread through infected USB drives or phishing emails containing malicious attachments or links. Ransomware has become a serious threat, often encrypting user data and demanding payment through difficult-to-trace bitcoin. Figure 1 provides a visual representation of ransomware.

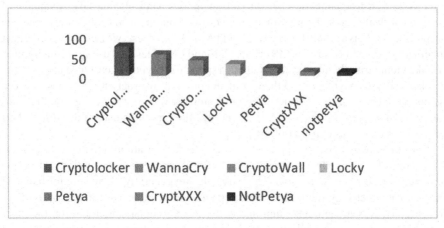

Fig. 1. List of Ransomware Attack [9]

1.2 Types of Ransomware Attacks

1) Crypto-Ransomware- Encrypts files on the victim's computer and demands a ransom for decryption. WannaCry, WannaCry, Petya, CryptoLocker [10].
2) Locker-Ransomware Locks the victim out of their system entirely, preventing access to any files or applications. Win locker, Police Trojan, FBI Virus [11].
3) Scareware Ransomware- Displays false warning messages to trick the victim into paying the ransom. Fake antiviruses, Tech support frauds.
4) RaaS (Ransomware-as-a-Service)- A business model where cybercriminals sell ransomware to other attackers for a share of the profits. Satan, Shark, Philadelphia.
5) Mobile Ransomware- target mobile devices, locking the user out or encrypting data on the device. Simplocker Android/Filecoder.C.

However, the role of operating systems in ransomware attacks cannot be overlooked. Observations have shown that devices utilizing the Windows operating system tend to be more susceptible to these attacks and are frequently singled out as targets [12]. Nevertheless, it's essential to recognize that other operating systems, such as iOS and MacOS, are not exempt from vulnerability. This underscores the fact that the threat of ransomware is pervasive and no operating system is impervious to it [13]. Figure 2 demonstrated in various instances.

Ransomware is a form of cyber-attack that involves the use of encryption to block access to a victim's data, and a demand for payment in exchange for the decryption key [14]. According to research conducted in the field, ransomware can be traced back to the

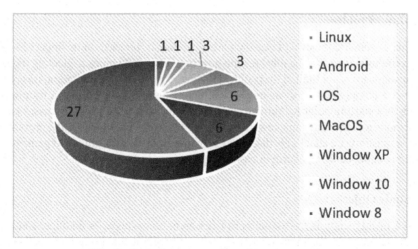

Fig. 2. Operating system effected by ransomware.

early 1990s, when cryptography was first used for exploitation purposes. However, at that time, it was not possible to demand money from victims because it was easy to trace the recipient. It was only with the introduction of cryptocurrency that the idea of using ransomware as a means of making money became viable. Therefore, the emergence of cryptocurrency can be linked to the rise of ransomware attacks.

Furthermore, a critical analysis of the impact of ransomware attacks on organizations in different countries was conducted. The analysis revealed that in 2021, approximately 50% of organizations in several countries were affected by ransomware attacks. The figure below depicts the countries where the highest number of organizations were negatively impacted by ransomware attacks (Fig. 3).

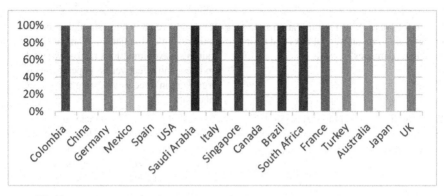

Fig. 3. Ransomware attack success rates in the past 12 months vary by country.

1.3 Major Problem

Previous systematic reviews of ransomware have mainly focused on its impact in specialized industries such as healthcare, and government organizations neglecting the fact that ransomware is not limited to specific domains. To address this limitation, this paper proposes a comprehensive evaluation of the detecting and mitigating of ransomware, serving as a starting point for further research. Furthermore, the paper discusses existing methods for detecting ransomware, analyzing their pros and cons. Lastly, prevention tools for ransomware attacks are discussed, providing valuable insights for organizations looking to enhance their security measures against ransomware threats.

1.4 Study Objectives

The aim of this study is to examine prior research, consolidate its findings, and concentrate on analyzing ransomware attacks, risks, mitigation, and prevention methods to control ransomware attacks. The study also aims to provide recommendations for the use of these techniques and tools, as well as identify areas for future research in this field. Ultimately, the objective would be to contribute to the development of more effective strategies for mitigating the impact of ransomware attacks. To achieve this goal, three research questions have been formulated, as shown in Table 1.

Table 1. Formulated Questions and discussion

Research Question	Discussion
What are the current state-of-the-art techniques and tools used for detecting ransomware?	The aim is to explain ransomware detection approaches without excessive technical detail. However, these techniques are not foolproof as attackers constantly develop new methods to evade detection [15, 16]
How effective are existing mitigation strategies in preventing ransomware attacks and their associated damages?	Ransomware prevention strategies (backup, antivirus, intrusion detection, and employee training) have limitations (zero-day attacks, updates) and effectiveness depends on an organization's security posture and threat landscape
What are the most common tactics and techniques used by ransomware attackers and how can these be thwarted?	To prevent ransomware attacks, use a multi-layered approach with technological and behavioral solutions, including multifactor authentication, regular backups, and system updates, as attackers use various tactics [15]

1.5 Contribution and Structure

This systematic literature review provides a valuable resource for individuals seeking to advance their knowledge in ransomware attacks and cyber security. By synthesizing previous research, it builds upon existing knowledge and makes new research, as discussed in Table 1.

- Our review identified 31 papers that are relevant to the topics of cyber security and ransomware threats and detection. This set of studies can serve as a resource for other researchers who seek to further investigate these areas.
- Organize and classify different methods of ransomware attacks into a specific taxonomy.
- We investigated the conditions utilized for evaluating defense, detection, mitigation, and prevention techniques against ransomware attacks.
- We identified available research data for a future analysis of ransomware and provided guidelines to assist in further research in this field.

The structure of this paper unfolds as follows: Sect. 2 explains the methodology employed to systematically select primary studies for our comprehensive analysis. In Sect. 3, we present the outcomes derived from our scrutiny of the selected primary research studies. Finally, Sect. 4 serves as the result of our research efforts, offering conclusions drawn from our findings and suggesting recommendations for future investigations.

2 Methodology

The research methodology section of this paper describes the systematic approach taken to look at previous studies about prospective ransomware attacks and their corresponding detection systems. Article offer details on the inclusion and exclusion criteria used to choose relevant research, also describe how we locate articles, papers, books, and journals about ransomware attacks.

2.1 Source Material

The study utilized a specific search engine and focused on entering relevant keywords to ensure the retrieval of primary research that would address the research questions. The selected keywords were carefully chosen to optimize the development of relevant findings. Boolean operators were limited to AND and OR. The search terms used were: (insert the specific keywords used).

("ransom" OR "ransom-ware" OR "ransomware" OR "Mal-ware" OR "Malware" OR "ransomware attacks") AND "information security" ("ransomware" OR "ransom" OR "Malware AND ("security" OR "cybersecurity" OR "cyber-security").

In the first phase, the task to be performed for the quality of research is to undertake an exhaustive literature search. Therefore, a search was conducted using six different electronic libraries namely IEEE Xplore, Science Direct, ACM, Springer, Web of Science, and Google Scholar to search for the relevant materials.

The search process for relevant studies involved using titles, keywords, and abstract depending on the platform used. All studies published up to a certain point were included and filtered based on the selection/eligibility criteria provided in Sect. 2.2. The search process was conducted iteratively, both forward and backward, until no further publications that met the selection criteria could be found.

According to [3, 17], ransomware refers to a type of malicious software that encrypts data and demands payment in exchange for its release. This literature review includes both published and ongoing research studies related to ransomware attacks. The review methodology involves a four-step process, which is illustrated in Fig. 4. The process includes library searches and various steps to identify and select relevant articles for analysis.

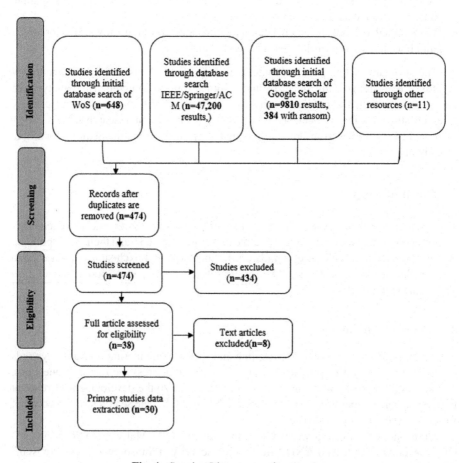

Fig. 4. Scoping Literature review process

To conduct the literature search, various search options were used in different databases. In IEEE, the search option "anywhere" was selected, while in Google Scholar, the "anywhere in the article" option was used. For Web of Science, the search was limited to the "subject" parameter. The search included a variety of publication types, such as journal articles, book sections, working papers, conference papers, dissertations, and reports.

Advanced search filters were used to refine search results, including past 13 years, document types, and English language. New keywords like "cyber risk" and "challenges and analysis" were added. A slimming approach was used to analyze articles, removing duplicates, and considering only English-language textual sources. 30 journal articles were selected for the literature study, as shown in Fig. 4.

2.2 Inclusion and Exclusion Criteria

A systematic literature review requires empirical evidence from case studies, new ransomware attacks, and advancements in ransomware mitigation technologies. English-written, peer-reviewed studies must meet standards, and only updated ones within recent years are considered. Google Scholar results may not meet standards, so all results are evaluated for compliance (Table 2).

Table 2. Inclusion and exclusion criteria for primary studies

Inclusion Criteria	Exclusion Criteria
The article offers insights and practical advice to protect against ransomware attacks and other cyber threats	The article should discuss papers that investigate the impact of ransomware attacks on businesses or the legal system
The document should provide an in-depth examination of ransomware or any other relevant technological advancement in your writing	Governmental documents and blogs should not be included in the article
The article must be a peer-reviewed paper published in a journal or conference proceedings	non-English publications

2.3 Selection Results

A total of 648 studies were searched, but duplicates were removed, leading to 474. After evaluating, 38 publications were identified. The criteria were applied again, reducing the number to 30 papers.

2.4 Quality Assessment

The primary studies were assessed for quality in accordance with the guidelines. The evaluation aimed to determine the relevance of the papers to the research questions while considering any possible research bias and the reliability of the experimental findings.

The evaluation process was modeled after similar literature reviews. To evaluate the effectiveness of randomly selected papers, a specific quality assessment procedure was implemented.

Step 1: Ransomware: The article should discuss multiple forms of ransomware attacks or security breaches and offer insightful commentary on a specific issue.
Step 2: Perspective: The research's objectives and conclusions should be properly contextualized to ensure a comprehensive understanding of the study.
Step 3: Ransomware detection Strategy: Study must provide enough information to show how technology is used to detect attacks and answer research questions, including specific tools and techniques used for detection and mitigation.
Step 4: Defense context: The document should explain the security issue to help answer research questions, including its nature, potential consequences, and challenges in addressing it.
Step 5: Security measures: The application of diverse security measures to alleviate several types of ransomware attacks.
Step 6: Data Recovery: Specifics on data collection, measurement, and reporting must be provided to assess accuracy.

2.5 Data Extraction

The data completeness and accuracy of articles were assessed by extracting data from quality-approved papers. The technique was tested on a preliminary investigation before being applied to the full set of research. Data was categorized and entered into a spreadsheet using the following categories.

Context Data: Information involving the study's performed objectives.

Qualitative Data: The author's findings and opinions.

Quantitative Data: Information collected through tests and research has been used in the study.

2.6 Meaningful Keywords Count

A keyword analysis was conducted on all 38 studies to identify the common themes among the selected primary research. The frequency of various words used across all studies was compiled and presented in Table 3. As observed in the table, "Machine Learning" is the third most frequent term in the dataset, following "ransomware" and "Trojan," and preceded only by the author's chosen keywords "ransomware" and "security".

Table 3. Keywords count from primary studies.

Keywords	Count
Ransomware	2451
Trojan	1752
Security	1664
Machine learning	1356
Information	853
Cybersecurity	334
Deep learning	675
Software	1320
Privacy	598
Attacks	486
Malware	475

3 Findings

Table 4 summarizes relevant qualitative and quantitative data extracted from the main research papers. Each primary study had a specific objective or theme related to previous research on ransomware attacks, which is also indicated in the table.

Table 4. Finding of the primary studies

PS	Key Qualitative	Type of research
[26]	The article covers the methodology and threats of Petya ransomware, as well as strategies for awareness and mitigation	effects
[27]	Healthcare companies can improve system defense through user-focused tactics like simulation and training on proper computer and network application usage [19]	Mitigation
[25]	The paper covers the impact of ransomware attacks on cloud service users and providers and proposes mitigating tactics.[28]	
[29]	To provide the decryption key for encrypted user data, hackers often demand a ransom or payment, typically in the form of digital currencies	
[19]	The paper stresses the importance of a written information security program mandated by Massachusetts law or other security frameworks	security
[30]	Memory forensics was conducted on volatile memory dumps of virtual machines using the Volatility framework for analysis	Detection
[9]	The report introduces Net Converse, a machine learning study for detecting ransomware network traffic reliably	
[18]	The article proposes DNA act-Ran, a digital DNA sequencing engine that uses machine learning to detect ransomware, utilizing frequency vectors and design limitations for digital sequencing	

3.1 RQ1: What Are the Current State-of-the-Art Techniques and Tools Used for Detecting Ransomware?

Ransomware detection techniques include behavioral analysis, signature-based detection, and machine learning. Popular tools include antivirus software, specialized ransomware detection tools, and managed detection and response services [32]. A combination of these techniques and tools can help detect and protect systems from ransomware attacks.

- Signature-based detection: Signature-based detection compares known malware signatures to identify malware (Malwarebytes)
- Heuristic-based detection: Heuristic-based detection analyzes the behavior of files or processes to detect malware. This can be more effect in detecting new or unknown ransomware
- Machine learning-based detection: Machine learning-based detection uses machine learning models to identify ransomware based on its behavior or characteristics, it may not be able to detect very new ransomware (Crowed strike falcon)
- Behavioral analysis: Behavioral analysis monitors process behavior to identify suspicious activity that may indicate the presence of ransomware, may generate false positive (McAfee)
- Network traffic analysis: Network traffic analysis examines network traffic to identify suspicious activity that may indicate the presence of ransomware
- Sandboxing: Sandboxing runs files or processes in a controlled environment to observe their behavior and identify ransomware

3.2 RQ2: How Effective Are Existing Mitigation Strategies in Preventing Ransomware Attacks and Their Associated Damages?

Mitigation strategies such as regular data backups, patch management, user education, and antivirus software can be effective in preventing ransomware attacks and their damages. However, their effectiveness depends on proper implementation and maintenance

Table 5. Mitigation Strategy

Mitigation Strategy	Effectiveness
Regular Data Backups	High
User Education and Awareness	High
Multi-factor Authentication	High
Network Segmentation	High
Vulnerability Patching	High
Endpoint Protection Software	Moderate
Intrusion Detection and Prevention Systems	Moderate
Security Information and Event Management (SIEM)	Moderate
Email Filtering and Spam Detection	Moderate
Encryption	Low
Incident Response Planning	Low

[33]. Organizations and individuals should prioritize these strategies to minimize the risk of ransomware attacks illustrated in Tables 5 and 6.

Table 6. Ransomware Tactic techniques

Tactic/Technique	Description	Possible Mitigations
Phishing Emails	Social engineering tricks users into clicking malicious links or opening infected attachments	User education and awareness, email filtering and spam detection, multi-factor authentication
Exploit Kits	Attackers use software vulnerabilities to gain access to systems or networks	Regular vulnerability patching, network segmentation; intrusion detection and prevention systems [27, 35]
Remote Desktop Protocol (RDP) Attacks	Attackers use brute-force methods to gain access to RDP connections [34]	Secure RDP access with strong passwords, MFA, IP whitelisting
Fileless Attacks	Fileless techniques evade detection and analysis, execute code sans disk [26]	Endpoint detection and response tools, intrusion detection and prevention systems, regular system auditing
Supply Chain Attacks	Attackers target third-party software providers to gain access to systems and networks [36]	Vendor risk management, regular patching and updates, network segmentation
Zero-Day Exploits	Attackers exploit unknown software vulnerabilities to access systems/networks [37]	Ensure security with scanning, IDS/IPS, and network segmentation

3.3 What Are the Most Common Tactics and Techniques Used by Ransomware Attackers and How Can These Be Thwarted?

Ransomware attackers commonly use social engineering, phishing, and software vulnerabilities to gain access to systems and demand payment [30]. To thwart these attacks, user education, software patching, data backups, network segmentation, and access controls can help prevent these attacks and limit their impact.

4 Mitigation and Prevention Techniques of Ransomware

Preventing ransomware is crucial to protect against its damaging effects on individuals and corporations. In case of infection, data recovery can be challenging and may require the help of a trusted specialist. Pre-encryption mitigation refers to the security measures taken before the encryption process to minimize the risk of security breaches.

- Implementing strict access policies, network segmentation, regular software, and hardware updates, password management and employee training and awareness
- Quarantine suspicious emails, inspect attachments in malware sandbox
- To identify unknown ransomware at pre-encryption stage
- During detection of ransomware, false positives, and false negatives high
- To prevent execution of exploits in a user's system
- Hibernate system to interrupt encryption and recover file encryption key
- To block ransomware when ransomware starts encryption, it is recommended

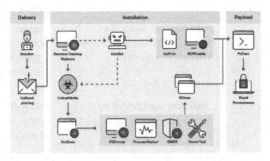

Fig. 5. Ransomware attack life cycle [32]

5   Recommendations

Ransomware is a major cybersecurity threat, with limitations in current prevention and detection methods. Improved prediction techniques are necessary to identify future attacks, along with cyber profiling and transaction tracing to track ransom payments and attackers. Despite significant research efforts, finding a long-term solution to pre-encryption of ransomware remains a critical challenge due to its dynamic nature. Organizations can minimize the risk of security breaches and protect sensitive information from unauthorized access, which can help them avoid costly security incidents and reputational damage (Fig. 5 and 6).

The ransomware mitigation paradigm focuses on defining parameters for the pre-encryption phase of the lifecycle, allowing the model to respond before sabotage occurs. This allocation prevents premature cutoff issues and allows for sufficient data collection. A temporally correlated pre-encryption description technique, based on the IRP-API, links resources to cryptography-related APIs. This API separates the pre-encryption phase and encryption phase for user-related files. Machine learning algorithms are applied to forecast ransomware or benign attacks, using pre-encryption border entries to identify ransomware instances [38].

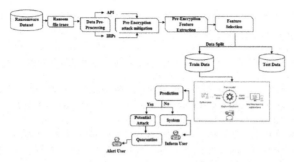

Fig. 6. Ransomware pre-encryption attack mitigation model

6 Conclusion

This paper discusses the emerging cyber-threat of ransomware and its monetary impact on organizations. It analyzes various security measures and proposes a model for preventive measures to avoid pre-encryption attacks. Tools like endpoint protection solutions, intrusion detection systems, and advanced threat detection technologies can help organizations detect and prevent ransomware attacks. Utilizing these tools enhances defense strategy effectiveness. In the future ransomware can be detected at early stage and also pre-encryption can be implemented with machine learning algorithm to reduce false positive and false negative rates, also can be improved using heuristic based to detect new and unknown ransomware.

Acknowledgement. This research work was supported by the Universiti Technologi PETRONAS, Malaysia STIRF Research Grant Project (Cost Centre No. 015LA0-036).

References

1. Kamil, S., Siti Norul, H.S.A., Firdaus, A., Usman, O.L.: The rise of ransomware: a review of attacks, detection techniques, and future challenges. In: 2022 Int. Conf. Bus. Anal. Technol. Secur. ICBATS 2022 (2022). https://doi.org/10.1109/ICBATS54253.2022.9759000
2. Yazdinejad, A., Parizi, R.M., Dehghantanha, A., Zhang, Q., Choo, K.K.R.: An energy-efficient SDN controller architecture for IoT networks with blockchain-based security. IEEE Trans. Serv. Comput.Comput. 13(4), 625–638 (2020). https://doi.org/10.1109/TSC.2020.2966970
3. Ekta, Bansal, U.: A review on ransomware attack. In: ICSCCC 2021 - Int. Conf. Secur. Cyber Comput. Commun., pp. 221–226 (2021). https://doi.org/10.1109/ICSCCC51823.2021.9478148
4. Sittig, D.F., Singh, H.: A socio-technical approach to preventing, mitigating, and recovering from Ransomware attacks. Appl. Clin. Inform. 7(2), 624–632 (2016). https://doi.org/10.4338/ACI-2016-04-SOA-0064
5. Monika, P.Z., Lindskog, D.: Experimental analysis of ransomware on windows and android platforms: evolution and characterization. Procedia Comput. Sci. 94, 465–472 (2016). https://doi.org/10.1016/j.procs.2016.08.072
6. Yazdinejad, A., Parizi, R.M., Dehghantanha, A., Choo, K.K.R.: P4-to-blockchain: a secure blockchain-enabled packet parser for software defined networking. Comput. Secur.. Secur. 88, 101629 (2020). https://doi.org/10.1016/j.cose.2019.101629

7. Zimba, A.: Malware-free intrusion: a novel approach to ransomware infection vectors. Int. J. Comput. Sci. Inf. Secur. **15**(2), 317–325 (2017). https://search.proquest.com/docview/1879494467?accountid=15977%5Cnhttp://su3pq4eq3l.search.serialssolution.com?ctx_ver=Z39.882004&ctx_enc=info:ofi/enc:UTF8&rfr_id=info:sid/ProQ%3Acriminaljusticeperiodicals&rft_val_fmt=info:ofi/fmt:kev:mtx:journal&rft.ge

8. Zimba, A., Wang, Z., Chen, H.: Multi-stage crypto ransomware attacks: a new emerging cyber threat to critical infrastructure and industrial control systems. ICT Express **4**(1), 14–18 (2018). https://doi.org/10.1016/j.icte.2017.12.007

9. Cohen, A., Nissim, N.: Trusted detection of ransomware in a private cloud using machine learning methods leveraging meta-features from volatile memory. Expert Syst. Appl. **102**, 158–178 (2018). https://doi.org/10.1016/j.eswa.2018.02.039

10. Reshmi, T.R.: Information security breaches due to ransomware attacks - a systematic literature review. Int. J. Inf. Manage. Data Insights **1**(2). Elsevier Ltd, Nov. 01, 2021. doi: https://doi.org/10.1016/j.jjimei.2021.100013

11. Maigida, A.M., Abdulhamid, S.M., Olalere, M., Alhassan, J.K., Chiroma, H., Dada, E.G.: Systematic literature review and metadata analysis of ransomware attacks and detection mechanisms. J. Reliab. Intell. Environ. **5**(2), 67–89 (2019). https://doi.org/10.1007/s40860-019-000 80-3

12. Alenezi, M.N., Alabdulrazzaq, H., Alshaher, A.A., Alkharang, M.M.: Evolution of malware threats and techniques: a review. Int. J. Commun. Networks Inf. Secur. **12**(3), 326–337 (2020). https://doi.org/10.17762/ijcnis.v12i3.4723

13. Yazdinejad, A., Dehghantanha, A., Parizi, R.M., Hammoudeh, M., Karimipour, H., Srivastava, G.: Block hunter: federated learning for cyber threat hunting in blockchain-based IIoT networks. IEEE Trans. Ind. Informatics **18**(11), 8356–8366 (2022). https://doi.org/10.1109/TII.2022.3168011

14. Abdullahi, M., Ngadi, M.A., Abdulhamid, S.M.: Symbiotic Organism Search optimization based task scheduling in cloud computing environment. Futur. Gener. Comput. Syst.. Gener. Comput. Syst. **56**, 640–650 (2016). https://doi.org/10.1016/j.future.2015.08.006

15. Urooj, U., Al-Rimy, B.A.S., Zainal, A., Ghaleb, F.A., Rassam, M.A.: Ransomware Detection using the dynamic analysis and machine learning: a survey and research directions. Appl. Sci. **12**(1) (2022). https://doi.org/10.3390/app12010172

16. Nadir, I., Bakhshi, T.: Contemporary cybercrime: a taxonomy of ransomware threats & mitigation techniques. In: 2018 Int. Conf. Comput. Math. Eng. Technol. Inven. Innov. Integr. Socioecon. Dev. iCoMET 2018 - Proc., vol. 2018-January, no. February, pp. 1–7 (2018). https://doi.org/10.1109/ICOMET.2018.8346329

17. Jegede, A., Fadele, A., Onoja, M., Aimufua, G., Mazadu, I.J.: Trends and future directions in automated ransomware detection. J. Comput. Soc. Informatics **1**(2), 17–41 (2022). https://doi.org/10.33736/jcsi.4932.2022

18. Khan, F., Ncube, C., Ramasamy, L.K., Kadry, S., Nam, Y.: A digital DNA sequencing engine for ransomware detection using machine learning. IEEE Access **8**, 119710–119719 (2020). https://doi.org/10.1109/ACCESS.2020.3003785

19. Naidu, P.S., Kharat, R.: Security in Computing and Communications, vol. 625 (2016). https://doi.org/10.1007/978-981-10-2738-3

20. Turner, A.B., McCombie, S., Uhlmann, A.J.: Discerning payment patterns in Bitcoin from ransomware attacks. J. Money Laund. Control **23**(3), 545–589 (2020). https://doi.org/10.1108/JMLC-02-2020-0012

21. Alhawi, O.M.K., Baldwin, J., Dehghantanha, A.: Leveraging machine learning techniques for windows ransomware network traffic detection. In: Advances in Information Security, vol. 70, Springer New York LLC, pp. 93–106 (2018). https://doi.org/10.1007/978-3-319-739 51-9_5

22. Humayun, M., Jhanjhi, N.Z., Alsayat, A., Ponnusamy, V.: Internet of things and ransomware: evolution, mitigation and prevention. Egypt. Informatics J. **22**(1), 105–117 (2021). https://doi.org/10.1016/j.eij.2020.05.003

23. Sajjan, R.S., Ghorpade, V.R.: Ransomware attacks: Radical menace for cloud computing. In: Proc. 2017 Int. Conf. Wirel. Commun. Signal Process. Networking, WiSPNET 2017, vol. 2018-January, no. May 2005, pp. 1640–1646 (2018). https://doi.org/10.1109/WiSPNET. 2017.8300039

24. Azzedin, F., Suwad, H., Rahman, M.M.: An asset-based approach to mitigate zero-day ransomware attacks. Comput. Mater. Contin. **73**(2), 3003–3020 (2022). https://doi.org/10.32604/cmc.2022.028646

25. Yeboah-ofori, A.: Mitigating Cybercrimes in An Evolving Organizational Landscape (2022)

26. Aslan, O., Samet, R.: A comprehensive review on malware detection approaches. IEEE Access **8**, 6249–6271 (2020). https://doi.org/10.1109/ACCESS.2019.2963724

27. Akhtar, M.S., Feng, T.: Malware analysis and detection using machine learning algorithms. Symmetry **14**(11) (2022). https://doi.org/10.3390/sym14112304

28. S. Sundaram, IEEE Computational Intelligence Society, and Institute of Electrical and Electronics Engineers, Proceedings of the 2018 IEEE Symposium Series on Computational Intelligence (SSCI 2018) : 18–21 November 2018, Bengaluru

29. Naeem, M.R., et al.: A malware detection scheme via smart memory forensics for windows devices. Mob. Inf. Syst. 2022, 2022, doi: https://doi.org/10.1155/2022/9156514

30. Kapoor, A., Gupta, A., Gupta, R., Tanwar, S., Sharma, G., Davidson, I.E.: Ransomware detection, avoidance, and mitigation scheme: a review and future directions. Sustain. **14**(1), 1–24 (2022). https://doi.org/10.3390/su14010008

31. Al-rimy, B.A.S., Maarof, M.A., Shaid, S.Z.M.: Ransomware threat success factors, taxonomy, and countermeasures: a survey and research directions. Comput. Secur.. Secur. **74**, 144–166 (2018). https://doi.org/10.1016/j.cose.2018.01.001

32. Maurya, A.K., Kumar, N., Agrawal, A., Khan, R.A.: Ransomware evolution, target and safety measures. Int. J. Comput. Sci. Eng.Comput. Sci. Eng. **6**(1), 80–85 (2018). https://doi.org/10.26438/ijcse/v6i1.8085

33. Maimó, L.F., Celdrán, A.H., Perales Gómez, Á.L., García Clemente, F.J., Weimer, J., Lee, I.: Intelligent and dynamic ransomware spread detection and mitigation in integrated clinical environments. Sensors **19**(5), 1–31 (2019). https://doi.org/10.3390/s19051114

34. Yazdinejad, A., Bohlooli, A., Jamshidi, K.: Performance improvement and hardware implementation of Open Flow switch using FPGA. In: 2019 IEEE 5th Conf. Knowl. Based Eng. Innov. KBEI 2019, no. February, pp. 515–520 (2019). doi: https://doi.org/10.1109/KBEI. 2019.8734914

35. Subedi, K.P., Budhathoki, D.R., Dasgupta, D.: Forensic analysis of ransomware families using static and dynamic analysis. In: Proc. - 2018 IEEE Symp. Secur. Priv. Work. SPW 2018, pp. 180–185 (2018). https://doi.org/10.1109/SPW.2018.00033

36. Beaman, C., Barkworth, A., Akande, T.D., Hakak, S., Khan, M.K.: Ransomware: Recent advances, analysis, challenges and future research directions. Comput. Secur. **111**, December 2021. https://doi.org/10.1016/j.cose.2021.102490

37. I. PES Institute of Technology (Bangalore, IEEE Communications Society, IEEE Photonics Society. Bangalore Chapter, IEEE Robotics and Automation Society. Bangalore Chapter, and Institute of Electrical and Electronics Engineers, 2018 International Conference on Advances in Computing, Communications and Informatics (ICACCI), 19–22 Sept. 2018

38. Alqahtani, A., Gazzan, M., Sheldon, F.T.: A proposed Crypto-Ransomware Early Detection (CRED) model using an integrated deep learning and vector space model approach. In: 2020 10th Annual Computing and Communication Workshop and Conference (CCWC), Las Vegas, NV, USA, 2020, pp. 0275–0279. https://doi.org/10.1109/CCWC47524.2020.9031182

A Systematic Literature Review of Intrusion Detection System in Network Security

Guntoro Guntoro[1,2](✉) 🔟 and Mohd. Nizam Bin Omar[1]

[1] University Utara Malaysia, 06010 Sintok, Kedah, Malaysia
guntoro_g@ahsg.uum.edu.my
[2] Universitas Lancang Kuning, Pekanbaru, Indonesia

abstract
Abstract. In the rapidly evolving information technology landscape, network attacks are becoming more sophisticated and pose significant threats. Intrusion Detection Systems (IDS) have emerged as crucial tools for mitigating network security risks. Despite the vast amount of research on IDS methods, there still remains a gap in comprehensive literature reviews that cover recent developments in techniques, datasets, and tools. This study conducted a comprehensive systematic literature review to address this gap, analyzing 67 selected articles. The review covered various aspects, including IDS research domains, techniques/methods, datasets, and simulators. By synthesizing the findings, the study provides valuable insights into the current state of IDS research and identifies future challenges and unexplored areas. This review sheds light on the strengths and limitations of existing IDS techniques and datasets, offering researchers and practitioners a holistic understanding of the field. The identified research gaps and unexplored topics will guide future research endeavors, leading to advancements in IDS techniques and bolstering network security.

Keywords: Intrusion Detection System · IDS · Network Security · Systematic Literature Review

1 Introduction

The advancement of computer technology continues in the modern era, providing network technology and the Internet of Things (IoT) for everyday use Kalimuthan and Arokia Renjit [1]. Indeed, this has led to the storage of vast amounts of personal, commercial, military, and government information through network infrastructure. As a result, security has become a major concern.

Information technology security is a crucial issue, and extensive research has been conducted on intrusion detection [2]. To enhance the performance of Intrusion Detection Systems (IDS), various techniques have been employed, both using machine learning methods [3] and deep learning approach [4, 5]. In addition to improving individual methods, another approach is to utilize ensemble learning techniques [6]. A network system can be disrupted by a variety of attacks, which are classified into two types: passive and aggressive attacks[7]. Intrusion Detection Systems (IDS) are considered

© The Author(s), under exclusive license to Springer Nature Singapore Pte Ltd. 2024
N. H. Zakaria et al. (Eds.): ICOCI 2023, CCIS 2001, pp. 96–107, 2024.
https://doi.org/10.1007/978-981-99-9589-9_8

the most efficient systems for detecting intrusions and protecting computer networks. Intrusion Detection Systems (IDS) are software applications that monitor computer networks for malicious activities such as information theft, tampering, or disrupting network protocols [8].

In recent years, several datasets and intrusion detection techniques have been available for building IDS. These datasets are divided into two categories: public datasets and private datasets. Some public datasets that can be used for testing IDS include KDD'99 [9], NSL-KDD [9] and CICIDS2017 [10]. Meanwhile, some private datasets used in IDS include In-vehicle network [11], Bot-IoT [12], ToN-IoT [12], and Virus Total [13]. Several techniques that can be implemented in intrusion detection systems include machine learning and deep learning.

Some machine learning methods that have been applied in IDS include Support Vector Machine (SVM) [14], Random Forest [15], Ensemble (Decision Tree + Random Forest) [16], and C5.0 [17]. Meanwhile, the most popular deep learning methods used in IDS are Convolutional Neural Network (CNN) [18] and Deep Neural Network (DNN) Vinayakumar et al. (2019) [19] Based on previous research, several studies can be conducted related to IDS:

- Researchers can determine which datasets are utilized most frequently due to the vast array of dataset categories available for IDS.
- Many IDS employ various intrusion detection methods; thus, understanding the techniques most commonly used by researchers currently is crucial.
- Several strategies have been implemented in Intrusion Detection Systems (IDS), but not all consistently identify intrusions with high accuracy.
- Many IDS use a range of simulators and programming languages; hence, it's vital to grasp the programming languages most often used by researchers.

As a result, this study aims to perform a Systematic Literature Review (SLR) to identify and assess trends in IDS research approaches, datasets, and methodologies from January 2019 through March 2023. The article is divided into five parts. Section 1 is an introduction, Sect. 2 is a review of relevant literature, Sect. 3 is the methodology, Sect. 4 is the study results, and Sect. 5 is a conclusion with recommendations for future research.

2 Related Work

There is a vast body of literature covering various aspects of intrusion detection. This section will present relevant existing works and compare them to our study. In a study [20], the researchers used the firefly optimization algorithm. This algorithm was employed to eliminate irrelevant features and reduce the dimensionality of the data, thereby improving the classification time. Additionally, SVM was used to evaluate the results obtained from the generated features. The proposed method achieved an accuracy of 78.89%.

According to [21], the researchers identified the necessary features in developing an intrusion detection model to achieve maximum accuracy. The model employed an ensemble approach, utilizing feature selection through the Chi-square method and an ensemble-based intrusion detection model consisting of Support Vector Machine (SVM), modified Naive Bayes (MNB), and LPBoost. The experimental results demonstrated that normal, DoS, and R2L attacks were detected with an accuracy of 99%, probe attacks with 98%, and U2R attacks with 100% accuracy.

[22] reported that an IDS based on Information Gain and Multi-layer Perceptron Artificial Neural Network was developed. The research selected 30 attributes from the UNSW-NB15 dataset. The experimental results showed an accuracy of 76.96% and a Matthews Correlation Coefficient (MCC) of 0.57. These results indicate that the developed technique can be used for real-time IDS.

Based on the mentioned studies, it can be concluded that each research has different approaches and methods for developing intrusion detection models. Each study achieved varying levels of accuracy, [21] obtaining the highest accuracy. Therefore, our study will compare and evaluate existing approaches and methods to develop a more optimal and accurate IDS model.

3 Methodology

3.1 Method of Reviewing

A Systematic Literature Review (SLR) on IDS utilizes a well-known literature review methodology known as a Systematic Literature Review, following the original guidelines proposed [23]. The Systematic Literature Review (SLR) process is divided into three primary phases: planning, execution, and reporting. These phases ensure a comprehensive and structured review of the literature related to IDS.

3.2 Research Questions

The primary aim of this study is to examine the new and developing subjects and patterns in scientific research within the broader field of Intrusion Detection Systems in Network Security [24]. Questions are essential to research. Table 1 answers this literature review's research questions.

3.3 Search Strategy

- Search Term and Literature Resource
     There are stages involved in constructing the search terms for this study [23]. The search string used is as follows: (("Title":"Intrusion Detection System" OR "IDS" OR "Intrusion Detection" and "Network Security") AND "Abstract":"Intrusion Detection System" OR "IDS" OR "Intrusion Detection" and "Network Security"). This study utilized four electronic databases to search for primary study sources, namely: IEEE Xplore (ieeexplore.ieee.org), ScienceDirect (sciencedirect.com), Springer (springerlink.com), and Google Scholar (scholar.google.com).
- Search Process
     The literature collection procedure yielded a total of 20,561 documents. After filtering based on full-text evaluation, only 67 relevant articles addressing IDS-related issues were identified. Figure 1 depicts the entire search and selection procedure. Table 1 provides a comprehensive listing of the selected studies included in this SLR.

Table 1. Research Questions

Number	Questions	Motivations
RQ1	What is the IDS research domain?	IDS research domain identification
RQ2	What is the technique used in IDS?	Identify the techniques used in IDS
RQ3	What is the dataset used in IDS?	Identification of datasets used in IDS
RQ4	What is the method used in IDS research?	Identification of the methods used in IDS research
RQ5	What is the method that is often used in IDS?	Identify methods that are often used in IDS
RQ6	Is the simulator or programming language used?	Identify the simulator or programming language used

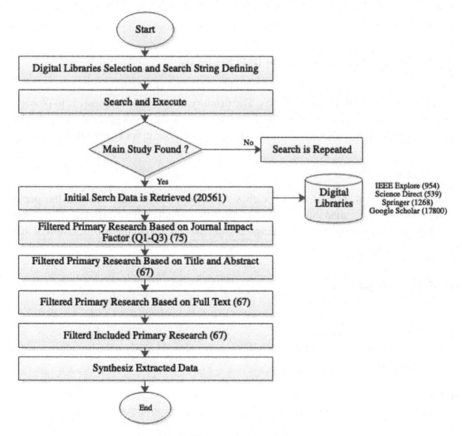

Fig. 1. Paper Selection Process

3.4 Study Selection

Specific inclusion and exclusion criteria are used to select the primary studies [25]. The inclusion criteria are as follows: 1) articles must be published in journals. 2) articles are selected based on the journal's impact factor, limited to Q1-Q3. 3) papers on the subject of IDS primarily compare algorithms or techniques. On the other hand, the exclusion criteria are as follows: 1) Research not written in English. 2) Literature review studies. 3) Studies without substantial IDS validation. 4) Research addressing intrusion methods and datasets unrelated to IDS contexts. 5) Studies not centered on relevant subjects.

3.5 Data Extraction

To address the research questions, data collection from primary studies is necessary. Following that, we will perform data extraction using the collected data. We will extract the IDS research area (to address RQ1), IDS techniques (to address RQ2), IDS datasets (to address RQ3), IDS methodologies (to address RQ3, RQ4, RQ5), and IDS simulators (to address RQ6).

3.6 Study Quality Assessment and Data Synthesis

Assessing the quality of studies is essential to enhance the understanding of synthesized findings and solidify conclusions. The primary aim of data synthesis is to provide comprehensive responses to all research inquiries. This data is organized based on the research question. It is then visualized using pie charts, bar graphs, and tables.

3.7 Threat Validation

There is a potential threat to this review's reliability. This occurs because the paper search solely entails manually reviewing the titles of all journal articles. Therefore, specific papers might have yet to undergo comprehensive screening for inclusion in this study.

4 Research Result

RQ1: IDS Research Domain
Table 2 presents the research domains of IDS are presented based on the literature review of 67 primary studies.

RQ3: IDS Datasets
A review of 67 primary studies identified 5 private and 100 public datasets. This indicates that 93% of the datasets are public, with only 7% are private. Table 3 illustrates the distribution of public and private IDS datasets between January 2019 and March 2023.

RQ4: Method Used in IDS
Twenty-seven classification algorithms are among the top IDS approaches based on

Table 2. Number of Papers by Domain in Intrusion Detection Methods

Domain	Number
Internet	57
Internet of Things (IoT)	6
Real Vehicle	1
Wireless Mesh Network	1
Wireless IDS	1

Table 3. The datasets used in papers

Dataset	Count
NSL-KDD	33
UNSW-NB15	25
KDD CUP99	19
CIC-IDS 2017	11
ISCX2012	4
CICDDoS2019	2
CSE-CIC-IDS 2018	2
ADFA-LD	1
AWID	1
Bot-IoT	1
CIDDS-001	1
Kyoto	1
Real Vehicle	1
ToN-IoT	1
VirusTotal	1
WSN-DS	1

primary investigations from January 2019 to March 2023. The number of studies per approach is as follows: SVM = 16, RF = 13, DT = 8, ANN = 6, LR = 5, BPNN = 5, KNN = 5, Auto-Encoder = 4, MLP = 3, NB = 3, CNN = 2, DNN = 2, etc. With 16 research studies, SVM is the most popular algorithm. Figure 2 displays the count of studies for each IDS algorithm.

RQ5: Most Used Methods in IDS

Based on Fig. 3, one can observe that the most frequently used methods in IDS are Support Vector Machine (SVM) (27%), Random Forest (RF) (22%), Decision Tree

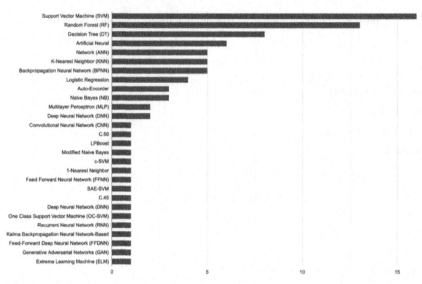

Fig. 2. Methods Used in IDS

(DT) (14%), Artificial Neural Network (ANN) (10%), K-Nearest Neighbor (KNN) (9%), Backpropagation Neural Network (BPNN) (9%), and Logistic Regression (9%).

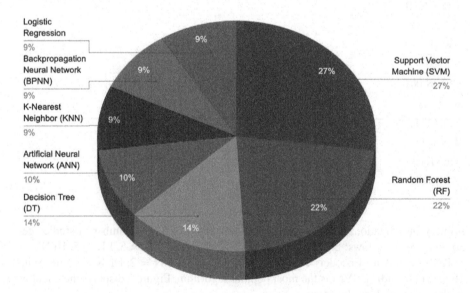

Fig. 3. Most Used Methods

RQ6: Is the Simulator or Programming Language Used?

The most popular simulators or programming languages between January 2019 and

March 2023, as indicated by the selected primary research, include Python (20), Matlab (20), Weka (4), Sucirata (1), Rapidminer (1), C# (1), and Java (1). This information is depicted in Fig. 4.

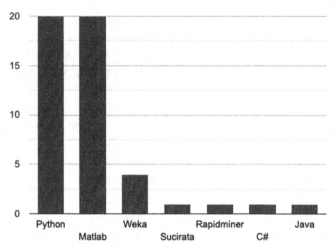

Fig. 4. Simulators Used

5   Conclusion

A literature review is required to find the most recent trends in the approaches, methods, and datasets used by IDS researchers. A survey of articles published in various major journals between January 2019 and March 2023 revealed 67 articles discussing IDS research. This study of the literature utilized a Systematic Literature Review (SLR).

Based on the conducted literature review, the research domain of IDS still predominantly focuses on the general internet. However, some IDS studies have begun to specifically target the field of IoT. Regarding the datasets used, the review found that 93% of the datasets were public, while only 7% were private.

Frequently used methods in IDS include Support Vector Machine (SVM) (27%), Random Forest (RF) (22%), Decision Tree (DT) (14%), Artificial Neural Network (ANN) (10%), K-Nearest Neighbor (KNN) (9%), Backpropagation Neural Network (BPNN) (9%), and Logistic Regression (9%). Regarding the commonly used simulators or programming languages, they include Python (20), Matlab (20), Weka (4), Sucirata (1), Rapidminer (1), C# (1), and Java (1).

Many researchers have developed methodologies and methods for reducing IDS datasets' characteristics to lower computational complexity. Furthermore, machine learning classification is commonly employed in IDS to enhance accuracy. Specifically, the combination of multiple machine learning methods, such as boosting, bagging, stacking, and others, has been utilized. Therefore, future work can explore feature selection combination methods to address the dimensionality issues in IDS datasets and employ classification methods to improve accuracy in intrusion detection (Table 4).

Table 4. The List of IDS Primary Studies

No	Ref	Year	Dataset
1	(Lee and Park 2019)	2019	CICIDS 2017
2	(Gurung et al. 2019)	2019	NSL-KDD
3	(Vinayakumar et al. 2019)	2019	KDD CUP99, NSL-KDD, UNSW-NB15, Kyoto, WSN-DS, CICIDS2017
4	(Ghanem and Jantan 2020)	2019	KDD CUP99, ISCX2012, NSL-KDD, UNSW-NB15
5	(Duan et al. 2019)	2019	NSL-KDD
6	(Binbusayyis and Vaiyapuri 2019)	2019	KDD CUP99, NSL-KDD, UNSW-NB15, CICIDS2017
7	(Gu et al. 2019)	2019	NLS-KDD
8	(Iqbal and Aftab 2019)	2019	KDD CUP99
9	(Al-Yaseen 2019)	2019	NSL-KDD
10	(Thaseen et al. 2019)	2019	NSL-KDD
11	(Mazini et al. 2019)	2019	NSL-KDD, ISCXIDS2012
12	(Mousavi et al. 2019)	2019	KDD CUP99
13	(Mohammadi et al. 2019)	2019	KDD CUP99
14	(Vijayanand and Devaraj 2020)	2020	CICIDS2017, ADFA-LD
15	(Li et al. 2020)	2020	CSE-CIC-IDS 2018
16	(Almomani 2020)	2020	UNSW-NB15
17	(Kunhare et al. 2020)	2020	NSL-KDD
18	(Kasongo and Sun 2020a)	2020	UNSW-NB15
19	(Almiani et al. 2020)	2020	NSL-KDD
20	(Devan and Khare 2020)	2020	NSL-KDD
21	(Sumaiya Thaseen et al. 2021)	2020	NSL-KDD, UNSW-NB15
22	(Chkirbene et al. 2020)	2020	NSL-KDD, UNSW-NB15
23	(Alzubi et al. 2020)	2020	NSL-KDD
24	(Song et al. 2020b)	2020	Real Vehicle
25	(Binbusayyis and Vaiyapuri 2020)	2020	NSL-KDD, UNSW-NB15
26	(Kasongo and Sun 2020b)	2020	UNSW-NB15
27	(Zhou et al. 2020)	2020	NSL-KDD, AWID, CIC-IDS2017
28	(Chen et al. 2020)	2020	UNSW-NB15, KDD CUP99
29	(Mebawondu et al. 2020)	2020	UNSW-NB15
30	(Maniriho et al. 2020)	2020	NSL-KDD, UNSW-NB15

(continued)

Table 4. (*continued*)

No	Ref	Year	Dataset
31	(Bhati and Rai 2019)	2020	NSL-KDD
32	(Meira et al. 2020)	2020	NSL-KDD, ISCXIDS2012
33	(Alamiedy et al. 2020)	2020	NSL-KDD
34	(Velliangiri 2020)	2020	KDD CUP99
35	(Ali et al. 2020)	2020	KDD CUP99
36	(Albahar et al. 2020)	2020	NSL-KDD, CIC-IDS-2017, UNSW-NB15
37	(Pawlicki et al. 2020)	2020	CIC-IDS2017
38	(Alzahrani et al. 2020)	2020	NSL-KDD
39	(Alazzam et al. 2020)	2021	KDD CUP99, NSL-KDD, UNSW-NB15
40	(Dwivedi et al. 2021)	2021	NSL-KDD, KDD CUP99
41	(Ajdani and Ghaffary 2021b)	2021	UNSW-NB15, KDD CUP99
42	(Ajdani and Ghaffary 2021a)	2021	Virus Total
43	(Lu et al. 2021)	2021	KDD CUP99, UNSW-NB15
44	(Almiani et al. 2021)	2021	CICDDoS2019
45	(Sekhar et al. 2021)	2021	NSL_KDD, UNSW-NB15
46	(Al-Daweri et al. 2021)	2021	KDD CUP99, UNSW-NB15
47	(Mighan and Kahani 2021)	2021	UNSW-NB15, UNB-ISCX 2012, CICIDS 2017
48	(Kshirsagar and Kumar 2021)	2021	UNSW-NB15
49	(Abdulrahman and Ibrahem 2021)	2021	CIC-IDS2017
50	(Anitha and Kaarthick 2021)	2021	KDD CUP99
51	(Farzadnia et al. 2021)	2021	UNSW-NB15
52	(Aziz and Ahmad 2021)	2021	NSL-KDD, UNSW-NB15
53	(Sharma and Yadav 2021)	2021	KDD CUP99
54	(Ajdani et al. 2022)	2022	VirusTotal
55	(Al-Yaseen et al. 2022)	2022	NSL-KDD
56	(Aziz and Alfoudi 2022)	2022	NSL-KDD
57	(Bhuvaneshwari et al. 2022)	2022	NSL-KDD
58	(Wu et al. 2022)	2022	NSL-KDD
59	(Almotiri 2022)	2022	CICDDoS2019
60	(Pranto et al. 2022)	2022	NSL-KDD
61	(Kurniabudi et al. 2022)	2022	CICIDS-2017
62	(Dwivedi et al. 2022)	2022	KDD CUP99, CIC-IDS 2017

(*continued*)

Table 4. (*continued*)

No	Ref	Year	Dataset
63	(Farooq 2022)	2022	KDD CUP99
64	(Kunhare et al. 2022)	2022	NSL-KDD
65	(Mokbal et al. 2022)	2022	CICIDS2017
66	(de Carvalho Bertoli et al. 2023a)	2023	UNSW-NB15, CSE-CIC-IDS-2018, Bot-IoT, ToN-IoT
67	(Abu Alghanam et al. 2023)	2023	UNSW-NB15, KDD CUP99, NSL-KKD

References

1. Kalimuthan, C., Renjit, J.A.: Review on intrusion detection using feature selection with machine learning techniques. Mater. Today Proc. **33**, 3794–3802 (2020)
2. Ring, M., Wunderlich, S., Scheuring, D., Landes, D., Hotho, A.: A survey of network-based intrusion detection data sets. Comput. Secur. **86**, 147–167 (2019)
3. Fagerholm, N., et al.: Perceived contributions of multifunctional landscapes to human well-being: evidence from 13 European sites. People Nat. **2**, 217–234 (2020). https://doi.org/10.1002/pan3.10067
4. Aleesa, A.M., Younis, M., Mohammed, A.A., Sahar, N.M.: Deep-intrusion detection system with enhanced UNSW-NB15 dataset based on deep learning techniques. J. Eng. Sci. Technol. **16**, 711–727 (2021)
5. Toth, T.: Improving Intrusion Detection Systems, p. 147 (2003)
6. Khonde, S.R., Ulagamuthalvi, V.: Ensemble-based semi-supervised learning approach for a distributed intrusion detection system. J. Cyber Secur. Technol. **3**, 163–188 (2019)
7. Khan, K., Mehmood, A., Khan, S., Khan, M.A., Iqbal, Z., Mashwani, W.K.: A survey on intrusion detection and prevention in wireless ad-hoc networks. J. Syst. Archit. **105** (2020)
8. Ozkan-Okay, M., Samet, R., Aslan, O., Gupta, D.: A comprehensive systematic literature review on intrusion detection systems. IEEE Access **9**, 157727–157760 (2021). https://doi.org/10.1109/ACCESS.2021.3129336
9. Rama Devi, R., Abualkibash, M.: Intrusion detection system classification using different machine learning algorithms on KDD-99 and NSL-KDD datasets - a review paper. Int. J. Comput. Sci. Inf. Technol. **11**, 65–80 (2019). https://doi.org/10.5121/ijcsit.2019.11306
10. Maseer, Z.K., Yusof, R., Bahaman, N., Mostafa, S.A., Foozy, C.F.M.: Benchmarking of machine learning for anomaly based intrusion detection systems in the CICIDS2017 dataset. IEEE Access **9**, 22351–22370 (2021). https://doi.org/10.1109/ACCESS.2021.3056614
11. Song, H.M., Woo, J., Kim, H.K.: In-vehicle network intrusion detection using deep convolutional neural network. Veh. Commun. **21**, 100–198 (2020)
12. de Bertoli, C., Gustavo, L.A.P.J., Saotome, O., dos Santos, A.L.: Generalizing intrusion detection for heterogeneous networks: a stacked-unsupervised federated learning approach. Comput. Secur. **127**, 103–106 (2023)
13. Ajdani, M., Noori, A., Ghaffary, H.: Providing a consistent method to model the behavior and modelling intrusion detection using a hybrid particle swarm optimization-logistic regression algorithm. Secur. Commun. Netw. **2022** (2022). https://doi.org/10.1155/2022/5933086
14. Dwivedi, S., Vardhan, M., Tripathi, S.: Defense against distributed DoS attack detection by using intelligent evolutionary algorithm. Int. J. Comput. Appl. **44**, 219–229 (2022)

15. Kunhare, N., Tiwari, R., Dhar, J.: Intrusion detection system using hybrid classifiers with meta-heuristic algorithms for the optimization and feature selection by genetic algorithm. Comput. Electr. Eng. **102**, 108383 (2022)
16. Chkirbene, Z., Erbad, A., Hamila, R., Mohamed, A., Guizani, M., Hamdi, M.: TIDCS: a dynamic intrusion detection and classification system based feature selection. IEEE Access **8**, 95864–95877 (2020). https://doi.org/10.1109/ACCESS.2020.2994931
17. Abdulrahman, A.A., Ibrahem, M.K.: Intrusion detection system using data stream classification. Iraqi J. Sci. **62**, 319–328 (2021). https://doi.org/10.24996/ijs.2021.62.1.30
18. Bhuvaneshwari, K.S., Venkatachalam, K., Hubálovský, S., Trojovský, P., Prabu, P.: Improved dragonfly optimizer for intrusion detection using deep clustering CNN-PSO classifier. Comput. Mater. Contin. **70**, 5949–5965 (2022). https://doi.org/10.32604/cmc.2022.020769
19. Devan, P., Khare, N.: An efficient XGBoost–DNN-based classification model for network intrusion detection system. Neural Comput. Appl. **32**, 12499–12514 (2020)
20. Al-Yaseen, W.L., Idrees, A.K., Almasoudy, F.H.: Wrapper feature selection method based differential evolution and extreme learning machine for intrusion detection system. Pattern Recogn. **132**, 108912 (2022)
21. Thaseen, I.S., Kumar, C.A., Ahmad, A.: Integrated intrusion detection model using chi-square feature selection and ensemble of classifiers. J. Sci. Eng. **44**, 3357–3368 (2019)
22. Mebawondu, J.O., Alowolodu, O.D., Mebawondu, J.O., Adetunmbi, A.O.: Network intrusion detection system using supervised learning paradigm. Sci. African. **9**, e00497 (2020). https://doi.org/10.1016/j.sciaf.2020.e00497
23. Kitchenham, B., Charters, S.: Guidelines for performing systematic literature reviews in software engineering version 2.3. Engineering **45**, 1051 (2007)
24. Katuk, N., Ku-Mahamud, K.R., Zakaria, N.H., Jabbar, A.M.: A scientometric analysis of the emerging topics. J. Inf. Commun. Technol. **19**, 583–622 (2020)
25. Ismail, N., Yusof, U.K.: Journal of information and communication technology. J. Inf. Commun. Technol. **21**, 337–381 (2022)

Cross-layer Based Intrusion Detection System for Wireless Sensor Networks: Challenges, Solutions, and Future Directions

Noradila Nordin[1,2](✉) and Muhammad Syafiq Mohd Pozi[2]

[1] School of Games and Creative Technology, University for the Creative Arts, Farnham GU9
7DS, England, UK
adila.nordin@uca.ac.uk
[2] School of Computing, University Utara Malaysia, 06010 Sintok, Kedah, Malaysia

Abstract. Wireless Sensor Networks (WSNs) consist of numerous affordable, energy-efficient, compact wireless sensors. These sensors are designed to collect, process, and communicate data from their surrounding environment. Several energy-efficient protocols have been created specifically for WSNs to optimize data transfer rates and prolong network lifespan. Multi-channel protocols in WSN are one of the ways to optimize efficiency and enable seamless communication between nodes, thereby reducing interference and minimizing packet loss through multiple channels. Despite their numerous advantages in data sensing and monitoring, various attacks can pose a threat to a WSN. There are several types of attacks that a WSN may encounter, including spoofing, eavesdropping, jamming, sinkhole attacks, wormhole attacks, black hole attacks, Sybil attacks, and DoS attacks. One of the strategies for enhancing security in WSNs is implementing a cross-layer intrusion detection system (IDS) that can detect initial indicators of attacks that target vulnerabilities across multiple WSN layers. This paper reviews the existing IDS at each layer and the challenges in an energy-efficient cross-layer IDS for WSN in terms of the attacks and IDS approaches.

Keywords: Cross-layer IDS · Wireless Sensor Network · Multi-channel protocol

1 Introduction

A Wireless Sensor Network (WSN) is a dispersed sensor system made up of small nodes called sensor nodes. These nodes are frequently used for monitoring and detecting different occurrences or events. WSNs are also utilized for target tracking, environment monitoring, and event detection. WSNs are easily deployable in a variety of situations because of their compact size and low power consumption. In WSNs, the sensor nodes often employ low-power radios like IEEE 802.15.4, a 2.4 GHz band radio transmission standard radio technology with a relatively small range of operation. Within this band, the standard permits broadcast on several various channels. Unfortunately, the channels used by this technology, such as Wi-Fi (IEEE 802.11) and Bluetooth (IEEE 802.15.1), frequently experience interference. In wireless networks, multi-channel communication

N. H. Zakaria et al. (Eds.): ICOCI 2023, CCIS 2001, pp. 108–121, 2024.
https://doi.org/10.1007/978-981-99-9589-9_9

can lessen the impacts of interference, enhancing network effectiveness, stability, and link dependability, minimizing latency, and reducing total energy usage. This, however, creates another issue.

A wireless sensor network is susceptible to several various attacks. Due to several flaws and, most crucially, the data involved, wireless sensor networks are continually vulnerable to serious attacks. Typically, the nodes in a WSN are tiny, battery-operated gadgets containing sensors, microcontrollers, and communication transcribers. Due to the node's limited resources, wireless sensor networks are susceptible to various threats that may jeopardize the security and integrity of the data. Nevertheless, WSNs are susceptible to risks despite the various benefits they offer regarding data sensing and monitoring. These risk factors include those caused by memory limitations, unreliable communication, higher communication latency, unattended network operation, deployment in an environment prone to attacks and scalability. Some of these attacks, such as random multi-channel jamming attacks that interfere with radio frequencies on wireless communication channels and cause channel congestion, are intended to take down the network. The challenge may be that random multi-channel jamming attacks are difficult to detect and eliminate due to their random jamming behaviors. Attackers have complete discretion over the time and the specific channels to jam. Other attacks aim to eavesdrop on communications. Others are made to introduce erroneous data into the network. This poses a danger to real-time, reliable WSNs. Security in WSNs is, therefore a difficult problem since it depends on the way to evaluate the reliability of sensor data.

Numerous studies on intrusion detection in WSNs have been done in recent years [1–5]. Intrusion detection is used to detect unauthorized activity in a system. It works well as a security measure to defend WSNs against intrusion. There have been a few studies on the security of WSNs. However, they have mostly emphasized attack prevention instead of attack detection. This is an important study area since an attacker who can go undetected might cause significant damage or disruption. Although several intrusion detection systems have been developed to support WSNs, the majority of these systems only work at one layer of the Open Systems Interconnection (OSI) model. Several proposed intrusion detection systems are based on a cross-layer approach. They comprise the physical, data link, and network layers that contribute to cross-layer intrusion detection systems (IDS) design. By detecting the attackers across multiple layers, cross-layer IDS secures the WSN.

The rest of the paper is organized as follows. Section 2 highlights various attacks and challenges associated with WSN at each layer. Section 3 presents and compares recent existing work in cross-layer IDS in WSN. Section 4 discusses the challenges and future directions on cross-layer IDS, and Sect. 5 concludes the paper.

2   Related Work

2.1   Wireless Sensor Network Cross-layer Protocols

WSNs are networks of many inexpensive, low-power, small wireless sensors. The sensors can gather, analyze, and transmit data from their environment. WSNs have gotten a lot of attention from several application sectors because of their capabilities, including military surveillance, industrial monitoring, target tracking, and environment monitoring. Numerous energy-efficient protocols have been developed for WSNs to maximize throughputs while extending the lifetime of the networks through the Medium Access Control (MAC) and routing protocols, power consumption, and energy harvesting. The protocols are a vital aspect of WSN communication. The protocols determine the allocation of channel resources among the network's nodes in a way that maximizes efficiency, manages channel constraint, and ensures that nodes communicate simultaneously in single or multiple channels effectively to reduce interference which leads to packet drop. The WSNs are susceptible to attacks due to the extensive nature of node dispersion and the hardware limitation of the nodes.

Numerous studies on single-channel WSN protocols such as LEACH [6], RPL [7] and multi-channel protocols such as Chrysso [8] and MiCMAC [9] that interface to the MAC and the network layers, as well as MCRP [10], that interfaces to the MAC, network, and application layers, have been conducted. The real-time nature of MCRP's multi-channel processing enables it to adjust to any location's local interference. MCRP is a cross-layer protocol that is decentralized and centrally controlled to reduce interference without knowing where the channels are occupied in advance. In order to effectively use the spectrum, MCRP considers all channels that are accessible and transmits on a number of them. This generality makes it possible for better channels to be selected based on the location the sensor nodes are deployed. As a result, the protocol reduces the impact of interference, improving network efficiency, stability, and link reliability. While MCRP exhibits promising results in terms of improved resilience to interference, significantly higher throughput, and link stability, extending the lifetime of WSNs, it is vulnerable to numerous attacks because security was not considered. The protocol is more susceptible to attacks due to the cross-layer attributes and usage of several channels which are necessary for proper data transmission and reception. Thus, the intrusion detection system is a potential approach to detect attacks.

2.2 Intrusion Detection Systems

The limitations of sensor nodes in WSNs prevent traditional IDSs from being directly implemented in WSNs. To resolve this issue, various IDSs have been proposed for WSNs. Due to its IDS mechanism and the high processing demands of the algorithms of the IDs, several extended protocols have negatively impacted the network's energy. An IDS tracks traffic data that may be used to spot and prevent intrusions that compromise the privacy, integrity, and accessibility of an information system. An IDS is a term for software or hardware devices that monitor networks for cyberattacks from inside or outside and trigger an alert.

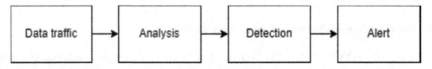

Fig. 1. Fundamental IDS architecture

The fundamental architecture of IDS as shown in Fig. 1, comprises four phases. The first phase is monitoring the captured data traffic, which will then be analyzed for any feature extraction or pattern identification in the second phase. The data that has been analyzed is examined in the third phase, the detection stage. Any possible harmful data is detected using IDS. The four types of intrusion detection techniques are signature-based, anomaly-based, specification-based, and hybrid-based IDS. These categories are based on the capability of detection algorithms. All these methods can be used to distinguish between trustworthy and malicious traffic. When a match is discovered, the IDS generates an alert.

Signature-Based IDS. The signature-based IDS is also called knowledge-based, misuse-based or rule-based IDS. This method depends on a database containing historical attack signatures and known system vulnerabilities. The signature-based IDS only detects known attacks and issues an alert for any matching signature patterns that have been recorded in the signature database. However, as sensor nodes in WSN have limited storage capacity, they could not store all the attack patterns. An example of a signature-based IDS is as proposed by Kurniawan & Yazid (2020) [11]. The IDS implements a blocking approach on the Denial-of-Service (DoS) attack node. It blocks all packets coming from the attacker's node until the attacker runs out of energy.

Anomaly-Based IDS. The anomaly-based IDS is also called behavior-based IDS. This method detects attacks based on the attack patterns which model the user, network, and host system behavior. An alert will be generated when the detected behavior deviates from the usual behavior. In contrast to the signature-based IDS, the anomaly-based IDS can identify known and unknown threats without prior knowledge of the attack. Based on their functions, anomaly-based detection approaches are divided into four categories: statistical, data mining, machine learning, and artificial intelligence.

Mohd et al. (2020) implemented IDS to detect Denial-of-Sleep (DoSL) attacks using support vector machine (SVM) learning in WSN [12]. Mehbodniya et al. (2021) suggested utilizing machine learning techniques like Naive Bayes, random forest, and logistic regression to calculate node packet delivery rates and detect assaults that use false identities, such as the Sybil attack [13]. Mounica et al. (2021) also suggested using machine learning to detect Sybil attacks that distinguish between authorized and illegal access points using the network's raw traffic data to evaluate the efficacy and accuracy of the machine learning approaches [14].

Specification-Based IDS. The advantages of signature-based and anomaly-based intrusion detection methods are combined in specification-based IDS. It learns the fundamental traits of attacks, identifies known attacks like a signature-based IDS, and also has the ability of anomaly-based IDSs to identify new attacks that do not fit into the system's normal conduct. Intrusion rules are manually developed in specification-based IDS to detect known and unknown attacks. The manual depiction of specification-based IDS produces few false positives. However, it is a lengthy process to establish the rules. Specification-based IDS can be utilized without the need for training after the rules have been established. Specification-based IDS is ineffective if the manually defined rules do not correspond with the real environment.

The forged rank and routing metric detector (FORCE) proposed by Althubaity et al. (2020) is a specification-based IDS. It makes use of the parent-child relationship in the

RPL topology, where the type of node is an essential part of detection [15]. Each node in FORCE examines the control messages it has received from its neighbors, performs local threat detection using the information supplied, and notifies other nodes when it finds threats in the neighborhood. Gothawal & Nagaraj (2019) suggested an IDS that utilizes the RPL's specifications, such as rank and DODAG version [16]. It monitors the network traffic to record normal network behavior and compares it with possible attacks.

Hybrid-Based IDS. The hybrid-based IDS is a combination of anomaly-based, signature-based or specification-based intrusion detection techniques. Most of the IDSs use any one of the intrusion detections. It is possible to utilize hybrid-based IDS since each intrusion detection technique has its own benefits and drawbacks. In order to increase accuracy and detection rates and reduce false alarm rates, hybrid-based IDS perform the detection by integrating signature-based, anomaly-based, or specification-based intrusion detection methods.

Bhushan & Sahoo (2019) proposed an Integrated IDS scheme (IIS), a hybrid IDS that combines clustering and digital signature [17], while Huang et al. (2022) suggested using multi-hop clustering. In their proposed IDS, to monitor the network and detect the intrusion, the cluster heads and the sink operate collaboratively as IDS agents [18]. Gandhimathi & Murugaboopathi (2020) proposed a two stages hybrid IDS that combines packet-based IDS using a cross-layer approach and flow-based IDS [19]. In the first stage, the sensor network's flow-based IDS differentiates malicious and normal flows. In the second stage, the entire packet's content is validated using cross-layer features by performing packet payload analysis. This increases the detection process's accuracy.

3   Wireless Sensor Network Intrusion Detection Systems

WSNs are vulnerable to various cyberattacks that might jeopardize the network's availability, privacy, control, and reliability. The nodes are usually deployed in hazardous and remote environments. Thus, they are frequently left unattended and unable to physically safeguard the information flow, which raises the risk of node compromise and lowers network security and protection. Therefore, securing such networks from breaches and assaults is vital where effective security measures are necessary. A possible approach to safeguard WSNs against cyberattacks is the cross-layer intrusion detection system, which protects multiple WSN layers.

3.1   Wireless Sensor Network Attacks

A WSN can be subjected to a variety of attacks, including spoofing, eavesdropping, jamming, sinkhole attack, wormhole attack, black hole attack, Sybil attack and DoS attack [1–5, 20]. Attacks that cause packet loss are among the most destructive and disruptive threats to WSNs. When such an attack occurs, normal network operations are disrupted because the received data packets or control messages are discarded instead of forwarded to other nodes. Attacks against WSNs can be grouped according to their OSI layers since each layer is vulnerable to multiple attacks.

Physical Layer. The physical layer in WSNs performs various operations, including the production of carrier signals, signal identification, modulation, and information cryptography to transfer data from the sensor nodes across wireless channels. The functions of sensor nodes are compromised when radio transmissions are obstructed or intercepted. A node might be the target of a DoS attack by jamming the physical channel. In this attack, an attacker constantly jams the communication frequencies by sending out unnecessary signals. A legitimate node becomes unavailable to the other nodes as it is occupied with receiving the signals from the malicious node, which jams the network [21].

Bengag et al. (2019) proposed a novel IDS approach based on the packet delivery ratio, energy consumption, signal strength indication received and bad packet ratios as the indicators for detecting jamming attacks in WBAN [22]. An alert is triggered when one of the indicators crosses the network threshold to indicate the presence of a jammer node. Bengag et al. (2023) improved their work by using a fuzzy logic system to identify jamming attacks in different network cases [23]. Savva et al. (2022) also proposed to detect jamming attacks through the use of fuzzy logic [24].

Data Link Layer. The link layer in WSNs, consisting of the MAC layer, is used to control errors and detect and access data frames. The MAC layer is vulnerable to several attack types, including back-off manipulation, denial of sleep and exhaustion attacks. A back-off manipulation attack is used to shorten the back-off time to get the channel priority. Ghugar & Pradhan (2020) proposed a MAC layer trust-based intrusion detection system, ML-IDS, based on the concept of a weighting method to detect back-off manipulation attacks [25].

A node subjected to a denial of service (DoS) attack, leading to a denial of sleep attack (DoSL) has its ability to sleep restricted. This raises the power needed for node data transmission and reception. It is also called an exhaustion attack. If no data has to be sent, the MAC protocols retain the node in sleep mode. The attacker attempts to keep the node awake by sending messages constantly, which results in an unnecessary transmission and increases energy consumption until all the node's energy is depleted.

Mohd et al. (2020) proposed an IDS using support vector machine learning in WSN to detect denial of sleep attacks [12]. It uses feature ranking and pruning based on performance analyzing parameters. Yaghoubi et al. (2022) on the other hand, proposed a Trust Value Based Intrusion Detection System (TIDS) that uses a genetic algorithm framework in WBAN to identify and prevent denial of sleep [26]. Hussain et al. (2019) proposed an IDS using a soft decision mechanism to identify, prevent and avoid exhaustion attacks [27].

Network Layer. In WSNs, the network layer manages the routes and data transmission using routing protocols to determine the best path from the source node to the destination node. At the network layer, the attacker attacks by gaining control of the data and interfering with its route. Attacks on the network layer can be severe because they compromise the entire network operation, particularly the routing part. Examples of attacks on this layer are Sybil, blackhole, and wormhole attacks.

Sybil attacks target fault-tolerance techniques, and as a result, they manifest in networks that utilize multiple paths for routing. In a Sybil attack, a malicious node assumes the identities of several other nodes to disguise its true identity. Sybil refers to these false identities that appear to be multiple nodes. These Sybil may develop their own identities or take on the identities of authorized nodes. Mehbodniya et al. (2021) proposed the use of machine learning approaches such as Naïve Bayes, Random Forest, and Logistic Regression to detect fake identity and Sybil attacks using the node's packet delivery rates [13]. Mounica et al. (2021) proposed a machine-learning model to evaluate the efficacy and precision of machine-learning techniques for identifying authorized and unauthorized access points in networks where raw internet traffic data has been gathered to detect Sybil attacks [14]. Arshad et al. (2022) proposed a Trust-based Hybrid cooperative RPL protocol (THC-RPL) that observes the directly connected neighbor node's behavior and calculates the trust value in detecting Sybil nodes [28].

Distance vector routing protocols are vulnerable to blackhole attacks where a malicious node claims a short routing distance from the source and the destination nodes. As a result, the attacker node is used to deceive the source node into passing data to the target node through it. The attacker node gets packets from the source node, but it drops them instead of delivering them to the destination node. Soni & Sudhakar (2020) proposed the Link Hop Value-based Intrusion Detection System (L-IDS) against the blackhole attack by establishing a wireless link between the nodes, exchanging data packets, and identifying the link hop value as the presence of the attacker by incorporating the data delivery in each hop [29]. On the other hand, Kumar et al. (2023) suggested anomaly-based hierarchical intrusion detection that uses a trust model and data routing with data type verification as the time of route to detect and prevent blackhole attacks [30].

Wormhole attacks are particularly common in WSNs, occurring on a low-latency bandwidth. The wormhole attack occurs within two independent network nodes containing distinctive portions of a message. The attacker uses a laptop or other wireless device to tunnel the packet to another area of the WSN over a low-latency link, where they are replayed. Deshmukh-Bhosale & Sonavane (2019) proposed an IDS for wormholes using RSSI to identify the attack and attacker node [31]. Bhosale & Sonavane (2021) further proposed an innovative intrusion detection system that detects wormhole attacks by analyzing the location information of any node and its neighbors, as well as the Received Signal Strength Indicator (RSSI) values and the hop count [32].

Transport Layer. WSNs' simplified or omitted transport layer protocols make this layer less vulnerable to attacks than the network layer. The transportation layer enables logical connections between two different sensor nodes. Examples of transport layer attacks are flood attacks, desynchronization attacks, and session hijacking attacks. The purpose of flooding is to drain a sensor node's memory by delivering a large number of connection setup requests. Desynchronization can be used to request retransmissions by transmitting packets with a different sequence number. Session hijacking occurs when an unsecured or inadequately protected session is hijacked at the start. When the right sequence number is discovered, the attacker spoofs the target node's IP address and launches a DoS attack. The attacker's goal is to get private information such as identities, passwords, and secret keys.

Application Layer. Protocols on the application layer are more vulnerable to DoS attacks. This layer holds user applications and data and is compatible with HTTP, Telnet, SMTP, and FTP protocols. The attacker is particularly interested in application layer information as it directly contains data about the user. At the application layer, a Man-in-the-Middle attack (MITM) is a type of eavesdropping which is also called a sniffing or snooping attack. It occurs when an outsider eavesdrops on the conversations of two or more exchange parties. Maniriho et al. (2020) presented an anomaly-based IDS approach that uses a hybrid feature selection engine. It chooses the most important information and uses the Random Forest algorithm to classify traffic as normal or abnormal [33]. The IDS can detect DoS and MITM attacks.

Table 1. Attacks in WSN based on the layers.

Layer	Attacks
Physical	Jamming, DoS, tampering, Sybil attack, interception, eavesdropping, active interference
Data link	Back-off manipulation, replay attack, interception, DoS, exhaustion attack, Sybil attack, collision, unfairness, traffic analysis and monitoring, spoofing and altering routing attack, selfish misbehavior, malicious misbehavior, Denial of sleep attack
Network	Selective forwarding attack, sinkhole attack, wormhole attack, black hole attack, Sybil attack, DoS, hello flood attack, Homing, spoofing attack, neglect and greed, grey-hole attack, misdirection attack, Internet smurf attack, rushing attack, replay attack, Byzantine attack
Transport	SYN flooding attack, desynchronization, session hijacking
Application	Eavesdropping, false data injection, spoofing and altering routing attack, malicious code attack, repudiation attack, DoS attack

Other attacks on all the layers are listed in Table 1 [1–5]. These cyber-attacks have a variety of objectives, including stealing, altering, hacking, and flooding the targeted nodes with excessive packets to deplete the sensors' battery power and disconnect them from the network, making them unusable and hindering them from sensing or routing traffic. The performance, effectiveness, and reliability of communication may suffer as a result of these attacks. To overcome these problems, effective security mechanisms, such as well-defined detection and mitigation procedures, must be put in place. As a result, intrusion detection methods to protect against such attacks are becoming increasingly important. An intrusion detection system (IDS) is a promising solution to identify intrusions in WSNs. However, the IDSs in WSNs face new challenges due to the characteristics of WSNs, thus, there is a need for an IDS to work interoperability across the layers.

3.2 Cross-layer Intrusion Detection Systems

Due to the numerous characteristics of sensor networks, such as their limited battery power supply, poor bandwidth support, self-organizing nature, and dependence on other nodes, there is a significant risk of security attacks in all OSI model layers. A single or a series of attacks may be made. Several specific attacks occur at regular intervals, such as blackhole attacks, rushing attacks, and flooding attacks. It has been noticed that circumstances may result in several attacks rather than a single attack. As a result, it is preferable to develop an effective Intrusion Detection System (IDS) capable of handling many attacks. Several proposed intrusion detection schemes are proposed based on a cross-layer approach, including the physical, data link and network layers that contribute towards the design of a cross-layer intrusion detection system. Cross-layer IDS secures WSNs by detecting various malicious activities and attackers at different layers.

Amouri et al. (2018) proposed an IDS that has a two-stage detection process that happens locally and globally [34]. The IDS system is for data collecting that works in situations that prohibit direct access to data on specific nodes. It uses dedicated sniffers to capture packets and generate correctly classified instances. The system establishes a detection threshold based on these instances. By analyzing the variation of correctly classified instances from different sniffers using a sliding window approach, the IDS detects malicious nodes in the network. Alharthi & Abdullah (2019) developed XLID, a cross-layer intrusion detection system between the network and MAC layers [35]. XLID detects intruders trying to communicate with network nodes by analyzing packet data and signal strength. It combines information from the MAC, network, and physical layers to identify potential attacks. XLID offers a unified system for detecting various intrusions at both layers, using cross-layer concepts.

Canbalaban & Sen (2020) proposed a novel intrusion detection system for RPL using neural networks [36]. It combines features from the link and network layers to detect specific attacks on RPL, such as version number, worst parent, and hello flood attacks. By analyzing packet drops at the link layer, the system distinguishes between natural losses and those caused by attacks. The system aims to process large amounts of data generated by RPL and accurately predict the type of attack, not just its presence. Ghugar et al. (2019) proposed LB-IDS, a layered-based intrusion detection system for Wireless Sensor Networks (WSNs) [21]. LB-IDS aims to detect various types of attacks, including jamming, back-off manipulation, sinkhole, and cross-layer attacks, occurring at different network protocol stack layers. The system calculates the trust value of a sensor node by analyzing the trust metrics' deviation at the physical, MAC, and network layers, considering trustworthiness in each layer individually. By utilizing this layered approach, LB-IDS provides a comprehensive means of identifying and mitigating attacks at multiple levels within the WSN.

Gandhimathi & Murugaboopathi (2020) proposed a hybrid IDS for WSN that consists of two stages [19]. The first stage utilizes cross-layer features, considering both the network and MAC layers. The network layer analyses packet routing, while the MAC layer considers medium access duration. If a compromised node is detected based on high MAC duration and packet drop rates, it is declared as an attacker. The second stage correlates the MAC and network layers to analyze IP flow records to detect network traffic attacks accurately.

Each of these proposed IDS in Table 2 showed to detect various types of attacks in WSN. Further improvements are required to enable these IDS to adapt to any changes in WSN, such as the limitations on the nodes and the attacks.

Table 2. Existing IDS in WSN based on the layers.

Authors	Intrusion Detection Approaches	Layers				
		P	D	N	T	A
Amouri et al. (2018) [34]	Traces packets	√	√	√		
Ghugar et al. (2019) [21]	Trust value	√	√	√		
Alharthi & Abdullah (2019) [35]	Combines information from layers		√	√		
Gandhimathi & Murugaboopathi (2020) [19]	Packet routing, medium access duration		√	√		
Canbalaban & Sen (2020) [36]	Neural networks		√	√		
Bengag et al. (2019) [22]	Packet delivery ratio, energy consumption, RSSI, bad packet ratios	√				
Bengag et al. (2023) [23]	Fuzzy logic system	√				
Hussain et al. (2019) [27]	Soft decision mechanism		√			
Ghugar & Pradhan (2020) [25]	Weighting method		√			
Mohd et al. (2020) [12]	Support vector machine learning		√			
Yaghoubi et al. (2022) [26]	Trust value		√			
Deshmukh-Bhosale & Sonavane (2019) [31]	RSSI			√		
Soni & Sudhakar (2020) [29]	Hop count			√		
Mehbodniya et al. (2021) [13]	Machine learning approaches			√		
Mounica et al. (2021) [14]	Machine learning approach			√		
Bhosale & Sonavane (2021) [32]	Location information, RSSI, hop count			√		
Arshad et al. (2022) [28]	Trust value			√		
Kumar et al. (2023) [30]	Trust model and verification			√		
Maniriho et al. (2020) [33]	Random Forest algorithm					√

P is physical, D is data link, N is network, T is transport and A is application

4 Challenges and Future Directions

The IDS schemes presently in use usually consider a few of the attacks. Attacks on other layers of the WSN are disregarded mainly by most currently employed techniques, which exclusively focus on one or more types of attacks on one layer of the WSN. In order to identify numerous attacks on distinct WSN layers, a cross-layer IDS needs to be devised. Future expansion of the types of attacks across the layers that an IDS must take into consideration when doing detection is intriguing. Additionally, multi-channel cross-layer protocols like MCRP were created to lengthen the lifespan of WSNs, but security was not a consideration. In order to safeguard the multi-channel cross-layer routing mechanism and make it resistant to both insider and external attackers, it might be expanded to add security features such as with an IDS.

WSNs use energy to gather information about their surroundings, process it, and send the resulting data. The IDSs must therefore use the least amount of energy feasible to leave enough for the WSN's vital operations. IDSs are crucial for the security of WSNs, and those created for them need to have specific features like low power usage. The success of an IDS in a WSN depends on the way it affects the network's energy usage as a WSN is resource constrained. Maintaining a network over its lifespan is one of the biggest issues in WSNs, so energy efficiency in IDSs is equally important. WSN sensor nodes have limited storage capacity. Therefore, it is challenging to meet the need to store attack signatures in sensor nodes.

In order to create an IDS in the WSN to identify various sorts of attacks, machine learning techniques were mostly utilized. The drawback of those techniques is that they require more memory to deploy a model to a sensor node and take longer for machine learning algorithms to build and evaluate data sets for WSN. It could be conceivable to develop a hybrid or cloud-based machine learning prototype for carrying out intrusion detection in the WSN to reduce the amount of memory required in the detection techniques. Another point to consider is many of the IDS schemes available do not provide self-defense. It is crucial because certain attackers may frequently generate false alarms by flooding the IDS host with irrelevant traffic. The host can run out of resources as a result, leaving the system open to intrusions. IDS's ability to protect itself is thus desirable.

5   Conclusions

WSNs face numerous cyberattacks that pose risks to the network's availability, privacy, control, and reliability. These attacks exploit the vulnerable nature of nodes deployed in hazardous and remote environments, where they often remain unattended, unable to protect the information flow physically. As a result, there is an increased likelihood of node compromise, leading to decreased network security and protection. It is crucial to implement robust security measures to safeguard these networks against breaches and assaults. One effective approach is the adoption of a cross-layer intrusion detection system, which provides comprehensive protection across multiple WSN layers. This paper reviews the existing IDS at each of the layers and cross-layers for WSN in terms of the attacks and approaches. Cross-layer IDS can detect early signs of advanced attacks exploiting multiple layers' vulnerabilities. They reduce evasion techniques by analyzing data from multiple layers, making it harder for attackers to evade detection. However, it's important to consider WSN's limited resources and constraints when designing and implementing cross-layer IDS. Thus, a more energy-efficient cross-layer IDS for WSN needs to be developed and improved from the existing IDS.

References

1. Khan, K., Mehmood, A., Khan, S., Khan, M.A., Iqbal, Z., Mashwani, W.K.: A survey on intrusion detection and prevention in wireless ad-hoc networks. J. Syst. Architect. **105**, 101701 (2020)
2. Pundir, S., Wazid, M., Singh, D.P., Das, A.K., Rodrigues, J.J., Park, Y.: Intrusion detection protocols in wireless sensor networks integrated to Internet of Things deployment: survey and future challenges. IEEE Access **8**, 3343–3363 (2019)
3. Elsaid, S.A., Albatati, N.S.: An optimized collaborative intrusion detection system for wireless sensor networks. Soft. Comput. **24**(16), 12553–12567 (2020)
4. Faris, M., Mahmud, M.N., Salleh, M.F.M., Alnoor, A.: Wireless sensor network security: a recent review based on state-of-the-art works. Int. J. Eng. Bus. Manag. **15** (2023)
5. Godala, S., Vaddella, R.P.V.: A study on intrusion detection system in wireless sensor networks. Int. J. Commun. Netw. Inf. Secur. **12**(1), 127–141 (2020)
6. Kong, H.Y.: Energy efficient cooperative LEACH protocol for wireless sensor networks. J. Commun. Netw. **12**(4), 358–365 (2010)
7. Winter, T., et al.: RPL: IPv6 routing protocol for low-power and lossy networks (No. RFC6550) (2012)
8. Iyer, V., Woehrle, M., Langendoen, K.: Chrysso—a multi-channel approach to mitigate external interference. In: 2011 8th Annual IEEE Communications Society Conference on Sensor, Mesh and Ad Hoc Communications and Networks, pp. 449–457. IEEE (2011)
9. Al Nahas, B., Duquennoy, S., Iyer, V., Voigt, T.: Low-power listening goes multi-channel. In: 2014 IEEE International Conference on Distributed Computing in Sensor Systems, pp. 2–9. IEEE (2014)
10. Nordin, N., Clegg, R.G., Rio, M.: Multi-channel cross-layer routing for sensor networks. In: 2016 23rd International Conference on Telecommunications (ICT), pp. 1–6. IEEE (2016)
11. Kurniawan, M.T., Yazid, S.: Mitigation and detection strategy of dos attack on wireless sensor network using blocking approach and intrusion detection system. In: 2020 International Conference on Electrical, Communication, and Computer Engineering (ICECCE), pp. 1–5. IEEE (2020)
12. Mohd, N., Singh, A., Bhadauria, H.S.: A novel SVM based IDS for distributed denial of sleep strike in wireless sensor networks. Wirel. Pers. Commun. **111**(3), 1999–2022 (2020)
13. Mehbodniya, A., Webber, J.L., Shabaz, M., Mohafez, H., Yadav, K.: Machine learning technique to detect Sybil attack on IoT based sensor network. IETE J. Res. 1–9 (2021)
14. Mounica, M., Vijayasaraswathi, R., Vasavi, R.: Detecting Sybil attack in wireless sensor networks using machine learning algorithms. IOP Conf. Ser. Mater. Sci. Eng. **1042**(1). IOP Publishing (2021)
15. Althubaity, A., Gong, T., Raymond, K.K., Nixon, M., Ammar, R., Han, S.: Specification-based distributed detection of rank-related attacks in RPL-based resource-constrained real-time wireless networks. In: 2020 IEEE Conference on Industrial Cyberphysical Systems (ICPS), vol. 1, pp. 168–175. IEEE (2020)
16. Gothawal, D.B., Nagaraj, S.V.: Intrusion detection for enhancing RPL security. Procedia Comput. Sci. **165**, 565–572 (2019)
17. Bhushan, B., Sahoo, G.: A hybrid secure and energy efficient cluster based intrusion detection system for wireless sensing environment. In: 2019 2nd International Conference on Signal Processing and Communication (ICSPC), pp. 325–329. IEEE (2019)
18. Huang, D.W., Luo, F., Bi, J., Sun, M.: An efficient hybrid IDS deployment architecture for multi-hop clustered wireless sensor networks. IEEE Trans. Inf. Forensics Secur. **17**, 2688–2702 (2022)

19. Gandhimathi, L., Murugaboopathi, G.: A novel hybrid intrusion detection using flow-based anomaly detection and cross-layer features in wireless sensor network. Autom. Control. Comput. Sci. **54**, 62–69 (2020)

20. Jilani, S.A., Koner, C., Nandi, S.: Security in wireless sensor networks: attacks and evasion. In: 2020 National Conference on Emerging Trends on Sustainable Technology and Engineering Applications (NCETSTEA), pp. 1–5. IEEE (2020)

21. Ghugar, U., Pradhan, J., Bhoi, S.K., Sahoo, R.R.: LB-IDS: securing wireless sensor network using protocol layer trust-based intrusion detection system. J. Comput. Netw. Commun. (2019)

22. Bengag, A., Moussaoui, O., Moussaoui, M.: A new IDS for detecting jamming attacks in WBAN. In: 2019 Third International Conference on Intelligent Computing in Data Sciences (ICDS), pp. 1–5. IEEE (2019)

23. Bengag, A., Bengag, A., Moussaoui, O., Mohamed, B.: A fuzzy logic-based intrusion detection system for WBAN against jamming attacks. In: Bekkay, H., Mellit, A., Gagliano, A., Rabhi, A., Amine Koulali, M. (eds.) ICEERE 2022. LNEE, vol. 954, pp. 3–11. Springer, Singapore (2023). https://doi.org/10.1007/978-981-19-6223-3_1

24. Savva, M., Ioannou, I., Vassiliou, V.: Fuzzy-logic based IDS for detecting jamming attacks in wireless mesh IoT networks. In: 2022 20th Mediterranean Communication and Computer Networking Conference (MedComNet), pp. 54–63. IEEE (2022)

25. Ghugar, U., Pradhan, J.: ML-IDS: MAC layer trust-based intrusion detection system for wireless sensor networks. In: Behera, H.S., Nayak, J., Naik, B., Pelusi, D. (eds.) Computational Intelligence in Data Mining. AISC, vol. 990, pp. 427–434. Springer, Singapore (2020). https://doi.org/10.1007/978-981-13-8676-3_37

26. Yaghoubi, M., Ahmed, K., Miao, Y.: TIDS: trust value-based IDS framework for wireless body area network. In: 2022 32nd International Telecommunication Networks and Applications Conference (ITNAC), pp. 142–148. IEEE (2022)

27. Hussain, I., Zahra, S., Hussain, A., Bedru, H. D., Haider, S., Gumzhacheva, D.: Intruder attacks on wireless sensor networks: a soft decision and prevention mechanism. Int. J. Adv. Comput. Sci. Appl. **10**(5) (2019)

28. Arshad, D., Asim, M., Tariq, N., Baker, T., Tawfik, H., Al-Jumeily OBE, D.: THC-RPL: a lightweight trust-enabled routing in RPL-based IoT networks against Sybil attack. PloS ONE **17**(7) (2022)

29. Soni, G., Sudhakar, R.: A L-IDS against dropping attack to secure and improve RPL performance in WSN aided IoT. In: 2020 7th International Conference on Signal Processing and Integrated Networks (SPIN), pp. 377–383. IEEE (2020)

30. Kumar, V.N., et al.: Anomaly-based hierarchical intrusion detection for black hole attack detection and prevention in WSN. In: Reddy, K.A., Devi, B.R., George, B., Raju, K.S., Sellathurai, M. (eds.) Proceedings of Fourth International Conference on Computer and Communication Technologies. Lecture Notes in Networks and Systems, vol. 606, pp. 319–327. Springer, Singapore (2023). https://doi.org/10.1007/978-981-19-8563-8_30

31. Deshmukh-Bhosale, S., Sonavane, S.S.: A real-time intrusion detection system for wormhole attack in the RPL based Internet of Things. Procedia Manuf. **32**, 840–847 (2019)

32. Bhosale, S.A., Sonavane, S.S.: Wormhole attack detection system for IoT network: a hybrid approach. Wirel. Pers. Commun. **124**(2), 1081–1108 (2022)

33. Maniriho, P., Niyigaba, E., Bizimana, Z., Twiringiyimana, V., Mahoro, L.J., Ahmad, T.: Anomaly-based intrusion detection approach for IoT networks using machine learning. In: 2020 International Conference on Computer Engineering, Network, and Intelligent Multimedia (CENIM), pp. 303–308. IEEE (2020)

34. Amouri, A., Morgera, S.D., Bencherif, M.A., Manthena, R.: A cross-layer, anomaly-based IDS for WSN and MANET. Sensors **18**(2), 651 (2018)

35. Alharthi, M., Abdullah, M.: XLID: cross-layer intrusion detection system for wireless sensor networks. Indian J. Sci. Technol. **12**, 3 (2019)
36. Canbalaban, E., Sen, S.: A cross-layer intrusion detection system for RPL-based Internet of Things. In: Grieco, L.A., Boggia, G., Piro, G., Jararweh, Y., Campolo, C. (eds.) ADHOC-NOW 2020. LNCS, vol. 12338, pp. 214–227. Springer, Cham (2020). https://doi.org/10.1007/978-3-030-61746-2_16

Digital Media and Information Literacy

A Feature-Based Optimization Approach for Fake News Detection on Social Media Using K-Means Clustering

Farzana Kabir Ahmad[1]([✉]) [iD], Siti Sakira Kamaruddin[1] [iD], Adnan Hussein Ali[1,2],
and Farah Lia Ibrahim[1]

[1] School of Computing, College of Arts and Sciences, Universiti Utara Malaysia, 06000 Sintok,
Kedah, Malaysia
farzana58@uum.edu.my

[2] Department of Computer Science, College of Computer Science and Engineering,
Al-Ahgaff University, Hadhramaut, Yemen

Abstract. The social networks and news ecosystem provide valuable social information, however, the rise of deceptive content such as fake news generated by social media users, poses an increasing threat to the propagation and diffusion of fake news over the social network and among users. Low-quality news and misinformation spread on social media had negative impacts on individuals and society. Hence, it is essential to detect fake news to ensure the spread of accurate and truthful information. To address this problem, a new approach using Binary Bat Algorithm (BBA) for fake news detection (FND) on Twitter data is proposed in this paper. Twitter data usually generates massive feature space which might consist of irrelevant features that could jeopardize the subsequent process. The proposed FND approach involves four stages, namely data collection, pre-processing, feature extraction, and fake news detection. The proposed techniques are tested on PHEME dataset, and the experimental results are measured in term average of Precision (PR), Recall (R), F-measure (F), and Accuracy (ACC). The experimental results show that the BBA algorithm has outperformed the Social Spider Optimization (SSO) algorithm. Thus, BBA is a promising solution for solving high-dimensionality feature space in fake news Twitter data.

Keywords: Fake news detection · Binary Bat Algorithm · Social Spider Optimization · Feature Selection · Text Mining

1 Introduction

The proliferation of fake news through social media in recent years has brought new challenges among researchers and rise global concerns. Fake news is described as misleading information that is intentionally spread through traditional or digital media to deceive and misinform the public and can be used to manipulate public opinion or to gain political or financial advantages. Generally, there are many forms of fake news which include fabricated stories, manipulated images or videos, or misleading headlines. These forms of fake news have the potential to spread rapidly, due to the development of new technologies and smartphones, causing harm to individuals, groups, and even entire nations.

Currently, the spread of fake news has become a substantial problem due to the vast amounts of information available on social media platforms [1]. The diffusion of fake news can have critical outcomes as it may jeopardize and create distrust in legitimate news sources, undermining democracy, and contributing to social and political conflict. Moreover, it is estimated that nowadays about 80–90% of unstructured data is generated which makes it difficult to gain insight into these current problems. Despite several efforts that have been taken [1, 2], fake news and misinformation continue to be a significant problem among researchers. Thus, the development of effective approaches for detecting fake news has become an urgent research area.

Despite the challenges posed by unstructured data, various techniques can be used to extract meaningful information from unstructured data, providing organizations with new insights and opportunities for innovation. One promising research area is to use feature-based optimization techniques that identify key characteristics of fake news [2]. Current years have witnessed that most fake new detection models are highly dependent on feature extraction techniques. Several studies are implemented by researchers to reduce the high-dimensionally features in fake news detection models using numerous feature extraction techniques, and to address issues related to redundant, irrelevant, and noisy features [1–3]. Feature extraction is mainly used for the identification of relevant patterns and characteristics in textual data that is used to differentiate between real and fake news. Several common feature extraction techniques used in fake news detection include:

i. Bag-of-words: This technique involves representing each document as a frequency distribution of the words it contains. However, the bag-of-words technique overlooks the order of words in the text yet captures the frequency of each word only, which later is used as a feature in machine learning models. The main disadvantage of this technique is that it ignores the rank of words in a text, which results in the loss of important semantic information.

ii. Term frequency-inverse document frequency (TF-IDF): TF-IDF is another feature extraction technique that is commonly used in fake news detection. The fundamental of this technique relies on weights measurement that offers the importance of each word in a document based on how frequently it appears in the document and across all documents in the corpus. Unlike bag-of-words, this technique is useful in identifying words that are unique to a particular document. Yet, TF-IDF requires a specific threshold to be determined in selecting the top features.

iii. Named Entity Recognition (NER): NER is used to indicate words that represent real-world objects, such as people, places, and institutes. Named entity recognition can be used to identify the named entities in a text, which can then be used as features in machine learning models to distinguish between real and fake news. NER is heavily determined by the comprehensiveness of existing lexicons or dictionaries for extracting different parts of words or named entities.

iv. Part-of-speech (POS) tagging: This technique involves identifying the grammatical components of a sentence, such as nouns, verbs, and adjectives. This information can be used to identify patterns in language use that may be associated with fake news. Like NER, POS is dependent on existing lexicons.

Besides the above studies, in some fake news detection models, several researchers have omitted the feature selection phase that caused poor performance since the training data can be biased and overwhelmed which ultimately hinders the subsequent process. Hence, this paper proposes a feature-based optimization approach for fake news detection on social media using BBA and SSO with K-Means clustering. The approach involves extracting relevant features from Twitter data, and optimizing these features before clustering them with K-Means. The resulting optimized features are to train a machine learning model for fake news detection. The proposed approach aims to achieve high accuracy in fake news detection.

The remainder of this paper is organized as follows. Section two provides related works in clustering analysis. The proposed feature-based optimization approach for fake news detection on social media using K-Means clustering is presented in section three. Section four describes the experimental setup and the results obtained. Finally, section five presents the conclusion and future work.

2   Related Works in Clustering Analysis

Cluster analysis is a technique for finding regions in n-dimensional space with large concentrations of data. These regions are called "clusters". Data are sorted into groups in clustering analysis based on predetermined principles. Its function is to categorize the data so that there is a significant degree of similarity within classes and a minor degree of similarity between classes. Although there are many different types of clustering algorithms available right now, each one has unique properties and applications. In general, there are different perspectives in categorizing the data, such as:

a) Partition method: The partition method is an iterative relocation algorithm that reduce the clustering criteria by reallocating the data points between clusters until convergence occurred. One of the common algorithms under this method is K- Means [4].

b) Hierarchical method: Hierarchical clustering is an algorithm that builds a hierarchy of clusters. This algorithm starts with all the data points assigned to a cluster of their own. Then two nearest clusters are merged into the same cluster. In the end, this algorithm terminates when there is only a single cluster left. The results of hierarchical clustering can be shown using a dendrogram. The issue with this method is the emerging and splitting of clusters are complex and errors generated cannot be revised. Moreover, this method is difficult to handle complex datasets.

c) Density-based method: Density-based Clustering method is based on determining regions where points are concentrated and those regions where the data points are separated by vacant or sparse regions [5]. Points that do not belong to any cluster are assigned as noise/outliers. One of the disadvantages of density-based clustering is it unable to handle high-dimensional datasets. Density-Based Spatial Clustering of Applications with Noise (DBSCAN) is representational of the density-based clustering method.

d) Grid-based method: grid-based approach mainly used quantized cells to divide the data space and conduct a necessary operation. The main advantage of the grid-based approach is it provides fast processing time which mainly depends on the number of quantized cells. Nevertheless, this approach is not able to cope with various data densities. Methods such as CLustering in QUEst (CLIQUE), STatistical INformation Grid (STING), Merging of Adaptive Intervals Approach to Spatial Data Mining (MAFIA), Wave Cluster, and Orthogonal partitioning CLUSTERing (O-CLUSTER) are examples of Grid-based method.

3   Methodology

This study proposed a fake news detection model using BBA and SSO with K-Means clustering. The proposed model is tested using Twitter data and measured based on several performance metrics as explained below. The proposed model is depicted in Fig. 1. The proposed fake news detection model consists of several phases which include Phase 1: Data Collection, Phase II: Data Pre-processing, Phase III: Feature Extraction, and Phase IV Feature Selection and Clustering. Each of these phases is explained in detail in the following sections.

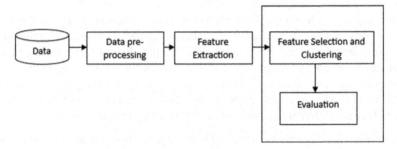

Fig. 1. The proposed fake news detection model.

3.1   Phase 1: Data Collection

The PHEME dataset is a publicly available dataset of Twitter conversations related to nine breaking news events. It was created to support research in the field of information verification and rumor detection on social media. The dataset consists of approximately 570,000 tweets from over 20,000 Twitter users. The tweets were collected between 2013 and 2015 and relate to nine different news events. However, in this study, only five breaking news events of The PHEME are included, which are:

1. Charlie Hebdo shooting in Paris (January 2015) - A terrorist attack on the offices of the French satirical magazine Charlie Hebdo resulted in the deaths of 12 people.
2. Sydney siege (December 2014) - A hostage-taking incident that occurred at the Lindt Cafe in Sydney, Australia, resulted in the deaths of two hostages and the gunman.

3. Ottawa shooting (October 2014) – An incident of a terrorist attack on the Canadian Parliament in Ottawa on October 22, whereby a Canadian soldier and a gunman were fatally shot.

4. Ferguson shooting (August 2014) - Protests that occurred in Ferguson, Missouri, which end up the firing of Michael Brown, an unarmed black teenager, by a white police officer.

5. Germanwings plane crash: An incident occurred on March 24, 2015, in which a passenger plane from Barcelona to Düsseldorf found collapsed in the French Alps. This event killed all passengers and crew. At last, the investigators have discovered that the plane was been intentionally crashed by the co-pilot of the plane.

Events that have been described above are from the Twitter threads that are collectively stored in PHEME dataset. Table 1 shows the statistical information for PHEME dataset, with events that have occurred and their respective rumors/non-rumors information (in percentage) (Table 2).

Table 1. The statistic information for PHEME dataset.

Events	Rumors	Rumors%	Non-rumors	Non-rumors%	Total
Charlie Hebdo	458	22.0	1621	78.0	2079
Sydney siege	522	42.75	699	57.25	1221
Ottawa shooting	470	52.81	420	47.19	890
Ferguson shooting	284	24.8	859	75.20	1143
Germanwings plane crash	238	50.75	231	49.25	469
	1972		3830		5802

Table 2. The output of feature extraction using the TF-IDF technique.

	children	fire	man	out	women	divorce	walk	shoot
0	0.00	0.00	0.69	0.00	0.55	0.43	0.00	0.46
1	0.41	0.50	0.37	0.32	0.00	0.43	0.00	0.46

Additionally, the PHEME dataset includes further metadata such as user profiles, tweet timestamps, and retweet and mention relationships. These metadata are useful to examine the spread of fake news on social media. PHEME dataset is used in this study as it has been widely used in many other studies which include studies on rumor detection, information verification, and social media analysis. This dataset is freely accessible at https://www.kaggle.com/datasets/nicolemichelle/pheme-dataset-for-rumour-detection.

3.2 Phase II Data Pre-processing

Data pre-processing is a crucial step in text mining, where the raw data is prepared for subsequent processes. In general, there are some common techniques used in data pre-processing such as (1) tokenization, (2) stop word removal, (3) stemming and lemmatization, (4) lowercasing, removing special characters and punctuation and (5) spell checking and correction. Some of these techniques can be applied to the raw dataset depending on its need and the requirement of the task at hand. At the stage of data pre-processing, several techniques have been applied and some parameters are adjusted to obtain optimal results. In this study, the TextBlob library is used to tokenize the words into features. TextBlob is a Python library for processing textual data.

3.3 Phase III Feature Extraction

Once the data is cleaned, the next phase is text feature extraction. Text feature extraction is the process to transform the pre-processed data into vectorization space which can be used as input for the machine learning model. The main aim of this phase is to reduce the high dimensionality features to more efficient and meaningful vector space. Generally, there are three common feature extraction techniques as explained below:

1. Bag of words: Bags of words is a representation of text according to its occurrence in the document. This technique counts the words and represents them based on their frequencies in a given document or corpus. The matrix created represents unique features however, this technique may lead to a spare matrix that often hinders the downstream process.
2. Term frequency-inverse document frequency (TF-IDF): TF-IDF is a technique based on a weighting mechanism that calculates the importance of words in a document or corpus. This technique measures the frequency of words and inverse document frequency of words across the documents [6].
3. Word embedding: Word embedding is a technique with a dense vector representation that captures the semantic relationships between words. Word embedding is usually trained with a large corpus and produces a small number of feature dimensionality in comparison to a bag-of-words or TF-IDF.

In this study, the TF-IDF technique is used to extract feature vectors. Two factors are measured, which are frequency (TF) and inverse document frequency (IDF). TF measures how many times the term appears in the document while the IDF indicates the scarcity of words across the documents. Formulas to calculate TF is given in Eq. (1) while Eq. (2) shows the IDF formula.

$$tf_{i,j} = \frac{n_{i,j}}{\sum_k n_{i,j}} \tag{1}$$

$$idf(w) = \log\left(\frac{N}{df_i}\right) \tag{2}$$

where tf is term frequency for word, i in document j divided by the total number of words in that document, k.

The TF-IDF on the other hand, is calculated by multiplying the term frequency (TF) by the inverse document frequency (IDF). The vector space produces by using TF-IDF illustrates the importance of the term in the document or corpus. Words with high TF-IDF weights are more important than ones with low TF-IDF weights [6].

$$w_{i,j} = tf_{i,j} * \log\left(\frac{N}{df_i}\right) \tag{3}$$

The vector space generated by TF-IDF is later used by the machine learning model to detect fake news. In this study, *sklearn* has been used and the example below shows the output of feature extraction using the TF-IDF technique.

3.4 Phase IV Feature Selection and Clustering

Feature selection is an essential process in fake news detection that involves identifying and selecting the most relevant features or attributes from a dataset that are likely to help distinguish between fake and genuine news. There are mainly three types of features that have been used by researchers for instance features related to news content which are known as content-based features and context features that are associated with social interaction between users. Some researchers also have proposed the integration of both types of features for a more reliable diffusion networks model. In this study, content-based features that rely on the TF-IDF technique are used to obtain the feature vectors. Figure 2 shows the feature vector space generated by using TF-IDF. The feature is denoted by F which consists of a set of features $\{f_1, f_2, f_3, f_4.... f_n\}$ where n is the number of features for each document, Doc = $\{Doc_1, Doc_2, Doc_3.... Doc_N\}$ where N is the number of documents in a dataset. However, TF-IDF generates a large sparse matrix, resulting in a high dimensionality feature space problem. Hence, this study presents a wrapper feature selection approach that used BBA_K-Means to determine the set of new informative features.

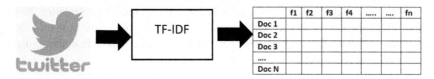

Fig. 2. Feature space generated using the TF-IDF

This paper aims to automate the discovery of the number of clusters and their respective centroids using BBA. The following section describes the K-Means clustering and BBA proposed in this study.

Binary Bat Algorithm (BBA). BBA is a meta-heuristic technique that is inspired by the behaviors of bats. This technique used the echo property of bats as a medium of communication in determining its prey [7–9]. Generally, BBA involves four phases as given below:

i. Initialization: At first, the population of bats, x_i is determined using a random number in obtaining the optimal solution for D space features. This solution is then evaluated by using Eq. (4).

$$x_{ij} = x_{min} + \varphi(x_{max} - x_{min}) \tag{4}$$

where x_{min} and x_{max} represent minimum and maximum margins for dimensional space of j in which $j = 1, 2.... D$, and population number of BA, $i = 1,2,3, ... N$. In this equation, φ value is set from $[0,1]$.

ii. Updating Frequency (f), Velocity (v), and New Solution (x^i): Later, the formulas below are used to update the location (position) of x^i and velocity v^i of a bat in a d-dimensional search space:

$$f_i = f_{min} + (f_{max} - f_{min})\beta, \tag{5}$$

$$v_i^t = v_i^{t-1} + \left(x_i^{t-1} - x_*\right)f_i \tag{6}$$

$$x_i^t = x_i^{t-1} + v_i^t, \tag{7}$$

iii. Updating r and A: In a nutshell, once a bat finds its prey, the A value decreases, while r increases. To imitate the mechanism, both A and r are updated using Eq. (8) and Eq. (9),

$$A_i^{t+1} = \alpha A_i^t, \tag{8}$$

$$r_i^{t+1} = r_i^0[1 - exp(-\gamma t)] \tag{9}$$

where γ and α are constants; and α is the cooling aspect of a cooling schedule in a simulated annealing algorithm.

iv. Evaluation, Saving, and Ranking Best Solutions: An evaluation procedure is employed to assess newly produced solutions for all bats after updating both A and r. The obtained solutions will be conditionally archived as the best solutions if they meet the specified requirement. All bats will then be ranked in determining the current top solution (x^*).

K-Means Clustering. K-means clustering is a technique that divides a dataset into k clusters/groups. This unsupervised learning algorithm attempts to group data points based on the sum of squared deviations between each data point and assigned centroid. Data points that are near centroid will be grouped in similar groups. Given below are the steps involved in the k-means clustering algorithm:

Step	Description
Step 1	Initialization: Initial centroid will be selected randomly
Step 2	Assignment: The Euclidean distance is used in determining data points that are the nearest to the centroid

(continued)

(*continued*)

Step	Description
Step 3	Recalculation: Recalculate the mean of all data points to assure all data points are assigned to the respective centroid
Step 4	Repetition of Step 2 and Step 3 until convergence occurred: Reallocating data points to their nearest centroid and recalculate the centroids until no data point changes its assigned cluster
Step 5	The final k centroids and the cluster assignments for each data point are determined

The k-means algorithm intends to reduce the within-cluster sum of squares, by measuring the distance between the data points to their assigned centroids. Data points that are close to assigned centroids will be grouped in the same cluster. In this study, we have used the elbow method or silhouette in determining the number of clusters, k.

4 Experimental Results and Discussion

The parameters for the proposed BBA in this study are set as follows, where values of A = 0.5; r = 0.5, $\alpha = 0.9$, and $\gamma = 0.9$. Meanwhile, the parameters for the SSO algorithm are set as given in Table 3. These values are given based on the suggestion of previous works that confirmed it could offer promising results. The iteration values of BBA are set max to 30 iterations and the evaluation is done by measuring an average of Precision (PR), Recall (R), F-measure (F), and Accuracy (ACC).

Table 3. Parameters setting for SSO algorithm.

Parameter	Value
Number of spiders	10
Dimension	9
Upper bound	50
Lower bound	0.01
Number of iterations	30

Based on the proposed method, several terms have been discovered to be prominent in PHEME dataset. To visualize these words, this study has used word clouds or tag clouds as a method of graphical representations to determine word frequency. Words with larger visuals indicate a significant prominence that has been repeatedly discovered in a source text. The figures below illustrate the words that are more common in Charlie Hebdo and Sydney Siege events (Fig. 3).

In this study comparison using different evaluation metrics on five events of PHEME dataset has been conducted as given in Table 4. The experimental results have shown that BBA has a better performance in comparison to SSO in terms of F measure, Precision,

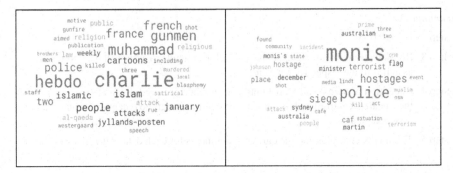

Fig. 3. Words cloud for Charlie Hebdo and Sydney Siege events.

and Recall for all events except for Ferguson shooting data. This is mainly due to the unbalanced dataset in Ferguson shooting data with 24.8% and 75.2% of data reported in non-rumors and rumors respectively (Figs. 4 and 5).

Table 4. Comparison of different evaluation metrics on five events in PHEME data.

Events	F_{Avg}		PR_{Avg}		R_{Avg}	
	BBA	SSO	BBA	SSO	BBA	SSO
Charlie Hebdo	**0.337**	0.220	**0.551**	0.443	**0.421**	0.325
Sydney siege	**0.524**	0.487	**0.657**	0.547	**0.524**	0.478
Ottawa shooting	**0.654**	0.613	**0.758**	0.687	**0.776**	0.689
Ferguson shooting	0.201	**0.211**	0.356	0.388	0.321	**0.257**
Germanwings plane crash	**0.711**	0.689	**0.778**	0.697	**0.879**	0.743

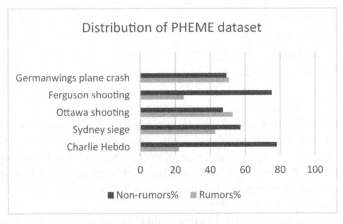

Fig. 4. Distribution of PHEME dataset.

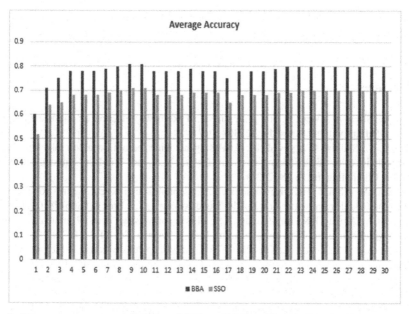

Fig. 5. The average accuracy of BBA and SSO on K-Mean clustering on Charlie Hebdo event.

In terms of average accuracy, the BBA has outperformed the SSO algorithm when trained with K-Means clustering as depicted in the figure above. BBA has achieved 80% of average accuracy whereas SSO has obtained 70% of average accuracy when tested on PHEME dataset. Although both algorithms have a novel optimization strategy, BBA has a better convergence rate than SSO with an increment of 10% of average accuracy.

5   Conclusion and Future Works

Social networks for instance Twitter offer useful social services to enable family members, family, and colleagues to stay connected and obtain quick information. However, the spread of false information, such as fake news created poses a growing threat among users which leads to a tremendous negative impact on people's lives and society. Therefore, it is crucial to identify fake news to ensure the dissemination of accurate and true information. To solve this issue, a novel method for detecting fake news using Twitter data is put forth in this research. The Binary Bat Algorithm (BBA) is suggested as a solution to problems with high-dimensional feature space brought on by a significant amount of Twitter data. In this study, BBA and SSO have trained with K-Means clustering on PHEME dataset. The data is tested o using the average of Precision (PR), Recall (R), F-measure (F), and Accuracy (ACC). The results show that the BBA algorithm outperforms the Social Spider Optimization (SSO) algorithm. Thus, BBA is a promising solution for solving high-dimensionality feature space in fake news Twitter data. For future works, an improved BBA will be developed and trained with other metaheuristic algorithms to extensively compare the performance of the proposed technique.

Acknowledgment. This research was supported by the Ministry of Higher Education (MoHE) of Malaysia through Fundamental Research Grant Scheme (FRGS/1/2020/ICT02/UUM/02/3).

References

1. Shu, K., Sliva, A., Wang, S., Tang, J., Liu, H.: Fake news detection on social media. ACM SIGKDD Explorations Newsl **19**, 22–36 (2017)
2. Mishra, S., Shukla, P. Agarwal, R.: Analysing machine learning enabled fake news detection techniques for diversified datasets. In: Hashmi, M.F., (ed) Wireless Communications and Mobile Computing, pp. 1–18 (2022)
3. Hussein, A., Ahmad, F.K., Kamaruddin, S.S.: Content-social based features for fake news detection model from twitter. Int. J. Adv. Trends Comput. Sci. Eng. **8**, 2806–2810 (2019)
4. Hussein, A., Ahmad, F.K., Kamaruddin, S.S.: Cluster analysis on Covid-19 outbreak sentiments from twitter data using K-means algorithm. J. Syst. Manage. Sci. **11**(4), 167–189 (2021)
5. Monshizadeh, M., Khatri, V., Kantola, R., Yan, Z.: A deep density based and self-determining clustering approach to label unknown traffic. J. Netw. Comput. Appl. **207**, 103513 (2022)
6. Ahuja, R., Chug, A., Kohli, S., Gupta, S., Ahuja, P.: The impact of features extraction on the sentiment analysis. Procedia Comput. Sci. **152**, 341–348 (2019)
7. Yang, X.-S.: Nature-Inspired Computation and Swarm Intelligence: Algorithms, Theory and Applications. Academic Press, Cambridge (2020)
8. Yang, X.S., He, X.: Bat algorithm: literature review and applications. Int. J. Bio-Inspired Comput. **5**, 141 (2013)
9. AL-Dyani, W.Z., Ahmad, F.K., Kamaruddin, S.S.: A survey on event detection models for text data streams. J. Comput. Sci. **16**(7), 916–935 (2020). https://doi.org/10.3844/jcssp.2020.916.935

Sentiment Analysis of Arabic Dialects: A Review Study

Abdullah Habberrih and Mustafa Ali Abuzaraida(✉)

Computer Science Department, Faculty of Information Technology, Misurata University, Misurata, Libya
{m09181037,abuzaraida}@it.misuratau.edu.ly

Abstract. Arabic people use Arabic dialects on social media platforms to express their opinions and connect. Due to the absence of standard rules or grammar, Arabic dialects are more challenging for NLP tools to analyze than standard Arabic. While most review studies in this field have focused on highly indexed databases such as Scopus, Web of Science, and IEEE, these databases are not accessible to many Arabic researchers in Arabic countries due to financial constraints. This review study explores recent research and studies published in different databases to address this gap. The study identifies the most common sentiment analysis approaches, preprocessing and feature extraction techniques, and classification and evaluation techniques used in this field. The authors found that Twitter is the most commonly utilized source for researchers to collect their datasets, and machine learning approaches are the most commonly used for sentiment analysis in Arabic dialects. Overall, this study provides valuable insights into the challenges and opportunities for sentiment analysis in Arabic dialects.

Keywords: Sentiment Analysis · Arabic Language · Arabic Dialects · Machine Learning · Classification

1 Introduction

The rise in social media platforms for expressing opinions on diverse products and topics [1] has generated the need for analyzing textual data. Researchers have turned to Natural Language Processing (NLP) methods to analyze the attitudes and opinions of people [2, 3]. Sentiment Analysis (SA) is an NLP method that enables machines to comprehend and evaluate sentiments expressed in a text. Texts are classified into positive, negative, and neutral categories, although some classifications may also include strongly negative and strongly positive sentiments [1, 4]. Nowadays, SA is considered an important field due to its applications in many domains, such as Decision-making support, finance, politics, predicting elections, and the Business [5].

According to [3], Arabic is considered the fifth most spoken language in the world. There are three variations of the Arabic language, including Classical Arabic (CA), Modern Standard Arabic (MSA), and Dialectal Arabic (DA) [2]. CA is used to write the holy book of Islam (Quran), while MSA is employed in politics, journalism, books,

N. H. Zakaria et al. (Eds.): ICOCI 2023, CCIS 2001, pp. 137–153, 2024.
https://doi.org/10.1007/978-981-99-9589-9_11

and education, whereas DA is an informal version of Arabic [2]. DA is used in daily life for communication. DA is different from country to country and even from city to city. However, there are six popular types of dialectal Arabic, namely Maghrebi, spoken in northern Africa, Khaliji spoken in the Arab Gulf area, Shami spoken in Jordan, Lebanon, Palestine, and Syria, Egyptian spoken in Egypt, Sudanese, and Iraqi spoken in Sudan and Iraq [4].

The Arabic language poses several challenges in SA, are addressed in [6, 11] and a study that focused on Saudi dialects, as described in [7, 10, 20]. One of the key complexities in dealing with dialectical Arabic is the absence of standard rules or grammar. Regarding sentence structure and morphology, Arabic sentences can start with a noun phrase, verb, or nominal phrase. Moreover, Arabic exhibits numerous syntactic variations within all sentence types. Additionally, dialect natives may express their opinions using different dialects and slang words and abbreviations. Furthermore, repetition of letters may be used to show emotion and emphasis, leading to spelling errors.

Many Arabic individuals use DA to convey their opinions on social media platforms like Twitter and Facebook. Consequently, many researchers have focused on studying DA rather than MSA [8, 20]. The main objective of this study is to examine the most notable research conducted on DA and emphasize the available datasets, common preprocessing techniques, and Machine Learning (ML) approaches commonly used to classify DA sentiment.

2 Methodology

This study conducts a comprehensive survey for the previous studies in Arabic dialect sentiment analysis. Here, the techniques used by the past studies in each phase of processing the Arabic sentences are highlighted. These phases are listed: Arabic dialect datasets, preprocess, feature extraction, and classification techniques. The search strategy of this study is explained in Sect. 2.1.

2.1 Search Strategy

Many recent studies have been carried out to present a systematic review in this field, as evidenced by the works of [2, 4, 7, 9]. However, these studies have exclusively employed highly indexed databases such as Scopus, Web of Science, and IEEE. Notably, publishing in these indexed databases is not preferred for many Arabic researchers in Arabic countries, mainly due to financial constraints. The primary reason for this reluctance is the lack of financial support, discouraging researchers from investing heavily in publication costs. Consequently, many researchers publish their work in local or non-indexed journals, even if their papers represent high-quality research. Against this backdrop, this study aims to conduct a comprehensive survey to review as many studies as possible instead of solely focusing on limited databases. The scope of this study is limited to cover the ML and Hybrid approaches of SA.

2.2 Arabic Dialect Datasets

The lack of accessible Arabic datasets on the internet has compelled several researchers to gather data independently from social media platforms to advance their research. Notwithstanding the significance of the Arabic language, it is deemed one of the languages that exhibit deficient content on the internet, with few web pages specifically devoted to Arabic reviews. Consequently, researchers have been encouraged to adopt Twitter as the principal source for acquiring vast amounts of data, as it offers a search application programming interface (API) that facilitates the retrieval of tweets in the desired language [10, 11, 15].

A study introduced a dataset called Corpus of Iraqi Arabic Dialect (CIAD) [13], comprising 1170 tweets. This dataset has been made publicly available on the GitHub platform and aims to facilitate the identification of hate speech from non-hate speech. Similarly, the study [14] built a Multi-Dialect Arabic Sentiment Twitter Dataset (MD-ArSenTD) from Twitter collected from 12 Arab countries, focusing on the dialects spoken in Egypt and the United Arab Emirates. They explored the discussed topics and dialectical differences and expressed sentiments between tweets from both countries. Additionally, various researchers compiled several Arabic datasets, as documented in [27, 30–35, 47], manually and publicly shared. Among these resources, [31] presented a comprehensive Arabic multi-domain corpus for sentiment analysis, comprising 33,000 annotated reviews from websites covering diverse domains such as hotels, products, movies, and restaurants. Furthermore, the authors created multi-domain lexicons from these datasets. The study [32] constructed a corpus of 2000 labeled tweets on politics and arts, written in Modern Standard Arabic (MSA) and Jordanian dialect. The study [33] introduced the Opinion Corpus for Arabic (OCA), which includes 500 movie reviews collected from multiple web pages and blogs. Another study [34] developed the Arabic Sentiment Tweets Dataset (ASTD), which contains approximately 10,000 tweets. Similarly, the study [35] proposed a Large-Scale Arabic Book Reviews Dataset (LSABR) comprising over 63,000 book reviews, each rated 1 to 5 stars. Finally, the study [30] utilized these publicly available datasets and data from [36] to create a new corpus consisting of 250,000 comments, 2000 of which were collected manually from Facebook pages in the Iraqi dialect.

2.3 Preprocessing and Feature Extraction Phases

The preprocessing phase is crucial in SA as it enhances the data quality and improves the analysis's overall performance. This phase can be carried out through various stages that depend on the language's nature and the analysis objectives. Most social media text is unstructured or noisy due to a lack of standardization, spelling mistakes, missing punctuation, non-standard words, and repetitions. The preprocessing process mainly comprises three steps: normalization, stemming, and stop-words removal [15]. The Normalization step involves transforming text to achieve consistency and putting it in a standard form, while the stemming step aims to reduce words to their uninflected base forms [15]. Finally, the stop words removal step entails eliminating natural language words that have little meaning, such as "إلى"(to), "حتى"(until), "انت"(you), "من"(of), and similar words [25].

After the preprocessing process, the next step is feature extraction, which involves identifying the most effective features for the sentiment analysis process and removing irrelevant, redundant, and noisy data. This step reduces the dimensionality of the feature space and the processing time, ultimately improving the efficiency and effectiveness of the analysis [17]. Feature frequency (FF), Term Frequency-Inverse Document Frequency (TF-IDF), feature presence (FP), Word Embedding (WE), Part of Speech (POS), and N-grams methods are the most commonly used methods for the features extraction phase [16].

2.4 Classification Techniques

The process of SA can be achieved through three primary approaches: Lexicon-Based (LB), Machine Learning (ML), and Hybrid approaches. The Lexicon-Based approach can be divided into two techniques: Corpus-based and Dictionary-based. Lexicon-Based techniques analyze a sentiment lexicon, a compilation of words with corresponding positive, negative, or neutral polarity labels [20]. However, this approach is excluded from this study due to its structure which is completely different from the ML and Hybrid approaches.

The ML approach involves the training of models on pre-labeled data, and it is categorized into three approaches: Supervised, Unsupervised, and Semi-supervised learning. The Supervised learning technique, also known as Classification or Regression, requires two subsets of data: a training set of labeled data and a testing set. The accuracy of this technique is dependent on the training set and the algorithm used. Unsupervised learning, also known as Clustering, is used for unlabeled data and aims to create clusters of data points, with similar points grouped in the same cluster and dissimilar points in different clusters. Semi-supervised techniques combine the advantages of both Supervised and Unsupervised techniques. The third approach used in SA is the Hybrid approach, which combines the Lexicon-Based and Machine Learning approaches [21].

Furthermore, a comparative study of some of the works invested in Arabic dialect sentiment analysis is presented in Table 1. Note that N/A means Not Available; DC: Data Cleaning; SWR: Stop-words removal; W2V: Word2Vec; NER: Named Entity Recognition; E: Evaluation; BR: Best Results; SR: Some Results.

3 Study Findings

Due to the lack of Arabic text resources on the internet, researchers have used social media platforms to collect their datasets. According to [7], Twitter is the most commonly used platform for constructing datasets for Arabic dialects. This can be observed by performing this study, including the works [11, 13, 14, 23, 26, 32, 40, 42, 44, 45, 47, 49, 51, 52, 54]. Facebook and YouTube have also been used as other resources for some researchers to collect their corpora, as in [8, 27, 29, 30, 38, 43, 45, 46]. However, websites that contain reviews for restaurants, movies, hotels, and products could be preferred resources for researchers to accumulate their datasets. Moreover, Fig. 1 illustrates the most Arabic dialects sources used.

Table 1. Comparative study of some works invested in Arabic dialect sentiment analysis.

Ref, Dataset size, Source, Annotated (Yes/No)	Preprocessing Techniques	Feature-extraction Techniques	Classification Approach, Techniques	Evaluations, Best Results (%)
[9] Emirati, About 216,000 comments, Instagram, Yes	1. Tokenization, 2. DC, 3. SWR, 4. Normalization, 5. Stemming	TF-IDF	ML, 1. LR, 2. MNB, 3. SVM, 4. DT, 5. RF, 6. MLP, 7. AdaBoost, 8. GBoost 9. Ensemble Model	E: Accuracy, Recall, F1-score, & Precision, BR: Ensemble Model with an accuracy of 80.88 on Unbalanced Dataset
[1] Libyan (Misurata sub-dialect), N/A. Manually with four poets. Yes	1. DC, 2. SWR, 3. Normalization	N/A	ML & DL, 1. LR, 2. SVM, 3. RF, 4. NB 5. Mazajak tool (CNN)	N/A. BR: ML with 68
[30] Iraqi, 252000 comments, Facebook pages and six publicly datasets, Yes	1. Tokenization, 2. Data cleaning, 3. SWR 4. Normalization	WE & Doc2Vec	ML, 1. LR, 2. DT, 3. SVM, 4. NB	E: Precision, Recall, & F-measure. BR: SVM with 82
[44] Tunisian, 204,097 items, 4 corpora & Twitter, Yes	1. DC 2. SWR, 3. Normalization, 4. Tokenization	BOW, TF-IDF, & avg-W2V	ML, DL, 1. Bi LSTM., 2. SVM. 3. DT, 4. NB, 5. CNN, 6. LSTM. 7. XGBoost	E: Accuracy, Recall, & F-measure. BR: ML: NB and LR with above 84, DL: Bi-LSTM with above 88
[45] Sudanese, 11,109 posts & tweets in two corpora, Facebook, YouTube, & Twitter, Yes	1. Sudanese SWR, 2. Data cleaning 3. Normalization	WE, TF-IDF, & W2V (AraVec)	ML & DL, 1. NB, 2. RF, 3. SVM, 4. LR, 5. RNN, 6. CNN, 7. CNN-LSTM, 8. MMA, 9. SCM	N/A. BR: SCM + MMA with 92.25

(continued)

Table 1. (*continued*)

Ref, Dataset size, Source, Annotated (Yes/No)	Preprocessing Techniques	Feature-extraction Techniques	Classification Approach, Techniques	Evaluations, Best Results (%)
[27] Tunisian, About 26000 comments, Facebook, Yes	1. DC, 2. SWR, 3. Normalization, 4. Tokenization	CV, TF-IDF, POS, & WE	ML DL, 1. KNN, 2. LR, 3. SVM, 4. AdaBoost, 5. RF. 6. DT, 7. BERT, 8. LSTM, 9. CNN	E: Accuracy, Recall, & Precision. BR: Ara-BERT with 76.9
[46] Algerian, 50572 comments, Facebook, Yes	1. Subject detection. 2. Tokenization. 3. SWR	WE & FT model	DL, 1. LSTM, 2. CNN	E: Error Rate, Accuracy, & F-measure. BR: LSTM + CNN with 85
[47] Saudi, 20,000 tweets, Twitter, Yes	N/A	TF & TF-IDF	ML, SVM	N/A. BR: AraCust + SVM with 91.0
[14] multi-dialects, 14,400 tweets, Twitter, Yes	1. Tokenization, 2. Normalization	Stem,W2V, N-grams, POS	ML & DL, 1. Lib-SVM, 2. LSTM	E: Accuracy & F-measure, BR: LSTM with 70.0
[13] Iraqi, 1170 tweets, Twitter. Yes	1. DC 2. SWR. 3. Tokenization	TF-IDF	ML, 1. SMO, 2. Lib-SVM	E: Accuracy, F1-Measure, Precision, & Recall. BR: Lib-SVM with 78.1
[26] Saudi, 5,500 tweets, Twitter, Yes	1. SWR, 2. Tokenization, 3. Stemming, 4. DC, 5. Normalization	N-grams	ML, 1. KNN, 2. SVM, 3. NB	E: Accuracy. BR: KNN + Stem with 59.22
[29] Algerian, 15,407,910 messages, Facebook. Yes	1. DC, 2. Exaggerations removal, 3. Stemming 4. Tokenization	BOW & Doc2vec	ML, 1. SVM, 2. NB, 3. LR, 4. DT, 5. RF	E: F-measure & Accuracy. BR: LR + BOW with 78

(*continued*)

Table 1. (*continued*)

Ref, Dataset size, Source, Annotated (Yes/No)	Preprocessing Techniques	Feature-extraction Techniques	Classification Approach, Techniques	Evaluations, Best Results (%)
[49] N/A, 22,550 tweets, Twitter. Yes	1. Tokenization 2. SWR 3. Stemming	N/A	ML, 1. NB, 2. SVM	E: Precision, Recall, & F-Measure BR: Exp1: NB with 99.8
[51] Sudanese,5456 tweets, Twitter. Yes	1. Tokenization 2. DC 3. SWR	N-gram	ML, 1. DT, 2. NB	N/A. BR: Exp1: DT with 60.85, Exp2: DT with 83.5
[52] MSA & Moroccan, 18,000 tweets, Twitter. Yes	1. Stemming. 2. Normalization. 3. DC	BOW	ML & DL, 1. SVM, 2. CNN, 3. LSTM, 4. LR	E: Precision & Accuracy. BR: LSTM 90.88
[11] Saudi, 4.000 tweets, Twitter. Yes	1. DC, 2. Tokenization, 3. Normalization	BOW & N-grams	ML, 1. SVM, 2. NB	E: F-measure. BR:SVM + BOW with 73
[31] MSA & DA, 33,000 reviews, Different Reviewing Websites. Yes	N/A	TF-IDF & Delta TF-IDF	Hybrid, 1. Linear-SVM, 2. LR, 3. BNB, 4. KNN, 5. SGD	N/A. BR: Exp1: SVM with 82.4, Exp2: SVM with 59.9
[32] MSA & Jordanian, 2000 tweets, Twitter. Yes	1. DC 2. SWR, 3. Normalization	Unigram	Hybrid, 1. SVM, 2. NB, 3. DT, 4. KNN	E: Precision, Recall, Accuracy. BR: Exp1: SVM with 84.7 of accuracy, Exp2: SVM with 85
[33] OCA, MSA & DA, 500 movie reviews, Different web pages & blogs. Yes	1. DC, 2. Spelling mistakes, 3. Tokenization, 4. SWR 5. Stemming	N-grams	ML, 1. SVM, 2. NB	N/A. BR: SVM with TF-IDF

(*continued*)

Table 1. (*continued*)

Ref, Dataset size, Source, Annotated (Yes/No)	Preprocessing Techniques	Feature-extraction Techniques	Classification Approach, Techniques	Evaluations, Best Results (%)
[34] ASTD, Egyptian, about 10,000 tweets, Twitter. Yes	N/A	N-grams	ML, 1. MNB, 2. BNB, 3. SVM, 4. SGD, 5. KNN	E: Accuracy, F1 measure, BR: SVM, Accuracy of 69, F1-score of 62.6
[35] LABR, MSA, With over 63,000 reviews, GoodReads, N/A	1. Tokenization 2. Punctuation removal	TF-IDF & N-grams	ML, 1. SVM, 2. BNB, 3. MNB	E: Accuracy & F-measure. BR: Balanced: MNB, Unbalanced: SVM
[38] TSAC, Tunisian, 17.000 comments, Facebook. Yes	DC	Doc2vec	ML, 1. MLP, 2. NB, 3. SVM	E: Error rate, Precision & Recall. BR: MLP, SVM
[40] Egyptian, 1000 tweets, Twitter. Yes	1. Egyptian SWR 2. DC	TF, N-grams	ML, 1. SVM, 2. NB	N/A. BR: SVM with an Accuracy of 72.6
[42] Kuwaiti, 340,000 tweets, Twitter. Yes	1. Tokenization, 2. Segmentation, 3. DC	TF & N-grams	ML, 1. SVM, 2. J48, 3. ADTREE, 4. Random Tree	E: Precision & Recall. BR: SVM with the precision of 76 and recall of 61
[43] Algerian, 49864 items, Facebook. Yes	1. Normalization 2. DC	W2V & TF-IDF	ML & DL, 1. SVM, 2.RNN (LSTM)	E: Accuracy, Precision, Recall & F1 score. BR: SVM Accuracy of 86
[23] MAC, Moroccan, 18,000 tweets, Twitter. Yes	1. Data cleaning, 2. Tokenization, 3. Normalization, 4. SWR	WE & TF-IDF	Hybrid, 1. SVM, 2. LR, 3. CNN, 4. LSTM	N/A. BR: Exp1: LSTM, Exp2: CNN

(continued)

Table 1. (*continued*)

Ref, Dataset size, Source, Annotated (Yes/No)	Preprocessing Techniques	Feature-extraction Techniques	Classification Approach, Techniques	Evaluations, Best Results (%)
[8] Algerian, 65,125 comments, Facebook. Yes	1. Data cleaning, 2. Tokenization, 3. Normalization	N/A	DL & ML, 1. CNN, 2. SVM	E: Precision & Recall. BR: CNN with Accuracy of 74.66
[54] MSTD, Moroccan, 35,000 tweets, Twitter. Yes	1. Data cleaning, 2. Tokenization, 3. Stemming, 4. SWR 5. Lemmatization	BOW & TF-IDF	ML, 1. SVM, 2. KNN, 3. BNB, 4. LR, 5. DT, 6. RF, 7. XGBoost	E: Accuracy. BR: LR & SVM
[55] SANA, Algerian, N/A. Newspapers. Yes	1. Data cleaning 2. Tokenization 3. Stemming 4. SWR	N-grams, TF & TF-IDF	ML, 1. SVM, 2. NB, 3. KNN	E:Precision, Recall, & Accuracy. BR: KNN
[18] Sudanese, 1,050 comments, Facebook. Yes	1. DC 2. SWR 3. Tokenization 4. Normalization 5. Lemmatization	N/A	ML, 1. SVM, 2. NB	E: Precision, Recall, Accuracy, & F-measure. BR: SVM with accuracy of 68.6
[53] ASTD, RES Egyptian & Multi-Dialect, N/A, Twitter & restaurant reviews, N/A	1- Tokenization 2. Normalization 3. Lemmatization 4. SWR 5. De-Noising	TF–IDF	ML, 1. SVM, 2. BNB, 3. DT, 4. SGD, 5. LR, 6. RF, 7. MNB	E: Accuracy, Precision, & Recall. BR: Exp1: BNB with 82 for ASTD, Exp2: SVM with 87.7 for RES
[48] N/A 8,053 comments, YouTube. Yes	1. Tokenization 2. Normalization	TF-IDF and N-grams	ML, 1. KNN, 2.SVM-RBF, 3. BNB	E: Precision, Recall, & F-measure BR: Exp3: SVM-RBF with 88.8 of f-measure

(*continued*)

Table 1. (*continued*)

Ref, Dataset size, Source, Annotated (Yes/No)	Preprocessing Techniques	Feature-extraction Techniques	Classification Approach, Techniques	Evaluations, Best Results (%)
[10] Saudi, 10,445 tweets, Twitter. N/A	1. Data cleaning 2. Tokenization 3. SWR 4. Stemming	N/A	ML, 1. NB, 2. RF, 3. KNN	E: N/A. BR: RF
[19] Jordanian, 2,500 reviews, Jordan website. Yes	1. DC 2. Normalization	N/A	Hybrid, 1. SVM, 2. NB, 3. RF, 4. KNN	E: Accuracy, Precision, Recall, & F-measure. BR: SVM with 92.3 accuracy
[12] Tunisian, 44,000 comments Facebook. Yes	1. Tokenization 2. Normalization 3. Stemming 4. DC	WE, W2V	DL, 1. CNN, 2. LSTM, 3. Bi-LSTM	E: F-measure, Precision, & Recall. BR: Exp1: LSTM & Bi-LSTM with 87
[22] MSAC, MSA & Moroccan, 2000 reviews, Hespress website, Facebook, Twitter, and YouTube. N/A	1. DC 2. Tokenization 3. Normalization 4. SWR 5. Stemming	BOW & Binary weighting	ML, 1. NB, 2. SVM, 3. ME	E: Precision, Accuracy, Recall, F-Measure. BR: Exp1: SVM with 82.5 of accuracy, Exp2: Ensemble classifier with 83.15
[41] MSA & Egyptian, 40,000 tweets, Twitter. Yes	1. Tokenization 2. SWR 3. Stemming 4. DC	WE	DL, 1. CNN, 2. LSTM, 3. Bi-LSTM 4. CNN LSTM	E: Accuracy, Precision, Recall, & F-Measure. BR: CNN with 99.65 accuracy

(*continued*)

Table 1. (*continued*)

Ref, Dataset size, Source, Annotated (Yes/No)	Preprocessing Techniques	Feature-extraction Techniques	Classification Approach, Techniques	Evaluations, Best Results (%)
[24] Saudi, 15,000 tweets, Twitter. Yes	1. DC2. Normalization 3. SWR	BOW & CV	Hybrid, 1. SVM, 2. DT, 3. MNB, 4. Popularity Scoring equation	E: Accuracy, Precision, Recall, & F-Measure. BR: Exp2: SVM for STC company was 97
[28] Jordanian, N/A. Facebook. N/A	1. DC 2. SWR 3. Negations	BOW	Hybrid, 1. SVM, 2. KNN, 3. NB	E: Accuracy. BR: SVM with 97.8
[37] Algerian, 11,760 comments, Facebook, YouTube, and Twitter. Yes	1. Tokenization 2. Normalization 3. SWR	Word2Vec (Skip-gram & CBOW)	ML & DL. 1. CNN, 2. SVM, 3. RNN, 4. BNB, 5. MNB, 6. GNB	E: Accuracy. BR: 1.ML: Exp1, Exp2, Exp4: SVM, Exp3: MNB 2.DL.: Exp1, Exp2, Exp3: CNN Exp4: RNN
[6] Jordanian, 3550 tweets, Twitter. Yes	1. DC 2. Tokenization 3. Normalization 4. SWR 5. Stemming 6. NER	N-grams	ML. 1. SVM, 2. NB	E: Accuracy, Precision, Recall, & ROC. BR: SVM with 82.1 accuracy
[56] MSA & Egyptian, 2,111 tweets. Two available datasets, N/A	1. DC 2. Normalization 3. Negations	N-grams & Sentiment Score	Hybrid. 1. Ensemble SVM, 2. RF, 3. Ensemble with RF	E: Accuracy, Precision, Recall & F-measure. BR: Exp1: Ensemble SVM with 90, Exp2: SVM with 90.4

(*continued*)

Table 1. (*continued*)

Ref, Dataset size, Source, Annotated (Yes/No)	Preprocessing Techniques	Feature-extraction Techniques	Classification Approach, Techniques	Evaluations, Best Results (%)
[50] SDCT, Saudi, 32063 tweets, Twitter. Yes	1. DC, 2. Normalization	Word2vec (CBOW)	ML & DL. 1. LSTM, 2. Bi-LSTM, 3. SVM	E: Accuracy. BR: Bi-LSTM with 94
[39] Libyan, 16,730 tweets, Twitter. Yes	1. DC, 2. Tokenization, 3. Normalization, 4. SWR	TF-IDF	ML. 1. SVM, 2. LR, 3. NB, 4. KNN, 5. DT	E: Accuracy, Recall, F-measure, & Precision. BR: Exp1: SVM with 80.67

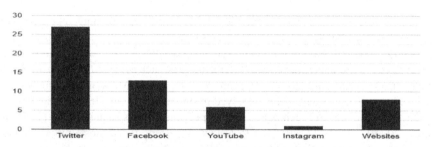

Fig. 1. Most Sources Used for Arabic Dialects.

According to [7], most research papers' authors did not specify the dialect type. This study showed that most of the researchers have indeed provided such specifications. For instance, the dialect type was identified in [10, 11, 24, 26, 47, 50] as Saudi, in [12, 27, 38, 44] as Tunisian, in [9] as Emirati, in [8, 29, 37, 43, 46, 55] as Algerian, in [6, 19, 28, 32] as Jordanian, in [13, 30] as Iraqi, in [1, 39] as Libyan, in [15, 34, 40, 56] as Egyptian, in [18, 45, 51] as Sudanese, in [42] as Kuwaiti, and in [23, 52, 54] as Moroccan dialects. In addition, the Arabic dialect types identified in the explored studies are shown in Fig. 2.

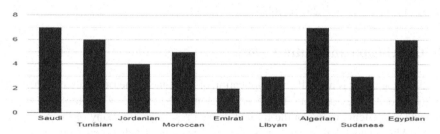

Fig. 2. Arabic Dialect Types Identified in The Explored Papers

As previously discussed, preprocessing is an essential step in Arabic sentiment analysis and poses a challenge for Arabic dialects. Tokenization, stop-word removal, normalization, and stems are the most common preprocessing techniques employed in the literature reviewed in this paper, as evidenced by studies such as [1, 9, 11, 13, 14, 26, 27, 29, 30, 44–46, 49, 51, 52]. Furthermore, studies like [1, 13, 26, 27, 29, 30, 44, 45, 51, 52] have employed additional techniques such as punctuation removal, repeated character removal, emoji removal, number removal, diacritic removal, and URL removal. Researchers in the field have mostly relied on Arabic NLP tools to implement these techniques. Some studies implemented Lemmatization techniques such as [18, 39, 54] and Negations techniques like [56].

Moreover, the most widely used feature-extraction techniques in Arabic dialects are TF-IDF, N-grams, and BOW. Studies such as [9, 11, 13, 14, 26, 27, 29, 44, 45, 47, 51, 52] have employed these techniques in machine learning approaches. Also, the authors in [31] have implemented Delta TF-IDF and compared it with TF-IDF. They claimed that "this method promises to be more efficient than traditional TF-IDF."

Other studies, such as [14, 27, 30, 45, 46], have used deep learning approaches and employed word embedding as a feature extraction technique. Furthermore, some studies, such as [27, 44, 45], have used Word2Vec, Average-Word2Vec, and CV techniques. However, only a few papers have used POS techniques, such as [14, 27], possibly because Arabic dialects lack standard rules or grammar compared to MSA or other languages.

Various approaches have been employed in studies on Arabic sentiment analysis, as evidenced by the range of techniques used in previous studies such as [1, 9, 11, 13, 14, 26, 27, 29, 30, 44, 45, 47, 49, 51, 52]. Machine learning is the most commonly used approach, with Support Vector Machine (SVM) and Naive Bayes (NB) being the most frequently utilized algorithms, as noted by [29] and supported by the studies reviewed in this study. Other algorithms, such as Decision Tree (DT), Random Forest (RF), Logistic Regression (LR), GBoost, K-Nearest Neighbors (KNN), and Lib-SVM, have also been widely employed in various studies [1, 9, 26, 27, 29, 30, 44, 45, 51, 52]. Deep learning (DL) techniques, including Convolutional Neural Networks (CNN), Recurrent Neural Networks (RNN), Long Short-Term Memory (LSTM), and Bi-LSTM, have also been employed in several studies [1, 9, 14, 27, 44–46, 52].

In contrast with doing the survey, only a few studies have employed Hybrid approaches, such as [19, 23, 24, 28, 31, 32, 56]. The performance metrics such as accuracy, recall, F1-score, precision, and error rate have been employed in many studies [1, 9, 11, 13, 14, 26, 27, 29, 30, 44, 47, 49, 51, 52].

4   Conclusion and Future Work

Sentiment analysis is a significant application of NLP due to the rich source of information provided by textual data. However, developing NLP models and tools for Arabic dialects is challenging, given the limited written resources for many of these dialects. Unlike MSA, which has a rich corpus of written resources such as news articles, books, and academic papers, Arabic dialects often lack standard written forms and are primarily used in spoken communication. This study has investigated the studies that have been recently published and revealed that most researchers collect their datasets from Twitter, Facebook, and YouTube. Furthermore, studies were predominantly applied to dialects spoken in Saudi Arabia, Tunisia, Iraq, Algeria, and Sudan, with fewer studies applied to Libyan, Syrian, and Yemeni dialects. Machine learning approaches were the most utilized in sentiment analysis of Arabic dialects, with the best results obtained using this approach—however, most papers employed Arabic NLP tools rather than building specific tools for the studied dialect. Future work will aim to build a sentiment analysis model and compare different machine learning classifiers for the Libyan dialect.

References

1. Abugharsa, A.: Sentiment analysis in poems in misurata sub-dialect--a sentiment detection in an Arabic Sub-dialect, arXiv Prepr. arXiv:2109.07203 (2021)
2. Alyami, S., Alhothali, A., Jamal, A.: Systematic literature review of Arabic aspect-based sentiment analysis. J. King Saud Univ. Inf. Sci. **34**(9), 6524–6551 (2022)

3. Alshutayri, A.O.O., Atwell, E.: Exploring Twitter as a source of an Arabic dialect corpus. Int. J. Comput. Linguist. **8**(2), 37–44 (2017)
4. Elnagar, A., Yagi, S., Nassif, A.B., Shahin, I., Salloum, S.A.: Sentiment analysis in dialectal Arabic: a systematic review. Adv. Mach. Learn. Technol. Appl. Proc. AMLTA **2021**, 407–417 (2021)
5. Mehta, P., Pandya, S.: A review on sentiment analysis methodologies, practices and applications. Int. J. Sci. Technol. Res. **9**(2), 601–609 (2020)
6. Atoum, J.O., Nouman, M.: Sentiment analysis of Arabic Jordanian dialect tweets, Int. J. Adv. Comput. Sci. Appl., **10**(2) (2019)
7. Al Shamsi, A.A., Abdallah, S.: A systematic review for sentiment analysis of arabic dialect texts researches. In: Proceedings of International Conference on Emerging Technologies and Intelligent Systems: ICETIS 2021, vol. 2, pp. 291–309 (2022)
8. Klouche, B.,. Benslimane, S.M., Mahammed, N.: Sentiment analysis of algerian dialect using a deep learning approach. In: Artificial Intelligence and Its Applications: Proceeding of the 2nd International Conference on Artificial Intelligence and Its Applications 2022, pp. 122–131 (2021)
9. Al Shamsi, A.A., Abdallah, S.: Sentiment analysis of emirati dialect. Big Data Cogn. Comput. **6**(2), 57 (2022)
10. Althagafi, A., Althobaiti, G., Alhakami, H., Alsubait, T.: Arabic tweets sentiment analysis about online learning during COVID-19 in Saudi Arabia. Int. J. Adv. Comput. Sci. Appl. **12**(3) (2021)
11. Alwakid, G., Osman, T., Hughes-Roberts, T.: Challenges in sentiment analysis for Arabic social networks. Procedia Comput. Sci. **117**, 89–100 (2017)
12. Masmoudi, A., Hamdi, J., Belguith, L.H.: Deep learning for sentiment analysis of Tunisian dialect. Comput. y Sist. **25**(1), 129–148 (2021)
13. Alharbi, H.A.-J.M.M., H., Almukhtar, A.F., Alnawas, A.A.: Constructing Twitter Corpus of Iraqi Arabic Dialect (CIAD) For Sentiment Analysis. In: Научно-технический вестник информационных технологий, механики и оптики, vol. 22, no. 2, pp. 308–316 (2022)
14. Baly, R., et al.: Comparative evaluation of sentiment analysis methods across Arabic dialects. Procedia Comput. Sci. **117**, 266–273 (2017)
15. Shoukry, A., Rafea, A.: Preprocessing Egyptian dialect tweets for sentiment mining. Fourth Workshop Comput. Approach. Arabic-Script-based Lang. **2012**, 47–56 (2012)
16. Haddi, E., Liu, X., Shi, Y.: The role of text preprocessing in sentiment analysis. Procedia Comput. Sci. **17**, 26–32 (2013)
17. Sayed, A.A., Elgeldawi, E., Zaki, A.M., Galal, A.R.: Sentiment analysis for Arabic reviews using machine learning classification algorithms. In: 2020 International Conference on Innovative Trends in Communication and Computer Engineering (ITCE), pp. 56–63 (2020)
18. Heamida, I.S.A.M., Ahmed, E.L.S.A.E., Mohamed, M.N.E., Salih, A.: Applying sentiment analysis on Arabic comments in sudanese dialect. Int. J. Comput. Sci. Trends Technol. **8** (2020)
19. Al-Harbi, O.: Classifying sentiment of dialectal Arabic reviews: a semi-supervised approach. Int. Arab J. Inf. Technol. **16**(6), 995–1002 (2019)
20. Alwakid, G.: Sentiment analysis of dialectical Arabic social media content using a hybrid linguistic-machine learning approach. Nottingham Trent University (United Kingdom) (2020)
21. Aurélien, G.: Hands-on machine learning with scikit-learn & TensorFlow, Geron Aurelien (2017)
22. Oussous A., Lahcen A.A., Belfkih, S.: Improving sentiment analysis of Moroccan tweets using ensemble learning, in Big Data, Cloud and Applications: Third International Conference, BDCA 2018, Kenitra, Morocco, April 4–5, 2018, Revised Selected Papers 3, 2018, pp. 91–104 (2018)

23. Garouani, M., Kharroubi, J.: MAC: an open and free Moroccan Arabic Corpus for sentiment analysis. In: Innovations in Smart Cities Applications Volume 5: The Proceedings of the 6th International Conference on Smart City Applications, pp. 849–858 (2022)

24. Abdullah, B., Alosaimi, N., Almotiri, S.: Reputation measurement based on a hybrid sentiment analysis approach for Saudi telecom companies. Int. J. Adv. Comput. Sci. Appl. **12**(6) (2021)

25. Birjali, M., Kasri, M., Beni-Hssane, A.: A comprehensive survey on sentiment analysis: approaches, challenges and trends. Knowl.-Based Syst. **226**, 107134 (2021)

26. Al-Harbi, W.A., Emam, A.: Effect of Saudi dialect preprocessing on Arabic sentiment analysis. Int. J. Adv. Comput. Technol. **4**(6), 91–99 (2015)

27. Mekki, A., Zribi, I., Ellouze, M., Belguith, L.H.: A Tunisian benchmark social media data set for COVID-19 sentiment analysis and sarcasm detection (2022)

28. Nahar, K.M.O., Jaradat, A., Atoum, M.S., Ibrahim, F.: Sentiment analysis and classification of arab jordanian Facebook comments for Jordanian telecom companies using lexicon-based approach and machine learning. Jordanian J. Comput. Inf. Technol., **6**(3) (2020)

29. Guellil, I., Adeel, A., Azouaou, F., Hussain, A.: Sentialg: automated corpus annotation for Algerian sentiment analysis. In: Advances in Brain Inspired Cognitive Systems: 9th International Conference, BICS 2018, Xi'an, China, July 7–8, 2018, Proceedings 9, 2018, pp. 557–567 (2018)

30. Alnawas, A., Arici, N.: Sentiment analysis of Iraqi Arabic dialect on Facebook based on distributed representations of documents. ACM Trans. Asian Low-Resource Lang. Inf. Process. **18**(3), 1–17 (2019). https://doi.org/10.1145/3278605

31. ElSahar, H., El-Beltagy, S.R.: Building large Arabic multi-domain resources for sentiment analysis. In: Gelbukh, A. (ed.) CICLing 2015. LNCS, vol. 9042, pp. 23–34. Springer, Cham (2015). https://doi.org/10.1007/978-3-319-18117-2_2

32. Abdulla, N.A., Ahmed, N.A., Shehab, M.A., Al-Ayyoub, M.: Arabic sentiment analysis: Lexicon-based and corpus-based. In: 2013 IEEE Jordan Conference on Applied Electrical Engineering and Computing Technologies (AEECT), pp. 1–6 (2013)

33. Rushdi-Saleh, M., Martín-Valdivia, M.T., Ureña-López, L.A., Perea-Ortega, J.M.: OCA: Opinion corpus for Arabic. J. Am. Soc. Inf. Sci. Technol. **62**(10), 2045–2054 (2011)

34. Nabil, M., Aly, M., Atiya, A.: ASTD: Arabic sentiment tweets dataset. In: Proceedings of the 2015 Conference on Empirical Methods in Natural Language Processing, 2015, pp. 2515–2519 (2015)

35. Aly, M., Atiya, A.: LABR: a large scale Arabic book reviews dataset. In: Proceedings of the 51st Annual Meeting of the Association for Computational Linguistics (Volume 2: Short Papers), pp. 494–498 (2013)

36. Banea, C., Mihalcea, R., Wiebe, J.: Multilingual subjectivity: are more languages better?. In: Proceedings of the 23rd International Conference on Computational Linguistics (Coling 2010), pp. 28–36 (2010)

37. Mazari, A.C., Djeffal, A.: Sentiment analysis of Algerian dialect using machine learning and deep learning with Word2vec. Informatica **46**(6) (2022).https://doi.org/10.31449/inf.v46i6.3340

38. Mdhaffar, S., Bougares, F., Esteve, Y., Hadrich-Belguith, L.: Sentiment analysis of Tunisian dialects: linguistic resources and experiments. In: Third Arabic Natural Language Processing Workshop (WANLP), pp. 55–61 (2017)

39. Omar, A., Essgaer, M., Ahmed, K.M.S.: Using machine learning model to predict libyan telecom company customer satisfaction. In: 2022 International Conference on Engineering & MIS (ICEMIS), pp. 1–6 (2022)

40. Shoukry, A., Rafea, A.: Sentence-level Arabic sentiment analysis. In: 2012 International Conference on Collaboration Technologies and Systems (CTS), pp. 546–550 (2012)

41. Mohamed, S.M., Mohamed, E.H., Belal, M.A.: Polarity detection of dialectal arabic using deep learning models. Int. J. Adv. Comput. Sci. Appl. **12**(11) (2021)

42. Ben Salamah, J., Elkhlifi, A.: Microblogging opinion mining approach for Kuwaiti dialect. In: The International Conference on Computing Technology and Information Management (ICCTIM), p. 388 (2014)

43. Abdelli, A., Guerrouf, F., Tibermacine, O., Abdelli, B.: Sentiment analysis of Arabic Algerian dialect using a supervised method. In: 2019 International Conference on Intelligent Systems and Advanced Computing Sciences (ISACS), pp. 1–6 (2019)

44. Jaballi, S., Zrigui, S., Sghaier, M.A., Berchech, D., Zrigui, M.: Sentiment analysis of tunisian users on social networks: overcoming the challenge of multilingual comments in the tunisian dialect. In: Computational Collective Intelligence: 14th International Conference, ICCCI 2022, Hammamet, Tunisia, September 28–30, 2022, Proceedings, 2022, pp. 176–192. (2022)

45. Mhamed, M., Sutcliffe, R., Sun, X., Feng, J., Almekhlafi, E., Retta, E.A.: A deep CNN architecture with novel pooling layer applied to two sudanese Arabic sentiment datasets. arXiv Prepr. arXiv2201.12664 (2022)

46. Bousmaha, K.Z., Hamadouche, K., Gourara, I., Hadrich, L.B.: DZ-OPINION: Algerian dialect opinion analysis model with deep learning techniques. Rev. d'Intelligence Artif. **36**(6), 897 (2022)

47. Almuqren, L., Cristea, A.: AraCust: a Saudi telecom tweets corpus for sentiment analysis. PeerJ Comput. Sci. **7**, e510 (2021)

48. Al-Tamimi, A.-K., Shatnawi, A., Bani-Issa, E.: Arabic sentiment analysis of YouTube comments. In: 2017 IEEE Jordan Conference on Applied Electrical Engineering and Computing Technologies (AEECT), pp. 1–6 (2017)

49. Duwairi R. M.: Sentiment analysis for dialectical Arabic. In: 2015 6th International Conference on Information and Communication Systems (ICICS), pp. 166–170 (2015)

50. . Alahmary, R.M., Al-Dossari, H.Z., Emam, A.Z.: Sentiment analysis of Saudi dialect using deep learning techniques. in 2019 International Conference on Electronics, Information, and Communication (ICEIC), 2019, pp. 1–6 (2019)

51. Abo M. E. M., Shah N. A. K., Balakrishnan V., Kamal M., Abdelaziz A., and Haruna K., Ssasda: subjectivity and sentiment analysis of Sudanese dialect Arabic. In: 2019 International Conference on Computer and Information Sciences (ICCIS), pp. 1–5 (2019)

52. Garouani, M., Kharroubi, J.: Towards a new lexicon-based features vector for sentiment analysis: application to Moroccan Arabic tweets. In: Advances in Information, Communication and Cybersecurity: Proceedings of ICI2C'21, pp. 67–76 (2022)

53. Hussein, A.H., Moawad, I.F., Badry, R.M.: Arabic sentiment analysis for multi-dialect text using machine learning techniques. Int. J. Adv. Comput. Sci. Appl. **12**(12) (2021).https://doi.org/10.14569/IJACSA.2021.0121286

54. Mihi, S., Ait, B., El, I., Arezki, S., Laachfoubi, N.: MSTD: Moroccan sentiment twitter dataset". Int. J. Adv. Comput. Sci. Appl. **11**(10), 363–372 (2020)

55. Rahab, H., Zitouni, A., Djoudi, M.: SANA: sentiment analysis on newspapers comments in Algeria. J. King Saud Univ. Inf. Sci. **33**(7), 899–907 (2021)

56. El-Naggar, N., El-Sonbaty, Y., Abou El-Nasr, M.: Sentiment analysis of modern standard Arabic and Egyptian dialectal Arabic tweets. In: 2017 Computing Conference, pp. 880–887 (2017)

Charting Inclusive Digital Society Research Trends: A Bibliometric Analysis of E-Participation Through Social Media

Hapini Awang[1]([✉]) [ID], Nur Suhaili Mansor[1] [ID], Maslinda Mohd Nadzir[1] [ID],
Osman Ghazali[1] [ID], Abderrahmane Benlahcene[2] [ID], Fadhilah Mat Yamin[3] [ID],
Isyaku Uba Haruna[1] [ID], Shakiroh Khamis[4] [ID],
and Abdulrazak F. Shahatha Al-Mashhadani[5] [ID]

[1] Institute for Advanced and Smart Digital Opportunities, School of Computing, Universiti Utara Malaysia, 06010 UUM Sintok Kedah, Malaysia
hapini.awang@uum.edu.my
[2] School of Government, Universiti Utara Malaysia, 06010 UUM Sintok Kedah, Malaysia
[3] School of Technology Management and Logistics, Universiti Utara Malaysia, 06010 UUM Sintok Kedah, Malaysia
[4] Faculty of Information and Communication Technology, Universiti Tuanku Abdul Rahman, 31900 Kampar, Perak, Malaysia
[5] Faculty of Business, Sohar University, Sohar 311, Oman

Abstract. This study analyzed 287 articles on e-participation within social media, which were retrieved from the Scopus online databases as of 11 December 2022. The aim was to identify crucial areas and significant contributors within the field and recent research trends. The findings indicate that the trend of e-participation was slow to start, with researchers primarily from Western nations. The field still struggles to establish itself as an independent area of research, and identity-related issues are prevalent. In addition, the subject of e-participation through social media has received limited attention in the literature, with a focus on politicians' groups and minimal consideration of government-driven initiatives. This study is among the first to analyze bibliometric trends in e-participation literature related to social media. It is revealed that the publication trends on e-participation did not portray any consistent increment over the years, although the adoption of ICT in public sectors is happening at a peak rate. The findings can guide future research in this area and underscore the importance of considering government-driven initiatives in e-participation research, as they play a critical role in shaping digital democracy. Nonetheless, it is essential to interpret these findings deliberately, as the dataset solely covers the Scopus database and may not comprehensively cover all available sources. Finally, the study serves as a basis for future investigations in the field of e-participation and social media.

Keywords: E-Participation · Digital Society · Social Media · Digital Solutions

N. H. Zakaria et al. (Eds.): ICOCI 2023, CCIS 2001, pp. 154–167, 2024.
https://doi.org/10.1007/978-981-99-9589-9_12

1   Introduction

Electronic participation (E-Participation) refers to the process of using technology to encourage stakeholders' involvement and interaction. Governments worldwide have adopted e-participation policies to promote citizens' participation in public decision-making [1]. The importance of Information and Communication Technology (ICT) in enabling citizen participation has grown significantly over the past few decades [2]. Moreover, e-participation is crucial in educating citizens about the complex decision-making process, enhancing their understanding and perception of the rationale behind a given policy. However, its implementation involves various complex aspects that impact the participation process beyond just technology capability or participation itself [3]. Existing research in this field has often focused on a single domain without considering its connections to other aspects [4].

In reality, while specific e-participation programs have shown significant effects, many of them have a low level of citizen involvement, and only a few have had a tangible impact on the decision-making process [5–9]. To improve citizens' e-participation, governments are advised to move to where citizens gather most, such as social media, instead of expecting them to move to traditional government websites [10]. However, despite social media's increasing popularity and extensive usage, little research has been conducted to encourage its users to participate in public decision-making [5, 11]. Although e-participation and social media have been analyzed regularly using various research methods, their literature analysis using bibliometrics is still relatively uncommon. This inadequacy leads to difficulties for future researchers in understanding research trends, identifying gaps, and proposing impactful studies. Hence, this article provides an overview of recent research trends in e-participation using bibliometric analysis techniques. It also seeks to evaluate the critical areas and significant applications of e-participation, particularly in social media.

2   Literature Review

Social media platforms have created new opportunities for e-participation, enabling citizens to engage in public decision-making through ICT. This trend has attracted researchers in the Information Systems (IS) field to explore the area. To facilitate knowledge growth, bibliometric analysis can shed light on the extent of research on e-participation via social media, providing a better understanding of current trends and identifying available gaps for future research. In light of this, it was found that most studies on e-participation have focused on general concepts rather than social media as a tool for e-participation. Only 10% of the analyzed studies specifically addressed social media, indicating a need for further research in this area [12].

The definition of e-participation remains unsettled among academics [9], and it is often used interchangeably with synonyms like "engagement," "involvement," and "empowerment," and occasionally with "political involvement." Consequently, this lack of agreement could hinder the growth and development of e-participation. E-participation was initially considered a sub-section of e-democracy aimed at encouraging representative democratic decision-making [13]. Nonetheless, e-participation is not limited to politics. In contrast to e-participation initiatives in the political context, there is a growing movement towards citizen-centric e-participation initiatives designed to involve citizens in policy-making processes [10]. These initiatives prioritize citizens' needs and interests over those of politicians and governments. The objective is to provide more interactive and participatory platforms, motivating citizens to participate in policy-making processes [10].

E-participation is a growing area that uses digital innovations to enhance citizen involvement in shaping public policy, especially for achieving the 2030 Sustainable Development Plan [5]. To encourage citizen e-participation, engaging them where they are most active, such as on social media platforms rather than relying solely on traditional government websites, is essential. Social media platforms provide a new dimension to the e-participation field and offer significant ability for improving citizen involvement in policy-making processes at various levels [2, 10, 14]. Despite the extensive use of social media, there has been limited research on encouraging its users to engage in public decision-making [5, 11].

Recent literature summarized the study trend on e-participation through social media [5, 10, 15]. A key emphasis was also placed on the difficulties in promoting e-participation initiatives that prioritize citizens, specifically elevating their engagement and participation on these platforms [5, 11]. Social media platforms provide an opportunity to increase citizen participation in e-participation initiatives, but recent research indicates that they tend to be more informative than interactive [16]. Efforts are needed to create more interactive and engaging e-participation initiatives that provide citizens with opportunities to express their opinions and contribute to policy-making processes [5, 15, 17].

Overall, e-participation is a growing field that aims to increase citizen participation in policy-making processes through the use of digital technologies. While e-participation has historically been associated with e-democracy and political contexts, there is a growing movement towards citizen-centric e-participation initiatives that prioritize citizens' needs and interests over those of politicians and governments. Efforts are needed to create more interactive and engaging e-participation initiatives that provide citizens with opportunities to express their opinions and contribute to policy-making processes. Therefore, bibliometric analysis is a good starting point for identifying recent trends and exploring future research directions. This can help increase the level of citizen engagement with the government in practice.

3   Methods

To conduct the bibliometric analysis for this study, it followed the suggestion by [18] and modified it based on the recommendations by [19]. The method was systematic and followed a specific process, which can be replicated in future studies. The study used 287 articles to answer the research questions. It employed the Preferred Reporting Items for Systematic Review and Meta-Analysis (PRISMA) method to select articles from the Scopus database. The study used categorical inclusion and exclusion criteria, which are specified in Fig. 1. The criteria were based on the relevance of the articles to the research questions, the quality of the articles, and the publication date. The inclusion criteria included articles published in the last five years, written in English, and related to the topic of interest. The exclusion criteria included articles not written in English, articles unrelated to the subject, and articles with low-quality scores.

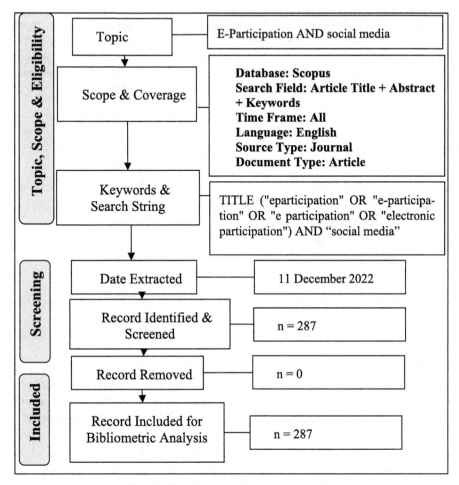

Fig. 1. Flow diagram of the search strategy.

To search for relevant papers, five sets of keywords were applied in the Scopus database, as displayed in Fig. 1. The primary keyword used was a combination of "eparticipation", "e-participation", "e participation", or "electronic participation" AND "social media".

4   Results

Through the implementation of bibliometric analysis, the study has derived outcomes related to document types, source types, language, subject area, research trends, keywords, authorship, and citations, which are explained in further detail in the following sections.

4.1 Documents Profiles

Table 1 illustrates the distribution of the various types of documents related to e-participation and social media examined in the Scopus database. Conference papers were the most common document type, accounting for 48% of the total. Articles represented 29.27%, followed by book chapters at 11.15% and conference reviews at 8.36%. The remaining documents were in the form of reviews (1.05%), books (0.70%), and editorials (0.70%), respectively. Conference papers in this context refer to papers presented at conferences that may have been published as full journal articles [20].

Table 1. Document type.

Document Type	Total Publications (TP)	Percentage (%)
Conference Paper	140	48.78%
Article	84	29.27%
Book Chapter	32	11.15%
Conference Review	24	8.36%
Review	3	1.05%
Book	2	0.70%
Editorial	2	0.70%
Total	**287**	**100.00**

Table 2 provides an overview of the source types related to e-participation, indicating that there are four types of sources. The most significant source type is conference proceedings, accounting for 39.37% of the total. Journals represent the succeeding greatest source type in e-participation research, comprising 31.36%, followed by book series at 20.56% and books at 8.71%.

Table 2. Source type.

Source Type	Total Publications (TP)	Percentage (%)
Conference Proceeding	113	39.37%
Journal	90	31.36%
Book Series	59	20.56%
Book	25	8.71%
Total	**287**	**100.00**

Table 3 shows the distribution of languages used in e-participation-related documents. English was the primary language for publication of most of the documents, representing 98.61% of the total. The remaining 0.35% were published in Italian, Portuguese, Russian, and Spanish, which were the least popular languages used in this study.

Table 3. Languages

Language	Total Publications (TP)*	Percentage (%)
English	284	98.61%
Italian	1	0.35%
Portuguese	1	0.35%
Russian	1	0.35%
Spanish	1	0.35%
Total	**288**	**100.00**

* One document was written in dual languages

Table 4 displays the 15 most productive journals in the e-participation field. The analysis revealed that the "Computer Science" category had the highest number of e-participation-related documents, accounting for 284 (74.22%). This may be due to its listing in the Scopus database, which could have contributed to its high percentage compared to other listed sources. The "Social Science" category had the second-highest percentage of published e-participation documents, contributing up to 36.59% with a total of 105 documents. The remaining journals had published less than 100 documents, with the lowest on the list publishing only 49 articles as of the data search date.

Table 4. Subject area.

Subject Area	Total Publications (TP)	Percentage (%)
Computer Science	213	74.22%
Social Sciences	105	36.59%
Mathematics	49	17.07%
Business, Management and Accounting	39	13.59%
Decision Sciences	26	9.06%
Engineering	21	7.32%
Environmental Science	6	2.09%
Economics, Econometrics and Finance	5	1.74%
Arts and Humanities	4	1.39%
Energy	3	1.05%

(continued)

Table 4. (*continued*)

Subject Area	Total Publications (TP)	Percentage (%)
Medicine	3	1.05%
Psychology	3	1.05%
Materials Science	1	0.35%
Pharmacology, Toxicology and Pharmaceutics	1	0.35%

4.2 Research Trends

Figure 2 illustrates the publication trend of e-participation research between 2007 and 2022. Although publications related to e-participation date back to 2007, there was no significant increase in the number of publications until recent years. Between 2007 and 2010, there were no publications, and the trend fluctuated until 2013. However, since 2013, the graph demonstrates a gradual but steady rise in the number of publications, indicating a growing interest in e-participation. It is worth mentioning that the number of documents for 2022 is relatively low, despite this study being conducted in February 2023. Table 5 provides a breakdown of publications from 2007 to 2022.

Table 5. Year of publication.

Year	TP	NCP	TC	C/P	C/CP	h	g
2022	14	4.88%	3	200	14.29	66.67	
2021	21	7.32%			0.00		
2020	23	8.01%			0.00		
2019	26	9.06%			0.00		
2018	34	11.85%			0.00		
2017	27	9.41%			0.00		
2016	34	11.85%			0.00		
2015	30	10.45%			0.00		
2014	24	8.36%			0.00		
2013	17	5.92%			0.00		
2012	27	9.41%			0.00		
2011	6	2.09%			0.00		
2010	3	1.05%			0.00		
2007	1	0.35%			0.00		
Total	287						

Notes: TP = total number of publications; NCP = number of cited publications; TC = total citations; C/P = average citations per publication; C/CP = average citations per cited publication

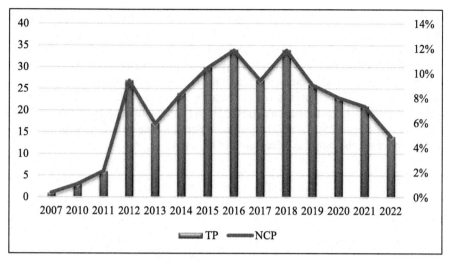

Fig. 2. Total publications and citations by year.

4.3   Citation Analysis

Table 6 presents citation metrics for the collected documents from 2007 to 2022, encompassing the overall number of citations and average citations per year for all retrieved articles. As per the table, the 286 retrieved articles received 52,608.85 citations over 15 years (2007–2022), with an average of 12.08 citations annually.

Table 6. Citations metrics.

Metrics	Data
Papers	286
Number of Citations	16
Years	15
Citations per Year	215.88
Citations per Paper	12.08
Cites_Author	52608.85
Authors_Paper	2.53
h_index	26
g_index	53

Table 7 provides an overview of the citation metrics for the collected documents as of February 2007, including the total number of citations and the mean citations per year for all retrieved articles. As indicated, there were 8,600 citations reported from 1992 to 2007 for 286 obtained articles, with an average of 302.85 citations per year.

The listed articles are related to social media and governance (which is very relevant to e-participation), and their names and affiliations are essential for readers to understand the backgrounds and expertise of the researchers who have contributed to the field. The top 5 highly cited articles cover a range of topics, including the impact of social media on corporate transparency [21], citizens' engagement on local government's Facebook sites [22], measuring participation in online political engagement [23], predicting changes in voting preferences using Twitter analytics [24], and factors influencing social media use in local governments [25]. Table 7 helps researchers spot the most dominant articles in the field and track the progress of research in this area.

Table 7. Top five highly cited articles.

No	Authors	Title	Year	Cites	Cites/Year
1	Bonsón et al. (2012)	Social media and corporate transparency in municipalities	2012	616	11
2	Bonsón et al. (2015)	Citizens' engagement on local governments' Facebook sites. An empirical analysis: The impact of different media and content types in Western Europe	2015	297	8
3	Gibson and Cantijoch (2013)	Conceptualizing and measuring participation in the age of the internet: Is online political engagement really different to offline?	2013	217	10
4	Grover et al. (2019)	Polarization and acculturation in US Election 2016 outcomes–Can Twitter analytics predict changes in voting preferences?	2019	129	4
5	Guillamón et al. (2016)	Factors influencing social media use in local governments: The case of Italy and Spain	2016	102	7

4.4 Keywords

Table 8 presents the top 10 keywords used in e-participation research, their total number of publications, and their percentage. VOS viewer is used to create a visual map (see Fig. 3) with a minimum threshold of five occurrences to analyze the keywords. The results demonstrated that "E-Participation" was the most frequently used keyword, appearing in 167 publications, followed by "Social Media" (163) and "Social Networking (online)"

(102). These three keywords covered over half of the total publications. The table also highlights other commonly used keywords such as "Egovernment", "Government Data Processing", "Decision Making", and "Public Policy." Overall, Table 8 helps researchers gain an understanding of the most frequent topics and themes in e-participation research.

Table 8. Top ten keywords.

Author Keywords	Total Publications (TP)	Percentage (%)
E-Participation	167	58.19%
Social Media	163	56.79%
Social Networking (online)	102	35.54%
E-Participation	40	13.94%
Government Data Processing	39	13.59%
Egovernment	36	12.54%
Decision Making	35	12.20%
EParticipation	28	9.76%
Public Policy	28	9.76%
Electronic Participation	21	7.32%

Figure 3 depicts a visualization map that demonstrates the connections among author keywords, citations by documents, and bibliographic coupling by authors. The varying colors, font sizes, and thickness of the connecting lines signify the strength of the relationships between the keywords. Keywords that share the same color are frequently listed together, indicating their close association and tendency to co-occur. For example, the diagram shows that E-Participation, Social Media, Social Networking (online), and Electronic Participation are highly related. Additionally, after excluding the core keyword (E-Participation) specified in the search query, the keywords with the highest occurrences are "Government Data Processing", "E-government", "Decision-Making", "Public Policy", and "Electronic Participation". This figure is helpful for researchers to visualize the relationships between different keywords in the field of E-Participation research and to identify potential research topics or themes.

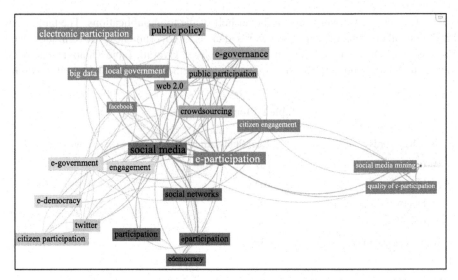

Fig. 3. Network visualization map of the author keywords.

5 Discussion and Conclusion

The study utilizes bibliometric analysis to identify the most researched topics and their relationships in e-participation through social media research from 2007 to 2022. The study presents twelve tables and a network visualization that includes document profiles, research trends, citation analysis and author keywords. All peer-reviewed journals available in the Scopus database that focus on e-participation in social media are reviewed. As a result, it is found that English is the dominant language in this research area, with approximately 98.70% of the retrieved documents written in this language. The trend also revealed that the literature on e-participation has not significantly increased over the years, despite the widespread adoption of ICT in public sectors. Although it has been researched for over 15 years, e-participation has faced challenges in establishing itself as an independent field, which calls for further research to strengthen it both theoretically and practically.

Theoretically, the result of this study advanced the academic understanding of e-participation. Several key discoveries have been made, including a declining trend in the number of authorships per document over time. Greece has reported the highest number of authors in this research domain, followed by Canada and Ireland as the primary contributing countries. Several other European countries have also supported scholarly works in this area. Another significant contribution of this study is that it identifies potential topics for future research by analyzing keywords with less frequent occurrences. The study fills a gap in the literature, as very little bibliometric analysis has been conducted to analyze e-participation in social media in the last decade. Therefore, this study has successfully updated and enriched the bibliometric literature, mainly since there has been a decline in e-participation in social media research since 2018. On the other hand, the practical impact of the study's results on e-participation lies in its ability to guide policymakers and practitioners in designing and implementing more tailored and effective e-participation initiatives. By identifying specific research areas and potential topics for further exploration, this study offers valuable direction to enhance citizen engagement, address challenges, and leverage the power of social media to foster meaningful and inclusive public participation in decision-making processes. In the long run, this will lead to more responsive and citizen-centric policies, greater transparency, and increased trust between governments and the public.

However, the study has certain limitations, primarily because it only uses datasets from the Scopus database, focusing primarily on peer-reviewed publications. Thus, future research should also consider using various online databases such as Web of Science (WoS), Springer, and IEEE Xplore, among others, to obtain a more comprehensive range of scientific contributions. Next, to avoid subjective assessment by authors, the results of the bibliometric analysis should be compared with different methods. While the study provides valuable insights into e-participation in social media literature, it is still vital to further broaden the analysis's scope and increase the reliability of the findings by exploring other databases and utilizing alternative methodologies, such as qualitative content analysis, systematic literature reviews, or meta-analysis. Furthermore, to build on this study, future researchers could highlight several important points extracted from the findings. For instance, Asian countries have not been thoroughly researched in terms of e-participation in social media, creating an opportunity for future research to explore how people in countries like Malaysia, with unique cultures, religions, nationalisms, and lifestyles, could influence e-participation. Investigating these unique characteristics could offer valuable insights into how e-participation can be tailored to specific cultural contexts. Overall, this study can provide useful information for researchers, practitioners, and policymakers to identify knowledge gaps, research opportunities, and potential collaborations in the field of e-participation in social media.

Acknowledgment. This research was supported by the Ministry of Higher Education (MoHE) of Malaysia through Fundamental Research Grant Scheme (FRGS/1/2022/ICT03/UUM/02/4).

References

1. United Nations: E-Government Survey. New York (2020)
2. Susha, I., Grönlund, Å.: EParticipation research: systematizing the field. Gov. Inf. Q. **29**, 373–382 (2012). https://doi.org/10.1016/j.giq.2011.11.005
3. Mat Nawi, H., Sapiai, N.S., Ishak, F.M., Mustapha, WMBW, Arifin, N.B., Mohd Zawawi, T.M.Z.: A bibliometric analysis on e-participation. Int. J. Acad. Res. Bus. Soc. Sci. **11**, 1201–1215 (2021). https://doi.org/10.6007/ijarbss/v11-i9/10846
4. Yusuf, M., Muntasa, A., Agustiono, W., Anamisa, D.R., Syarief, M.: A novel conceptual model of e-participation using biometrics technologies. J. Phys. Conf. Ser. **1569**(2), 022069 (2020). https://doi.org/10.1088/1742-6596/1569/2/022069
5. Alarabiat, A., Soares, D.S., Estevez, E.: Electronic participation with a special reference to social media - a literature review. In: Tambouris, E., Panagiotopoulos, P., Sæbø, Ø., Wimmer, M.A., Pardo, T.A., Charalabidis, Y., Soares, D.S., Janowski, T. (eds.) Electronic Participation: 8th IFIP WG 8.5 International Conference, ePart 2016, Guimarães, Portugal, September 5-8, 2016, Proceedings, pp. 41–52. Springer, Cham (2016). https://doi.org/10.1007/978-3-319-45074-2_4

6. Demirdoven, B., Cubuk, E.B.S., Karkin, N.: Establishing relational trust in e-participation: a systematic literature review to propose a model. In: ACM International Conference Proceeding Series, pp. 341–348 (2020). https://doi.org/10.1145/3428502.3428549

7. Charalabidis, Y., Loukis, E.N., Androutsopoulou, A., Karkaletsis, V., Triantafillou, A.: Passive crowdsourcing in government using social media. Transform. Gov.: People Process Policy **8**, 283–308 (2014)

8. Charalabidis, Y., Loukis, E.N., Androutsopoulou, A., Karkaletsis, V., Triantafillou, A.: Passive crowdsourcing in government using social media. Transforming Government: People, Process and Policy **8**(2), 283–308 (2014). https://doi.org/10.1108/TG-09-2013-0035

9. Rustad, E., Sæbø, Ø.: How, why and with whom do local politicians engage on Facebook? In: Wimmer, M.A., Tambouris, E., Macintosh, A. (eds.) ePart 2013. LNCS, vol. 8075, pp. 69–79. Springer, Heidelberg (2013). https://doi.org/10.1007/978-3-642-40346-0_7

10. Johannessen, M.R., Elvestad, E.: Participation in a new media landscape - a literature review of participation tools. In: CEUR Workshop Proceedings, pp. 27–35 (2021)

11. Hariguna, T., Rahardja, U., Aini, Q.: Nurfaizah: effect of social media activities to determinants public participate intention of e-government. Procedia Comput. Sci. **161**, 233–241 (2019). https://doi.org/10.1016/j.procs.2019.11.119

12. Kahne, J., Bowyer, B.: Educating for democracy in a partisan age: confronting the challenges of motivated reasoning and misinformation. Am. Educ. Res. J. **54**, 3–34 (2017). https://doi.org/10.3102/0002831216679817

13. Macintosh, A.: Characterizing e-participation in policy-making. In: Presented at the 37th Annual Hawaii International Conference on System Sciences (HICSS 2004) (2004)

14. Medaglia, R.: eParticipation research: moving characterization forward (2006–2011). Gov. Inf. Quarterly **29**, 346–360 (2012). https://doi.org/10.1016/j.giq.2012.02.010

15. Dini, A.A., Øystein, S.: The current state of social media research for eParticipation in developing countries: a literature review. In: Presented at the 2016 49th Hawaii International Conference on System Sciences (HICSS) (2016)

16. Johannessen, M.R.: New vs old media a case study of political protest groups' media use in a Norwegian municipality. Int. J. Public Inf. Syst. **11** (2015)

17. Tambouris, E., et al.: Eparticipation in Europe: Current State and Practical Recommendations, in EGovernment Success around the World: Cases, Empirical Studies, and Practical Recommendations (2013)

18. Moher, D., Liberati, A., Tetzlaff, J., Altman, D.: Preferred Reporting Items for Systematic Reviews and Meta-Analyses (2009)

19. Zakaria, R., Ahmi, A., Ahmad, A.H., Othman, Z.: Worldwide Melatonin Research: A Bibliometric Analysis of the Published Literature between 2015 and 2019, Chronobiology International (2020)

20. Ahmi, A., Elbardan, H., Ali, R.H.R.M.: Bibliometric analysis of published literature on industry 4.0. In: 2019 International Conference on Electronics, Information, and Communication (ICEIC) (pp. 1–6). IEEE (2019)

21. Bonsón, E., Torres, L., Royo, S., Flores, F.: Local e-government 2.0: Social media and corporate transparency in municipalities. Gov. Inf. Q. **29**, 123–132 (2012). https://doi.org/10.1016/j.giq.2011.10.001

22. Bonsón, E., Royo, S., Ratkai, M.: Citizens' engagement on local governments' Facebook sites. an empirical analysis: the impact of different media and content types in Western Europe. Gov. Inf. Q. **32**(1), 52–62 (2015). https://doi.org/10.1016/j.giq.2014.11.001

23. Gibson, R., Cantijoch, M.: Conceptualizing and measuring participation in the age of the internet: Is online political engagement really different to offline? J. Polit. **75**, 701–716 (2013). https://doi.org/10.1017/S0022381613000431

24. Grover, P., Kar, A.K., Dwivedi, Y.K., Janssen, M.: Polarization and acculturation in US Election 2016 outcomes – Can Twitter analytics predict changes in voting preferences. Technol. Forecast. Soc. Change. **145**, 438–460 (2019). https://doi.org/10.1016/j.techfore.2018.09.009
25. Guillamón, M.D., Ríos, A.M., Gesuele, B., Metallo, C.: Factors influencing social media use in local governments: the case of Italy and Spain. Gov. Inf. Q. **33**, 460–471 (2016). https://doi.org/10.1016/j.giq.2016.06.005

Systematic Literature Review and Bibliometric Analysis on Addressing the Vanishing Gradient Issue in Deep Neural Networks for Text Data

Shakirat Oluwatosin Haroon-Sulyman[1]([email]) [ID], Mohammed Ahmed Taiye[2] [ID],
Siti Sakira Kamaruddin[3] [ID], and Farzana Kabir Ahmad[3] [ID]

[1] Department of Information and Communication Science, Faculty of Communication and Information Sciences, University of Ilorin, Ilorin 240003, Nigeria
sulyman.sh@unilorin.edu.ng
[2] Department of Cultural Sciences, Faculty of Arts and Humanities, Linnaeus University, 351 95 Vaxjo, Sweden
[3] School of Computing, Universiti Utara Malaysia, 06010 Sintok, Kedah, Malaysia

Abstract. The feature to learn complex text representations enabled by Deep Neural Networks (DNNs) has revolutionized Natural Language Processing and several other fields. However, DNNs have not developed beyond all challenges. For instance, the vanishing gradient problem remains a major challenge. This challenge hinders the ability of the system to capture long-term dependencies in text data. This challenge limits the ability to understand context, implied meanings, semantics, and to represent intricate patterns in text. This study aims to address the prevalent vanishing gradient problem encountered in DNNs when dealing with text data. Text data's inherent sparsity and heterogeneity exacerbate this issue, increasing computational complexities and processing time. To tackle this problem comprehensively, we will explore existing literature and conduct a bibliometric analysis to identify potential solutions. The findings will contribute to a comprehensive review of the existing literature and suggest effective strategies for mitigating the vanishing gradient problem in the context of NLP tasks. Ultimately, our study will pave the way for further advancements in this area of research.

Keywords: Vanishing gradient · Text data · Natural Language Processing · Deep Neural Network

1 Introduction

In recent years, the ability of Deep Neural Networks (DNN) to learn complex representations of data has brought significant attention to them. A crucial element for knowledge acquisition and information extraction in different applications is data representation. Consequently, understanding the efficacy of DNN is important in domains like speech recognition, computer vision, and Natural Language Processing (NLP) [2, 3]. However, the vanishing gradient problem is frequently encountered in DNNs, which often

N. H. Zakaria et al. (Eds.): ICOCI 2023, CCIS 2001, pp. 168–181, 2024.
https://doi.org/10.1007/978-981-99-9589-9_13

impedes or hinders the training and learning process, resulting in computational complexities and time consumption of data processing [4]. More importantly, the vanishing gradient problem is commonly observed in gradient-based learning and extends beyond image datasets. It applies to various other data types, including text data. Despite the improved results in gradient-based learning for NLP methods, the vanishing gradient remains a challenge that has hindered the effective training of long-term dependencies, a common feature in unstructured texts [5]. Thus, NLP tasks such as text classification, sentiment analysis, question-answering, and text anomaly detection must investigate ways to overcome these issues by proffering possible solutions for better model performance [3]. It is noteworthy that text data holds a substantial amount of information. It is also believed that a significant portion (around 80–90 percent) of forthcoming data growth resides within unstructured text databases, potentially holding valuable patterns and trends [6].

Considering the paramount importance of text data, this research will primarily address the vanishing gradient problem, specifically in textual data. The sparsity and heterogeneous nature of text data influence the vanishing gradient problem encountered in DNNs. Textual information often exhibits sparsity, characterized by the abundance of zero or near-zero values, resulting in numerous inactive or uninformative features [7]. Consequently, during the backpropagation phase, gradients associated with these inactive features diminish rapidly, impeding effective weight updates and hindering learning [8]. Moreover, the heterogeneity of text data, stemming from its diverse vocabulary, sentence structures, and semantic variations, presents additional challenges [9]. Gradients exhibit significant variations across different text segments, introducing inconsistent propagation throughout the network and further aggravating the vanishing gradient problem.

Inherent sparsity and heterogeneity of text data pose significant obstacles to gradient-based learning algorithms, undermining the convergence and training efficiency of DNNs. This study explores the vanishing gradient problem in DNN applicable to textual data by looking into the solutions proffered in literature. The study, therefore, seeks to answer the questions; What are the current state-of-the-art approaches and emerging trends to address the vanishing gradient challenge in DNNs for text data? This study adopts a different viewpoint by conducting a bibliometric analysis to examine the literature review using the Preferred Reporting Items for Systematic Reviews and Meta-Analysis (PRISMA) guideline. The aim is to explore the existing studies and their solutions to the vanishing gradient problem in deep neural networks.

This article is organized into 5 sections as follows; The introductory section elaborates on the background, motivation, problem statement, and research questions of the study. Section 2 gives an overview of relevant and related studies; Sect. 3 discusses the study methods; Sect. 4 sheds light on study findings; Sect. 5 sheds light on future recommendations and conclusions.

2   Review of Related Literature

2.1   Algorithmic Features

In recent times, researchers have examined the simultaneous use of models such as Convolutional Neural Network (CNN) and Long Short-term Memory (LSTM) [3], Convolutional Neural Network (CNN) with Bidirectional Long Short-term Memory (BiLSTM) [10], Long Short-term Memory (LSTM) with Bidirectional Long Short-term Memory (BiLSTM) [11, 12] to mitigate text data vanishing gradient issues. CNNs commonly used in image data contain spatial features that, when combined with LSTM, are effective in handling sequential and temporal text data; this sometimes results in a potential model for the vanishing gradient. CNNs can extract local text features, while LSTMs capture contextual features and long-term dependencies. However, as much as this approach has shown promising results in research, its limitations still lie in unsuitability for large-scale datasets as it requires time and multiple network layers, leading to model complexity and lack of interpretability. [3] used CNN and LSTM for sentence classification, which is an NLP approach. The study observed that even though the model could learn long-term dependencies, their experiments show that the model performance is affected by dataset size, classifiers, and gradients vanishing. A similar study [10] used CNN and BiLSTM deep neural networks for a text sequence classification task. The model was able to extract semantics, which is an essential feature in long text sequences, though the delay was encountered in the processing time due to the sequential process in the BiLSTM architecture. Similarly, the sentiment analysis task was performed using deep networks. Authors observed that the proposed framework is prone to limitations in cases of imbalanced or text bias in capturing diversity [11].

To improve performance, especially in the case of imbalanced datasets, some studies used multiple embedding techniques in addition to the network layers. [13] proposed a model that combines CNN and LSTM with word2vec and GloVe word embedding representations for sentence-level classification. Their model was able to capture different various representations of word embedding in the input layer. The results showed that it outperformed the models with a single embedding technique though it is time-consuming and may not be efficient for large datasets. Also, [14] proposed a model on CNN-LSTM with an attention mechanism, where the attention mechanism is useful to focus and capture relevant information. However, its use is dedicated to the specific study, which may not be suitable in all cases.

Other algorithmic features that have been commonly used in research to mitigate the vanishing gradient problem is the combination of activation functions [15–24] such as Rectified Linear Unit (ReLU), sigmoid, tanh, and SoftMax function, which has been used to improve the deep learning training by involving them in one or more of the network layers. A commonly used activation function is ReLU which has been used in various NLP tasks [15–18, 25]. Studies show that its major challenge is the dying ReLU which causes neurons to stop learning and eventually die.

2.2   Regularization Technique

This has been widely used as a means of mitigating the vanishing gradient challenge with techniques such as dropout [13, 26, 27], early stopping [13, 15, 28, 29], batch normalization [18, 26, 30]. It is commonly used in the data training phase. [30] made use of dropout, batch normalization, and a fast gradient sign procedure to add noise to the training data and avoid overfitting. Specific regularization technique was also considered in the case of large datasets, such as adaptive batch normalization as used in [31] to adjust the dimensionality of the input data representations. Research shows that more than one regularization or normalization technique has been used together for improved performance. Overfitting and noise in data rather than the underlying pattern arising due to model complexity in using algorithmic features [17] can lead to poor model performance on unseen data, which can cause vanishing gradient issues. To prevent such, these regularization techniques adjust the model during training to avoid overfitting and improve the model. However, this method is quite complex and sensitive to hyperparameters which may be time-consuming and require more computational resources [32].

2.3 Optimization Technique

This set of techniques focuses on finding the model's optimal parameters that minimize the loss function, such as gradient descent [22], weight clipping [33], stochastic gradient descent [25, 34, 35], Adam [36, 37]. Research shows that optimization techniques are combined with regularization and algorithmic features to speed up the process [3, 5, 29]. Stochastic Gradient Descent, used in [25] as an optimization technique to measure text novelty, improves the model's ability to detect rare texts. However, hyperparameters and large datasets are likely to affect its performance. [36] used Adam Optimizer in their study on social media industry review detection, whose aim was to speed up the process.

3 Methods and Interpretation of Findings

An extensive review of existing literature was carried out on the vanishing gradient in text data to identify specific methods used to handle the vanishing gradient issue of text data which was done using both the PRISMA and bibliometric analysis using VOS viewer.

3.1 Data Collection

The data was collected using the search string; *(TITLE-ABS-KEY ("Vanishing Gradient") OR ("backpropagation") AND ("text data")* from the Scopus database so as to get relevant recent studies on the search domain. Studies outside text data, such as image data, were not included. This is required to not digress from this study's domain. The next section is detailed on the PRISMA and bibliometric analysis respectively.

Step 1
The PRISMA analysis is a recognized framework for conducting and reporting systematic reviews and meta-analyses. It includes guidelines and a checklist to ensure reliability and transparency. The key steps involve defining the research question, conducting a thorough literature search, selecting relevant studies, extracting data, assessing study

quality, synthesizing data, and reporting results. This approach enhances the quality and reproducibility of these types of studies.

To retrieve literature on gradient vanishing and text data. The search yielded 141 results which were all considered for the bibliometric analysis. However, 31 documents were found relevant after the screening process. Figure 1 shows the PRISMA flow search strategy depicted in this study.

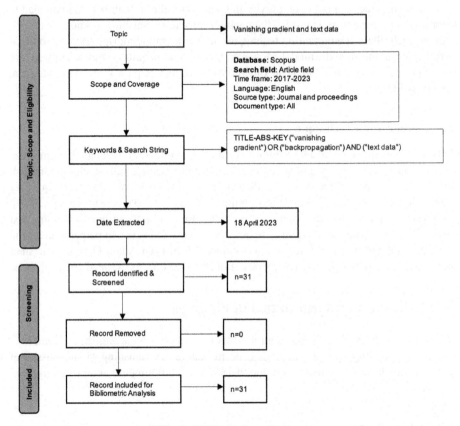

Fig. 1. PRISMA flow diagram

Step 2

VOSviewer is a valuable tool for researchers in bibliometric analysis. It helps visualize and understand complex networks from scholarly literature and identify research trends and gaps, thereby making informed decisions regarding collaboration, resource allocation, and future research directions surrounding the DNN and vanishing gradient issue.

Combining these analytical approaches aims to ensure quality information can be reproduced from the study. Furthermore, the Scopus database was chosen to gather relevant bibliographical data due to its functionality in generating a wide range of results.

Microsoft Excel was also used to collect data in structured form for a rigorous review of literature related to "vanishing gradients" and "text data." This has enabled easy identification of patterns from the existing studies and suggests new ideas to overcome the challenges for further research.

3.2 Data Analysis Process

This is important to achieve the aim of this study and guide further research. The data analysis includes literature selection, information extraction, information synthesis, and bibliometric analysis.

Table 1 further shows the top 10 most cited documents related to DNN and their various NLP applications. It is observed that the most common NLP applications focus on short-text sentence tasks such as sentiment analysis and text classification. It also provided insights into the various techniques for handling the vanishing gradient problem. As a result, the information provided in the table should be valuable to researchers in this domain and serve as a reference point for future work.

Table 1. Top 10 highly cited documents

No	Author/Title	Task performed	Method	Number of current citations
1	Zhang, Z., Robinson, D., & Tepper, J. (2018). Hate Speech Detection Using a Convolution-LSTM Based Deep Neural Network	Proposed a model to enhance performance in DNN for hate speech detection	CNN-LSTM, Dropout	576
2	Hassan, A., & Mahmood, A. (2018). Convolutional Recurrent Deep Learning Model for Sentence Classification	Proposed a model to capture long-term dependencies in short texts efficiently	LSTM, Stochastic Gradient Descent	221
3	Pham, D. H., & Le, A. C. (2018). Learning multiple layers of knowledge representation for aspect-based sentiment analysis	To improve capturing of long-range dependencies and semantic information for sentiment analysis	CNN, LSTM, Stochastic Gradient Descent	107

(continued)

Table 1. *(continued)*

No	Author/Title	Task performed	Method	Number of current citations
4	Plaza-del-Arco, F. M., Molina-González, M. D., Ureña-López, L. A., & Martín-Valdivia, M. T. (2021). Comparing pre-trained language models for Spanish hate speech detection	To detect hate speech on social media	CNN, LSTM. BiLSTM, Early stopping	79
5	Sadiq, S., Mehmood, A., Ullah, S., Ahmad, M., Choi, G. S., & On, B. W. (2021). Aggression detection through the deep neural model on Twitter	To detect aggression on Twitter	MLP, ReLU	77
6	Chandra, R., & Krishna, A. (2021). COVID-19 sentiment analysis via deep learning during the rise of novel cases	To explore the temporal nature of sentiments on covid-19	LSTM	62
7	Ma, Q., Yu, L., Tian, S., Chen, E., & Ng, W. W. (2019). Global-local mutual attention model for text classification. IEEE/ACM Transactions on Audio, Speech, and Language Processing, 27(12), 2127–2139	To capture both semantic features and long-term dependencies	CNN-BiLTSM, ReLU	31
8	Baccouche, A., Ahmed, S., Sierra-sosa, D., & Elmaghraby, A. (2020). *Malicious Text Identification: Deep Learning from Public Comments and Emails*	Proposed a model to identify malicious emails and comments	LSTM, Early stopping	28

(continued)

Table 1. (*continued*)

No	Author/Title	Task performed	Method	Number of current citations
9	Nguyen, V. Q., Anh, T. N., & Yang, H. J. (2019). Real-time event detection using recurrent neural network in social sensors	Proposed a model to detect temporal occurrence and improve LSTM performance	CNN, LSTM, dropout	28
10	Khan, M. U., Javed, A. R., Ihsan, M., & Tariq, U. (2020). A novel category detection of social media reviews in the restaurant industry	Proposed a customer detection opinion model	CNN, BiLSTM, Adam	25

Table 1 provides a comprehensive overview of techniques and models used in various NLP tasks, highlighting ongoing efforts to improve accuracy and effectiveness across domains. Key trends include the integration of RNNs and CNNs, utilizing regularization techniques and optimization algorithms, and emphasis on capturing semantic information and considering temporal aspects. These trends reflect the continuous pursuit of improved performance by addressing challenges such as overfitting and capturing contextual and temporal nuances in NLP tasks.

The VOS viewer visualization technique provides a clear understanding of the relationship between frequently occurring keywords and identifies research trends in the field. The process involves selecting a data file, creating a map based on the text, and applying a counting method. This study used the full counting method, and a controlled number of relevant terms were manually selected after verification. The threshold for word appearance was set to 12. As a result, 81 terms were used to generate clusters of terms. Some of the visualizations of these terms can be seen in the Figures.

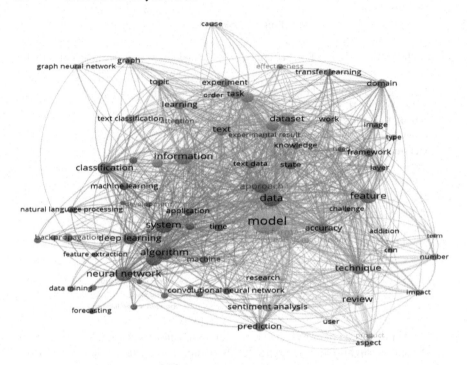

Fig. 2. VOS viewer General visualization of literature analysis results

Figures 2, 3, 4 give insights into exploring the selected text data. The next section will discuss observations and trends obtained from this data.

Cluster 1 centers on text data, classification, and sentiment analysis. It provides potential insights into methodologies for analyzing and classifying textual data and provides insights into exploring the performance evaluation, methodologies for exploring transfer learning, and experimental outcomes analyses within the dataset.

Cluster 2 This cluster highlights deep learning, recurrent neural networks RNNs, and NLP. It offers insights into the practical application of deep learning models, RNN architectures, and NLP techniques relevant to the dataset.

4   Findings

The clusters and their associated terms provide an overview of the various approaches and techniques employed in research to address the vanishing gradient issue in text data. It is, however, important to note that this review paper serves as only a starting point in the analysis of this challenge. There is a need for further research in terms of other domain–specific contextual analysis for a more explicit solution to the vanishing gradient issue in text data.

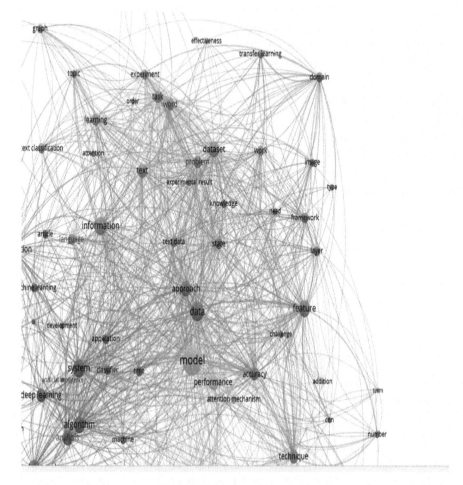

Fig. 3. VOS viewer Cluster one

5   Conclusion with Future Recommendation

A significant challenge presented by the vanishing graduating problem is encountered while training DNNs for NLP tasks. This study, among others, examines how the diminishing gradients perform during backpropagation and how this performance hinders the learning process by impeding effective and regular updates of weight parameters. Some of the approaches explored throughout this review in a bid to mitigate the vanishing gradient challenge and its impact on text data, include but are not limited to regularization, optimization techniques, and algorithmic features. However, there's a pressing need for further research to understand and solve this problem. For a more comprehensive understanding, easier reach of the solutions, and a broader perspective, it is crucial that more extensive analyses are conducted. These analyses will delve more into the understanding

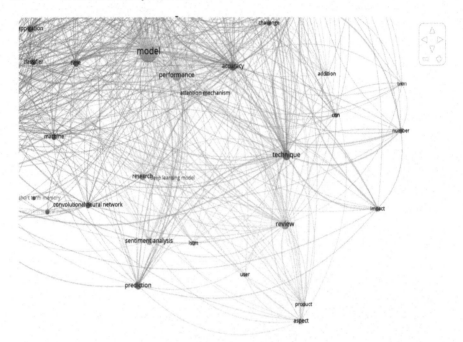

Fig. 4. VOS viewer Cluster two

of the vanishing gradient issue in text data and will be able to provide more tailored solutions and approaches that can be taken to avoid the issue in DNNs. To better understand how these techniques can be effectively applied in DNNS for NLP tasks, researchers can and should examine a broader range of data tests. It is also recommended that future studies adopt a comparative approach by evaluating and comparing existing methods to solve the vanishing gradient problem and assessing their specific effects on text data.

This comparative analysis will juxtapose different approaches and allow the researchers to see through their respective merits and demerits, thereby enabling researchers to make informed decisions regarding the most effective strategies for mitigating the vanishing gradient issue in text data. To further enhance our understanding of the datasets used in this study, it is recommended to explore additional explorative analyses. Deeper insights can be provided into the characteristics and patterns of the data through Techniques such as keyword extraction, phrase extraction, or text prediction. By employing advanced text mining approaches, researchers can better understand the relationships between the vanishing gradient problem and the text data. By conducting further investigations, employing advanced text mining techniques, and performing comparative analyses, researchers can make significant advancements in overcoming the challenges posed by the vanishing gradient problem. These efforts will ultimately contribute to improved performance and effectiveness of DNNs in NLP tasks.

References

1. Aldhyani, T.H.H., Al-Adhaileh, M.H., Alsubari, S.N.: Cyberbullying identification system based deep learning algorithms. Electronics **11**(20), 3273 (2022). https://doi.org/10.3390/electronics11203273

2. Acharya, J., Basu, A.: Deep neural network for respiratory sound classification in wearable devices enabled by patient specific model tuning. IEEE Trans. Biomed. Circuits Syst. **14**(3), 535–544 (2020). https://doi.org/10.1109/TBCAS.2020.2981172

3. Hassan, A., Mahmood, A.: Deep learning approach for sentiment analysis of short texts. In: The 3rd International Conference on Robotics, Automation, and Artificial Intelligence, ICCAR 2017, pp. 705–710 (2017). https://doi.org/10.1109/ICCAR.2017.7942788

4. Sun, X., Zhang, C., Ding, S., Quan, C.: Detecting anomalous emotion through big data from social networks based on a deep learning method. Multimed. Tools Appl. **79**(13–14), 9687 (2020). https://doi.org/10.1007/s11042-018-5665-6

5. Pham, D.H., Le, A.C.: Learning multiple layers of knowledge representation for aspect based sentiment analysis. Data Knowl. Eng. **114**, 26–39 (2018). https://doi.org/10.1016/j.datak.2017.06.001

6. Zainol, Z., Jaymes, M. T. H., Nohuddin, P. N. E.: VisualUrText: a text analytics tool for unstructured textual data. J. Phys. Conf. Ser. **1018**(1) (2018). https://doi.org/10.1088/1742-6596/1018/1/012011

7. Li, A., Sun, J., Zeng X., Zhang, M., Li, H., Chen, Y.: FedMask: joint computation and communication-efficient personalized federated learning via heterogeneous masking. In: SenSys 2021 – Proceedings of 2021 19th ACM Embedded Networked Sensor Systems, pp. 42–55 (2021). https://doi.org/10.1145/3485730.3485929

8. Hoefler, T., Alistarh, D., Ben-Nun, T., Dryden, N., Peste, A.: Sparsity in deep learning: pruning and growth for efficient inference and training in neural networks. J. Mach. Learn. Res. **22**, 1–124 (2021)

9. Kamaruddin, S.S., Yusof, Y., Bakar, N.A.A., Tayie, M.A., Alkubaisi, G.A.A.J.: Graph-based representation for sentence similarity measure: a comparative analysis. Int. J. Eng. Technol. **7**(2), 32–35 (2018). https://doi.org/10.14419/ijet.v7i2.14.11149

10. Ma, Q., Yu, L., Tian, S., Chen, E., Ng, W.W.Y.: Global-local mutual attention model for text classification. IEEE/ACM Trans. Audio Speech Lang. Process. **27**(12), 2127–2139 (2019). https://doi.org/10.1109/TASLP.2019.2942160

11. Chandra, R., Krishna, A.: COVID-19 sentiment analysis via deep learning during the rise of novel cases. PLoS ONE **16**(8), 1–26 (2021). https://doi.org/10.1371/journal.pone.0255615

12. Tarnate, K.J.M., Devaraj, M., De Goma, J.C.: Overcoming the vanishing gradient problem of recurrent neural networks in the ISO 9001 quality management audit reports classification. Int. J. Sci. Technol. Res. **9**(3), 6683–6686 (2020)

13. Nguyen, V.Q., Anh, T.N., Yang, H.-J.: Real-time event detection using recurrent neural network in social sensors. Int. J. Distrib. Sens. Netw. **15**(6), 155014771985649 (2019). https://doi.org/10.1177/1550147719856492

14. Zhang, L.: The evaluation on the credit risk of enterprises with the CNN-LSTM-ATT model. Comput. Intell. Neurosci. **2022**, 1–10 (2022). https://doi.org/10.1155/2022/6826573

15. Baccouche, A., Ahmed, S., Sierra-Sosa, D., Elmaghraby, A.: Malicious text identification: deep learning from public comments and emails. Information **11**(6), 312 (2020). https://doi.org/10.3390/info11060312

16. Ghosal, T., Edithal, V., Ekbal, A., Bhattacharyya, P., Chivukula, S.S.S.K., Tsatsaronis, G.: Is your document novel? Let attention guide you. An attention-based model for document-level novelty detection. Natl. Lang. Eng. **27**(4), 427–454 (2021). https://doi.org/10.1017/S1351324920000194

17. Kamyab, M., Liu, G., Adjeisah, M.: Attention-based CNN and Bi-LSTM model based on TF-IDF and GloVe word embedding for sentiment analysis. Appl. Sci. **11**(23) (2021). https://doi.org/10.3390/app112311255

18. Khan, U., Khan, S., Rizwan, A., Atteia, G., Jamjoom, M.M., Samee, N.A.: Aggression detection in social media from textual data using deep learning models. Appl. Sci. **12**(10), 5083 (2022). https://doi.org/10.3390/app12105083

19. Kowsher, M., et al.: LSTM-ANN & BiLSTM-ANN: hybrid deep learning models for enhanced classification accuracy. Procedia Comput. Sci. **193**, 131–140 (2021). https://doi.org/10.1016/j.procs.2021.10.013

20. Naseem, U., Razzak, I., Musial, K., Imran, M.: Transformer based deep intelligent contextual embedding for twitter sentiment analysis. Future Gener. Comput. Syst. **113**, 58–69 (2020). https://doi.org/10.1016/j.future.2020.06.050

21. Rosa, R.L., et al.: Event detection system based on user behaviour changes in online social networks: Case of the covid-19 pandemic. IEEE Access **8**, 158806–158825 (2020). https://doi.org/10.1109/ACCESS.2020.3020391

22. Sadiq, S., Mehmood, A., Ullah, S., Ahmad, M., Choi, G.S., On, B.W.: Aggression detection through deep neural model on Twitter. Futur. Gener. Comput. Syst. **114**, 120–129 (2021). https://doi.org/10.1016/j.future.2020.07.050

23. Schulte, J.P., et al.: ELINAC: autoencoder approach for electronic invoices data clustering. Appl. Sci. **12**(6) (2022). https://doi.org/10.3390/app12063008

24. Ullah, W., Ullah, A., Hussain, T., Khan, Z.A., Baik, S.W.: An efficient anomaly recognition framework using an attention residual LSTM in surveillance videos. Sensors **21**(8), 2811 (2021). https://doi.org/10.3390/s21082811

25. Bhattarai, B., Granmo, O.C., Jiao, L.: Measuring the novelty of natural language text using the conjunctive clauses of a Tsetlin machine text classifier. In: ICAART 2021 – Proceedings of 13th International Conference Agents Artificial Intelligence, vol. 2, pp. 410–417 (2020). https://doi.org/10.5220/0010382204100417

26. Thomas, J.G., Mudur, S.P., Shiri, N.: Detecting anomalous behaviour from textual content in financial records. In: Proceedings of 2019 IEEE/WIC/ACM International Conference of Web Intelligence WI 2019, pp. 373–377 (2019). https://doi.org/10.1145/3350546.3352550

27. Zhang, Z., Robinson, D., Tepper, J.: Hate speech detection using a convolution-LSTM based deep neural network. In: Proceedings of ACM Web Conference (WWW 2018), pp. 1–10 (2018)

28. Kumari, R., Ashok, N., Ghosal, T., Ekbal, A.: Misinformation detection using multitask learning with mutual learning for novelty detection and emotion recognition. Inf. Process. Manag. **58**(5), 102631 (2021). https://doi.org/10.1016/j.ipm.2021.102631

29. Plaza-Del-Arco, F.M., Molina-Gonzalez, M.D., Urena-Lopez, L.A., Martin-Valdivia, M.T.: A multi-task learning approach to hate speech detection leveraging sentiment analysis. IEEE Access **9**, 112478–112489 (2021). https://doi.org/10.1109/ACCESS.2021.3103697

30. Rohanian, O., et al.: Privacy-aware early detection of COVID-19 through adversarial training. IEEE J. Biomed. Heal. Inform. **27**(3), 1249–1258 (2022). https://doi.org/10.1109/JBHI.2022.3230663

31. Yi, P., Zubiaga, A.: Cyberbullying detection across social media platforms via platform-aware adversarial encoding. Proc. Int. AAAI Conf. Web Soc. Media **16**, 1430–1434 (2022). https://doi.org/10.1609/icwsm.v16i1.19401

32. Gorokhov, O., Petrovskiy, M., Mashechkin, I.: Convolutional neural networks for unsupervised anomaly detection in text data. In: Yin, H., Gao, Y., Chen, S., Wen, Y., Cai, G., Tianlong, G., Junping, D., Tallón-Ballesteros, A.J., Zhang, M. (eds.) Intelligent Data Engineering and Automated Learning – IDEAL 2017, pp. 500–507. Springer International Publishing, Cham (2017). https://doi.org/10.1007/978-3-319-68935-7_54

33. Ilie, V.I., Truica, C.O., Apostol, E.S., Paschke, A.: Context-aware misinformation detection: a benchmark of deep learning architectures using word embeddings. IEEE Access **9**, 162122–162146 (2021). https://doi.org/10.1109/ACCESS.2021.3132502
34. Agbaje, M.: Neural network-based cyber-bullying and cyber-aggression detection using twitter text (2022). https://doi.org/10.21203/rs.3.rs-1878604/v1
35. Hajek, P., Barushka, A., Munk, M.: Fake consumer review detection using deep neural networks integrating word embeddings and emotion mining. Neural Comput. Appl. **32**(23), 17259–17274 (2020). https://doi.org/10.1007/s00521-020-04757-2
36. Khan, M.U., Javed, A.R., Ihsan, M., Tariq, U.: A novel category detection of social media reviews in the restaurant industry. Multimed. Syst. (2020). https://doi.org/10.1007/s00530-020-00704-2
37. Woo, J., Yun, J.: Content noise detection model using deep learning in web forums. Sustain. **12**(12), 1–16 (2020). https://doi.org/10.3390/su12125074

A Test Dataset of Offensive Malay Language by a Cyberbullying Detection Model on Instagram Using Support Vector Machine

Nurulhuda Ismail[1]([✉]), David Enrique Losada[2] [iD], and Rahayu Ahmad[1] [iD]

[1] School of Computing, University Utara Malaysia, 06010 Sintok, Kedah, Malaysia
nurulhuda_ismail2@ahsgs.uum.edu.my
[2] Centro Singular de Investigación en Tecnoloxías Intelixentes, Universidade de Santiago de Compostela, Rúa de Jenaro de La Fuente Domínguez, 15782 Santiago de Compostela, Spain

Abstract. Social media services have become a prevalent communication tool due to their capability to instantly share information with a large number of people for free. However, social media also facilitate cyberbullying, and studies have shown that cyberbullying on social media has a severe impact compared to other platforms. In some cases, cyberbullying provokes tragic problems, such as suicide. The information shared on social media services provides a massive amount of textual data, which can be used to explore patterns of human behaviors including cyberbullying. This paper aims to build a dataset of offensive language for research on cyberbullying in the Malay language through a series of baseline experiments by implementing SVM classifiers. These preliminary experiments helped to understand the performance of automatic tools that mine for abusive language within a corpus of Malay texts. To achieve the objectives, social media extraction methods and new crawling technologies oriented have been developed to monitor the Instagram accounts of popular Malaysian celebrities. The resulting collection contains 165,239 real-world comments associated with 27 Instagram public accounts. A sample of this corpus was manually labelled in terms of cyberbullying categories. After the dataset was cleaned, normalized, and vectorized, this led to a collection of 527 comments. Following a standard training (70%) and test (30%) split, the SVM classifier was developed and evaluated. These initial experiments produced a model accuracy of 75% and f1-scores of around 75%.

Keywords: Support Vector Machines · supervised machine learning · Instagram · cyberbullying · Malay language

1 Introduction

With more than four billion users worldwide, social media services have become a prevalent medium to express opinions about individuals, organizations, products, or events [1]. Social media services offer the capability to instantly disseminate information to a huge number of people, basically, for free. Unfortunately, the open nature of these information services also facilitates cyberbullying. It is common that people share offensive, insulting, and hateful messages toward others [2, 3].

As its name implies, cyberbullying is an intimidating action perpetrated by someone in an online setting to cause harm to the victim(s) [4–6]. Cyberbullying may lead to severe impacts on general well-being, mental health, and social issues. For example, it can lead to depression, low self-esteem and even suicide [7, 8].

The increasing volume of user-generated content (UGC) on social media platforms provides a vast amount of data, which can be accessed and explored to understand patterns of human emotions, behaviours, and sentiments [9]. With these data, Machine Learning approaches such as Support Vector Machine (SVM) and Random Forest (RF) can utilize the data to perform predictions [10]. For instance, cyberbullying behaviour can be detected based on the textual data accessed from comment or caption sections of a social media post.

Text mining techniques are among the most effective tools for cyberbullying detection [2]. Early cyberbullying detection is crucial in order to identify and classify the activities encompassing the attributes of cyberbullying to curb the problem and minimize the risks of cyberbullying victimization [8]. However, early detection technologies need language resources, such as corpora of labelled cyberbullying sentences, and these textual collections are scarce for many languages, including Malaysian.

This paper aims to discuss a preliminary study for developing a test collection of offensive Malay language from a number of Malaysian celebrities Instagram accounts and tracked cases of cyberbullying. Automatic cyberbullying detection on social media is crucial to minimize the impact of cyberbullying and it has potential to support law enforcement authorities in witnessing how social media foster the dissemination of offensive remarks [2, 8, 10]. Thus, this research developed a tool to automate cyberbullying detection and utilized standard effectiveness metrics to evaluate the classification models. The experimental report includes the F1 score, precision, accuracy, and recall of cyberbullying comments in Instagram. Results from these initial experiments could be used as a reference for future research related to cyberbullying detection on social media.

This paper is organized as follows. The next section explains the offensive Malay language used in Malaysia. Section 3 presents the process of building the textual collection for cyberbullying including the process of preparing the dataset, the methods used in the experiments and the results from the experiments. Section 4 provides the conclusion of this research.

2 Offensive Words in the Malay Language

English language datasets are the focus of most current research compared to other languages [11]. English, Spanish and French is recognized as high-resource languages [12]. In contrast, Malay is one of the low-resource languages [14]. High-resource language refers to numerous datasets that are currently available, and low-resource language refers to limited datasets [13].

Malay is spoken in Malaysia, Indonesia, Singapore, and Brunei. Despite their shared basis and incredible similarities, Malay dialects vary in each country [14]. Due to its low-resource nature, there are very few datasets related to cyberbullying in the Malay language [15]. Most recent studies on cyberbullying detection utilize Twitter datasets in the Indonesian language [2, 16–18].

Due to the close similarity of the Malay language used in Malaysia and Indonesia, this research adopted the guideline of determining offensive words from the research conducted by Ibrohim and Budi [18]. Offensive words are usually associated with conditions, animals, astral beings, objects, parts of a body, family members, activities, or professions. Table 1 explains further about the categories of offensive words referenced in the Indonesian language, which are also relevant to the Malay language in Malaysia.

Table 1. Categories of offensive words in Indonesian and Malay languages.

Category	Explanation	Examples	Malay language used in	
			Indonesia	Malaysia
Conditions	Words that express certain conditions in a conversation are sometimes used as abusive words (e.g., with a negative tone or offensive intention)	i. Mental Disorder	gila, bego, goblok, idiot, sinting, bodoh, tolol, sontoloyo, geblek, sarap	gila, bodoh, bengong, bangang, mereng, cacat otak, sakit otak, meroyan
		ii. Sexual Orientation	lesbian, homo, banci	lesbian, gay, pondan, bapok, jantan, betina
		iii. Lack of Modernization	kampungan, udik, alay	kampung, ulu, jakun, sakai
		iv. Physical Disability	buta, budek, bolot, bisu	buta, pekak, bisu, tuli
		v. Conditions where someone doesn't have etiquette	berengsek, bejat	biadap, kurang ajar, bedebah
		vi. Conditions that are not sanctioned by god or religion	keparat, jahanam, terkutuk, kafir, najis	keparat, jahanam, kafir, najis, murtad
		vii. Conditions that are related to unfortunate circumstances	celaka, mati, modar, sialan, mampus	celaka, mati, mampus, sial, miskin, papa kedana
Animals	Animals that represent offensive words and negative characteristics	i. Disgusting for certain people	anjing	anjing

(continued)

Table 1. (*continued*)

Category	Explanation	Examples	Malay language used in	
			Indonesia	Malaysia
		ii. Disgusting and forbidden by certain religions	babi	babi, khinzir
		iii. Annoying	bangsat, monyet, kunyuk	monyet, kera, beruk
		iv. Parasitic	lintah	lintah, pacat
		v. Lusty	buaya, bandot	buaya, kambing, lembu
		vi. Noisy	beo	murai
Astral Beings	Astral beings are often used as abusive words because they are believed to often interfere with human lives	-	setan, setan alas, iblis, tuyul, kunti	setan, syaitan, iblis, toyol, pontianak, dajjal
An Object	Like animals and astral beings, some objects or features can be employed as abusive words (based on their negative aspects):	i. Bad Smell	tai, tai kucing, bangkai	tahi, taik, bangkai, busuk
		ii. Dirty and Worn Out	gembel, gombal	kain buruk, sampah
Body Parts	Certain body parts that represent abusive language and often associated with sexual activities	-	kontol, memek, tempik, jembut	kote, punai, puki, pantat, bontot, punggung, cipap, tetek
Activity	Abusive words related to activity are usually associated to some sexual-related aspects	-	ngentot, ngewe	menyundal
Professions	Related to someone's employment, particularly low-class or religion-prohibited occupations	-	maling, sundal, bajingan, copet, lonte, cecenguk, kacung, pelacur, pecun, jablay, perek	pencuri, penyangak, penyamun, penipu, pelacur, sundal, peminta sedekah

The last category of offensive words is Family Members. Indonesians often add the suffix -mu on words that insinuate to family members as a curse, such as ibu-mu (your mother), bapak-mu (your father), kakek-mu (your grandfather), and nenek-mu (your grandmother). While in Malaysia, Malaysians usually pair the words of family members with another word that carries the meaning of 'your'. For example, *mak kau* (your mother), *bapa kau* (your father) and *atok kau* (your grandfather). The word '*kau*' is a word used to address someone in a rude way. Therefore, the combination of words of family members and '*kau*' is generally considered offensive in the Malaysian language.

According to the list of the aforementioned offensive words, the usage of those words in cursing others in the Indonesian language can be categorized into three types. Table 2 describes the three types of offensive Malay language used in Indonesia and Malaysia in the form of words, phrases, and clauses.

Table 2. Three types of offensive Malay language used in Indonesia and Malaysia.

Country	Types	Examples
Indonesia	Word	*Anjing!* (Dog!)
	Phrase	*Dasar bodoh!* (You stupid!)
	Clause	*Goblok lu, gitu aja ga bisa!?* (Idiot, you can't even do something like this!?)
Malaysia	Word	*Anjing!* (Dog!)
	Phrase	*Memang bodoh!* (You are stupid!)
	Clause	*Bangang betul, mcm ni pon tak reti!?* (Idiot, you can't even do something like this!?)

In modern conversation in Malaysia, it is noted that not all offensive words or phrases are used to curse others. Some Malaysians use offensive words to convey astonishment or wonder. For instance, the clause '*Cantik sial rumah kau!*' is not to curse someone as damned or unlucky. In this context, the offensive word '*sial*' is used to convey amazement or admiration for someone or something. Therefore, the clause '*Cantik sial rumah kau!*' is meant to be 'Wow! Your house is so beautiful!'. A clause as such is related to abusive language, but not offensive.

3   Building a Test Textual Collection for Cyberbullying

A survey conducted in 2017 ranked Instagram first as the most prevalent platform for cyberbullying [11]. Instagram provides some features to reduce the occurrences of cyberbullying. These features are reporting to Instagram, hiding offensive comments based on keywords that have been provided by Instagram, and disabling comments for a post [19]. However, despite these features, many comments on Instagram still have the traits of cyberbullying [19]. Thus, automatic cyberbullying detection on social media is crucial to minimize the impact of cyberbullying and for the law enforcement authorities to witness how social media facilitate the dissemination of offensive remarks [12, 20].

Malay is one of the low-resource languages [15]. Malaysia, Indonesia, Singapore, and Brunei are using the Malay language. Malay originates from the same root and shares incredible similarities, but every country has their own variant [14, 15]. Very limited datasets related to cyberbullying in the Malay language used in Malaysia can be found due to its low-resource nature [15].

Most of the current cyberbullying detection studies utilize datasets in the Indonesian language from Twitter [2, 17, 18]. To the best of our knowledge, there is one dataset developed by Zainol and others for cyberbullying in the Malay language [21]. They gathered the data from Twitter using RapidMiner studio based on keywords such as *'bodoh'*, *'sial'*, *'gila'*, *'babi'*, *'haram'*, and *'anjing'*. These words are often used for cyberbullying on Malaysian Twitter. In addition, there is also a third-party API called Malaya developed by Zolkepli Husein that serves as a repository for storing Malay corpus with datasets of various subjects such as political landscape, emotion, sarcastic news headlines, and stopwords [22]. The live data was collected from Facebook, Twitter and Instagram using crawlers. The API also provides a number of models trained with its relevant datasets with 80% of training and 20% of testing datasets [15]. Nevertheless, both of the datasets are not developed for Instagram and cyberbullying. Hence, this research developed a new Instagram dataset in Malay, specifically for cyberbullying detection.

3.1 Preparing the Dataset

Several aspects need to be taken into consideration during the process of data source selection, namely, the size and quality of the data sources, the difficulty to distinguish data consist of with and without the elements of cyberbullying, and the data redistribution terms and conditions [22]. This research performed baseline experiments using a real-world dataset from Instagram, as the platform that has the most prevalent cyberbullying incidents. The experiments were performed based on the flowchart, described in Fig. 1 [20].

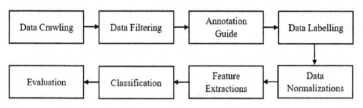

Fig. 1. Experiment flowchart.

The first step is to gather data from Instagram accounts using Instagrapi, a Python library for the Instagram API. The raw dataset consists of 165239 comments crawled from 27 public accounts of Malaysian famous people. To make the labelling more manageable, this research attempted for a smaller subset which focused on the accounts that have a high percentage of negative comments in their postings. It is more likely to give a higher probability of identifying cyberbullying once the data was properly labelled [19].

A total of 831 data was randomly selected for the subset. From the subset, the data was filtered by erasing comments that: (i) have only one word, (ii) are written in English, and (iii) contain product or business advertisements. The filtering process gives us 528 data that are ready to be labelled. The dataset was manually labelled into two respective classes, namely, Bullying and Non-bullying. Due to the small number of data, the dataset was labelled by only one annotator who is a native speaker of the Malay language. Figure 2 shows some of the data that have been labelled as Bullying and Non-bullying.

comment	label
@haziqmat_ jgn kacau dia tuhan dalam instagram ni ♣ü§£	Bullying
@asyrafikhmall hahahah apa seda pendek gilk owh ♣üòÇ	Bullying
Cantik betul la eak (moto nie)	Non-bullying
@_firdaussahrudin_ apa babi nia buat daus hahahahaha	Bullying
@manchester_city_222 org bodo mcm kau nih xpyh jdik manusia	Bullying
Pehhh bapak barai doh ♣üòÇ.	Bullying
Hudoh babi	Bullying
Semua cantik2 ♣üòç♣üòç♣üòç	Non-bullying
Boooo bibiorr ikan talapia kaki drama	Bullying
Muka kau pon mcm org terencat akal	Bullying
Dato ni mcm mulut/bibir ikan tilapia besar sangat haha	Bullying
moga murah rezeki dato,ù§Ô∏è	Non-bullying
Walau apa org kta sy ttp mnyokong dsv...	Non-bullying
Moga DSV selalu dimurahkn rezeki.. sebak tngok	Non-bullying
Subhanallah. .. semoga Allah pelihara dan merahmati Dato Vida sekeluarga... pemurah seperti Rasulullah saw... Laju bersedekah	Non-bullying
Bibir tebal ♣üòÇ	Bullying

Fig. 2. Examples of the labelled data.

After completing the labelling, symbols, punctuations, special characters, hashtags, emojis, and emoticons were deleted from the dataset. The next step is data normalization, where the non-standard words were changed into standard ones using Dewan Bahasa dan Pustaka (DBP) database [22]. DBP is one of the most reliable resources for reference and accommodating tasks, including semantic recognition, syntactic disambiguation, and sentence structure in the Malay language [23]. Figure 3 illustrates the labelled data after normalization.

3.2   Feature Extraction

Some application features such as TF-IDF will be applied to further clean the dataset by converting the comments into lowercase. The number of times a term appears in a document in relation to the total number of words is calculated using TF, whereas the importance of a phrase is calculated using IDF. This technique can quantify a word in documents, to compute a weight onto each word which highlights the importance of the word [18]. In this experiment, the Malay language stop words were utilized from Kaggle which consists of 364 words [24].

comment	label
haziqmat jangan kacau dia tuhan dalam instagram ini	Bullying
asyrafikhmall hahahah apa pendek gila oh	Bullying
cantik betullah ya (motor ini)	Non-bullying
firdaussahrudin apa babi ini buat hahahahaha	Bullying
manchester_city_222 orang bodoh macam kau ini tidak payah jadi manusia	Bullying
sudah hancur teruk	Bullying
hodoh babi	Bullying
semua cantik-cantik	Non-bullying
boooo bibir ikan talapia kaki drama	Bullying
muka kau pun macam orang terencat akal	Bullying
dato ini macam mulut/bibir ikan tilapia besar sangat haha	Bullying
moga murah rezeki dato	Non-bullying
walau apa orang kata saya tetap menyokong dsv	Non-bullying
moga dsv selalu dimurahkn rezeki sebak tengok	Non-bullying
subhanallah semoga allah pelihara dan merahmati dato vida sekeluarga pemurah seperti rasulullah saw laju bersedekah	Non-bullying
bibir tebal	Bullying

Fig. 3. Examples of the labelled data after normalization.

3.3 Baseline Experiments

After the feature extraction process, the data were ready for classification. This research implemented the Support Vector Machine (SVM) technique and ran a series of experiments to evaluate the performance. These experiments produced a test collection of text for cyberbullying detection that could be used by others as a reference. The implementation of those classifiers was accomplished using a library from Scikit-Learn, a library that provides widely-used classification algorithms in Python language. This library is often used in research related to text classification, including the SVM library [18].

The dataset was randomly split into two types, with 70% for the training set and 30% for the testing set. The training set consisted of 370 comments and the test set consisted of 157 comments. Next, the dataset was vectorized into numerical vectors, where a list of unique integers is assigned to each row and its associated importance as calculated by the TF-IDF method. After that, the training and testing set were transformed into vectorized datasets. Afterwards, the vectorized training set was used to fit into the SVM classifiers and the vectorized testing set was validated to get the prediction of the labels. This experiments used the default SVM classifier (C = 1.0, kernel = 'rbf') and generated

Table 3. Classification results.

	Precision	Recall	F1-score	Support
0.0	0.76	0.70	0.73	77
1.0	0.73	0.79	0.76	80
Accuracy			0.75	157
Macro avg	0.75	0.74	0.74	157
Weighted avg	0.75	0.75	0.74	157

0.0 = Bullying.

the best fit. This allows the machine learning algorithm to learn from the dataset and generate predictions (Yin et al., 2021). Finally, the f1_score, accuracy, precision, and recall were produced using the *classification_report* function. The results are shown in Table 3 as follows.

Based on Table 3, it was observed that with the SVM classifier, there is an accuracy of 0.75, which implies that the model correctly predicted 75% of the comments labelled as Bullying or Non-bullying. In general, a score between 0.50 to 0.80 is considered acceptable. The model also exhibits a precision score of 0.76 for Bullying indicating that 76% of the comments that the model predicted as Bullying are Bullying and 0.73 for Non-bullying indicating that 73% of the comments that the model predicted as Non-bullying are Non-bullying.

The model also shows a recall score of 0.70 for Bullying and 0.79 for Non-bullying indicating that the model was able to discover 70% of the comments the model predicted as Bullying and 79% of the comments the model predicted as Non-bullying in the pool of comments. The model reveals the F1-score of 0.73 (73%) for Bullying and 0.76 (76%) for Non-bullying as the weighted average of the precision and recall. The rule of thumb is that the closer the F1-score to the maximum value of 1 (minimum value is 0), the better the performance is [29]. The Confusion Matrix of the classification result for SVM is illustrated in Table 4.

Table 4. Confusion Matrix.

	Positive	Negative
Positive	63	23
Negative	17	54

Based on Table 4, the observations were recorded as follows:

i. True Positive (TP): 63 out of 80 comments were predicted as non-bullying and were actually classified as non-bullying.
ii. True Negative (TN): 54 out of 77 comments were predicted as bullying and were actually classified as bullying.
iii. False Positive (FP): 23 out of 157 comments were predicted as non-bullying but were classified as bullying.
iv. False Negative (FN): 17 out of 157 comments were predicted as bullying but were classified as non-bullying.

4   Conclusions

This paper presented a new test collection for cyberbullying and language in the Malaysian language. Additionally, this paper outlined the methodology to build a test collection that includes a series of offensive language written by Instagram users. A series of baseline experiments were performed to evaluate the model performance and provided a report.

This paper also discussed the types of offensive language identified in the Malay language used in Malaysia. Due to the limited number of cyberbullying datasets for the Malaysian language, this new collection can be used as a reference to foster research related to cyberbullying in Malaysia.

Future works aims to extend this research by exploring cyberbullying behaviour in the bystanders' comments and building a corpus specifically for Instagram in the Malay language. This research would be beneficial for facilitating cyberbullying research in Malaysia by providing a complete corpus in the Malay language. Furthermore, it is also important in supporting society's awareness of their roles in the effort to curb cyberbullying as well as for the authorities to witness the cyberbullying incidents in Malaysia.

References

1. Kumar, A., Albuquerque, V.H.C.: Sentiment analysis using XLM-R transformer and zero-shot transfer learning on resource-poor Indian language. ACM Trans. Asian Low-Resource Lang. Inf. Process. **20** (2021). https://doi.org/10.1145/3461764
2. Theng, C.P., Othman, N.F., Syahirah, A.R., Anawar, S., Ayop, Z., Ramli, S.N.: Cyberbullying detection in twitter using sentiment analysis. Int. J. Comput. Sci. Netw. Secur. **21**, 1–10 (2021)
3. Scott, G.G., Wiencierz, S., Hand, C.J.: The volume and source of cyberabuse influences victim blame and perceptions of attractiveness. Comput. Human Behav. **92**, 119–127 (2019)
4. Patchin, J.W., Hinduja, S.: Measuring cyberbullying: Implications for research. Aggress. Violent Behav. **23**, 69–74 (2015)
5. Patchin, J.W., Hinduja, S.: Digital self-harm among adolescents. J. Adolesc. Heal.Adolesc. Heal. **61**, 761–766 (2017)
6. Whittaker, E., Kowalski, R.M.: Cyberbullying via social media. J. Sch. Violence **14**, 11–29 (2015)
7. Hinduja, S., Patchin, J.W.: Connecting adolescent suicide to the severity of bullying and cyberbullying. J. Sch. Violence **18**, 33–346 (2019)
8. Azeez, N.A., Misra, S., Lawal, O.I., Oluranti, J.: Identification and detection of cyberbullying on facebook using machine learning algorithms. J. Cases Inf. Technol. **23**, 1–21 (2021). https://doi.org/10.4018/JCIT.296254
9. Jamil, N.S., Kamaruddin, S.S., Ahmad, F.K., Angeli, C.: Social tension detection on social media textual data: A literature review. Model. Simul. In: 2020 - European Simulation and Modelling Conference, ESM 2020, pp. 77–81 (2020)
10. Ismail, N., Yusof, U.K.: Recent trends of machine learning predictions using open data: a systematic review. J. Inf. Commun. Technol. **21**, 337–381 (2022)
11. Bozyiğit, A., Utku, S., Nasibov, E.: Cyberbullying detection: Utilizing social media features. Expert Syst. Appl. **179** (2021). https://doi.org/10.1016/j.eswa.2021.115001
12. Magueresse, A., Carles, V., Heetderks, E.: Low-resource Languages: A Review of Past Work and Future Challenges. (2020)
13. Almansor, E., Al-Ani, A.: A hybrid neural machine translation technique for translating low resource languages. In: Machine Learning and Data Mining in Pattern Recognition: 14th International Conference, MLDM, pp. 347–356 (2018)
14. Lin, N., Fu, S., Jiang, S., Zhu, G., Hou, Y.: Exploring lexical differences between indonesian and malay (2018)
15. Maskat, R., Faizzuddin Zainal, M., Ismail, N., Ardi, N., Ahmad, A., Daud, N.: Automatic labelling of malay cyberbullying twitter corpus using combinations of sentiment, emotion and toxicity polarities. In: ACM International Conference Proceeding Series (2020). https://doi.org/10.1145/3446132.3446412

16. Hidayatullah, A.F., Ma'arif, M..: Pre-processing tasks in Indonesian twitter messages This. J. Phys. Conf. Ser. **755** (2016). https://doi.org/10.1088/1742-6596/755/1/011001

17. Ibrohim, M.O., Budi, I.: A dataset and preliminaries study for abusive language detection in indonesian social media. Procedia Comput. Sci. **135**, 222–229 (2018). https://doi.org/10.1016/j.procs.2018.08.169

18. Yin, C.J., Ayop, Z., Anawar, S., Othman, N.F., Mohd Zainudin, N.: Slangs and short forms of malay twitter sentiment analysis using supervised machine learning. IJCSNS Int. J. Comput. Sci. Netw. Secur. **21**, 294–300 (2021)

19. Naf'an, M.Z., Bimantara, A.A., Larasati, A., Risondang, E.M., Nugraha, N.A.S.: Sentiment analysis of cyberbullying on instagram user comments. J. Data Sci. Its Appl. **2**, 88–98 (2019). https://doi.org/10.21108/jdsa.2019.2.20

20. Fati, S.M.: Detecting cyberbullying across social media platforms in saudi arabia using sentiment analysis: a case study. Comput. J.. J. **65**, 1787–1794 (2022)

21. Zainol, Z., Wani, S., Nohuddin, P.N.E., Noormanshah, W.M.U., Marzukhi, S.: Association analysis of cyberbullying on social media using apriori algorithm. Int. J. Eng. Technol. **7**, 72–75 (2018)

22. Losada, D.E., Crestani, F.: A test collection for research on depression and language use. In: Fuhr, N., Quaresma, P., Gonçalves, T., Larsen, B., Balog, K., Macdonald, C., Cappellato, L., Ferro, N. (eds.) Experimental IR Meets Multilinguality, Multimodality, and Interaction, pp. 28–39. Springer International Publishing, Cham (2016). https://doi.org/10.1007/978-3-319-44564-9_3

23. Bakar, J.A., Omar, K., Nasrudin, M.F., Murah, M.Z.: NUWT: Jawi-specific buckwalter corpus for Malay word tokenization. J. Inf. Commun. Technol. **15**, 107–131 (2016). https://doi.org/10.32890/jict2016.15.1.5

24. AlBeladi, A.A., Muqaibel, A.H.: Evaluating compressive sensing algorithms in through-the-wall radar via F1-score. Int. J. Signal Imaging Syst. Eng. **11**, 164–171 (2018)

TikTok Video Cluster Analysis Based on Trending Topic

Juhaida Abu Bakar[1,2(✉)] 🆔, Nur Azmielia Muhammad Sharimi[2],
Mohd Azrul Edzwan Shahril[2], Nur Syafiqah Azmi[2], Nor Hazlyna Harun[2,3] 🆔,
Hapini Awang[3] 🆔, and Nur Syafiqah Abu Bakar[4]

[1] Data Management and Software Solution Research Lab, School of Computing,
Universiti Utara Malaysia, 06010 Sintok, Kedah, Malaysia
juhaida.ab@uum.edu.my
[2] Data Science Research Lab, School of Computing, Universiti Utara Malaysia, 06010 Sintok,
Kedah, Malaysia
[3] Institute for Advanced and Smart Digital Opportunities, School of Computing,
Universiti Utara Malaysia, 06010 Sintok, Kedah, Malaysia
[4] Faculty of Medicine and Health Sciences, Universiti Sains Islam Malaysia, 71800 Nilai,
Negeri Sembilan, Malaysia

Abstract. TikTok is a popular social networking application that offers trend research and is a valuable source for users. However, this is often misconstrued for content, which may not be suitable for children due to misappropriate content. This study aims to improve user perception of TikTok by using topic modelling and clustering techniques to identify trending topics in TikTok videos. The research uses Latent Dirichlet Allocation (LDA) and K-means clustering techniques to enhance the recognition of local and global topics across text documents. The methodology includes data collection, data pre-processing, clustering, topic modelling, and results. Ten subjects associated with trending TikTok videos are displayed using the LDA algorithm, and the generated topics are used to produce an Inter-topic Distance Map. The method's effectiveness is evaluated using log-likelihood score and perplexity measurements. It has a log-likelihood score of 5579 and a perplexity score of 287. A good model is one with a higher log-likelihood and lower perplexity. The study ex-tracts popular TikTok topics using both the LDA topic modelling technique and the K-means clustering algorithm.

Keywords: social networking application · topic modelling · clustering analysis · latent dirichlet allocation · tiktok

1 Introduction

Trending analysis is the practice of gathering data and attempting to identify patterns or trends in data. It can also determine whether an organization's objectives have been met. Nowadays, Tik Tok is a new source and one of the most interesting and useful sources of information in social networking applications involved in trend analysis. TikTok was the most common application that grew faster and attracted 1.5 billion active users [1] of the hundreds of millions of users from children and young adults. This application lets users create short video content, sharing 15-s and up to 60-s videos on any topic. Influencer Marketing Hub said Tik Tok was formerly known as Musical.ly until ByteDance, a Chinese company, took over the app, and users were transferred to Tik Tok.

TikTok is a popular app among children and adults, often viewed as having disadvantages rather than advantages [2]. However, it offers interesting content such as business tips, cooking tips, and many other types of information. The study aims to classify video content into categories to improve user perception of TikTok. Users can better understand its features and avoid inappropriate content by analyzing the content.

The primary contribution of this study is the use of clustering and topic modelling methods to uncover hot topics from Tik Tok videos. The goal of the effort was to improve the recognition of local topics within a single document and a group of global topics across a series of text documents using Latent Dirichlet Allocation (LDA) and K-Means clustering algorithms. The remainder of the document is structured as follows: Sect. 2 includes a literature review; Sect. 3 describes data preparation and methodology; Sect. 4 illustrates experiments and results; and Sect. 5 concludes the paper.

2   Related Work

A topic modelling experiment based on user comments on social media is shown in the study [3]. The author conducted an experiment using two datasets from Yahoo and Tokyo Electric Power Company (TEPCO), which covered the most popular news stories and video streaming comments, respectively. LDA was used to implement topic clustering based on topic modelling. This experiment received 15,000 comments throughout the same period. The results of the modelling are displayed in Fig. 1.

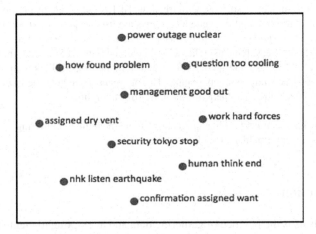

Fig. 1. Modelling's outcome

In the [4] study, Twitter social media was searched for information about the Covid-19 epidemic from March 3rd to March 31st. This author copied ten thousand tweets. The outcomes of clustering based on latent semantic analysis produced more clusters than clustering based on LDA. Because the largest cluster would show the day of trend, it was used as a comparison. The total number of confirmed cases in each nation and worldwide are shown in Fig. 2 [4].

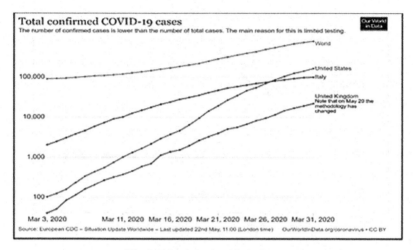

Fig. 2. Number of confirmed cases

This study [5] focuses on the two-step problem of extracting semantically relevant themes and trend analysis of these subjects from a large temporal text corpus utilising an end-to-end unsupervised technique. The author first created word clouds based on the frequency of terms in each cluster of abstract text. As a result, terms that were less prevalent and significant to the cluster were deleted from word clouds. The author generated word clouds based on the TF-IDF scores of phrases belonging to a cluster. The TF-IDF based on a word cloud of four distinct clusters is displayed in Fig. 3 [5].

Fig. 3. TF-IDF based on a word cloud of 4 different clusters

The study from [6] has addressed the issue by focusing on Facebook fan pages. The type of special account that has more significance than standard Facebook accounts.

Using a combination of LDA-based topic distribution and post interaction indices, the authors presented a vector for Facebook fan pages. Figure 4 shows the process of LDA to obtain the topic distribution vector for a specific document in a fan pages text corpus.

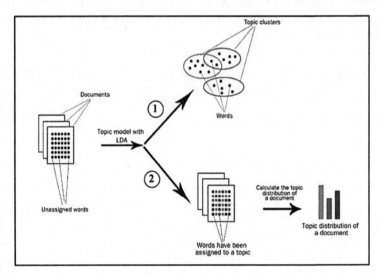

Fig. 4. Process of LDA

In [7], a new spammer classification method is based on the LDA topic model. This technique captures the spamming essence by retrieving global and local data regarding topic distribution patterns. Clustering based on online spam detection is proposed to discover spammers that appear to be posting legal tweets but are difficult to identify using existing spammer categorization methods. The examination of the K-means technique produces an accurate result, and it also identifies spammers on social media.

A past study from [8] explained the process of document clustering by using K-means and K-medoids algorithm (see Table 1.). This study focuses on hundreds of documents collected from Entertainment, Literature, Sports, Political, and Zoology. The authors implement the K-means algorithm on the WEKA tool and K-medoids on the Java platform. Both results of each algorithm are compared to get the best cluster.

Based on Table 1, each cluster defines documents of a particular domain topic. According to the result, the authors conclude that the K-means algorithm is more efficient than the clusters obtained from the K-medoids algorithm [8].

The following word clustering experiment, carried out by [9], focuses on grouping Chinese words using LDA and K-means in accordance with five categories: politics, economics, culture, people's livelihood, and science and technology. The Latent Dirichlet Allocation (LDA) algorithm and the k-means clustering algorithm are combined in a novel approach that is put forth in this work. The highest probability of each topic is picked as the centroids of k-means after some topics are retrieved using LDA. In the final stage, the K-means algorithm is employed to group every word in the text [9]. The authors calculate the K-means centroids using the LDA algorithm findings and utilise the Chinese word similarity calculation method to calculate the distance between the

Table 1. Comparison of K-means and K-medoids algorithm.

COMPARISON			
Algorithm	Cluster number	Number of documents	Efficiency
K-means	0	18	27.78%
	1	3	66.67%
	2	39	25.64%
	3	25	24%
	4	15	26.67%
K-medoids	0	43	18.60%
	1	11	54.15%
	2	7	42.85%
	3	35	14.2%
	4	4	50%

words. The authors calculate the K-means centroids using the LDA algorithm findings and utilise the Chinese word similarity calculation method to calculate the distance between the words. As a result, the suggested algorithm's average similarity is higher than that of the K-means algorithm.

To group Arabic documents, they were analysed using K-means and topic modelling [10]. LDA and K-means clustering methods were coupled in this study's dataset of Arabic text texts. Datasets that represent news stories are obtained from the internet. The experiments choose and apply TF-IDF weighting. This work's authors conclude that using topic modelling techniques during the clustering process enhances the quality of clusters for Arabic text texts [10].

Using the K-means technique, the study in [11] carried out text document clustering. The comparison of K-means clustering and K-Means clustering using Dimension Reduction approaches is covered in this work. The BBCSports dataset, which comprises five categories, including athletics, cricket, football, rugby, and tennis, is used for the comparison. The authors' evaluation metrics include accuracy, precision, recall, and f-measure. The efficiency of K-means clustering with and without DR methods is seen in the following figure [11]. K-means with information gain DR is superior to K-means clustering without dimension reduction approaches, as shown in Fig. 5.

A study on document feature extraction using LDA was conducted in [12]. The information was collected from websites of Indonesian news media by choosing news categories and saving them as text files. The TF-IDF K-Means methodology and the LDA method were used to compare the document clustering results.

Thus, based on previous studies, trend topics in social networking sites such as Tik Tok are still new in the current study. Hence, the use of topic modeling and clustering techniques to identify trending topics in Tik Tok videos is proposed in this study. In

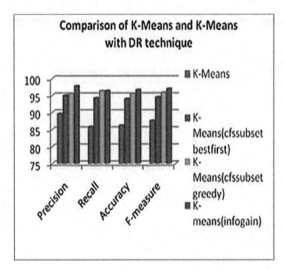

Fig. 5. Comparison of K-Means and K-Means with DR techniques

addition, this research also aims to improve the recognition of local topics in one document and a group of global topics across a collection of text documents using Latent Dirichlet Allocation (LDA) and K-Means clustering techniques.

3   Material and Methods

This study followed the four steps of trending topic analysis of TikTok videos, as shown in Fig. 6: data collection, preprocessing, clustering, and topic modelling algorithms and results. The following subsections clarify each step in detail.

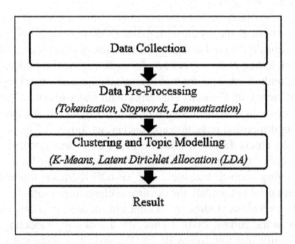

Fig. 6. Steps of Trending Topics Analysis of Tik Tok Video

3.1 Data Collection

This work mined Tik Tok data between April 25th and May 11th, 2021, for our experiment. The data was gathered by randomly extracting Tik Tok metadata such as number of views, number of likes, number of plays, video descriptions, etc. The Tik Tok API was utilized to collect 7552 data elements with 8 attributes at random, and this work used Python language software for data analysis and topic modelling tasks. The data was filtered based on the description's most frequently used terms and hashtags. Figure 7 shows the overview of the dataset.

```
In [9]: dataset.shape
        dataset.head()
```

Out[9]:

	user_name	video_desc	video_length	video_link	n_likes	n_shares	n_comments	n_plays
0	eijaanuar_	Pandai sorok kamera dah sekarang 😉 had to do t...	21	https://www.tiktok.com/@eijaanuar_/video/69523...	261400	3536	1695	4000000
1	khaby.lame	#πPerfavore non fare questo con la Pizza😡😡 #u...	20	https://www.tiktok.com/@khaby.lame/video/69554...	5600000	38100	46900	41300000
2	runningchan3	Benda paling kita takut terjadi lagi.. kwangso...	45	https://www.tiktok.com/@runningchan3/video/695...	48200	2846	1386	324500
3	tra_ahmad	#shouldbeme #fyp #esekeli #suekhaizhar #tribe769	6	https://www.tiktok.com/@tra_ahmad/video/694945...	12500	120	488	271500
6	areppo_	#spm #projekanchorspm #esekeli #fyp	15	https://www.tiktok.com/@areppo_/video/69555294...	33800	808	504	486800

Fig. 7. Tik Tok Datasets

3.2 Data Preprocessing

The first data preprocessing steps were carried out to eliminate noise from the dataset. It started by removing the following terms as noise from Tik Tok data: text and symbols that are not standard, mentions, hashtags, emoji, null values, and unwanted characters from the Tik Tok descriptions. In addition, to reduce dimensionality and promote the topic coherence, all words were transformed to lowercase. Following that, the preprocessing steps listed below were carried out:

Tokenization: This process changes a string sequence into words, keywords, phrases, symbols, and other items known as tokens. Each sentence is divided into a list of words, with all punctuation and extra characters removed.

Stop Word Removal: Words that are often used but have no effect on the data's meaning were also eliminated from the corpus. The LDA algorithm could only use the most important words as input by deleting such sentences from the text, yielding more accurate results. The work combines English and Malay stop words to remove the mixed term from the corpus. The work also extends the stop word by adding related words, as shown in Fig. 8.

Lemmatization: Lemmatization is the process of converting words to their base word. For instance, 'playing becomes 'play,' 'running becomes 'run,' and 'meeting becomes 'meet'. The benefit is that it can minimize the dictionary's overall number of unique terms. As a result, the number of columns in the document-word matrix will be reduced, resulting in a denser matrix with fewer columns.

```
# NLTK Stop words
from nltk.corpus import stopwords
stop_words = stopwords.words('english') + stopwords.words('malay')
stop_words.extend(['foryoupage', 'fyp', 'for', 'you', 'page',
                'esekeli', 'tiktok', 'foryou', 'fypppppppppppppppp', 'foryourpage', 'stitch', 'viral',
                'forpage', 'part', 'be', 'go', 'point', 'reply', 'fypage', 'untuk', 'fypviral' , 'take', 'help',
                'video', 'get', 'rise', 'always', 'want', 'comment', 'look', 'link', 'try', 'let', 'see', 'time',
                'do', 'babi', 'come', 'bro', 'lot', 'choice', 'follow', 'new', 'still', 'eskeli', 'trend', 'kira',
                'tiktokmalaysia', 'masing'])
```

Fig. 8. Stop word by adding some related words.

3.3   Clustering and Topic Modelling

The K-means clustering and LDA topic modelling methods are employed to the sets used in this work to identify patterns for trending topic discovery. The detail of following algorithm listed below:

K-means Clustering: K-means is a conventional clustering technique that seeks for each observation of each attribute value and compares it to the nearest mean, and it is used to define clusters that are similar to one another [13]. The k-means algorithm takes the input parameter k and partitions a set of n-objects into k-clusters. Cluster similarity is calculated using the mean value of the objects in the cluster, which serves as the cluster's centre of gravity. Steps that this work take for text clustering using k-means algorithm is (i) determine the k value, (ii) identify the segregation of topic clusters, and (iii) clustering evaluation model using Euclidean distance. Figure 9 shows the k-means algorithm.

Algorithm 1: k-means algorithm

1: Specify the number k of clusters to assign
2: Randomly initialize k centroids.
3: **repeat**
4:     **expectation:** Assign each point to its closest centroid.
5:     **maximization:** Compute each cluster's new centroid (mean).
6: **until** The centroid positions do not change.

Fig. 9. k-means algorithm

Latent Dirichlet Allocation (LDA): Topic modelling is unsupervised natural language processing used to represent text with the help of several topics. A generative model called LDA explains sets of observations made by unseen groups and explains why certain parts of the data are similar [14]. LDA is also a generative probabilistic model that is commonly utilized in the field of information retrieval [15]. Depending on the input settings, the generated topics can be highly generic or very specific [16].

3.4   Experimental Setup

The experiment started by preprocessing the TikTok Metadata by subsetting video descriptions with Python code. A word cloud was used to ensure that no unwanted content was included in the text corpus created from the video descriptions. Additionally, the word cloud can be utilised to verify the results of the preprocessing technique. The corpus was then represented using the bag of words characteristics representation technique. The bag of word words in the text corpus were therefore subjected to the LDA topic modelling technique.

By creating a topic per document and a word per topic model, LDA algorithms classify documents into themes. A keyword distribution is used to represent each processed video description. The LDA also assumes that the data used for the analysis are a mixture of subjects. The subject will next generate phrases depending on their likelihood matrix. Five topics were initially taken out of the data. However, to determine the ideal number of topics in the corpus, later found to be 10, the best model estimators were used.

4   Experiments and Results

The experiment yielded a word cloud of the Tik Tok description of frequent words, as seen in Fig. 10.

Fig. 10. Word Cloud of The Tik Tok Description

According to the word cloud, the majority of the words throughout the period are related to funny videos, food content, and Korean music videos. Hence, some of their words were included in 'Food,' 'Movie,' 'Korean' and 'Comedy' topics. Furthermore, some of the other words are related to the 'Pets', 'Tutorial' and 'Sports' topics. In addition, this work created an Intertopic Distance Map using the generated subjects. It gives a broad overview of the topics and how they differ from one another. It also allows for a detailed analysis of top phrases associated with each topic. The right panel, as illustrated in Fig. 11, presents a horizontal bar chart representing the top keywords that can be used to understand the topics.

Table 2 shows the results of applying the LDA algorithm to extract ten topics related to trending videos on Tik Tok. Topic 0 is about sharing material regarding drawing and painting. Other common words in this category include 'artwork,' 'animation,' and so on. Furthermore, as shown in Table 2, topic 1 is about creating Autonomous Sensory

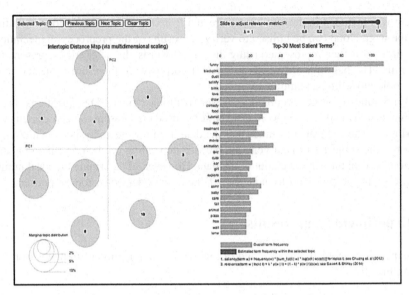

Fig. 11. Inter-topic distance plot of the 10 topics

Meridian Response (ASMR) video material or any enjoyable video. Some popular words associated with this topic include 'ear,' 'foodie,' 'food,' and so on. As a result, this form of ASMR content.

Table 2. Results of Applying The LDA Algorithm

	Topic 0	Topic 1	Topic 2	Topic 3	Topic 4	Topic 5	Topic 6	Topic 7	Topic 8	Topic 9	Topics
Topic 0	draw	art	share	hkfoodmoment	single	satisfaction	vietmyusa	freepalestine	mobilelegend	drawe	Art/Creative Content
Topic 1	satisfy	ear	asmr	rich	poor	country	teach	office	firework	hairpiece	Asmr/Satisfy Content
Topic 2	treatment	animation	care	soonent	respect	skill	toenail	epic	compilation	boss	Animation/Treatment/Sing Content
Topic 3	food	movie	main	satisfying	cartoon	eat	music	nailsmanicure	popularscience	hoove	Food/Movie/Music Content
Topic 4	blackpink	fish	guy	cute	member	release	read	support	amazing	content	Korean/Game Content
Topic 5	duet	comedy	explore	genshinimpact	good	malaysian	check	feature	male	ngakak	Comedy/Cooking Content
Topic 6	free	wait	lame	shipping	live	answer	ice	question	giant	work	Business/Work Content
Topic 7	funny	blink	fail	animal	challenge	tiktokmalaysia	tiktokguru	football	funnygame	pedicure	Funny/Sports Content
Topic 8	tutorial	day	edit	education	science	didyouknow	trick	change	warning	hagtt	Tutorial/Education/Tricks Content
Topic 9	love	girl	baby	pizza	car	beautiful	sport	woman	sikit	nail	Love Content

This work uses log likelihood score and perplexity measures to assess the algorithm's performance on the dataset. It acquired a perplexity score of 287 and a log likelihood score of 5579. A model with a greater log likelihood and a lower perplexity is regarded as good. The degree of perplexity is a measure of how well a model predicts a sample. Following that, this model was put to the test by predicting the topic using the newly developed LDA Model. Before predicting the topics, the work uses a random text using the same preprocessing technique. The transformation order and the result are shown in Fig. 12. Figure 13 shows the code to get similar documents.

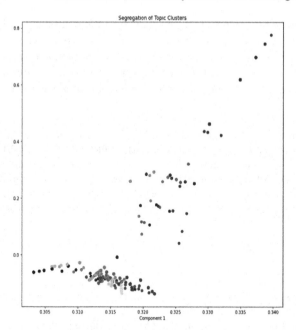

Fig. 12. Segregation of Topic Clust

```
# Get similar documents
mytext = ["i like to eat food and cook"]
doc_ids, docs = similar_documents(text=mytext, doc_topic_probs=lda_output, documents = data, top_n=1, verbose=True)
print('\n')

Topic KeyWords: ['movie', 'main', 'satisfying', 'cartoon', 'eat', 'music', 'nailsmanicure', 'popularscience', 'hoove', 'Food/Movie/Music Content']
Topic Prob Scores of text: [[0. 0. 0. 0.7 0. 0. 0. 0. 0. ]]
Most Similar Doc's Probs: [[0. 0. 0. 0.7 0. 0. 0. 0. 0. ]]
Topics:   Food/Movie/Music Content
```

Fig. 13. Similar Documents

In conclusion, this work uses K-Means clustering on the document's topic probability matrix with k-10 since the optimal model has 10 clusters to cluster video descriptions that share similar subjects and plots. To depict X and Y columns, singular value decomposition (SVD) is employed. SVD ensures that the two columns collect the most information available for the LDA model. Hence, Euclidean distance and the likelihood score are employed to find similar subjects. The themes that are the most comparable are classified with the shortest distance.

5   Conclusion

This study encompasses the LDA topic modelling technique and the K-means clustering algorithm, both used to extract trending topics from Tik Tok. The study aimed to locate and extract the most popular Tik Tok content. The LDA method obtained a perplexity score of 287 and a log likelihood score of 5579 from 7552 video data. The perplexity score evaluates how well the probability models predict. However, this measure is insufficient unless accompanied by a manual topic evaluation. Some of the study findings are trendy topics, such as comedy and sports content. As a result, because data is a multi-language combination, future work will need to incorporate the extraction of keywords from the data. This work is also interested in evaluating different topic extraction algorithms, such as a combination of natural language processing and machine learning, and comment analysis [17].

Acknowledgment. This research was supported by the Ministry of Higher Education (MoHE) through the Fundamental Research Grant Scheme (Ref: FRGS/1/2021/ICT02/UMK/02/1). The content of this article is solely the responsibility of the authors and does not necessarily represent the official views of MoHE, Malaysia. The authors would also like to extend their gratitude to the Data Management & Software Solution Research Lab, School of Computing, Universiti Utara Malaysia for their generous support in sponsoring the publication of this article.

References

1. Weimann, G., Masri, N.: The virus of hate: Far-right terrorism in cyberspace. International Institute for Counter-Terrorism (2020). https://www.ict.org.il/Article/2528/The_Virus_of_Hate
2. Jing, P., et al.: Listen to social media users: Mining Chinese public perception of automated vehicles after crashes. Transport. Res. F: Traffic Psychol. Behav. **93**, 248–265 (2023)
3. Ramamonjisoa, D.: Topic modeling on users's comments. In: 2014 Third ICT International Student Project Conference (ICT-ISPC), pp. 177–180. IEEE (2014)
4. Sheikha, H.: Text mining Twitter social media for Covid-19: Comparing latent semantic analysis and Latent Dirichlet Allocation (2020)
5. Mann, J.K.: Semantic Topic Modeling and Trend Analysis (2021)
6. Phan, V.H., Ninh, D.K., Ninh, C.K.: An effective vector representation of Facebook fan pages and its applications. In: Hernes, M., Wojtkiewicz, K., Szczerbicki, E. (eds.) ICCCI 2020. CCIS, vol. 1287, pp. 674–685. Springer, Cham (2020). https://doi.org/10.1007/978-3-030-63119-2_55
7. Jose, T., Babu, S.S. Detecting spammers on social network through clustering technique. J. Ambient Intell. Humanized Comput., 1–15 (2019)
8. Rakesh Chandra Balabantaray, C.S.: Document clustering using K- means and K-Medoids. Elixir Inter. J., 16773–16777 (2013)
9. Qiu Lin, X.J.A.: Chinese Word Clustering Method using Latent Dirichlet Allocation and K-means. In: 2nd International Conference on Advances in Computer Science and Engineering , pp. 267–270 (2015)
10. Alhawarat, M., Hegazi, M.: Revisiting k-means and topic modeling, a comparison study to cluster arabic documents. IEEE Access **6**, 42740–42749 (2018)
11. Ramkumar, A.S., Nethravathy, R.: Text document clustering using k-means algorithm. Int. Res. J. Eng. Technol **6**, 1164–1168 (2019)
12. Prihatini, P.M., Suryawan, I.K., Mandia, I.N. Feature extraction for document text using Latent Dirichlet Allocation. J. Phys. Conf. Ser. 953(1), 012047 (2018)
13. Sapul, M.S C., Aung, T.H., Jiamthapthaksin, R.: Trending topic discovery of Twitter Tweets using clustering and topic modeling algorithms. In: 2017 14th International Joint Conference on Computer Science and Software Engineering (JCSSE) (2017)
14. Tong, Z., & Zhang, H. A text mining research based on LDA topic modelling. In: International Conference on Computer Science, Engineering and Information Technology, pp. 201–210 (2016)

15. Chyi-Kwei Yau, A.L.: Clustering scientific documents with topic modeling . Scientometrics, 767–786 (2014)
16. Blair, S.J., Bi, Y., Mulvenna, M.D.: Aggregated topic models for increasing social media topic coherence. Appl. Intell. **50**(1), 138–156 (2020)
17. Chumwatana, T.: Comment analysis for product and service satisfaction from Thai customers' review in social network. J. Inform. Commun. Technolo. **17**(2), 271–289 (2018)

Navigating AI Development and Deployment

A Video Summarization Method for Movie Trailer-Genre Classification Based on Emotion Analysis

Wan En Ng[1], Muhammad Syafiq Mohd Pozi[2](✉) ⓘ, Mohd Hasbullah Omar[2] ⓘ,
Norliza Katuk[2] ⓘ, and Abdul Rafiez Abdul Raziff[3]

[1] Faculty of Computer Science and Information Technology, Universiti Malaya, Kuala Lumpur, Kuala Lumpur 50603, Malaysia
[2] School of Computing, Universiti Utara Malaysia, 06010 Sintok, Kedah, Malaysia
syafiq.pozi@uum.edu.my
[3] Kulliyyah of Information and Communication Technology, International Islamic University Malaysia, 50728 Kuala Lumpur, Gombak, Malaysia

Abstract. We live in an information world where visual data undergo exponential growth within a very short time window. With diverging content diversity, we simply have no capacity to keep track of those data. While short video platforms (such as TikTok™ or YouTube Shorts™) can helped users viewing relevant videos within the shortest time possible, those videos might have misleading information, primarily if it is derived from long videos. Here, we analyzed several short videos (in terms of movie trailers) from YouTube and established a correlation between one movie trailer and the classified movie genre based on the emotion found in the trailer. This paper contributes to (1) an efficient framework to process the movie trailer and (2) a correlation analysis between the movie trailer and movie genre. We found that every movie genre can be represented by two unique emotions.

Keywords: movie analytic · face detection · emotion recognition · video summarization

1 Introduction

The emergence of social video platforms such as TikTok™ and YouTube Shorts™ have enabled people to consume several videos within a short time window [1]. This benefits both viewer and content creator, as only important and concise information is relayed from creator to viewer. However, some of these videos are redundant, misleading, clickbait or simply misrepresentations of reality [2]. As a result, many resources, such as computing capacity and (most importantly) people's time, have been wasted just to process and consume these short videos.

The misrepresentation issue can be largely observed in many movie trailers. A movie trailer (which is a very short video clip made of multiple scenes derived from the promoted movie) is usually composed when a movie producer needs to promote a new movie to the public. However, in recent times, many have complained that some of the produced movie trailers are misrepresenting the promoted movie [3]. For example, one of the issues is that some movie trailers' scenes are unavailable or probably edited out from the promoted movie [4]. This false representation is why some people spend their money and 1 - 2 h of their life watching that movie. There is a case where a fan threatened legal action over a particular when the final movie did not include scenes that were promoted in the movie trailers[1].

As the number of movies released to the public increases over time, many producers want to ensure their movies are watched by many people worldwide. This will also increase the number of movie trailers released to the public. Hence, to facilitate consumers in visualizing many movie trailers without having to spend minutes watching the trailer, we introduce a method to summarize the movie trailers into metadata and perform data analytics in determining the relationship between the movie genre and emotion recognition, that occur in the movie trailer.

This paper is organized as follows. Section 2 overviews the previous works on video summarization from the year 1997 to the year 2022. Section 3 explains the used in this work. Section 4 describes the results of the conducted experimentation on several movie trailers. Finally, Sect. 5 presents the conclusion and future perspectives related to the main findings.

2   Related Works

The exponential growth of video data has been overwhelming that it requires some sort of summarization so users can consume many videos within a short period of time [5]. Even though video summarization has recently engaged growing attention in computer vision communities, the research on video summarization can be dated back to 1997 [6]. Here, we categorized the changes in video summarization corpus into three categories, image features statistical analysis, graph-based analysis, and semantic analysis.

2.1   Image Features Statistical Analysis

From 1997 to 2005, video summarization is mainly focused on statistical analysis of the extracted image features. Hence, many efforts are focused on building quality image features from a given video, based on low-level image analysis [7]. For example, a novel technique based on SVD (Singular Value Decomposition) which derives the refined feature space for clustering visual similar frames and a metric from measuring the amount of visual content available in each frame based on the degree of visual changes [8]. Some have proposed an automatic construction of video summarization based on similarities of images in the video which will be used to select key frames of video segments [9]. Later, a more robust two-stage clustering based video summarization technique has also been proposed to improve the relevancy of the generated video summary, whereby, the first stage provided shot separation and determined the periods of stable content with good keyframe candidates while the second stage selected the final set of key-frames [10]. A

---

[1] https://bit.ly/3VTwcWS.

much more sophisticated low-level image analysis to select representative frames based on the result of analysis of the events has also been proposed as a method to improve the relevancy of the generated video summary [11].

2.2 Graph Based Analysis

From 2005 to 2015, video summarization is slowly transformed into graph- based analysis. Chong-Wah Ngo *et. al* have proposed a unified approach for video summarization based on video structure analysis and video highlights, consisting of two major components: scene modelling and high- light detection [12]. The scene modelling consists of a normalized cut algorithm and temporal graph analysis meanwhile the highlight detection focuses on the motion attention modeling [12]. In 2006, Yuxin Peng and Chong-Wah Ngo proposed an algorithm for similarity measure of video clips based on bipartite graph matching algorithms which are Maximum Matching (MM) and Optimal Matching (OM) [13]. Maximum matching can filter the irrelevant video clips meanwhile Optimal Matching is able to rank the similarity of the clips based on visual and granularity factors [13]. D. Besiris *et. al* have proposed an automatic video summarization technique based on graph theory methodology and the dominant sets clustering algorithm [14]. Graph clustering and mining for multi-video summarization were proposed at the year of 2010 which the separated shot from visual data and extracted keywords from transcripts are structured into a complex graph and perform clustering while the hidden topics in the keyframes and keywords will be mined from clustered complex graph to maximize the coverage of summary over the original video [15]. A video summarization based on the Segments Summary Graphs is proposed, which is the coherency analysis of segmented video frames as represented by region adjacency graphs [16].

2.3 Semantic Analysis

Nowadays, many authors approach video summarization tasks within semantic analysis methodology, using every bit of video data and metadata. For example, in 2015, Yale Song *et. al* proposed TVSum. This unsupervised video summarization framework uses video title to find visually important scenes [17]. In 2016, Aidean Sharghi *et. al* proposed the Sequential and Hierarchical Determinantal Point Process (SH-DPP) for query-focused extractive video summarization, in which, given a user query and a long video sequence, the algorithm will generate a summary by selecting key shots from the video [18]. Later, Mohaiminul Al Bahian *et. al* proposed a convolutional neural network (CNN)-based architecture to mimic the frame-level shot for user-oriented video summarization [19]. Kaiyang Zhou *et. al* proposed a deep summarization network (DSN) that predicts a probability for each video frame which indicates how likely a frame is selected, selects the frames based on probability distributions and generates a video summary [20]. Lebron Casas et. Proposed two models which are Video Summarization Long Short-Term Memory (vsLSTM) and Determinantal Point Process Long Short-Term Memory (dppLSTM) deep network that enable model frame relevance and similarity and additionally incorporate attention mechanism to model user interest [21]. LSTM generate a summary from the video by extracting the most relevant segments and vsLSTM contains the bidirectional chains of LSTM units [21]. The dppLSTM combines vsLSTM with Determinantal Point Process (DPP) to model pair-wise repulsiveness within video frames [21]. In 2020, Wencheng Zhu *et al. proposed a Detect-to-Summarize network (DSNet) framework containing* anchor-based and anchor-free counterparts [22]. The anchor-based method generates temporal interest proposals to determine and localize the representative contents of video sequences while the anchor-free method eliminates the predefined temporal proposals and directly predicts the importance scores and segment locations [22]. Later, UN Yoon *et. al* proposed an unsupervised video summarization method with piecewise linear interpolation (In-terp-SUM) that improve summarization performance and generate a natural sequence of keyframes by predicting importance scores of each frame utilizing the interpolation method [23]. Figure 1 summarizes how video summarization research domain evolves over time.

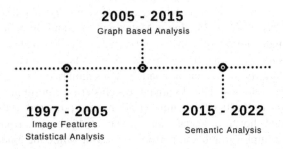

Fig. 1. A temporal summary of video summarization literature from 1997 to 2022.

3   Methodology

Figure 2 shows the overview of our methodology. In the first step, we collect several movie trailers from YouTube™, and group it based on the genre of the movie. Then, each video is splitted into several chunks, so that every chunk can be processed in parallel. Each chunk is processed to achieve the following tasks:

1. Face detection task, where we are going to identify whether there is at least one person in each chunk.
2. Emotion detection task, where we will identify the detected person's emotion.

Finally, a video summary will be produced by analyzing the distribution of detected emotion in each movie genre.

3.1   Data Collection

We used the movie trailers, downloaded from YouTube™ as our main data. Each movie trailer is based on 5 movie genres: Comedy, Action, Fantasy, Horror and Romance. A total of 25 trailers have been selected with five trailers for each movie genre. The duration of each movie trailer is about 3 to 4 min. Table 1 shows the list of movies that have been selected for each movie genre.

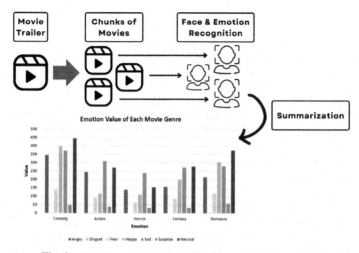

Fig. 2. Overview of our methodology used in this research.

Table 1. Table captions should be placed above the tables.

Movie Genre	Movie Title
Comedy	Ghostbusters, 2016 Once Upon a Time in Hollywood, 2019 Tag, 2018 The Intern, 2015 The Bucket List, 2007
Action	The Tomorrow War, 2021 The Finest Hours, 2016 Shooter, 2007 Security, 2017 Wonder Woman, 2017
Fantasy	Fantastic Beasts: The Secrets of Dumbledore, 2022 Dolittle, 2020 The Lord of the Rings: The Two Towers, 2002 Miss Peregrine's Home for Peculiar Children, 2016 A Monster Calls, 2016
Horror	No One Gets Out Alive, 2021 The Conjuring, 2013 Don't Breathe 2, 2021 The Silence, 2019 The Invisible Man, 2020

(continued)

Table 1. (*continued*)

Movie Genre	Movie Title
Romance	Little Women, 2019 Passengers, 2016 Crazy Rich Asians, 2018 Beauty and the Beast, 2017 Titanic, 1997

3.2 Data Processing

Each movie trailer is around 3 to 4 min. Even though the duration is shorter compared to the full movie, we still chunk the video into several chunks to benefit from the parallel processing facility provided by Python programming language. Prior to face detection and emotion recognition tasks, the movie trailer is chunked into multiple smaller chunks, in which each chunk only consists of 60 s short video data. These chunks are then processed in parallel for face detection and emotion recognition tasks.

3.3 Face Detection Task

A pretrained face detection model is used to identify faces from the video. It is based on Facial Emotion Recognition [24] and has been implemented as an open-source Python library[2] for emotion analysis of images and videos data which will categorize each of the faces based on the emotion into angry, disgust, fear, happy, sad, surprise and neutral. By default, Facial Emotion Recognition (FER) uses OpenCV's HaarCascade classifier to detect faces in image. However, to increase the face detection accuracy, FER implemented MTCNN network 3 in their face detection model. MTCNN is a Multi-task Cascaded Convolutional Networks which is a framework that consists of three stages of convolutional networks: Proposal Network (P-Net), Refine Network (R-Net), and Output Network (O-Net), that are able to recognize face based on the eye, nose and lip's location in an image frame [25, 26]. Figure 3 illustrates MTCNN network architecture, and how it relates to our dataset.

Stage 1: Proposal Network (P-Net).

This stage is a fully convolutional network which is known as Proposal Network (P-Net) which obtains the candidate windows and the bounding box regression vectors [25]. The bounding box regression vectors will be used to calibrate the candidate. Next, Non-Maximum Suppression (NMS) is employed to merge the highly overlapped candidates.

Stage 2: Refine Network (R-Net).

The candidates are fed to Refine Network (R-Net) to further reject a huge number of false candidates, calibrate the candidate with bounding box regression and merge the highly overlapped candidates with NMS.

Stage 3: Output Network (O-Net).

---

[2] https://pypi.org/project/facial-emotion-recognition/.

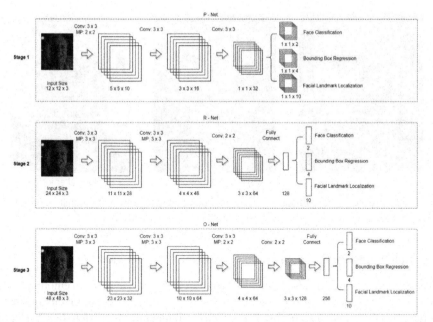

Fig. 3. An illustration of MTCNN network architecture. "Conv" refers to convolution while "MP" refers to max pooling.

Output Network (O-Net) is similar to the R-Net but it describes the detected face in more detail. At the end, the network will output the five facial landmarks' positions as shown in Fig. 4.

When the MTCNN parameter is set to'True', the FER model will use MTCNN network to detect faces meanwhile if it set to'False', OpenCV HaarCascade classifier will be used to detect the faces. The model will run analysis on each frame of the video chunk and create a rectangle box around the face on every image which the emotion values next to it. It will publish a processed video which will have a rectangle box around the detected faces with live emotion values. Figure 5 shows the example of a detected face with live emotion values of comedy movie title with the name of The Bucket List.

Fig. 4. The detected faces with facial landmark.

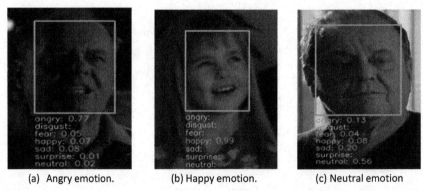

(a) Angry emotion.   (b) Happy emotion.   (c) Neutral emotion

Fig. 5. Each detected face will have 7 emotions quantified with probability of that emotion to be true. The emotions are angry, disgust, fear, happy, sad, surprise and neutral.

3.4 Emotion Recognition Task and Computing Emotion Value

The FER implementation also has a function that can be used to perform emotion detection tasks. The function can be used to classify detected faces into seven emotion categories: angry, disgust, fear, happy, sad, surprise and neutral, as shown in Fig. 5. Hence, for each detected face, there will be seven emotion values associated with the face. Each emotion value is a probability for that emotion to be true in that specific face instance (detected face in one frame).

Figure 6 tracks the emotion value and score of each of the emotions of the movie named "The Bucket List". In Fig. 6, every emotion in one frame is a probability value of all possible emotions, that sum up to 1, such as in Eq. 1:

$$frame = \sum\nolimits_{j=1}^{k} p(y_j) \tag{1}$$

where each frame represents the probability of every emotion to be true in relative to all available emotions: $y_j \in \{$angry, disgust, fear, happy, sad, surprise, neutral$\}$.

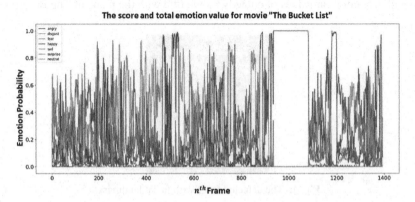

Fig. 6. The score and total emotion value for movie trailer "The Bucket List".

In the movie "The Bucket List", we can see that happy is the dominant emotion in that movie, especially at around 1000th frames, and disgust is the uncommon emotion in that movie.

4   Results and Analysis

Next, we compute the cumulative emotion value e_{ij} of video i, with emotion j, such as defined in Eq. 2:

$$ei, j = \sum_{m=1}^{n} (p(yj|f\ (face)))\qquad(2)$$

where $y_j \in$ {angry, disgust, fear, happy, sad, surprise, neutral} and $f\ (face)$ is a function that describes the emotion of detected face, for every m face detected in the video up to n faces.

Figure 7 shows the cumulative emotion value of each movie genre, in which each genre is represented by 5 movie trailers. Note that a -second clip has 30 frames, hence why Fig. 7 showing values greater than 1.

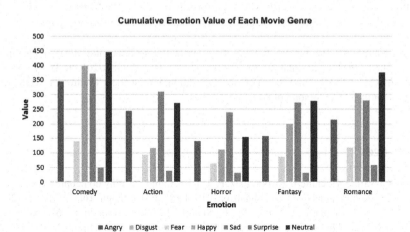

Fig. 7. Cumulative emotion value of each movie genre.

Based on Fig. 7, we found that:

1. We could not associate a movie genre with just one single emotion.
2. This experiment suggests each movie genre could be represented by the top three highest cumulative emotion value, such as:
    (a) *Comedy* genre movies can be represented by *Neutral, Happy,* and *Sad* emotions.
    (b) *Action* genre movies can be represented by *Sad, Neutral,* and *Angry* emotions.
    (c) *Horror* genre movies can be represented by *Sad, Neutral,* and *Angry* emotions.
    (d) *Fantasy* genre movies can be represented by *Neutral, Sad,* and *Happy* emotions.
    (e) *Romance* genre movies can be represented by *Neutral, Happy,* and *Sad* emotions.

3. Some of the movie trailers that we collected could overlap with other genres. For example, the *"Crazy Rich Asians, 2018"* movie can also be considered a Romance and Comedy genre movie, instead of a Romance-only movie. Hence, we found that *Neutral* and *Happy* are mostly associated with *Romance* and *Comedy* movie genres.
4. For *Action* and *Horror* movies, three common emotions associated with those genres are *Sad*, *Neutral* and *Angry*.
5. Based on our dataset, emotion *Disgust* is not a popular emotion to be portrayed in a movie.

5   Conclusion and Future Works

In this paper, we run an experiment to investigate the relationship between short videos that are derived from long videos, based on the description of the long videos. We done this by collecting 25 movie trailers, classified based on 5 movie genres. Next, we establish a relationship between emotion found in the movie trailers and with its movie genres, respectively. We found that a single emotion cannot represent each movie genre. In our case, at least 2 emotions are required to represent a movie genre.

In the future, we plan to collect much more movie trailers and build a more accurate emotion detection tool to verify the relationship between emotions detected in each movie trailer and classified movie genre, which has been established in paper.

Acknowledgments. The authors thank the Ministry of Higher Education Malaysia for funding this study under the Fundamental Research Grant Scheme (Ref: FRGS/1/2019/ICT02/UUM/02/2, UUM S/O Code: 14358), and Research and Innovation Management Centre, Universiti Utara Malaysia for the administration of this study.

References

1. Cuesta-Valiño, P., Gutiérrez-Rodríguez, P., Durán-Álamo, P.: Why do people return to video platforms? millennials and centennials on TikTok. Media Commun. **10**(1), 198–207 (2022)
2. Gothankar, R., Troia, F.D., Stamp, M.: In: Stamp, M., Aaron Visaggio, C., Mercaldo, F., Di Troia, F. (eds.) Clickbait Detection for YouTube Videos, pp. 261–284. Springer, Cham (2022). https://doi.org/10.1007/978-3-030-97087-1_11
3. Korsgaard, M.B.: Fake trailers as imaginary paratexts. MedieKultur: J. Media Commun. Res. **36**(68), 107–125 (2020)
4. Garcia, R., Watson, W.: Fake it while you make it: When do fantasy and science fiction movie trailers become deceptive advertising? In a Stranger Field. Studies of Art, Audiovisuals and New Technologies in Fantasy, SciFi and Horror Genres., 122
5. En, N.W., Mohd Pozi, M.S., Jatowt, A.: A face recognition module for video content analysis in malaysian parliament sessions. In: Proceedings of the ACM/IEEE Joint Conference on Digital Libraries in 2020, JCDL 2020, pp. 533–534. Association for Computing Machinery, New York (2020).https://doi.org/10.1145/3383583.3398628
6. DeMenthon, D., Kobla, V., Doermann, D.: Video summarization by curve simplification. In: Proceedings of the Sixth ACM International Conference on Multimedia, pp. 211–218 (1998)
7. Zhang, H.J., Wu, J., Zhong, D., Smoliar, S.W.: An integrated system for content-based video retrieval and browsing. Pattern Recogn. **30**(4), 643–658 (1997)

8. Gong, Y., Liu, X.: Video summarization using singular value decomposition. In: Proceedings IEEE Conference on Computer Vision and Pattern Recognition, CVPR 2000 (Cat. No. PR00662), vol. 2, pp. 174–180. IEEE (2000)

9. Yahiaoui, I., Merialdo, B., Huet, B.: Automatic video summarization. In: Proceeding of CBMIR Conference (2001)

10. Farin, D., Effelsberg, W., de With, P.H.: Robust clustering-based video-summarization with integration of domain-knowledge. In: Proceedings of IEEE International Conference on Multimedia and Expo, vol. 1, pp. 89–92. IEEE (2002)

11. Corchs, S., Ciocca, G., Schettini, R.: Video summarization using a neurodynamical model of visual attention. In: IEEE 6th Workshop on Multimedia Signal Processing 2004, pp. 71–74. IEEE (2004)

12. Ngo, C.-W., Ma, Y.-F., Zhang, H.-J.: Video summarization and scene detection by graph modeling. IEEE Trans. Circuits Syst. Video Technol. 15(2), 296–305 (2005)

13. Peng, Y., Ngo, C.-W.: Clip-based similarity measure for query-dependent clip retrieval and video summarization. IEEE Trans. Circuits Syst. Video Technol. 16(5), 612–627 (2006)

14. Besiris, D., Makedonas, A., Economou, G., Fotopoulos, S.: Combining graph connectivity & dominant set clustering for video summarization. Multimedia Tools Appli. 44(2), 161–186 (2009)

15. Shao, J., Jiang, D., Wang, M., Chen, H., Yao, L.: Multi-video summarization using complex graph clustering and mining. Comput. Sci. Inf. Syst. 7(1), 85–98 (2010)

16. Demir, M., Isil Bozma, H.: Video summarization via segments summary graphs. In: Proceedings of the IEEE International Conference on Computer Vision Workshops, pp. 19–25 (2015)

17. Song, Y., Vallmitjana, J., Stent, A., Jaimes, A.: Tvsum: Summarizing web videos using titles. In: Proceedings of the IEEE Conference on Computer Vision and Pattern Recognition, pp. 5179–5187 (2015)

18. Sharghi, A., Gong, B., Shah, M.: Query-focused extractive video summarization. In: Leibe, B., Matas, J., Sebe, N., Welling, M. (eds.) Computer Vision – ECCV 2016, Part VIII, pp. 3–19. Springer International Publishing, Cham (2016). https://doi.org/10.1007/978-3-319-464 84-8_1

19. Al Nahian, M., Iftekhar, A., Islam, M.T., Rahman, S.M., Hatzinakos, D.: Cnn-based prediction of frame-level shot importance for video summarization. In: 2017 International Conference on New Trends in Computing Sciences (ICTCS), pp. 24–29. IEEE (2017)

20. Zhou, K., Qiao, Y., Xiang, T.: Deep reinforcement learning for unsupervised video summarization with diversity-representativeness reward. In: Proceedings of the AAAI Conference on Artificial Intelligence, vol. 32 (2018)

21. Lebron Casas, L., Koblents, E.: Video summarization with lstm and deep attention models. In: International Conference on MultiMedia Modeling, pp. 67–79. Springer (2019).

22. Zhu, W., Lu, J., Li, J., Zhou, J.: Dsnet: a flexible detect-to-summarize network for video summarization. IEEE Trans. Image Process. 30, 948–962 (2021).https://doi.org/10.1109/TIP. 2020.3039886

23. Yoon, U.-N., Hong, M.-D., Jo, G.-S.: Interp-sum: Unsupervised video summarization with piecewise linear interpolation. Sensors 21(13), 4562 (2021)

24. Goodfellow, I.J., et al.: Challenges in Representation Learning: A Report on Three Machine Learning Contests. In: Lee, M., Hirose, A., Hou, Z.-G., Kil, R.M. (eds.) Neural Information Processing, pp. 117–124. Springer, Heidelberg (2013). https://doi.org/10.1007/978-3-642-42051-1_16

25. Zhang, K., Zhang, Z., Li, Z., Qiao, Y.: Joint face detection and alignment using multitask cascaded convolutional networks. IEEE Signal Process. Lett. **23**(10), 1499–1503 (2016)
26. Saini, P., Kumar, K., Kashid, S., et al.: Video summarization using deep learning techniques: a detailed analysis and investigation. Artif. Intell. Rev. (2023). https://doi.org/10.1007/s10 462-023-10444-0

E-Nose: Spoiled Food Detection Embedded Device Using Machine Learning for Food Safety Application

Wan Nur Fadhlina Syamimi Wan Azman[1,2]([✉]), Ku Nurul Fazira binti Ku Azir[1,2], and Adam bin Mohd Khairuddin[1,2]

[1] Faculty of Electronic Engineering, Universiti Malaysia Perlis (UniMAP), Perlis, Malaysia
syamimifadhlina@gmail.com
[2] Advanced Computing Engineering, Center of Excellence (CoE), Universiti Malaysia Perlis (UniMAP), Perlis, Malaysia

Abstract. This research aims to employ machine learning (ML) to classify the degree of contamination in leftover cooked foods based on their smell. This study evaluates the odour characteristics of typical leftover cooked lunch or dinner meals that are consumed locally in Malaysia. An easy-to-use e-nose application was attached to the food containers, consisting of four different types of sensors sensitive to various gases, to collect the data. RStudio is used to analyze samples in order to identify the odour classification of leftover Malaysian food. The accuracy ranged from 90% to 100% when using the oversampling and undersampling techniques. The results of this re-search showed satisfactory performances by Support Vector Machines (SVM) is superior compared to that of k-Nearest Neighbours (k-NN) in classifying the samples' contamination degree. As a result, the findings showed that the electronic nose used in this study was a promising method for classifying the degree of contamination in leftover cooked foods and predicting whether food is still edible or not.

Keywords: classification · machine learning · food waste

1 Introduction

Food loss and waste (FLW) was a serious issue due to the huge socioeconomic costs involved and its connection to issues with waste management and climate change [1]. Globally, it had also become a major issue, especially in developing countries like Malaysia where the issue has gotten out of hand. Food waste is the use of food intended for human consumption for non-human consumption, the repurposing of food for animal consumption, or the discarding of edible food [2]. Certain academics have referred to food loss and food waste interchangeably. Food waste happens most frequently, but not always, at the retail and consumption stages of the food value chain. It is typically the result of carelessness or a deliberate decision to throw away food [4].

Furthermore, according to [2], there are three types of food waste: (a) prevent-able waste, which refers to food that was once edible but has turned inedible by the time it

N. H. Zakaria et al. (Eds.): ICOCI 2023, CCIS 2001, pp. 221–234, 2024.
https://doi.org/10.1007/978-981-99-9589-9_17

reaches disposal; (b) unavoidable waste, which refers to non-edible items; and (c) food waste that is potentially preventable, which refers to waste that is occasionally but not always consumed. Food waste generation at the consumption level is a form of avoidable waste typically produced at the household level. Consumer-level food waste can result from customer behaviours such as overbuying, poor planning, lack of information about their food storage, confusion over "best before" and "use by" dates, and more.

According to Khazanah Research Institute (KRI), the household sector accounts for 44.5% of all solid waste collected, or 6.1 million metric tons annually. Food waste made up 50% of all waste composition in MSW, one of 20 major groups, and food scrap dumping is anticipated to increase greenhouse gas emissions by 50% by 2020 [5].

The primary objective of this research is to identify and forecast contamination levels using a machine-learning algorithm. This study aims to categorize cooked contamination levels and evaluate the accuracy of machine learning in classifying various levels of contamination and identifying spoiled food using taste, texture, and colour in addition to odour.

Many studies have been conducted on integrating electronic noses and machine learning algorithms. Due to its rapid speed, highly reliable, straightforward operation, and cost-effectiveness, an electronic nose is a chemical measurement instrument that measures the chemical characteristics of volatile gases. It is frequently used to identify the quality and safety of food [6]. However, research on the issue of food waste in the context of leftover cooked food is presently lacking. Section II will discuss related studies on the combination of electronic nose and machine learning and how this research differs from the related studies.

2 Related Works

The use of electronic nose machine learning for identifying the various characteristics of foods or drinks was covered in a number of literature studies. Conventional techniques like high performance liquid chromatography (HPLC), microbiological cell counting, mass spectrometry, and gas and liquid chromatography are cumbersome because they require time-consuming and laborious sample processing [7]. To run these conventional methods, skilled personnel were also required. Therefore, e-nose technology has been used in the food industry due to its ease, cost effectiveness, and close connection to sensory panels.

In a number of areas of food safety assessment, electronic noses have recently become known as potential tools for quick, early detection of contamination and defects in the food production chain. By identifying its distinctive components and studying its chemical components, an e-nose may recognize an odour [8, 9]. The electronic nose (E-nose) is a group of electronic gas sensors that can detect volatile compounds in the headspaces of food product samples with high sensitivity and selectivity [10]. It resembles the human sense of smell to some extent [10–12]. Figure 1 shows the correlation of human nose with electronic nose.

According to Fig. 1 above, gas sensors and sensing materials were used in place of the odour receptor cells to mimic a biological olfactory system. A computational algorithm, an artificial neural network, and data analysis software are used in place

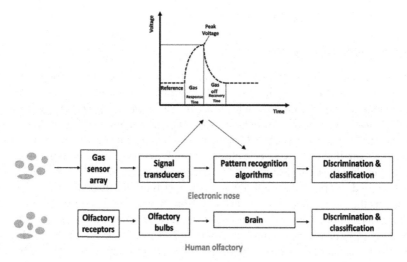

Fig. 1. Sensing-interpreting-discriminating process of an electronic nose [13].

of the brain and neural network [14]. During the detection process, numerous various volatile compounds interact with each other on the sensor array, and the data from each sensor is retained as a distinct pattern or "fingerprint" [15–17]. These signals are sent to a computer system, which recognizes the signals and distinguishes the fingerprinting of measured samples using multivariate data analysis (MVDA) methods [15].

As an objective automated non-destructive technology with significant benefits like high sensitivity, simplicity in construction, and cost-effectiveness, e-nose has gained popularity and become a prominent detection system in many sectors [12]. A number of studies demonstrated the widespread use of e-nose in assessing food quality-related properties, including the detection of wine properties [18], the classification of Chinese libations [19, 20], the quality status of fruits [21, 22], the quality of olive oils [23, 24], and the detection of contaminated foods [7, 25]–[27].

The integration of an electronic nose and machine learning to evaluate the quality of leftover food after days of storage, however, set this study apart from other similar works done in. A similar study recently have been done by [28], yet the method of classification was different as this study utilized multi-classification and obtained different result. It is crucial for the electronic nose to identify the contaminated food accurately as this will help the consumers decide which food to discard. It was believed that the suggested machine learning and method for classifying contamination levels in this research would help create a special framework for improving environmental protection and food waste management in Malaysia.

3   Materials and Methods

3.1   Food Sample Preparation

In this study, six (6) food samples of leftover cooked food—typically found in typical Malaysian households—are utilized to analyze the odour released and identify the indicator of contamination. These include *Nasi Goreng Daging, Sup Daging, Ayam Masak Lemak, Ayam Masak Kunyit, Ayam Goreng Berempah,* and *Sawi Masak Air*. These food samples were chosen to investigate how the way they were cooked affected their spoilage rate. Apart from that, they were also chosen to study whether different types of cooking affected the classification results.

These food samples were stored in a pristine, airtight plastic container with sensors fastened to the lid for five days. Every day from 8.30 am to 5.30 pm, the study was conducted. The container lid will be opened every 15 min for sensor cleaning. The experiment took place in a room temperature (28°C - 30°C). Figure 2(a) – Fig. 2(f) shows the food samples in Fresh condition. These food samples will be observed for five days in a row with the purpose of detecting any visible changes.

(a)   (b)   (c)   (d)   (e)   (f)

Fig. 2. Food Samples in Fresh Condition: (a) *Sup Daging,* (b) *Nasi Goreng Daging,* (c) *Ayam Masak Kunyit,* (d) *Ayam Masak Lemak,* (e) *Ayam Goreng Berempah* and (f) *Sawi Masak Air.*

3.2   Experimental Setup

The food's emissions of gases can be detected using four (4) gas sensors. The data from the sensor to the computer in this study is processed and converted using an Arduino microcontroller and a data collection programme called PLX-DAQ. The list of sensors utilized in this investigation was provided in Table 1 below, along with the types of gases the sensors detected.

3.3   Data Analysis Methods

The present study involved the utilization of Support Vector Machines (SVM) and k-Nearest Neighbors (k-NN) in the analysis of data gathered from gas sensors, as well as the classification of the degree of food contamination. The datasets utilized in this study were characterized by an imbalance in the amounts of dependent variables, which may result in inaccurate classification algorithm performance due to unevenly distributed class label characteristics. To address this issue, oversampling and undersampling techniques were

Table 1. Sensors Used in the Study.

Sensor Name	Types of Gas Detected	Types of Gas Detected in this Study
MQ-2	LPG, Propane, Hydrogen, Methane, Smoke	Methane
MQ-136	Hydrogen Sulphide	Hydrogen Sulphide
MQ-137	Ammonia	Ammonia
MQ-138	n-Hexane, Benzene, NH3, Alcohol, Smoke, CO	NH3, Alcohol

employed to balance the imbalanced datasets. Oversampling is the act of increasing the number of minority class instances or samples produced, as well as repeating some instances. Contrary to that, reducing the number of majority target instances or samples was known as undersampling. The data analysis tool of choice in this study was R Studio.

This study evaluated 300 rows of sensor values and 17 covariates for multi-classification. The categories "Fresh," "Semi-Fresh," and "Spoiled" were utilized as the reference group for the multi-classification, based on observations made of the food sample during the experiment's five-day course. The food sample was deemed "Fresh" on Days 1 and 2, "Semi-Fresh" on Days 3 and 4, and "Spoiled" on Days 4 and 5.

Following the loading of datasets into the software, a data partition process was carried out, whereby the datasets were partitioned using an 80:20 ratio, with 80% of datasets serving as training sets and the remaining 20% serving as test sets. Each data point belonging to respective classes was chosen randomly during this process. A control function was also established for multi-classification, using k-cross validation with a value of k equal to 10, which is consistent with past studies.

4   Results and Discussion

This section will be using confusion matrices to explain the classification task outcomes. For each class, the various rows reflect the prediction, while the various columns show the actual number of samples for each class. Each food sample will have three (3) confusion matrices representing the classification tasks for unbalanced, over-sampled, and undersampled datasets, respectively. In addition, the classification result will be divided into two sections: the k-NN classification results and the SVM classification results.

4.1   K-NN Classification Result

Figure 3 shows the confusion matrices for the food sample *Ayam Goreng Berempah*. The first confusion matrix shows that when the dataset for *Ayam Goreng Berempah* was unbalanced, k-NN could not classify the levels of food contamination accurately.

Hence, the average accuracy for this dataset was 50%. On the other hand, the average accuracy rose to 92.86% and 91.07%, respectively, after the dataset was balanced using the oversampling and undersampling techniques.

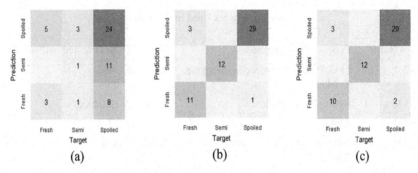

Fig. 3. k-NN Confusion Matrix for Classification of *Ayam Goreng Berempah*: (a) Unbalanced, (b) Oversampled, and (c) Undersampled.

The confusion matrices for the meal sample *Ayam Masak Kunyit* were displayed in Fig. 4. The confusion matrix for the unbalanced dataset demonstrated that the k-NN could not effectively classify food contamination levels. As a result, this dataset's average accuracy was 42.86%. Yet, the average accuracy rose to 91.07% and 92.86%, respectively, when the dataset was balanced using the oversampling and undersampling technique.

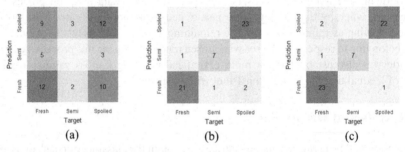

Fig. 4. k-NN Confusion Matrix for Classification of *Ayam Masak Kunyit:* (a) Unbalanced, (b) Oversampled, and (c) Undersampled.

Next, Fig. 5 shows the confusion matrix for classification tasks done on *Ayam Masak Lemak*. When the datasets were unbalanced, the average accuracy for this food sample was 51.8%.

The average accuracy rose to 89.29% and 91.07% when the dataset was balanced using oversampling and undersampling techniques, respectively. In oversampling, only 2 samples were misclassified as "Fresh" from the "Semi-Fresh" class and 4 samples were misclassified as "Fresh" from the "Spoiled" class. For the undersampling datasets, 2 samples were misclassified as "Fresh" from the "Semi-Fresh" class and 3 samples from the "Spoiled" class.

Meanwhile, Fig. 6 below shows the confusion matrix for the classification tasks done *Nasi Goreng Daging*. When the datasets were unbalanced, the average accuracy for this

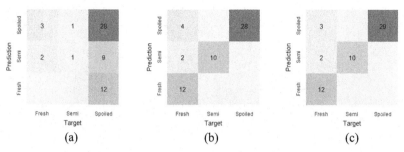

Fig. 5. k-NN Confusion Matrix for Classification of *Ayam Masak Lemak:* (a) Unbalanced, (b) Oversampled, and (c) Undersampled.

food sample was 37.5%. The classification average accuracy rose to 91.07% when the dataset was balanced using oversampling and undersampling.

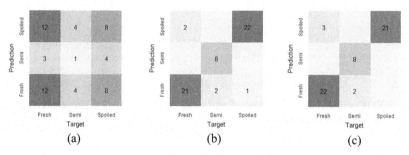

Fig. 6. k-NN Confusion Matrix for Classification of *Nasi Goreng Daging:* (a) Unbalanced, (b) Oversampled, and (c) Undersampled.

In oversampling, 2 samples from "Fresh" class were misclassified as "Semi-Fresh" and 1 sample were misclassified as "Spoiled", whereas 2 samples were misclassified as "Fresh" from the "Spoiled" class. Meanwhile, in undersampling, only 3 samples from "Spoiled" class were misclassified as "Fresh" class and 2 samples were misclassified as "Semi-Fresh" from the "Fresh" class.

Figure 7 below shows the confusion matrices for the food sample *Sup Daging*. The first confusion matrix shows that when the dataset for *Sup Daging* was unbalanced, k-NN could not accurately classify food contamination levels. Hence, the average accuracy for this dataset was 26.78%.

Yet, when the dataset were balanced using the oversampling and undersampling technique, the average accuracy increased to 96.43% and 98.21%, respectively.

On the other hand, Fig. 8 shows the confusion matrix for the classification tasks done *Sawi Masak Air*. From the first figure, it can be observed that the k-NN algorithm could not classify the samples into their respective classes accurately. Hence, the average accuracy for this dataset was 41.07%.

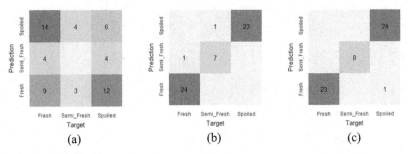

Fig. 7. k-NN Confusion Matrix for Classification of *Sup Daging:* (a) Unbalanced, (b) Over-sampled, and (c) Undersampled.

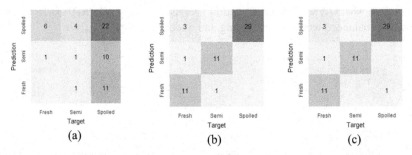

Fig. 8. k-NN Confusion Matrix for Classification of *Sawi Masak Air:* (a) Unbalanced, (b) Over-sampled, and (c) Undersampled.

Nevertheless, when the oversampling technique was used to balance the dataset, the classification average accuracy rose to 91.07%. The classification average accuracy for when the dataset was balanced using the undersampling method also increased to 91.07%. In oversampling, only 3 samples were misclassified as "Fresh" from the "Spoiled" class and 1 sample was misclassified as "Fresh" from the "Semi-Fresh" class. There was also 1 sample was misclassified as "Semi-Fresh" from the "Fresh" class.

For the undersampling datasets, 3 samples were misclassified as "Fresh" from the "Spoiled" class and 1 sample was misclassified as "Fresh" from the "Semi-Fresh" class. Meanwhile, 1 sample from the "Fresh" class was misclassified as "Spoiled".

4.2 SVM Classification Result

This section will discuss on the classification results for the SVM algorithm. Figure 9 below shows the confusion matrices for the food sample *Ayam Goreng Berempah*. The first confusion matrix shows that when the dataset for *Ayam Goreng Berempah* was un-balanced, only 1 sample were misclassified as "Fresh" from "Spoiled" class. In contrast, the data points for "Fresh" and "Semi-Fresh" class were misclassified completely.

Thus, the average accuracy for this dataset was 55.36%. On the other hand, the average accuracy rose to 100% after the dataset was balanced using the oversampling and undersampling techniques.

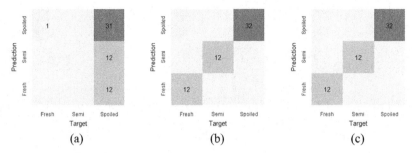

Fig. 9. SVM Confusion Matrix for Classification of *Ayam Goreng Berempah*: (a) Unbalanced, (b) Oversampled, and (c) Undersampled.

Meanwhile, the confusion matrices for the meal sample *Ayam Masak Kunyit* are displayed in Fig. 10. Similar to the previously mentioned food sample, the confusion matrix for the unbalanced dataset demonstrated that the SVM could not effectively classify food contamination levels. As a result, this dataset's average accuracy was 33.93%. Yet, the algorithm managed to achieve average accuracy of 100% when the dataset was balanced using the oversampling and undersampling technique.

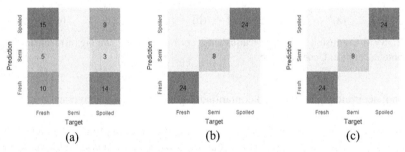

Fig. 10. SVM Confusion Matrix for Classification of *Ayam Masak Kunyit*: (a) Unbalanced, (b) Oversampled, and (c) Undersampled.

Next, Fig. 11 shows the confusion matrix for classification tasks done on *Ayam Masak Lemak*. This food sample's average accuracy was 57.14% when the datasets were out of balance. Nevertheless, when the dataset was balanced with the help of the oversampling and undersampling techniques, the classification accuracy was 100%, respectively, and there were no misclassifications.

Figure 12 below shows the confusion matrix for the classification tasks done *Nasi Goreng Daging*. When the datasets were unbalanced, the average accuracy for this food sample was 41.07%.

The classification average accuracy for this particular food sample dataset also achieved 100% when oversampling and undersampling technique were applied to balance the dataset.

Figure 13 below shows the confusion matrices for the food sample *Sup Daging*. The first confusion matrix shows that when the dataset for *Sup Daging* was unbalanced, SVM

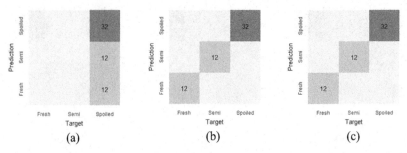

Fig. 11. SVM Confusion Matrix for Classification of *Ayam Masak Lemak*: (a) Unbalanced, (b) Oversampled, and (c) Undersampled.

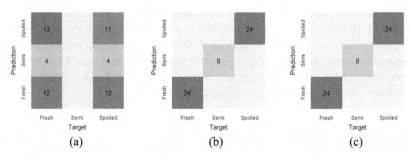

Fig. 12. SVM Confusion Matrix for Classification of *Nasi Goreng Daging*: (a) Unbalanced, (b) Oversampled, and (c) Undersampled.

could not accurately classify food contamination levels. Thus, the average accuracy for this dataset was 39.29%.

However, when the dataset was balanced using the oversampling and undersampling techniques, no misclassification error occurred as the algorithm could classify the food sample into the respective classes correctly (classification accuracy 100%).

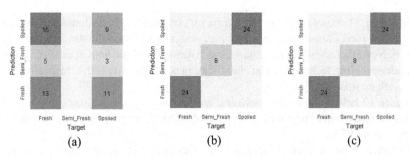

Fig. 13. SVM Confusion Matrix for Classification of *Sup Daging*: (a) Unbalanced, (b) Over-sampled, and (c) Undersampled.

On the other hand, Fig. 14 shows the confusion matrix for the classification tasks done *Sawi Masak Air*. From the first figure, it can be observed that the SVM algorithm can only classify the "Spoiled" class accurately, leading to the average accuracy for this dataset being 57.14%.

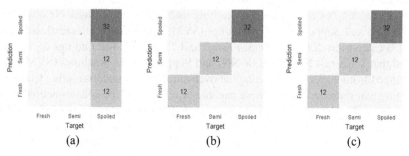

(a)   (b)   (c)

Fig. 14. SVM Confusion Matrix for Classification of *Sawi Masak Air*: (a) Unbalanced, (b) Oversampled, and (c) Undersampled.

Nevertheless, when the dataset was balanced using the oversampling and under-sampling techniques, no misclassification error occurred as the algorithm could classify the food sample into the respective classes correctly. Table 2 be-low shows the summarization of the k-NN and SVM classification results based on the accuracy.

Table 2. Summary of Accuracy Results for k-NN and SVM

MULTI CLASSIFICATION ACCURACY %						
Food Sample	k-NN			SVM		
	Unbalanced	Oversampled	Undersampled	Unbalanced	Oversampled	Undersampled
AGB	50.00	92.86	91.07	55.36	100.00	100.00
AMK	42.86	91.07	92.86	33.93	100.00	100.00
AML	51.80	89.29	91.07	57.14	100.00	100.00
NGD	37.50	91.07	91.07	41.07	100.00	100.00
SD	26.78	96.43	98.21	39.29	100.00	100.00
SMA	41.07	91.07	91.07	57.14	100.00	100.00

Based on the summarized outcomes presented in Table 2, it is apparent that the level of accuracy in food classification varies between different food samples. This difference is due to the various ways of cooking the food samples such as frying, cooking proteins or vegetables in soups and cooking proteins or vegetables using coconut milk. These different cooking methods can also influence the spoilage rate of the food samples. Hence, it can be inferred that the accuracy of classification outcomes is impacted by the techniques employed for preparing the food samples.

5   Conclusion

With the aid of machine learning (ML) and the scent of the foods, a friendly electronic nose (e-nose) application was created to recognize and classify the degree of contamination in leftover cooked food. The meal sample for this study was made up of typical local Malaysian lunch and dinner items that were afterwards saved as leftovers. This work analyzed the samples using machine learning techniques, including k-Nearest Neighbors (k-NN) and Support Vector Machines (SVMs). The samples were classified into three (3) categories: "Fresh," "Semi-Fresh," and "Spoiled". The findings of this study showed that k-Nearest Neighbors (k-NN) and Support Vector Machines (SVMs) accuracy ranged from 90% to 100% using the oversampling and undersampling techniques, indicating that these techniques were capable of classifying the contamination level of the food sample. However, SVM outperforms k-NN in terms of classification since it can accurately categorize every food sample when the dataset is balanced using oversampling and undersampling. Thus, the findings indicated that the electronic nose used in this study was a potential tool for classifying the degree of contamination in leftover cooked dishes.

Acknowledgement. This research is supported by the Ministry of Higher Education through Fundamental Research Grant Scheme (FRGS/1/2022/STG07/UNIMAP/02/5).

References

1. Chauhan, C., Dhir, A., Akram, M.U., Salo, J.: Food loss and waste in food supply chains. a systematic literature review and framework development approach. J. Cleaner Prod. **295**, 126438 (2021). https://doi.org/10.1016/j.jclepro.2021.126438
2. Dhir, A., Talwar, S., Kaur, P., Malibari, A.: Food waste in hospitality and food services: A systematic literature review and framework development approach. J. Clean. Prod. **270**, 122861 (2020). https://doi.org/10.1016/j.jclepro.2020.122861
3. Betz, A., Buchli, J., Göbel, C., Müller, C.: Food waste in the Swiss food service industry - Magnitude and potential for reduction. Waste Manag. **35**, 218–226 (2015). https://doi.org/10.1016/j.wasman.2014.09.015
4. Lipinski, B.: By the numbers: reducing food loss and waste, *World Resour. Inst.*, pp. 1–6, 2013
5. Ismail, M.H., et al.: Impact of movement control order (Mco) due to coronavirus disease (covid-19) on food waste generation: A case study in klang valley, malaysia. Sustain. **12**(21), 1–17 (2020). https://doi.org/10.3390/su12218848
6. Changquan Huang, Y.: A machine learning method for the quantitative detection of adulterated meat using a MOS-Based E-Nose. Foods **11**(4), 602 (2022). https://doi.org/10.3390/foods11040602
7. Qiu, S., Wang, J.: The prediction of food additives in the fruit juice based on electronic nose with chemometrics. Food Chem. **230**, 208–214 (2017). https://doi.org/10.1016/j.foodchem.2017.03.011
8. J. Gębicki and B. Szulczyński, "Discrimination of selected fungi species based on their odour profile using prototypes of electronic nose instruments," *Meas. J. Int. Meas. Confed.*, vol. 116, no. November 2017, pp. 307–313, 2018, doi: https://doi.org/10.1016/j.measurement.2017.11.029.

9. M. Roy and B. K. Yadav, "Electronic nose for detection of food adulteration: a review," *J. Food Sci. Technol.*, vol. 59, no. 3, pp. 846–858, 2022,https://doi.org/10.1007/s13197-021-050 57-w

10. Gu, S., Wang, J., Wang, Y.: Early discrimination and growth tracking of Aspergillus spp. contamination in rice kernels using electronic nose. Food Chem. **292**(April), 325–335 (2019). https://doi.org/10.1016/j.foodchem.2019.04.054

11. Abu-Khalaf, N.: Identification and quantification of olive oil quality parameters using an electronic nose. Agriculture **11**(7), 674 (2021). https://doi.org/10.3390/agriculture11070674

12. Liu, H., Li, Q., Yan, B., Lei Zhang, Y.: Bionic electronic nose based on mos sensors array and machine learning algorithms used for wine properties detection. Sensors **19**(1), 45 (2018). https://doi.org/10.3390/s19010045

13. Tan, J., Xu, J.: Applications of electronic nose (e-nose) and electronic tongue (e-tongue) in food quality-related properties determination: a review. Artif. Intell. Agric. **4**, 104–115 (2020). https://doi.org/10.1016/j.aiia.2020.06.003

14. Hsieh, Y., Yao, D.: Intelligent gas-sensing systems and their applications. J. Micromech. Microeng. **28**(9), 093001 (2018). https://doi.org/10.1088/1361-6439/aac849

15. Jiang, S., Liu, Y.: Gas sensors for volatile compounds analysis in muscle foods: A review. TrAC - Trends Anal. Chem. **126**, 115877 (2020). https://doi.org/10.1016/j.trac.2020.115877

16. Oates, M.J., Fox, P., Sanchez-Rodriguez, L., Carbonell-Barrachina, Á.A., Ruiz-Canales, A.: DFT based classification of olive oil type using a sinusoidally heated, low cost electronic nose. Comput. Electron. Agric. **155**, 348–358 (2018). https://doi.org/10.1016/j.compag.2018. 10.026

17. Oates, M.J., Abu-Khalaf, N., Molina-Cabrera, C., Ruiz-Canales, A., Ramos, J., Bahder, B.W.: Detection of lethal bronzing disease in cabbage palms (Sabal palmetto) using a low-cost electronic nose. Biosensors **10**(11), 188 (2020). https://doi.org/10.3390/bios10110188

18. Qiang Li, Y., Jia, J.: Classification of multiple chinese liquors by means of a QCM-based e-nose and MDS-SVM classifier. Sensors **17**(2), 272 (2017). https://doi.org/10.3390/s17020272

19. Li, Q., Gu, Y., Wang, N.F.: Application of Random Forest Classifier by Means of a QCM-Based E-Nose in the Identification of Chinese Liquor Flavors. IEEE Sens. J. **17**(6), 1788–1794 (2017). https://doi.org/10.1109/JSEN.2017.2657653

20. Qiu, S., Wang, J., Tang, C., Du, D.: Comparison of ELM, RF, and SVM on E-nose and E-tongue to trace the quality status of mandarin (Citrus unshiu Marc.). J. Food Eng. **166**, 193–203 (2015). https://doi.org/10.1016/j.jfoodeng.2015.06.007

21. Qiu, S., Gao, L., Wang, J.: Classification and regression of ELM, LVQ and SVM for E-nose data of strawberry juice. J. Food Eng. **144**, 77–85 (2014). https://doi.org/10.1016/j.jfoodeng. 2014.07.015

22. Buratti, S., Malegori, C., Benedetti, S., Oliveri, P., Giovanelli, G.: E-nose, e-tongue and e-eye for edible olive oil characterization and shelf life assessment: a powerful data fusion approach. Talanta **182**(February), 131–141 (2018). https://doi.org/10.1016/j.talanta.2018.01.096

23. Ordukaya, E., Karlik, B.: Quality control of olive oils using machine learning and electronic nose. J. Food Qual. **2017**, 1–7 (2017). https://doi.org/10.1155/2017/9272404

24. Kiani, S., Minaei, S., Ghasemi-Varnamkhasti, M.: Integration of computer vision and electronic nose as non-destructive systems for saffron adulteration detection. Comput. Electron. Agric. **141**, 46–53 (2017). https://doi.org/10.1016/j.compag.2017.06.018

25. Tian, X., Wang, J., Cui, S.: Analysis of pork adulteration in minced mutton using electronic nose of metal oxide sensors. J. Food Eng. **119**(4), 744–749 (2013). https://doi.org/10.1016/j. jfoodeng.2013.07.004

26. Tian, X., Wang, J., Ma, Z., Li, M., Wei, Z.: Combination of an E-Nose and an E-Tongue for adulteration detection of minced mutton mixed with pork. J. Food Qual. **2019**, 1–10 (2019). https://doi.org/10.1155/2019/4342509

27. Leggieri, M.C., et al.: An electronic nose supported by an artificial neural network for the rapid detection of aflatoxin B1 and fumonisins in maize. Food Control **123**, 107722 (2021). https://doi.org/10.1016/j.foodcont.2020.107722

28. Wan Azman, W. N. F. S., Ku Azir, K. N. F., Amir, A.: *Classification of Odour in the Leftover Cooked Food to Determine Contamination Using Machine Learning*, vol. 835. 2022. doi: https://doi.org/10.1007/978-981-16-8515-6_63

An Analysis of Objective Function Modification Approaches in Routing Protocols for Low Power and Lossy Networks: A Fuzzy Logic-Based Perspective

Laila Al-Qaisi[1,2](✉) [iD], Suhaidi Hassan[2] [iD], and Nur Haryani Zakaria[3] [iD]

[1] Computer Network and Information Systems Department, The World Islamic Sciences Education University, Amman, Jordan
laila.qaisi@wise.edu.jo

[2] InterNetWorks Research Lab, School of Computing, Universiti Utara Malaysia, Kedah, Malaysia

[3] Data Management and Software Solution Research Lab, School of Computing, Universiti Utara Malaysia, Kedah, Malaysia

Abstract. The routing protocol known as RPL is employed in low power and lossy networks. It makes use of an objective function (OF) to establish a Destination Oriented Directed Acyclic Graph (DODAG) and ascertain the most suitable parental candidate or trip route. Nevertheless, the task of identifying a suitable OF in Low Power and Lossy Networks (LLN) is a significant challenge. The RPL was intentionally designed to possess a high degree of flexibility, allowing for the construction of routing topologies without imposing any specific routing metric or constraint. This design choice was made to accommodate the diverse range of LLN that exist. This study provides a critical overview of recent literature pertaining to the topic of RPL and specifically focuses on the many strategies aimed at enhancing OF inside the RPL protocol. The objective of this study is to provide an analysis of relevant endeavors, including the development of innovative metrics and the application of fuzzy logic techniques in the combination of OF metrics. Furthermore, this paper discusses the recommended augmentation strategies, as well as constraints and future development directions. The research community can employ the findings to gain a deeper comprehension of objective functions and improve the performance of RPL in the face of security problems.

Keywords: RPL · OF enhancement · IoT · RPL performance · Fuzzy Logic

1 Introduction

Connecting commonplace items to the web is an innovative concept made possible by the Internet of Things (IoT) [1]. Intending to improve our quality of life and keep us safe, it spans various fields, from medicine and military services to industry and smart home monitoring. Lossy, low-powered and resource-constrained best describe the tiny devices utilized on IoT [2]. Hence, an efficient routing protocol in this setting is both a requirement and a difficult problem to study [3]. A new IPv6 protocol, termed Routing Protocol for Low Power and Lossy Networks (RPL), has been suggested by the IETF ROLL working group to address the needs of low-power and lossy networks (LLN) [4].

As a promising protocol, RPL offers various benefits for tiny devices, that it can adapt to and manage shifts in network architecture and implementation, which is one of its primary strengths. It is also employed to address issues unique to LLN, such as traffic congestion [5], imbalanced consumed energy [6], and load balancing [7]. Yet, choosing the best route to the destination still represents a significant challenge for RPL [8]. Consequently, numerous research studies have addressed this concern and recommended various enhancements for the best parent/best path [9].

For advanced IoT applications to succeed, it's essential to select a path between sensors that is both fast and has minimal data loss [10]. The routing quality can be enhanced by employing a suitable objective function (OF). Yet, several scenarios, including network scalability, mobility [11], security [12, 13], and topology changes, might pose challenges for applications built on LLNs. More packet loss, shorter network life, higher overhead, and higher energy consumption are all possible outcomes of certain worst-case scenarios [10–13].

This article will focus on OF enhancements. The OF in routing protocols finds the optimum path to a destination. A good route meets power consumption, network durability, convergence speed, and connection quality parameters like ETX and PDR. The rapid development of OF attracts LLN researchers. This paper discusses the most important efforts to assess and enhance the objective function, prompted by the lack of earlier RPL objective function surveys.

This research critically evaluates OF modification methods for RPL routing service improvement. RPL should be explained thoroughly. Discussing OF modification approaches. Then fuzzy logic is discussed. The rest of the paper is organized: Prelims are explained in Sect. 2. The paper's methodology is in Sect. 3. Modification procedures are in Sect. 4. The results are thoroughly discussed in Sect. 5. Section 6 discusses directions and opportunities.

2 The Objective Function in RPL

It's one of the most important parts of RPL because it helps build the topology using the Directed Acyclic Graphs (DAG) concept and the distance vector technique to create a tree-like structure, or Destination Oriented Directed Acyclic Graph (DODAG), which regulates links between reachable nodes [14]. DODAG root and RPL routers exchange data between source and destination nodes [15]. RPL's DODAG construction process depends heavily on the networks OF. Route selection also affects network efficiency. The metrics and limitations used to establish the ideal path from a node to the root can improve or damage network performance [16].

2.1 Standard Objective Functions (oF)

RPL defines two standards OF, Objective Function zero (OF0) and Minimum Rank with Hysteresis Objective Function (MRHOF).

OF0 [17] uses hop count by default. As the purpose is to find the shortest path from root to grounded node, the optimal parent is chosen based on node rank, with the root always having the lowest rank. As topology descends, node ranks rise. OF0 keeps a backup successor in case the chosen parent fails. Depending on the linkages, the node forwards all upward traffic to the root via the designated parent or backup successor. As OF0 does not attempt load balancing, if the chosen parent cannot transfer a packet to the root node, the backup successor is used instead [18]. A node's rank is calculated by adding its preferred parent's rank to **rank_increase**, which is calculated using Eq. 1 and specified values:

$$R(n) = R(p) + RI \tag{1}$$

R(n) is the new rank for node n, R(p) is the preferred parent node, and RI is the **rank_increase**, derived in Eq. 2:

$$RI = (Rf * Sp + Sr) * MHRI \tag{2}$$

The adjustable rank factor Rf has a default value of 1, the rank step is Sp, the largest rank level value is Sr, and the minimum hop rank increase is MHRL, which is 256 in RFC6550 [19]. However, using a node routing metric will lower link quality, which is one of OF0's main downsides. Besides, an increase in retransmissions and packet loss may occur when selecting the shortest route in terms of minimal hop count if the path is unreliable.

MRHOF [20] It was created to identify the option with the lowest cost without shifting the chosen parent. Therefore, MRHOF uses two ways to do this. The first finds the quickest route, while the other is hysteresis. Hysteresis method selects a candidate parent as the preferred parent if and only if its path cost is less than the current preferred parent, minus a threshold value [21].

MRHOF defaults to the expected transmission count (ETX) metric for path cost calculation [22]. Periodically recalculating path cost keeps the network working smoothly. The preferred parent is only selected when a neighbor's path cost is updated, or a new neighbor is added to the neighbor's table. As mentioned, the hysteresis condition must be managed to replace the chosen parent and protect the offspring from a never-ending cycle of parental turnover. By default, MRHOF-ETX prioritizes linkages by ETX value, choosing paths. The links' ETX is calculated using Eq. 3.

$$ETX = \frac{1}{Df * Dr} \tag{3}$$

Dr is the likelihood of neighbor to get acknowledgment packet, and Df is probability that it reaches neighbor [23]. The traditional OF relies on single metrics, which is a major challenge for choosing the best parent and getting the best network performance. This is when a routing metrics combination is proposed to research to overcome this challenge. As per [24], In highly dynamic or heterogeneous networks, combining metrics improves routing decisions and network performance. Combining link quality, latency, energy usage, bandwidth, dependability, and other application-specific indicators gives a more holistic network picture. Resources will be better used. Additionally, offering network-condition-based routing flexibility. Metrics give RPL extensions a complete network picture and enable intelligent routing decisions that improve energy efficiency, dependability, latency, and service quality. RPL routes data in resource constrained and lossy IoT environments using many variables.

2.2 Routing Metrics

RPL was ratified by the IETF ROLL working group as an IPv6 routing protocol to meet LLN lossy link and limited node requirements. RPL supports point-to-point, multipoint-to-point, and point-to-multipoint topologies [9]. RPL updates routing topology and information using four ICMPv6 control packets. DODAG Information Object (DIO) preserves node rating and root distance before finding best parent. Second, send DAO-containing up-ward traffic to parents. Third, joinable nodes receive a DODAG Information Solicitation for DIO messages. Finally, the DAO receiver confirms receipt with a DAO-ACK message [13].

LLN have distinct behavioral characteristics compared to wired and ad hoc networks. The most notable is that RPL is being used as the major routing protocol in these networks. Because of the OF, this protocol offers tremendous freedom in choosing routing metrics [25]. Routing metrics ensure path cost evaluation and the least restrictive path selection. Certain RPL implementations require multiple routing metrics and limitations, whereas others require only one [26]. Routing metrics can be static or dynamic, focus on the link or the node, emphasize quality or quantity, etc. However, routing metrics and constraints are different. The routing protocol may consider Both of these factors when determining the best route to take. In order to avoid potentially problematic links, a routing protocol may take advantage of a routing constraint. A routing metric selects its path according to the links that guarantee a certain level of reliability.

The requirements for RPL implementation will determine which metrics or constraints will be imposed. The routing metrics also need to consider the network's dynamic nature. LLN networks' link or node metrics are dynamic and subject to change as the network functions. Here, we'll look at the residual energy as a node metric for choosing a route. The network nodes' inability to maintain their energy reserves gradually decreases their remaining power. Thus, the path calculation using this metric shift as the measure itself shifts and evolves. Both node and link metrics are explained as per [27, 28] and [29].

1. Node Metrics:
- Hope Count: a common wireless network routing metric It is deployed for measuring network path length.
- Energy: reports network node power consumption. Location and distance from the sink may cause some nodes to lose energy faster than others.
2. Link Metrics:
- Throughput: amount of data to be exchanged between nodes over the network in a certain timeframe. More throughput means better performance.
- Latency: time to transport data across the network. The latency of a network is measured in milliseconds, and lower latency indicates a quicker reaction time.

- Expected Transmission Count (ETX): checks network reliability. It shows how many transmissions the destination needs to confirm data receipt. The root is best reached via the lowest ETX path. ETX's high value shows the network's instability.
- RSSI/LQI: The physical layer may precisely set a network's signal, frequency, voltage, etc. RSSI and LQI are the most common radio link estimators. RSSI checks received frequency signals as a radio transceiver. Thus, a greater RSSI indicates a stronger radio signal and closer destination. LQI rates link reliability from 0 to 7.

3   Methodology

The main objective of this study is to provide in-depth coverage of available modifications and enhancements proposed in the literature on RPL OF. The method proposed by Arksey and O'Malley [30] and Pham et al. [31] was applied to identify the studies related to RPL OF modifications for the IoT environment. It consisted of five steps: formulating research questions (RQ), searching for relevant studies, selecting the best matching studies, organizing, and documenting data, and finally, reporting the findings.

In identifying the RQ, two major questions were set. RQ1: What is the modification approach used? And RQ2: What are the metrics combined? Keywords for step 2 of the method's database search were determined in based on the (RQs) provided, which were "Fuzzy logic OF", "Lexical OF", "Additive OF" or "Enhanced OF". The timeframe was set to include studies published within the last 4 years, 2019 to 2023. Afterward, the abstracts of the documents were analyzed, and then the search results were filtered, the shortlisted papers were discussed and summarized in Tables 1 and 2.

4   Objective Function Modification Approaches

4.1   Lexical and Additive Composition

WERTGHJ In most cases, using a single metric for OF rank computation degrades other metrics while ensuring fascinating network parameter performances [32]. Thus, this part identifies and evaluates literature-based approaches to constructing superior OF for RPL using combination methods.

Lexical Metric Method
Lexical composition in RPL combines metrics to create a composite measure for route selection. RPL uses a tree-like component hierarchy with a root node. The lexical composition of routing metrics determines the rank of each network node, which determines its tree location [33].

Additive Metric Method
As explained by [34], The additive technique's aggregated metrics are promoted by DIO messages using a predetermined OF. Aggregated routing metrics from all path nodes are in the DAG Metric Container Object. The additive composition should have this form:

$$w = (a1 * HP) + (a2 * ETX) \tag{4}$$

Noting that both a1 and a2 are values that must meet both conditions, $0 < = a1, a2 < = 1$ and $a1 + a2 = 1$.

Many studies examined the effects of lexical and additive methods, [35] proposed EHA-RPL, a composite routing technique that combined ETX, HC, and available energy (AE) using the two methods. Results showed its superior performance.

Moreover, [36] applied a lexical and additive composition method informed by learning automata to combine vital routing metrics, including HC, ETX, and traffic-related metric. Focusing on expected transmission energy (ETT) to balance energy in a network helps prevent hotspots and wasteful energy routing.

Lazarevska et al. [37] stated that the additive composition strategy is more effective in their research, which balances three metrics. The new OF defines how network nodes create pathways to efficiently and optimally route data packets. Thus, ETX, RE, and RSSI represent the best path computation metrics in the new OF (NEWOF). NEWOF improved EC and total traffic control overhead with a slight decrease in PDR.

Furthermore, [38] proposed a new OF based on combining three metrics; RE, the load metric, and ETX. Each node has the least ETX, minimum load, and maximum node RE while selecting the parent and constructing the DODAG from the candidate parent nodes. Results evaluated the proposed OF registered performance improvement by reducing PDR, the packet loss ratio and EC.

The Energy and Load aware RPL (EL-RPL) protocol was proposed by [39] to improve RPL. It used an additive route selection method with a composite metric based on ETX, Load, and BDI. The shortest path with the least traffic in EL-RPL is the one with the lowest OF value and transmits data to the DODAG root. The COOJA simulator compared EL-RPL to RERBDI and OF-FL RPL. Results demonstrated that EL-RPL outperformed RERBDI RPL and OF-FL RPL in terms of network lifetime, packet delivery ratio, and end-to-end delay.

Also, [40] Smart Energy Efficient OF (SEEOF) was designed to optimize energy consumption and network life. Link quality and lifespan EC were combined to create SEEOF for parent selection. The existing MRHOF with ETX was compared to SEEOF using COOJA. The simulation results showed that SEEOF can extend BPD longevity and balance EC while maintaining PDR.

Moreover, a new OF called IRH-OF was designed by [41], choosing RSSI for link reliability and HC for shortest path. Cooja Simulator evaluated both metrics after additively combining them. Compared to standard OF, IRH-OF maintained a PDR of over 98% regardless of network density, reduced the network's average EC by nearly 45%, and reduced convergence time and latency.

Another study by [42] proposed two new OFs, weighted combined metrics objective function (WCM-OF) and non-weighted combined metrics objective function (NWCM-OF), based on the additive combination of node EC and link quality ETX, with equal and non-equal weights, respectively, to increase reliability, maximize network lifetime, and decrease parent changes.

4.2 Fuzzy Logic Composition

Fuzzy logic is a frequently used heuristic approach to solving complex communication and computer network issues grounded in an AI process as per. The fuzzy logic method has witnessed extensive application in literature to integrate sets of information with dissimilar features. Fuzzy logic uses membership to condense numerous independent variables into one result. It classifies data using linguistic variables and determines their relationship as per [43]. The procedures required to implement the fuzzy process model are laid forth in Fig. 1.

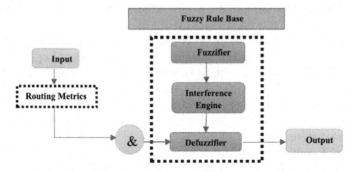

Fig. 1. Fuzzy Interference System (FIS) applied to the output metric.

- Fuzzification: to create a fuzzy set, one must first "fuzzify" an input variable by defining its membership degree (fuzziness).
- Fuzzy inference: permits fuzzified input combination followed by output calculation.
- Aggregation: If the results are contingent on multiple rules, they can be aggregated into a single result.
- Defuzzification: converts a fuzzy result to a definitive number.

It was mentioned by [44], Fuzzy logic allows for more sophisticated decisions. Where a third option is a medium ground between True and False. It works effectively in IoT by considering numerous metrics in a dynamic node deployment context. Fuzzy-based OF(F-OF) was proposed, which included HC, ETX, and RE, improved throughput by 15% and PDR by 14% without reducing energy utilization.

Also, a new fuzzy logic OF called (OF-EC) was designed by [6] that combined link and node metrics, especially ETX, HC, and EC, to overcome single-metric limitations. Simulations showed that the novel OF-EC outperforms MRHOF, ENTOT, and OF-FUZZY in PDR, network lifetime, convergence time, latency, overhead, and EC. OF-EC maintained RPL's efficiency regardless of network structure or distance. An opportunistic fuzzy logic based OF (OPP-FL) that accounted for the neighbor load was proposed by [45]. Children Number (CN) was added to the IETF ROLL routing metrics along with ETX and HC metrics. The simulation results revealed that a fuzzy logic-based OF had greater PDR and acceptable delay when the network size expanded without causing substantial traffic overhead compared to MRHOF and OF-EC.

As per [46] rapid internode connectivity, low energy usage, and reliable data delivery are signs of improved QoS. Considering this, RPL-FZ fuzzy logic OF has been proposed to make routing decisions based on RE, Delay, and ETX. Fuzzy logic combines metrics into quality, which all neighbor nodes can use. The nearest neighbor with the highest quality value is picked as the ideal parent to send sensed data to the collection unit. COOJA simulations and RPL-FZ integration were done. RPL-FZ outperformed OF0 and MRHOF by 7% in PDR, 8% in EC, and 8% in delay.

A Combined Metric OF(COM-OF) was proposed by [47], by which several key metrics were integrated to create a load-balanced DODAG to distribute traffic load evenly among nodes and extend network lifetime. The estimated lifetime, number of children, EC, and link reliability were investigated. The Cooja simulator compared COM-OF to OF0 and MRHOF. COM-OF surpassed OF0 and MRHOF by 33% EC reduction, 97% PDR increase, and 45% network lifespan extension.

Furthermore, [48] created and proposed the Fuzzy Analytic Hierarchy Process OF (FAHP-OF), a soft criterion decision-making system using Fuzzy Logic and AHP as Multi-Criteria Decision Making (MCDM). This method feeds the Fuzzy system three quantitative metrics—HC, ETX, and RSSI—of a collection of possible parents to evaluate if a node should swap parents. After ranking potential parents by AHP, the highest scorer is chosen. Cooja simulator findings revealed better End-to-End Delay (E2ED) and PDR than standard OF.

Moreover, To solve load balancing, fuzzy logic and the well-known multi-criteria decision-making procedure for the order of priority by resemblance to the ideal solution (TOPSIS) were used [49]. This is done using HC, ETX, and RSSI, which are link and node routing metrics. Simulated results showed that this strategy could enhance QoS for PDR and average E2ED.

Another study by [50] Another study [50] presented ERAOF, a fuzzy logic OF for RPL. The key goal was low-power, dependable IoT data transmission. ERAOF used EC and ETX routing metrics to determine the best data transmission path. The performance investigation showed that the ERAOF improved PDR without affecting EC or network topology.

A fuzzy logic-based energy aware routing protocol (FLEA-RPL) used load, RE, and ETX routing metrics to find the most cost-effective route [51]. A COOJA simulator evaluates the proposed FLEA-RPL's effectiveness. FLEA-RP increases network longevity by 10–12% and PDR by 2–5% compared to standard RPL, MRHOF-RPL, and FL-RPL.

5 Discussion

As the previous section discussed in-depth enhancement approaches applied on OF for better RPL performance. This section summarizes papers conducted with lexical, additive, and fuzzy logic.

Table 1 lists papers using lexical and additive techniques, as most papers did. To combine metrics, ETX and Energy were chosen most. This is because energy is limited in nodes and ETX represents link quality, which affects performance. More importantly, PDR was chosen to assess the offered methodologies' performance. That's because it indicates network packet transmission success. All publications used Contiki/Cooja simulator to test the proposed OF because it is reliable for IoT and RPL research.

Research papers proposed OF with combined metrics based on fuzzy logic are summarized in Table 2. Most used metrics were HC, ETX and energy either EC or RE, while RSSI and HC metrics were used in fuzzy logic combination studies more than lexical and additive ones. Almost all papers used PDR to evaluate the proposed fuzzy logic OF and E2ED were used for the same purpose more than studies of lexical and additive approaches. Again, the Cooja simulator was the chosen tool to test the proposed work just as in lexical and additive papers.

Table 1. Summary of papers for Lexical and Additive Composition

Ref	Combined metrics	Evaluation Metrics
[35]	ETX, HC, and AE	EC, NL, and PDR
[36]	HC, ETX, and ETT	Overhead
[37]	ETX, RE and RSSI	EC, total traffic control overhead and PDR
[38]	RE, load and ETX	PDR, the packet loss ratio and EC
[39]	ETX, Load, and BDI	Network lifetime, PDR, and E2ED
[40]	Link quality and EC	PDR, EC and lifetime
[41]	RSSI and HC	PDR, EC and latency
[42]	EC and ETX	Reliability, Network lifetime and parent changes

Table 2. Summary of papers for Fuzzy Logic Composition

Ref	Combined metrics	Evaluation Metrics
[44]	HC, ETX and RE	Throughput and PDR
[6]	ETX, HC, and EC	PDR, network lifetime, convergence time, latency, overhead, and EC
[45]	ETX and HC	PDR and delay
[46]	RE, Delay, and ETX	PDR, EC and delay
[47]	Node's lifetime, Children number, Node's EC, and Reliability of its links	PDR, EC and network lifetime
[48]	HC, ETX, and RSSI	E2ED and PDR
[49]	HC, ETX, and RSSI	E2ED and PDR
[50]	EC and ETX	PDR and EC
[51]	Load, RE, and ETX	Network lifetime and PDR

6 Opportunities and Future Work

Most of the enhancement approaches mentioned above were subject to combining two or a maximum of three metrics, and most of them were used in the basic RPL OF, OF0 and MRHOF. Yet, approaches like fuzzy logic might be exploited to include further metrics on multiple levels to improve RPL basic functions such as parent selection. Most importantly, improvements on OF were conducted in terms of load balancing and Quality of services (QoS), while other critical aspects were not studied, discussed, or examined, such as security, which forms one of the most vital challenges facing RPL.

7 Conclusion

As the core of the RPL routing function, this study focused on OF RPL improvement efforts. First, an overview of the RPL protocol's architecture, DODAG construction, and various traffic patterns was presented. Then, the actions of researchers to improve the RPL protocol were discussed thoroughly. An analysis of collected publications addressing significant RPL OF enhancements was considered. Then categorized into lexical, additive, and fuzzy logic-based approaches for metrics-combination-based OF, which is the prevalent technique. Also, the necessity for future research was stressed to concentrate on the security challenge of RPL and their actual implementation and experimentation.

Acknowledgement. This research was supported by the Ministry of Higher Education (MoHE) through the Fundamental Research Grant Scheme (Ref: FRGS/1/2020/ICT03/UUM/02/1). The content of this article is solely the responsibility of the authors and does not necessarily represent the official views of MoHE, Malaysia. The authors would also like to extend their gratitude to the Data Management & Software Solution Research Lab, School of Computing, Universiti Utara Malaysia for their generous support in sponsoring the publication of this article.

References

1. Lin, J., Yu, W., Zhang, N., Yang, X., Zhang, H., Zhao, W.: A survey on Internet of Things: architecture, enabling technologies, security and privacy, and applications. IEEE Internet Things J. **4**, 1125–1142 (2017). https://doi.org/10.1109/JIOT.2017.2683200
2. Díaz, M., Martín, C., Rubio, B.: State-of-the-art, challenges, and open issues in the integration of Internet of things and cloud computing. J. Netw. Comput. Appl. **67**, 99–117 (2016). https://doi.org/10.1016/j.jnca.2016.01.010
3. Tasneem, B., Wahid, M.: A review of secure routing challenges in low power and lossy networks. In: 2021 International Conference on Communication Technologies (ComTech), pp. 120–125. IEEE (2021). https://doi.org/10.1109/ComTech52583.2021.9616966
4. Krishna, G.G., Krishna, G., Bhalaji, N.: Analysis of routing protocol for low-power and lossy networks in IoT real time applications. Procedia Comput. Sci. **87**, 270–274 (2016). https://doi.org/10.1016/j.procs.2016.05.160
5. Musaddiq, A., Zikria, Y.B., Zulqarnain, Kim, S.W.: Routing protocol for Low-Power and Lossy Networks for heterogeneous traffic network. EURASIP J. Wirel. Commun. Netw. **2020**, 21 (2020). https://doi.org/10.1186/s13638-020-1645-4
6. Lamaazi, H., Benamar, N.: OF-EC: a novel energy consumption aware objective function for RPL based on fuzzy logic. J. Netw. Comput. Appl. **117**, 42–58 (2018). https://doi.org/10.1016/j.jnca.2018.05.015
7. Qasem, M., Al-Dubai, A., Romdhani, I., Ghaleb, B., Gharibi, W.: A new efficient objective function for routing in Internet of Things paradigm. In: 2016 IEEE Conference on Standards for Communications and Networking (CSCN), pp. 1–6. IEEE (2016). https://doi.org/10.1109/CSCN.2016.7785168
8. Kim, H.-S., Ko, J., Culler, D.E., Paek, J.: Challenging the IPv6 routing protocol for low-power and lossy networks (RPL): a survey. IEEE Commun. Surv. Tutorials. **19**, 2502–2525 (2017). https://doi.org/10.1109/COMST.2017.2751617

9. Kharrufa, H., Al-Kashoash, H.A.A., Kemp, A.H.: RPL-based routing protocols in IoT applications: a review. IEEE Sens. J. **19**, 5952–5967 (2019). https://doi.org/10.1109/JSEN.2019.2910881

10. Kassab, W., Darabkh, K.A.: A-Z survey of Internet of Things: architectures, protocols, applications, recent advances, future directions and recommendations. J. Netw. Comput. Appl. **163**, 102663 (2020). https://doi.org/10.1016/j.jnca.2020.102663

11. Jeong, S., Park, E., Woo, D., Kim, H.-S., Paek, J., Bahk, S.: MAPLE: mobility support using asymmetric transmit power in low-power and lossy networks. J. Commun. Netw. **20**, 414–424 (2018). https://doi.org/10.1109/JCN.2018.000057

12. Muzammal, S.M., Murugesan, R.K., Jhanjhi, N.Z.: A comprehensive review on secure routing in Internet of Things: mitigation methods and trust-based approaches. IEEE Internet Things J. **8**, 4186–4210 (2021). https://doi.org/10.1109/JIOT.2020.3031162

13. Al-Qaisi, L., Hassan, S., Zakaria, N.H.B.: Secure routing protocol for low power and lossy networks against rank attack: a systematic review. Int. J. Adv. Comput. Sci. Appl. **13** (2022). https://doi.org/10.14569/IJACSA.2022.0130539

14. Sobral, J.V.V., Rodrigues, J.J.P.C., Rabêlo, R.A.L., Al-Muhtadi, J., Korotaev, V.: Routing protocols for low power and lossy networks in Internet of Things applications. Sensors **19**, 2144 (2019). https://doi.org/10.3390/s19092144

15. Sankar, S., Srinivasan, P., Luhach, A.K., Somula, R., Chilamkurti, N.: Energy-aware grid-based data aggregation scheme in routing protocol for agricultural internet of things. Sustain. Comput. Inf. Syst. **28**, 100422 (2020). https://doi.org/10.1016/j.suscom.2020.100422

16. Kamgueu, P.O., Nataf, E., Ndie, T.D.: Survey on RPL enhancements: a focus on topology, security and mobility. Comput. Commun. **120**, 10–21 (2018). https://doi.org/10.1016/j.comcom.2018.02.011

17. Thubert, P.: Objective Function Zero for the Routing Protocol for Low-Power and Lossy Networks (RPL). https://www.rfc-editor.org/rfc/rfc6552

18. Onwuegbuzie, I.U., Razak, S.A., Isnin, I.F.: Control messages overhead impact on destination oriented directed acyclic graph—a wireless sensor networks objective functions performance comparison. J. Comput. Theor. Nanosci. **17**, 1227–1235 (2020). https://doi.org/10.1166/jctn.2020.8794

19. Winter, T., et al.: RPL: IPv6 routing protocol for low-power and lossy networks. https://www.rfc-editor.org/rfc/rfc6550.html

20. Gnawali, O., Levis, P.: The minimum rank with hysteresis objective function. https://www.rfc-editor.org/rfc/rfc6719.html?theme=2019

21. Manvi, S., Shobha, K.R., Vastrad, S.: Performance analysis of routing protocol for low power and lossy networks (RPL) for IoT environment (2023).https://doi.org/10.1007/978-3-031-24848-1_25

22. Cyriac, R., Durai, M.A.S.: RPL enhancement with mobility-aware two-stage objective function for improving network lifetime in IoT. Int. J. Electron. Bus. **17**, 244 (2022). https://doi.org/10.1504/IJEB.2022.124325

23. Jamil, M.Z., Khan, D., Saleem, A., Mehmood, K., Iqbal, A.: Comparative performance analysis of RPL for low power and lossy networks based on different objective functions. Int. J. Adv. Comput. Sci. Appl. **10**, 183–190 (2019). https://doi.org/10.14569/ijacsa.2019.0100524

24. Lemercier, F., Montavont, N.: Performance Evaluation of a RPL Hybrid Objective Function for the Smart Grid Network (2018).https://doi.org/10.1007/978-3-030-00247-3_3

25. Lamaazi, H., Benamar, N.: A novel approach for RPL assessment based on the objective function and trickle optimizations. Wirel. Commun. Mob. Comput. **2019**, 1–9 (2019). https://doi.org/10.1155/2019/4605095

26. Lamaazi, H., Benamar, N., Jara, A.J.: RPL-based networks in static and mobile environment: A performance assessment analysis. J. King Saud Univ. - Comput. Inf. Sci. **30**, 320–333 (2018). https://doi.org/10.1016/j.jksuci.2017.04.001

27. Abdel Hakeem, S., Hady, A., Kim, H.: RPL routing protocol performance in smart grid applications based wireless sensors: experimental and simulated analysis. Electronics **8**, 186 (2019). https://doi.org/10.3390/electronics8020186

28. Bisen, A., Matthew, J.: Performance evaluation of RPL routing protocol for low power lossy networks for IoT environment. In: 2018 International Conference on Circuits and Systems in Digital Enterprise Technology (ICCSDET), pp. 1–8. IEEE (2018). https://doi.org/10.1109/ICCSDET.2018.8821163

29. Hassan, A., Alshomrani, S., Altalhi, A., Ahsan, S.: Improved routing metrics for energy constrained interconnected devices in low-power and lossy networks. J. Commun. Netw. **18**, 327–332 (2016). https://doi.org/10.1109/JCN.2016.000048

30. Arksey, H., O'Malley, L.: Scoping studies: towards a methodological framework. Int. J. Soc. Res. Methodol. **8**, 19–32 (2005). https://doi.org/10.1080/1364557032000119616

31. Pham, M.T., Rajić, A., Greig, J.D., Sargeant, J.M., Papadopoulos, A., McEwen, S.A.: A scoping review of scoping reviews: advancing the approach and enhancing the consistency. Res. Synth. Methods. **5**, 371–385 (2014). https://doi.org/10.1002/jrsm.1123

32. Alsukayti, I.S., Alreshoodi, M.: Toward an understanding of recent developments in RPL routing. IET Netw. **8**, 356–366 (2019). https://doi.org/10.1049/iet-net.2018.5167

33. Ullah, R., Faheem, Y., Kim, B.-S.: Energy and congestion-aware routing metric for smart grid AMI networks in smart city. IEEE Access **5**, 13799–13810 (2017). https://doi.org/10.1109/ACCESS.2017.2728623

34. Mishra, S.N., Chinara, S.: CA-RPL: A Clustered Additive Approach in RPL for IoT Based Scalable Networks (2019)https://doi.org/10.1007/978-3-030-20615-4_8

35. Mishra, S.N., Elappila, M., Chinara, S.: EHA-RPL: A Composite Routing Technique in IoT Application Networks (2020).https://doi.org/10.1007/978-981-15-0029-9_51

36. Anita, C.S., Sasikumar, R.: Learning automata and lexical composition method for optimal and load balanced RPL routing in IoT. Int. J. Ad Hoc Ubiquitous Comput. **40**, 288 (2022). https://doi.org/10.1504/IJAHUC.2022.124560

37. Lazarevska, M., Farahbakhsh, R., Shakya, N.M., Crespi, N.: Mobility supported energy efficient routing protocol for IoT based healthcare applications. In: 2018 IEEE Conference on Standards for Communications and Networking (CSCN), pp. 1–5. IEEE (2018). https://doi.org/10.1109/CSCN.2018.8581828

38. Hadaya, N.N., Alabady, S.A.: Improved RPL protocol for low-power and lossy network for IoT environment. SN Comput. Sci. **2**, 1–11 (2021). https://doi.org/10.1007/s42979-021-00742-1

39. Sankar, S., Srinivasan, P.: Energy and load aware routing protocol for Internet of Things. Int. J. Adv. Appl. Sci. **7**, 255 (2018). https://doi.org/10.11591/ijaas.v7.i3.pp255-264

40. Shakya, N.M., Mani, M., Crespi, N.: SEEOF: smart energy efficient objective function: adapting RPL objective function to enable an IPv6 meshed topology solution for battery operated smart meters. In: 2017 Global Internet of Things Summit (GIoTS), pp. 1–6. IEEE (2017). https://doi.org/10.1109/GIOTS.2017.8016252

41. Eloudrhiri Hassani, A., Sahel, A., Badri, A.: IRH-OF: a new objective function for RPL routing protocol in IoT applications. Wirel. Pers. Commun. **119**, 673–689 (2021). https://doi.org/10.1007/s11277-021-08230-8

42. Eloudrhiri Hassani, A., Sahel, A., Badri, A.: A new objective function based on additive combination of node and link metrics as a mechanism path selection for RPL protocol. Int. J. Commun. Netw. Inf. Secur. **12**, 63–68 (2022). https://doi.org/10.17762/ijcnis.v12i1.4446

43. Zadeh, L.A.: Fuzzy logic. Computer (Long. Beach. Calif) **21**, 83–93 (1988). https://doi.org/10.1109/2.53

44. Fabian, P., Rachedi, A., Gueguen, C., Lohier, S.: Fuzzy-based objective function for routing protocol in the Internet of Things. In: 2018 IEEE Global Communications Conference (GLOBECOM), pp. 1–6. IEEE (2018). https://doi.org/10.1109/GLOCOM.2018.8647969

45. Kechiche, I., Bousnina, I., Samet, A.: A novel opportunistic fuzzy logic based objective function for the routing protocol for low-power and lossy networks. In: 2019 15th International Wireless Communications & Mobile Computing Conference (IWCMC), pp. 698–703. IEEE (2019). https://doi.org/10.1109/IWCMC.2019.8766691

46. Kuwelkar, S., Virani, H.G.: Design of an efficient RPL objective function for Internet of Things applications. Int. J. Adv. Comput. Sci. Appl. **12**, 228–235 (2021). https://doi.org/10. 14569/IJACSA.2021.0120625

47. Venugopal, K., Basavaraju, T.G.: A Combined Metric Objective Function for RPL Load Balancing in Internet of Things. **10**, 22–31 (2022).https://doi.org/10.5923/j.ijit.20221001.02

48. Koosha, M., Farzaneh, B., Alizadeh, E., Farzaneh, S.: FAHP-OF: a new method for load balancing in rpl-based Internet of Things (IoT). In: 2022 12th International Conference on Computer and Knowledge Engineering (ICCKE), pp. 471–476. IEEE (2022). https://doi.org/ 10.1109/ICCKE57176.2022.9960073

49. Ahmed, A.K., Farzaneh, B., Boochanpour, E., Alizadeh, E., Farzaneh, S.: TFUZZY-OF: a new method for routing protocol for low-power and lossy networks load balancing using multi-criteria decision-making. Int. J. Electr. Comput. Eng. **13**, 3474 (2023). https://doi.org/ 10.11591/ijece.v13i3.pp3474-3483

50. Sousa, N., Sobral, J.V.V., Rodrigues, J.J.P.C., Rabêlo, R.A.L., Solic, P.: ERAOF: a new RPL protocol objective function for Internet of Things applications. 2017 2nd Int. Multidiscip. Conf. Comput. Energy Sci. Split. **2017**, 1–5 (2017)

51. Sankar, S., Srinivasan, P.: Fuzzy logic based energy aware routing protocol for internet of things. Int. J. Intell. Syst. Appl. **10**, 11–19 (2018). https://doi.org/10.5815/ijisa.2018.10.02

An Empirical Study of Label Size Effect on Classification Model Accuracy Using a Derived Rule from the Holy Quran Verses

Ghaith Abdulsattar A. Jabbar Alkubaisi[1]([envelope]) [iD], Siti Sakira Kamruddin[2,2] [iD], and Husniza Husni[2,2] [iD]

[1] University of Technology and Applied Sciences, Al Khuwair 133, Muscat, Oman
ghaith.alkubaisi@utas.edu.om
[2] University Utara Malaysia, Sintok, 06010 Kedah, Malaysia

Abstract. Machine Learning (ML) has become more and more significant in various applications, such as sentiment analysis and topic modelling, due to its ability to handle large volumes of text data and achieve high accuracy. Thus, the accuracy of the classification model using sentiment analysis has gained important heed recently because of its potential to provide valuable insights into customer preferences and public opinions. Accuracy is largely dependent on the quality and quantity of labelled data. This study aims to manifest the impact of label size on classification model accuracy by applying a derived rule from the Holy Quran verses which focuses on the useability of binary classification with two labels and comparing the accuracy models trained on a dataset labelled based on that rule and three-labelled dataset. The results show that the accuracy of the models trained on the binary-labelled dataset was higher than the accuracy of the models trained on the three-labelled dataset. The study's findings will have implications for future research in ML models by applying the observed semantics from Quranic exegesis and analysis to improve the performance of ML models.

Keywords: Machine Learning · Sentiment Analysis · Classification Accuracy

1 Introduction

Developing efficient algorithms and models capable of learning from data and making predictions or decisions based on patterns and relationships specified in the data [1] has become a significant focal point in the realm of Machine Learning (ML). ML's capacity to handle vast and intricate datasets while streamlining decision-making processes has contributed to its widespread adoption across diverse sectors, including healthcare, finance, manufacturing, and others [2]. ML algorithms can be broadly classified into three categories: supervised learning, unsupervised learning, and reinforcement learning, each possessing distinct advantages and limitations [3].

Despite the remarkable performance of ML models in various tasks, achieving high accuracy remains a substantial challenge. The quality, quantity, representativeness, and diversity of data used for training are key factors influencing ML models' accuracy [4,

N. H. Zakaria et al. (Eds.): ICOCI 2023, CCIS 2001, pp. 248–259, 2024.
https://doi.org/10.1007/978-981-99-9589-9_19

5]. Inadequate or biased data, along with insufficient label size, can lead to model under-fitting or overfitting, resulting in poor generalization and low accuracy on unseen data [4–7]. Accuracy plays a crucial role in classification models as it assesses the model's ability to accurately assign the correct label or class to new data. Misclassification in real-world applications can result in serious consequences, such as financial losses or harm to individuals, underscoring the significance of high accuracy [8, 9]. To ensure the effectiveness and reliability of classification models, achieving high accuracy is of utmost importance. As a result, researchers and practitioners continuously explore novel techniques and approaches, such as data preprocessing, feature selection, model selection, and labelling processes, among others, to enhance classification models' accuracy [10, 11]. The accuracy of a classification model can be significantly influenced by the label or target variable's size.

As previously mentioned, using varying numbers of labels, such as two, three, or multiple labels on the same dataset, can have different impacts on classification accuracy. Notably, the utilization of binary labels has been demonstrated to enhance classification model accuracy compared to three-labelled datasets. This finding is supported by a rule derived from specific Quranic verses, which highlight the existence of only two classes for every word: positive and negative, without any additional categories. The relevant verses are 24 and 26 of Surah Ibrahim in the Quran (14:24 and 26) (Translation by [12]):

أَلَمْ تَرَ كَيْفَ ضَرَبَ اللّٰهُ مَثَلًا كَلِمَةً طَيِّبَةً كَشَجَرَةٍ طَيِّبَةٍ أَصْلُهَا ثَابِتٌ وَفَرْعُهَا فِي السَّمَاءِ (24)

Have you not considered how Allah presents an example, [making] a good word like a good tree, whose root is firmly fixed and its branches [high] in the sky (24).

وَمَثَلُ كَلِمَةٍ خَبِيثَةٍ كَشَجَرَةٍ خَبِيثَةٍ اجْتُثَّتْ مِن فَوْقِ الْأَرْضِ مَا لَهَا مِن قَرَارٍ (26)

And the example of a bad word is like a bad tree, uprooted from the surface of the earth, not having any stability (26).

In the context of data science and ML, this analogy emphasizes the importance of utilizing high-quality labelled data in classification tasks. Binary labels, in particular, simplify the classification task, reduce noise and ambiguity in the labelled data, and consequently lead to higher accuracy in ML models. The Quranic verses provide compelling semantic insights into the significance of data quality and label quantity in classification tasks, thereby suggesting the potential benefits of incorporating binary labels in ML models.

This study leverages the semantic meanings extracted from the aforementioned Quranic verses to compare the performance of classification models using binary and three labels on the exact dataset. The evaluation takes into account various factors, such as class distribution, data quality, and the complexity of classification problems. The primary focus of this study is to assess the performance of models in terms of their accuracy, precision, and recall.

From a standpoint of contribution and uniqueness, this study presents an innovative method for examining how the number of labels affects classification accuracy. Specifically, the practical application of semantic interpretations extracted from verses in the Holy Quran supports the notion that words can be classified into just two categories: positive and negative. This approach offers a fresh perspective on the matter and emphasizes the potential of incorporating semantic interpretations from Holy Quran verses into data science and ML research.

2 Literature Review

In this section, an overview of recent studies concerning the utilization of binary and multi-label datasets in ML classification models is presented. Labelling features constitutes a common practice in classification models, and the effectiveness of these feature labels in enhancing the accuracy of various classifiers has been the subject of several investigations. To offer a comprehensive review of the current state of research, the section summarizes recent studies that employed widely adopted ML techniques, including Naive Bayes (NB), Support Vector Machines (SVM), and Decision Trees (DT), to assess the efficacy of binary labelled datasets in comparison to datasets with three or more labels.

2.1 Overview

Understanding the impact of label size on text classification model accuracy holds significance for several reasons. Firstly, it aids in optimizing resource allocation by determining the minimal labelled data required to attain a desired level of accuracy. This is crucial, as labelling substantial data volumes can be both time-consuming and costly. Secondly, it assists in assessing model generalizability and detecting potential biases or errors. Models trained on a limited set of labelled data may fail to fully represent the diversity and intricacy of the target domain. Understanding the relationship between label size and model accuracy empowers researchers and practitioners to evaluate model generalizability [13, 14]. Furthermore, it enables them to pinpoint methods for enhancing model performance by selecting the most effective training data and refining the model architecture. This holds particular importance in the realm of text classification models, extensively employed in applications such as sentiment analysis and spam filtering. Lastly, comprehending this relationship contributes to the development and refinement of theories regarding text classification's nature and the factors influencing model performance. Such insights can lead to fresh discoveries within the broader domains of Natural Language Processing (NLP) and ML [13, 14].

This study investigates how the size of labels affects the accuracy of text classification models. This exploration holds significance as it can guide decisions regarding the requisite amount of labelled data for efficient training of text classifiers. The existing understanding of this subject is encapsulated in the literature review, which scrutinizes prior research endeavors in this domain. Subsection 2.2 subsequently conducts an in-depth analysis of each study, encompassing their headings, goals, theoretical underpinnings, methodologies, outcomes, and conclusions, along with offering insights and recommendations derived from these studies.

2.2 Related Work

The research by Shamantha, Shetty, and Rai [15] focuses on conducting sentiment analysis of tweets and reviews shared on Twitter. Its objective is to categorize opinions expressed in the text as positive, negative, or neutral. ML classifiers, including Naïve Bayes, Random Forest, and Support Vector Machine (SVM), are employed to assess sentiments using specific keywords. The theoretical framework of this work is rooted in sentiment analysis, a subset of natural language processing (NLP). The methodology blends techniques from NLP and ML to carry out sentiment analysis, involving the identification of particular keywords in tweets and reviews to discern expressed sentiment. Classifier performance is measured in terms of accuracy, precision, and processing time. Additionally, feature selection is applied to pinpoint the most relevant aspects for sentiment analysis.

The results indicate that the NB Classifier outperforms the other two classifiers in both accuracy and speed. Moreover, concerning sentiment model performance, the study suggests that employing binary labels for sentiment analysis of tweets or reviews can be a beneficial approach for gauging overall sentiment as it simplifies classification and reduces complexity. Similarly, with binary labels, text sentiment can be categorized as either positive or negative, facilitating result interpretation. Additionally, binary labels prove valuable when text sentiment isn't distinctly positive or negative, enabling a more nuanced sentiment analysis.

As well, Wang and Wang [16] emphasize the need to safeguard plant biodiversity, which necessitates the identification of plant species. However, traditional plant species identification is challenging for the general public and even experts. In response, the study presents a few-shot learning method for leaf classification with a small sample size based on the Siamese network framework. The neural network architecture in this study consists of two identical subnetworks that share weights and distinguish between similar and dissimilar inputs. To extract features from two distinct images, a Siamese network structure is used, involving a parallel two-way Convolutional Neural Network (CNN). The learned metric space is then used for leaf classification with a K-Nearest Neighbor (KNN) classifier. The loss function used to generate this metric space aims to place analogous leaf samples close together and different leaf samples far apart. Additionally, the study proposes a Spatial Structure Optimizer (SSO) method to enhance leaf classification accuracy.

The proposed method is evaluated on three datasets (Flavia, Swedish, and Leafsnap). Despite the limited size of supervised samples, it achieves high classification accuracy. The proposed method's effectiveness is evaluated using the average classification accuracy as a performance metric and it achieves high accuracy with a small size of supervised samples. The use of the SSO method further enhances the accuracy of leaf classification. However, the study does not provide a comparison of the proposed method with other state-of-the-art methods for leaf classification, which may limit its applicability. Despite this limitation, the proposed method shows promise as a solution for leaf classification with a small sample size. The use of binary labels in the Siamese network suggests a recommendation for future studies.

Similarly, in their study, Xiao, Huang, Chen, and Jing [17] present a Label-Specific Attention Network (LSAN) for multi-label text classification, a crucial task in text mining that involves categorizing a single document into several topics. The LSAN utilizes label semantic information to establish the semantic relationship between labels and documents, creating label-specific document representations. The self-attention mechanism identifies label-specific document representations using document content information. An adaptive fusion strategy seamlessly integrates these two components, creating comprehensive label-specific document representations that can be used to build multi-label text classifiers.

The LSAN is presented as a theoretical framework that constructs label-specific document representations using label semantic information and establishes a semantic connection between labels and documents. The self-attention mechanism identifies label-specific document representations using document content information. The adaptive fusion strategy seamlessly integrates the two components, creating comprehensive label-specific document representations that can be used to build multi-label text classifiers. The LSAN methodology involves extracting label-related elements from each document using both document content and label texts and adaptively extracting relevant information from both aspects. The classification model can be trained using the fused label-specific document representations. The study provides a detailed explanation of the LSAN architecture and the training process.

In terms of performance, the LSAN beats the state-of-the-art methods on four different datasets, especially on the prediction of low-frequency labels using binary labels.

Moreover, Alrehili and Albalawi [18] have highlighted the importance of customer reviews in e-commerce and online shopping. Specifically, they aimed to conduct sentiment analysis on a set of customer reviews gathered from Amazon. The sentiment analysis approach employed classified each review into either a positive or negative class. To achieve greater accuracy in classification, the study utilized an ensemble ML method called the Voting algorithm, which combined the results of five different classifiers. To assess the proposed model against five classifiers, we tested six different scenarios using unigram, bigram, and trigram models, both with and without stop word removal. The study's theoretical framework centers on sentiment analysis, entailing the categorization of customer reviews as either positive or negative. The methodology employed involved gathering customer reviews from Amazon and applying the Voting algorithm, an ensemble ML technique, to classify each review. This research aimed to offer insights into the significance of customer reviews in online shopping and e-commerce.

The voting algorithm blends five distinct classifiers, namely NB, SVM, Random Forest, Bagging, and Boosting, to enhance the accuracy of classifying customer reviews. The research reveals that ensemble ML techniques, with particular emphasis on the Voting algorithm, prove highly proficient in discerning positive and negative customer feedback. By combining the results of these classifiers, the Voting algorithm achieves higher accuracy in classification. The study shows that using the Random forest technique with unigram and stop word removal provides the highest accuracy rate of 89.87%. However, in other scenarios, the Voting algorithm outperforms other methods. The research focuses on binary labels, which categorize customer reviews as either positive or negative. The ensemble ML approach aims to classify each review into one of these two categories. Based on the study's experiments, the ensemble ML method, particularly the Voting algorithm, is suggested for accurate classification of customer reviews as positive or negative.

Likewise, Hartmann, Huppertz, Schamp, and Heitmann [19] discuss the growth of unstructured text data on online social media platforms and the need for methods to automatically classify this data at large scales. The study compares the performance of ten different approaches for automatically classifying unstructured text data, including five lexicon-based methods and five ML algorithms. The study covers 41 social media datasets from various platforms, sample sizes, and languages. The goal is to determine which methods perform best in terms of correctly identifying sentiment and other researcher-defined content categories. The study describes the methods used to compare the performance of different approaches for automatically classifying unstructured text data from social media platforms. The authors used a variety of datasets from different social media platforms, sample sizes, and languages to evaluate the performance of five lexicon-based methods and five ML algorithms. The study provides a detailed description of the methods used to preprocess the data, train, and test the models, and evaluate their performance. The authors also discuss the limitations of their study and suggest directions for future research.

After conducting the study, the results indicate that the random forest or NB algorithms were the most effective in correctly uncovering human intuition for all tasks using binary labelled datasets. In contrast, the SVM algorithm never performed better than the other methods. Furthermore, the lexicon-based approaches, especially Linguistic Inquiry and Word Count, were not as successful as ML methods in terms of performance.

Correspondingly, Farisi, Sibaroni, and Al Faraby [20] conducted a study on classifying hotel reviews as positive or negative. They emphasized the importance of online reviews in the tourism industry and compared different models using preprocessing, feature extraction, and feature selection to achieve the best results. The study is based on the Multinomial NB Classifier method, which is a probabilistic algorithm used for text classification. They collected hotel reviews from various online sources and preprocessed the data by removing stop words, stemming, and converting the text to lowercase. The authors used different feature extraction and selection techniques to represent the text data and select the most relevant features for classification.

They evaluated the performance of the different models using metrics such as accuracy, precision, recall, and F1-score, and achieved the best results using preprocessing and feature selection with 10-fold cross-validation, with an average F1-score of over 91%. The study concluded that the use of binary labels is recommended for classifying hotel reviews, and the Multinomial NB Classifier method was effective in distinguishing between positive and negative reviews.

Furthermore, Saifullah, Fauziyah, and Aribowo [21] examine the impact of the COVID-19 pandemic, which has caused anxiety and uncertainty for everyone, including the government and the community in Indonesia. The study aims to detect anxiety in social media comments related to government programs for dealing with the pandemic using machine learning. However, the study is based on the concept of sentiment analysis, which is a common approach used in NLP to identify and extract subjective information from text. In addition, it discusses the use of ML methods, which are widely used in sentiment analysis tasks. Therefore, the theoretical framework of this study can be considered as the combination of sentiment analysis and ML.

The study utilized six ML methods, which were K-NN, Bernoulli, DT Classifier, Support Vector Classifier, Random Forest, and XG-Boost. YouTube comments were crawled to gather the data sample, and the ML methods were processed using count-vectorization and TF-IDF for feature extraction. Results indicated that the Random Forest method with feature extraction of vectorization count and TF-IDF was the most accurate in detecting anxiety with an accuracy rate of 84.99% and 82.63%, respectively. Furthermore, binary labels (negative and positive) were recommended for identifying anxiety in social media comments related to government programs aimed at dealing with the COVID-19 pandemic.

Also, Onan [22] investigates the utilization of Massive Open Online Courses (MOOCs) in distance education and proposes an effective sentiment classification scheme for MOOC reviews. The study employs both ensemble learning and deep learning paradigms to achieve superior predictive performance. It evaluates the performance of various traditional supervised, ensemble, and deep learning methods, as well as different text representation and word-embedding schemes for sentiment analysis on MOOC evaluations. Additionally, the study provides a detailed analysis of a corpus containing 66,000 MOOC reviews.

Indeed, they found that deep learning-based architectures outperformed other methods, with the highest accuracy reached by using long short-term memory networks in conjunction with the GloVe word-embedding scheme-based representation, with a classification accuracy of 95.80%. Finally, the study recommends using binary labels for sentiment classification in MOOC reviews. The researchers used binary labels to classify each review as either positive or negative sentiment and achieved high predictive performance using deep learning-based architectures.

In summary, the reviewed studies indicate that binary labels prove highly advantageous for specific classification tasks. Hence, it is advisable to employ binary labelling whenever feasible. Binary labelling is favoured over using three or more classes as it consistently yields more precise and dependable outcomes. Additionally, it streamlines the classification process and minimizes computational expenses, enhancing efficiency, particularly with extensive datasets. Nonetheless, it remains crucial to assess the unique demands and attributes of each classification task before selecting the appropriate labelling strategy.

3   Experimental Design and Implementation

The goal of this study is to empirically explore the influence of label size on the accuracy of classification models. This will be achieved by contrasting the performance of models trained on a dataset labelled according to a rule derived from Holy Quran verses with those trained on a three-label dataset. This section outlines the experimental design and implementation of the study, encompassing the datasets employed, the classification algorithms utilized, and the evaluation metrics. Additionally, it elaborates on the measures taken to guarantee the accuracy and reliability of the obtained results. Figure 1 below shows the experimental model.

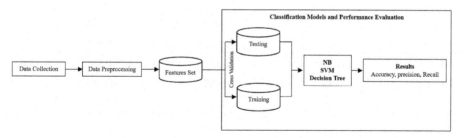

Fig. 1. Experimental Model.

The implemented model consisted of several stages, including dataset preparation, text preprocessing, feature extraction, classification, and evaluation. In the dataset preparation stage, a set of 3,000 customer reviews was collected. The reviews were then labelled first based on the derived rule from Holy Quran verses, resulting in a binary-labelled dataset (positive and negative), and secondly, based on three labels, resulting in a three-labelled dataset (positive, negative, and neutral).

Next, the text preprocessing stage was performed to clean and normalize the text data. This stage involved several techniques, such as tokenization, stop-word removal, and stemming. Feature extraction was then performed to transform the text data into numerical vectors that could be used as input for the classification model. The feature extraction technique used was the Bag-of-Words (BoW) model.

During the classification phase, the dataset underwent division into training and testing sets. Various models, namely NB, SVM, and DT, were employed for training and testing on both binary-labeled and three-labeled datasets. To gauge each model's performance, evaluation metrics such as accuracy, precision, and recall were utilized.

Accuracy signifies the model's capability to correctly classify instances across all classes. It is determined by the ratio of correctly classified instances to the total number of instances [5]. Additionally, precision measures the proportion of instances correctly classified as positive among all instances labelled as positive by the model. This metric is calculated by dividing true positives by the sum of true positives and false positives [6]. Conversely, recall assesses the proportion of instances correctly classified as positive out of all actual positive instances. It is computed by dividing true positives by the sum of true positives and false negatives [7].

4   Results and Discussion

In this section, the results of experiments comparing the performance of binary-label and three-label classification models with a customer review dataset are presented. The study evaluated the performance of three algorithms (NB, SVM, and DT) on both a balanced and an imbalanced dataset. Results for the binary-label model are shown first in Tables 1 and 2, which display all metrics for each algorithm on both balanced and imbalanced datasets. Results for the three-label model are then presented in the same manner in Tables 3 and 4.

Table 1. Binary-label balanced dataset.

Model	Accuracy	Precision	Recall
NB	0.8700	0.8719	0.8672
SVM	0.9183	0.9218	0.9149
DT	0.8467	0.8494	0.8465

Table 2. Binary-label imbalanced dataset.

Model	Accuracy	Precision	Recall
NB	0.8833	0.9123	0.8435
SVM	0.9283	0.9402	0.9209
DT	0.8567	0.8708	0.8446

Table 3. Three-label balanced dataset.

Model	Accuracy	Precision	Recall
NB	0.8583	0.8576	0.8623
SVM	0.9050	0.9037	0.9089
DT	0.8200	0.8196	0.8192

Table 4. Three-label imbalanced dataset.

Model	Accuracy	Precision	Recall
NB	0.8717	0.8723	0.8733
SVM	0.9128	0.9109	0.9205
DT	0.8222	0.8236	0.8209

Following the presentation of the results in Tables 1–4, the subsequent Sects. (4.1 to 4.4) provide in-depth analysis and explanations for the observed outcomes.

4.1 Comparison of Binary-Label and Three-Label Models

The presented results demonstrate that the binary-label model consistently outperforms the three-label model across all metrics in both datasets. For instance, in the balanced dataset, the binary-label model achieved higher accuracy (NB: 0.8700 vs. 0.8583), (SVM: 0.9183 vs. 0.9050), and (DT: 0.8467 vs. 0.8200) compared to the three-label model. Similarly, in the imbalanced dataset, the binary-label model exhibited better accuracy (NB; 0.8833 vs. 0.8717), (SVM: 0.9283 vs. 0.9128), and (DT: 0.8567 vs. 0.8222) compared to the three-label model.

4.2 Effectiveness of Binary-Label Model

The results strongly suggest that a binary-label model trained on a dataset labelled based on a derived rule from the Holy Quran verses may be a more effective approach to sentiment analysis than a three-label model. The binary-label model consistently achieves higher accuracy and performs better in correctly identifying positive and negative sentiments.

4.3 Importance of Dataset Balancing

The findings also highlight the importance of dataset balancing. Using a balanced dataset significantly improves the performance of both binary-label and three-label models. The binary-label model benefits from dataset balancing, achieving enhanced precision and recall, while the three-label model also exhibits improved accuracy, precision, and recall.

4.4 Implications for Sentiment Analysis and Future Research

In summary, this study provides valuable insights into how label size impacts the accuracy of sentiment analysis models. The findings suggest that utilizing binary labels with a balanced dataset and a rule drawn from Holy Quran verses has the potential to enhance sentiment analysis tasks. Furthermore, this study opens the door to future investigations, including exploring alternative labelling rules and examining the influence of dataset size on model performance.

To conclude, the presented results and analysis strongly validate the hypothesis that a binary-label model, trained on a balanced dataset using rules from Holy Quran verses, outperforms a three-label model in sentiment analysis. The study's findings have significant implications for sentiment analysis research and underscore the importance of dataset balancing and rule-based labelling approaches to enhance model accuracy.

5 Conclusion

To sum up, this study's assessment of classification models using Semantics from the Holy Quran verses illuminates the effect of label quantities on classification accuracy. The study's practical implications for businesses that utilize sentiment analysis imply that a binary-label model trained on a well-proportioned dataset utilizing the Quranic Semantics principle can result in more accurate outcomes and enhanced customer satisfaction. Further exploration can investigate the utilization of alternative labelling principles and the influence of dataset size on model performance to build on this study's conclusions.

In conclusion, this study's approach and outcomes emphasize the importance of taking into account Quranic Semantics in data science research. Nonetheless, it's essential to recognize that the recommendation to use binary labelling must not be employed indiscriminately in all classification tasks without assessing their specific needs and characteristics.

References

1. Choi, Y.: GeoAI: Integrating Artificial Intelligence, Machine Learning, and Deep Learning with GIS. Appl. Sci. **13**(6), 3895 (2023)
2. Javaid, M., Haleem, A., Singh, R.P., Suman, R., Rab, S.: The significance of machine learning in healthcare: features, pillars, and applications. Int. J. Intell. S **3**, 58–73 (2022)
3. Chiche, A., Yitagesu, B.: A systematic review of deep learning and machine learning approaches for part-of-speech tagging. J. Big Data **9**(1), 1–25 (2022)
4. Leenings, R., Winter, N.R., Dannlowski, U., Hahn, T.: Recommendations for neuroimaging machine learning benchmarks. Neuroimage **257**, 119298 (2022)
5. Hurtado Bodell, M., Magnusson, M., Mützel, S.: A framework for ensuring total corpus quality: from documents to data. Socius **8**, 23780231221135524 (2022)
6. Alkubaisi, G. A. A., Kamaruddin, S. S., Husni, H.: A conceptual framework for stock market classification models using sentiment analysis on twitter based on hybrid naive bayes classifiers. Int. J. Eng. Technol. 7(2.14), 57–61 (2018)
7. Alkubaisi, G. A. A. J.: The role of ensemble learning in stock market classification model accuracy enhancement based on naïve bayes classifiers. Int. J. Stat. Probab. **9**(1), 1–36 (2020)
8. Alkubaisi, G. A. A. J., Kamaruddin, S. S., Husni, H., Al-Saifi, N. S.: A GCC stock market classification model using sentiment analysis based on HNBCs. Int. J. **9**(4) (2020)
9. Raschka, S.: Python Machine Learning (3rd ed.). Packt Publishing Ltd. (2021)
10. Brownlee, J.: Machine Learning Mastery with Python: Understand Your Data, Create Accurate Models, and Work Projects End-to-End. Machine Learning Mastery (2016)
11. Raschka, S., Liu, Y. H., Mirjalili, V., Dzhulgakov, D.: Developing machine learning and deep learning models with python: Machine Learning with PyTorch and Scikit-Learn. Packt Publishing Ltd. (2022)
12. Sahih International: The Quran: English translation and commentary. Retrieved from https://quran.com/ (2017)
13. Elnagar, A., Al-Debsi, R., Einea, O.: Arabic text classification using deep learning models. Inf. Process. Manage. **57**(1), 102121 (2020)
14. Aljedani, N., Alotaibi, R., Taileb, M.: HMATC: hierarchical multi-label Arabic text classification model using machine learning. Egypt. Inf. J. **22**(3), 225–237 (2021)
15. Rai, B. S., Shetty, S. M., Rai, P.: Sentiment Analysis Using Machine Learning Classifiers: Evaluation of Performance. In: 9th International Proceedings on Proceedings, pp. 21–25. Publisher, Location (2019)
16. Wang, B., Wang, D.: Plant leaves classification: a few-shot learning method based on Siamese network. IEEE Access **7**, 151754–151763 (2019)
17. Xiao, L., Huang, X., Chen, B., Jing, L.: Label-Specific document representation for Multi-Label text classification. In: Proceedings of the 2019 Conference on Empirical Methods in Natural Language Processing and the 9th International Joint Conference on Natural Language Processing (EMNLP-IJCNLP), pp. 466–475 (2019)
18. Alrehili, A., Albalawi, K.: Sentiment analysis of customer reviews using ensemble method. In: 2019 3rd International Conference on Computational Intelligence and Applications (ICCIA), pp. 1–6 (2019)

19. Hartmann, J., Huppertz, J., Schamp, C., Heitmann, M.: Comparing automated text classification methods. Int. J. Res. Mark. **36**(1), 20–38 (2019)
20. Farisi, A.A., Sibaroni, Y., Al Faraby, S.: Sentiment analysis on hotel reviews using multinomial naïve bayes classifier. J. Phys. Conf. Ser. **1192**(1), 012024 (2019)
21. Shoffan, S., Fauziah, Y., Aribowo, A.S.: Comparison of machine learning for sentiment analysis in detecting anxiety based on social media data. arXiv: Computation and Language (2021)
22. Onan, A.: Sentiment analysis on massive open online course evaluations: a text mining and deep learning approach. Comput. Appl. Eng. Educ.. Appl. Eng. Educ. **29**(3), 572–589 (2021)

Anomalies in Mooring (Thin) Lines: Causes, Risk Mitigations, and Real Time Consequences of Failure – A Comprehensive Review

Tarwan Kumar Khatri[1,3]([✉]) [ID], Manzoor Ahmed Hashmani[1,2] [ID], Hasmi Taib[4], Nasir Abdullah[5], and Lukman Ab. Rahim[1,2]

[1] Department of Computer Science and Information Sciences, Universiti Teknologi PETRONAS (UTP), 32610 Seri Iskandar, Perak, Malaysia
tarwan_22008482@utp.edu.my
[2] High Performance Cloud Computing Centre (HPC3), UTP, 32610 Seri Iskandar, Perak, Malaysia
[3] Department of Computer Science, Bahria University Karachi Campus, Karachi, Sindh, Pakistan
[4] Floating Production Facilities, Civil and Structural Section, Engineering Department, Group Technical Solutions, Project Delivery & Technology Division, Petroleum Nasional Berhad (PETRONAS), Kaula Lumpur, Selangor, Malaysia
[5] Metocean Engineering, Petroleum Nasional Berhad (PETRONAS), Kaula Lumpur, Selangor, Malaysia

Abstract. Mooring (Thin) lines are fabricated of polyester ropes, steel wire ropes, and chains. These are considered the essential components which are used to secure offshore marine vessels and floating facilities by keeping them in a fixed place and resisting external loads. However, the failure of any mooring lines because of anomalies can cause severe consequences including financial losses, loss of life, and harm to the environment. Thus, it is essential to determine the anomalies in mooring lines beforehand to ascertain reliable and safe offshore mooring operations. This paper furnishes a comprehensive review of various types of anomalies in mooring lines with their underlying causes, and risk mitigation tactics. Furthermore, the types of mooring lines including polyester ropes, chain, and steel wire ropes have been discussed with their advantages and disadvantages. Additionally, the real-time consequences of failure in mooring lines are explored which occur due to the anomalies in the mooring lines including but not limited to environmental damage, vessel drift, and collision. In order to reduce the risks associated with mooring line anomalies, this review concludes by summarizing the major findings and emphasizing the significance of proactive monitoring and maintenance.

Keywords: Anomalies in Mooring Lines · Mooring Systems · Mooring (Thin) Line Failure

1 Introduction

Mooring systems consist of mooring (Thin) lines that are used to keep floating structures and the offshore vessel stationary in deep water during the unloading of the hydrocarbon production. These offshore vessels shape like ships or boats. The mooring lines are disseminated into polyester or fiber ropes, chain, and steel wire ropes, and such types are utilized to fix a floating vessel in one place by connecting the mooring lines to the vessel which is further anchored to the seafloor [1]. However, mooring systems are used to prevent the offshore floating structure from drifting and to keep the vessels fixed from being affected due to the external force that offshore waves, currents, and strong winds may cause. Mooring systems fall under numerous categories which are considered based on the length, floating structure type, offshore water depth, and external sea conditions. Besides, many factors are involved in the design of the mooring system such as seabed constitution, length of the mooring ropes, and the strength of the anchors and weight [2]. However, the maintenance and the proper installation of the mooring systems are critical for protecting the marine environment and keeping the vessel safe [3].

Mooring lines have great importance in the offshore marine environment and failure of any line in the mooring system due to anomalies in the mooring lines can cause severe consequences. The anomalies in the mooring lines induce a substantial risk to the safety of the floating facilities. These anomalies are posed by numerous factors that may include poor maintenance, broken wires or chains, corrosion, and loose connections [4]. These issues can lead to a loss of stability or position of the vessel or structure, increasing the risk of collisions or damage to equipment, and posing a threat to the safety of personnel onboard. Besides, if a mooring line fails due to the existence of an anomaly in the mooring systems, it can cause the vessel or offshore structure to drift, potentially colliding with other vessels, structures, or even shorelines, resulting in severe damage or loss of life [4, 5].

Additionally, failure in the mooring system can cause hydrocarbon spills, leading to environmental damage and financial losses. Furthermore, the failure of a single mooring line can result in increased tension on the remaining mooring lines, potentially causing them to fail as well, leading to a catastrophic situation. Therefore, it is essential to regularly inspect, monitor and maintain mooring lines and address anomalies promptly to prevent any potential safety or environmental risks caused by the failure of the mooring system [6].

Before monitoring and addressing the anomalies in mooring lines, it is crucial to identify the different types of anomalies in mooring lines with their causes and risk mitigation strategies [4]. However, no comprehensive review paper defines the various anomalies in different types of mooring lines except [1, 7], along with their underlying causes and prevention. Besides, no real-time consequences of failure in mooring lines have been discussed in the literature except for a few instances in [8]. Therefore, this paper comprehensively reviews anomalies in different types of mooring lines, including polyester ropes, chains, and steel wire ropes, along with their underlying causes and risk mitigation strategies, as part of mooring systems. Additionally, the paper explores the real-time consequences of mooring line failure due to anomalies in the offshore marine environment, including vessel drift, collision, and environmental damage.

Furthermore, these objectives have been accomplished by an extensive analysis of research articles, existing studies, publications, and reports associated with the various types of mooring lines and their anomalies, causes, risk tactics, and real-life consequences of line failure. However, the said comprehensive information has been gathered by searching prestigious databases, conference proceedings, academic journals, and industry reports which have been found available through online sources and other technical websites. To the best of our knowledge, this paper represents the first attempt to comprehensively review the different anomalies in various types of mooring lines with their underlying causes and risk mitigation strategies while also discussing their real-time reported consequences of failure.

This review paper is structured into the following sections. Section 2 describes the anomalies in mooring systems, their underlying causes, and risk mitigation strategies. A comparative analysis is also depicted in this section based on the advantages and drawbacks of each type of mooring line. The real-time reported consequences of failure in mooring lines are demonstrated in Sect. 3 with some examples. Finally, the entire study is concluded in Sect. 4.

2 Anomalies in Mooring Lines

Mooring (Thin) lines normally comprise polyester or fiber ropes, steel wire ropes, and the chain. Each form of these mooring lines is thoroughly discussed in the following subsections with respect to the different types of anomalies in various sorts of mooring lines, their underlying causes, and the risk prevention tactics. Properly implementing the risk mitigation tactics can prevent the mooring lines from failing and may also assure the marine vessels' reliable and safe mooring operation. Furthermore, Table 1 presents a comparative analysis aimed at selecting the most suitable mooring lines solution from among all available types, based on their respective advantages, and disadvantages in the context of mooring systems.

2.1 Anomalies in Polyester Mooring Ropes

Fiber ropes are utilized in mooring operations in a wide range because of their durability, ability to withstand abrasion, and great strength. Even so, these ropes may still fail in a case when not maintained in the right manner or if they are experienced with specific anomalies. The following subsections discuss typical anomalies by which the polyester ropes are caused to fail when the mooring operations are carried out.

Cut or Abrasion Damage. Abrasion takes place when the polyester ropes are rubbed in contact with the seafloor, other fiber ropes, or hull. It induces the fibers in the ropes to undergo scratches and wear which may result in undermining the structure of the ropes and can be susceptible to failure or breakage in the mooring rope. Abrasion in ropes can be caused by various factors, including but not limited to the rough sea, strong current, and acute edges of the surface by which the rope is rubbed [9]. Furthermore, some examples of damage in the fiber ropes are shown in Fig. 1.

To mitigate the risk of such failure, obviating contact with abrasive surfaces or rough seas is essential. Besides the ropes need to be cautiously inspected to identify the damage or wear signs. In case of abrasion is observed, it must be either replaced with new material or completely removed to assure the unity of the rope. Thorough storage of the rope aids in precluding abrasion by storing the rope on a reel or drum from being tangled and avoiding rubbing the rope in contact with other surfaces [10].

UV Degradation. The exposure of sunlight to the polyester rope causes the fibers of the mooring rope to collapse overtime because of ultraviolet (UV) radiation in the sunlight that breaks down the fibers of the mooring rope which result in deterioration of the rope strength and may be susceptible to fail [11]. To mitigate the risk of such type of failure, placing the mooring ropes away from sunlight is significant when these are not in function.

Chemical Damage. The damage to polyester mooring ropes is done when the ropes are in contact with solvent and oil chemicals which causes the fibers of the ropes to become weak and increases the chances of the rope failing [12]. The risk of such failure can be mitigated by obviating the leakage and spilling of oil close to mooring ropes. Besides, the ropes should be stored in a dry and well-ventilated area when they are not functioning.

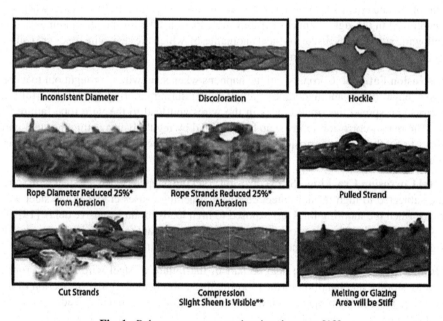

Fig. 1. Polyester rope cut or abrasion damages [13].

Knotting. The fibers in the polyester ropes are compressed and deformed when the rope is knotted. Over time, this anomaly weakens the rope and makes it more susceptible to failure [14]. The risk of such an anomaly can be mitigated by avoiding the knot that may create unneeded stress on the rope [15].

Manufacturing Defects. The structure of the rope can be weakened due to the manufacturing defects in the polyester ropes. These defects may contain wear spots, defects in the construction of the rope, or incompatibility in the fibers [16]. The risk of these defects can be mitigated by utilizing good quality mooring ropes that are constructed and produced by good manufacturers [15, 16].

Heat Damage. Polyester mooring lines are caused by heat damage which fails the mooring rope. When a rope is subjected to extreme temperatures, heat damage happens. Hot surfaces induce this anomaly, the friction generated by the motion of the fiber rope through equipping and the exposure to flames [7, 17]. It is crucial to place the ropes away from the heat origins to mitigate the heat damage anomaly in the fiber mooring rope. Besides, the ropes must be avoided in close contact with the hot surfaces and flames. In addition, it is very important to inspect the rope regularly to determine the signs of heat damage which may include melting of the fibers. To reduce the risk of failure, the rope must be replaced immediately if heat dam-age is suspected [18].

2.2 Anomalies in Steel Wire Mooring Ropes

Steel wire ropes are utilized in mooring operations in a wide range because of their durability and great strength. Even so, these ropes may still fail in a case when not maintained in the right manner or if they are experienced with specific anomalies. The following subsections discuss typical anomalies by which the steel wire ropes are caused to fail when the mooring operations are carried out.

Corrosion Fatigue. Coronary fatigue happens when steel wire is brought out to a corrosive environment and undergoes cyclic loading during mooring operations. Multiple factors can spread the small cracks in the wires and lead to the wire rope failure [1, 7]. The risk of corrosion fatigue can be mitigated by regularly inspecting the steel wire ropes to get the sign of corrosion and obviate revealing the mooring lines to extravagant loads.

Steel Corrosion Cracking. Steel corrosion cracking happens when the steel wire ropes are subjected to high tension. Steel corrosion cracking causes cracks in the steel wire ropes when the mooring lines are exposed to high loads for an extensive delay [19]. To mitigate the risk of steel corrosion cracking, it is significant to determine the corrosion signs by regular inspection and avoid disclosing the line under high tension [20].

Human Error. Humans can also be part of the failure of steel wire mooring ropes. Wrong storage and handling of the mooring lines, absence of regular inspection of the mooring lines, and improper training of the staff are the factors that may lead to problems that enhance the chances of failure in the mooring line [1]. Establishing accurate processes, inspection, and monitoring procedures is crucial to reduce the risk of human error. Furthermore, proper training and supervision are necessary for the staff who perform mooring operations [20].

Vibration. When the frequency of vibration coincides with the natural frequency of the steel wire then the steel wire is more likely to become worn out and break. Over time, the lines are caused to fail [20]. The risk of such anomaly can be mitigated by measuring the length and the load of the mooring lines properly and obviating the reveal of mooring lines to the high frequency of vibrations [21].

Environmental Factors. Exposure to sunlight that causes to generate ultraviolet radiation may weaken the steel wire mooring ropes. Over time, it may enhance the chances of failure in steel wire rope [7, 20]. To prevent environmental degradation, inspecting the mooring lines for signs of damage regularly and storing the lines in a cool, dry, and protected environment when not in use [20].

Creep. Creep occurs when the wire is under a constant load for an extended period, which can cause slow, permanent deformation of the wire [21]. To prevent creep, it is important to properly size the mooring lines and avoid exposing them to excessive loads for extended periods [1].

Manufacturing Defects. Manufacturing defects can occur during the wire drawing process, heat treatment, or quality control procedures. These defects can cause weaknesses in the wire, leading to failure over time [7]. To prevent manufacturing defects, it is important to work with reputable manufacturers and inspect the mooring lines for any signs of defects before using them [20].

Overloading and Broken Wires. Overloading occurs when the mooring lines are subjected to loads that exceed their capacity. This can cause the wire to stretch, deform, or even break. Very few amounts of broken wires in a steel rope at termination show high tension. This may be because of inaccurate fixing of the steel rope at the endpoints, managed badly at the time of recovery and deployment, some fatigue, or the due to overloading [22]. The local damage is caused by broken wires which are grouped in a neighboring strand or one strand. This is considered the worst situation when finding such a breakage of steel wire rope and this constraint can disturb the load balance that is conveyed by steel rope strands as shown in Fig. 2.

To prevent overloading, it is important to properly size the mooring lines for the vessel and operating conditions and to avoid exposing the lines to extreme weather conditions or other sources of excessive loading [22].

Fig. 2. Broken wires at wire rope endpoint [1].

2.3 Anomalies in Mooring Chains

Mooring chains are commonly used in mooring operations due to their high strength and durability. However, these chains can still fail if they are not properly maintained or if they are subjected to certain anomalies. Some of the common anomalies that can cause mooring chains to fail during mooring operations include:

Corrosion. Corrosion is a chemical reaction between metal and its environments, such as saltwater or moisture. Corrosion can lead to the loss of metal mass, weakening the chain's structural integrity, and eventually causing it to fail. Corrosion can be accelerated by factors such as high humidity, exposure to saltwater, and extreme temperatures. Regular inspection and maintenance of the mooring chains are essential to detect and address any corrosion promptly [23].

Chemical reactions between the material and the environment can cause rust and corrosion. Expanding marine life may also increase the need for new mooring lines to pre-vent failure [7]. The mooring chains are typically found with corrosion in the splash zone as demonstrated in Fig. 3 (a and b). It is very belligerent to have a corrosion rate greater than 1 mm per year by relying on the temperate of the seafloor and the quality [1].

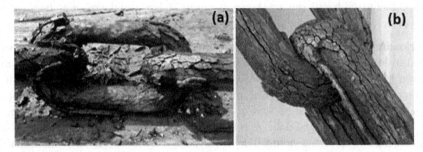

Fig. 3. Mooring chain with dense corrosion [1].

The submerged chains can also cause the prominent cavities in the top field of the water as shown in Fig. 4 (a and b). The unreasonable corrosion enhances the chances of mooring chain failure from fatigue or when being overloaded [1].

Fig. 4. Mooring chain with heavy corrosion cavities [1].

Fatigue. Fatigue failure occurs when a material is subjected to repeated loading and unloading. This repeated stress can cause small cracks to develop in the material, which can eventually grow into larger cracks that weaken the chain and cause it to fail. The risk of fatigue failure can be reduced by ensuring that the mooring chains are designed and manufactured to withstand repeated stress cycles and that the loading is distributed evenly across all chain links [23].

Overloading. Overloading occurs when the mooring chain is subjected to loads that exceed its maximum capacity. This can cause the chain to deform, stretch, or even break. Overloading can occur due to factors such as high winds, waves, or improper mooring techniques. To mitigate the risk of such anomaly, mooring chains are properly managed for the expected tension concerning their design, installation, and size to function within their great capacity [24].

Wear and Tear. Another anomaly known as wear and tear contributes to failure in the mooring chain. This type of anomaly occurs due to the friction of the chain tied to the seabed, other chain links, or the mooring chain connected to the Catenary Anchor Leg Mooring (CALM) mooring buoy [1]. It causes the materials to wear down, which reduces the diameter of the chain, loss of the metal, and finally leads to failure in the mooring chain [7].

Such anomaly can be mitigated by properly classifying the chain loads and it can be done by regularly inspecting the mooring chain to identify the signs of wear and tear in the form of reduction in the chain diameter and distortion. Furthermore, the proper maintenance and lubrication of the chain can also help to reduce friction and wear and tear [23]. In addition, it is important to monitor the mooring environment and take appropriate measures to reduce the risk of wear and tear, such as using a protective covering over the chain in areas where it is likely to come into contact with other surfaces or reducing the intensity of loading on the chain by using multiple mooring points [24].

Abrasions. Abrasion can occur when the mooring chain is subjected to contact with other surfaces or when the chain is bent and flexed. Over time, abrasion can weaken the chain and make it more susceptible to failure [7, 25]. Besides, Sediments on the seafloor can be abrasive, and friction can erode the chain when it encounters the bottom of the ocean [1].

Fig. 5. Ground touching mooring chain with one side material loss [1].

The mooring chain can also fail due to ground touching region as shown in Fig. 5 and such causes are considered seafloor abrasion [1]. To prevent abrasion, it is important to ensure that the mooring lines are properly sized, positioned, and secured to avoid contact with other surfaces [24].

Deformation. Deformation occurs when the mooring chain is subjected to excessive bending or torsional stress, causing it to deform or bend out of shape. This can weaken the chain and eventually lead to failure [22]. Deformation is caused by overloading, and environmental conditions (waves, strong wind, and current). It can also be due to not properly installing the mooring system during the operation [1, 7].

The deformation risk can be reduced by checking the proper installation of the mooring chains that will be utilized for bearing the high loads, which is limited to their design capacity. Besides, causes of deformation can also be addressed promptly by regularly monitoring the mooring chains to diagnose the deformation-affected factors and then perform the required maintenance to fix them [4].

Chain Links. Chain links anomaly concerned with the failure in mooring chains which is caused by wear and tear, overloading, wear and tear and most often it can be found due to manufacturing faults. A failure of a chain link causes the adjacent links of the chains to fail and finally result in the failure of the entire mooring chain [23].

These anomalies can be mitigated by monitoring the mooring chain regularly to confront the signs of the above-mentioned factors and fixing them appropriately through proper maintenance of the mooring chains where the faults actually exist. Additionally, assurance of the designed mooring chain, manufacturing materials, and knowing the installation base for the expected load to be borne by mooring chains can aid in minimizing the risk of failure of chain links and deformation and results in ensuring secured and reliable mooring operations [4].

Improper Handling. The failure of morning chains also happens due to improper installation and handling them inappropriately. Several examples lead to improper handling anomalies. These include distortion or weakening of the chain [23], letting the chain fall to the surface can induce cracks in the chains, and improper handling of the mooring chain throughout the storage, installation, and transportation. All of these contribute to damage in the chain and finally cause mooring chains to fail [24].

The risk of such anomaly can be reduced by following the appropriate procedures and thumb rules, including properly giving up the components, keeping the mooring chain secure, and obviating the high tension and load that causes the chains to bend over time [24]. Additionally, the mooring chains must be inspected and monitored before and during the commencement of the mooring operations to eliminate the damages through repairing or completely replacing the chains that may turn to fail the mooring chains after a long [4, 26].

Table 1. Comparison of different types of mooring (Thin) lines for effective selection.

Types of Mooring Lines	Advantages	Disadvantages
Polyester Ropes	Lightweight and easy to handle	Sensitive to abrasion and can be damaged easily
	Has high strength-to-weight ratio	Can weaken over time when exposed to UV radiation and chemical degradation
	Good shock absorption and stretching properties	Can absorb moisture and become heavier, reducing its strength
	Resistant to UV radiation and chemical degradation	Limited maximum breaking strength compared to steel wire or chain
	Can be easily spliced and repaired	Low thermal conductivity, making it less effective in certain environments
	Cost-effective compared to steel wire or chain	Not suitable for use in high-tension applications
Steel Wire Ropes & Mooring Chains	High strength and durability	Heavy and difficult to handle
	Resistant to abrasion and corrosion	Limited shock absorption and stretching properties
	Can withstand high loads and tension	Can be prone to deformation and failure due to repeated bending and straightening
	Resistant to UV radiation and chemical degradation	Expensive compared to polyester rope
	Can be easily spliced and repaired	Can cause damage to vessels and ports if not handled properly

3   Real-Time Consequences of Failure in Mooring (Thin) Lines

Mooring (Thin) line failure can have serious consequences for marine vessels and structures such as FPSOs, commonly used in offshore oil and gas production and can lead to various potential risks and hazards. Some of the consequences of mooring line failure include:

1. Loss of Control: When a mooring line fails, the vessel or structure it is holding can lose control and be subject to the forces of wind, waves, and currents. This can cause the vessel or structure to drift or even capsize [27].
2. Collision: If a mooring line fails while a vessel or structure is moored, it can cause the vessel or structure to collide with other nearby vessels or structures. This can lead to property damage, injury, or loss of life [26].

3. Environmental Damage: Mooring line failure can also result in environmental damage if the vessel or structure carrying hazardous materials or oil spills into the ocean or causes damage to underwater ecosystems [6, 28].
4. Loss of Equipment: If an FPSO breaks free from its moorings due to a mooring line failure, it can result in damage to the vessel or loss of equipment (Cargo containers). This can be expensive to repair or replace, resulting in further production downtime [29, 30].
5. Production Downtime: FPSOs are typically used to produce and store oil or gas, and mooring line failure can result in production downtime, leading to significant financial losses for the operator [6, 8].

There have been several real-life incidents where mooring line failure has resulted in serious consequences. For example, in 2013, the oil rig Kulluk broke free from its moorings in Alaska and ran aground, leading to the loss of the rig and significant environmental damage [31]. In 2019, a mooring line failure caused a container ship to collide with a dock in Taiwan, resulting in significant property damage and several injuries [32]. In addition, there have been several incidents where mooring line failure has resulted in fatalities. A tugboat overturned accidentally in the Hudson River due to failure in a mooring line in 2015, resulting in the death of three crews [33]. An incident happened in 2018 where a boat was affected due to a collision with a barge that was broken because of the failure in a mooring line which led to result in the death of two people [32]. In 2019, an incident happened in the United Kingdom in which a mooring line was broken due to high friction and load when the vessel was being moored. This resulted in severe injuries of three onboard officers during the mooring operation [34].

Besides these examples, there have been a few more real-time incidents due to the failure of a mooring line in the Floating-Point Storage Offshore (FPSO) vessel, leading to several consequences. In Brazil, the FPSO vessel underwent a failure in a mooring line throughout the strong environmental condition (storm in this case) in 2011. As a result, the vessel was caused to drift and collide with another vessel, leading to the death of nine persons. Besides, oil was spilled, resulting in production shutdown from the vessel [35]. Moreover, in 2016, the FPSO in the United Kingdom North Sea underwent a failure in the mooring line during a high storm. As a result, the vessel drifted off to the original location, leading to the consequence of suspension in production [36]. However, all these incidents reveal the importance of thorough maintenance and the requirement of a real-time accurate mooring monitoring system to perform secure mooring operations on FPSOs and other offshore floating structures to prevent and mitigate the risk of hazards linked with failure in a mooring line.

4 Conclusion

Mooring (Thin) lines are considered essential to secure offshore marine vessels and floating facilities by keeping them in a fixed place and resisting external loads. However, the failure of any mooring line because of anomalies can cause severe consequences including financial losses, loss of life, and harm to the environment. This review paper has comprehensively reviewed various types of anomalies in mooring lines with their underlying causes and risk mitigation tactics. Besides, the real-time consequences of failure in mooring lines have also been demonstrated in association with various anomalies in the mooring system. Furthermore, the three most common types of mooring lines including polyester ropes, chains, and steel wire ropes have been manifested with numerous anomalies such as fatigue, corrosion and cut or broken lines, abrasion, and extra by which mooring lines are caused to damage and finally subjected to the failure. Thus, appropriate measures are needed to obviate such failure in mooring lines. Hence, this review paper has presented the proper prevention and risk mitigation tactics to obviate damages that occur due to the anomalies and causes the mooring line to fail. Moreover, the importance of proactive inspection, monitoring of mooring lines, and maintenance to reduce the risk in conjunction with damages in mooring lines have also been highlighted. The mooring operators may determine and improve the potential problems and minimize the risk of catastrophic failure at an early stage before they intensify more crucial issues by adopting the proactive measurements mentioned in this review paper. Eventually, this review paper has focused on and underlined the need for progressive research and development in the field of marine technology to improve the safety and reliability of the critical components of the mooring lines during mooring operations. By addressing the underlying causes of mooring line anomalies, marine operators can ensure the long-term sustainability of their operations while minimizing the risks associated with these vital components.

Acknowledgement. The authors would like to extend their deepest gratitude to the High Performance Cloud Computing Centre (HPC3), Universiti Teknologi PETRONAS and Yayasan UTP (YUTP) - Grant number 015LC0-332 for provision of materials and resources to carry out this research work.

References

1. Ma, K.-T., Luo, Y., Kwan, C.-T.T., Wu, Y.: Mooring System Engineering for Offshore Structures. Gulf Professional Publishing (2019)
2. Xu, S., Wang, S., Soares, C.G.: Review of mooring design for floating wave energy converters. Renew. Sustain. Energy Rev. **111**, 595–621 (2019)
3. Minnebo, J., Aalberts, P., Duggal, A.: Mooring system monitoring using DGPS. In: International Conference on Offshore Mechanics and Arctic Engineering, p. V01BT01A035. American Society of Mechanical Engineers (2014)
4. Wang, S., Lu, P.: On the monitoring of mooring system performance. In: SNAME 21st Offshore Symposium. OnePetro (2016)
5. Soares, C.G., Teixeira, A.: Risk assessment in maritime transportation. Reliab. Eng. Syst. Saf. **74**, 299–309 (2001)
6. Jaffari, R., Hashmani, M.A., Taib, H., Abdullah, N., Rizvi, S.S.H.: A novel image-based framework for process monitoring and fault diagnosis of mooring lines. J. Hunan Univ. Nat. Sci. **47**(10), (2020)
7. Acteon Group Ltd. https://acteon.com/blog/seven-mechanisms-that-contribute-to-mooring-line-failure/
8. Lugsdin, A.: Real-time monitoring of FPSO mooring lines, risers. Sea Technol. **53**, 21–24 (2012)

9. Vlasblom, M.: The manufacture, properties, and applications of high-strength, high-modulus polyethylene fibers. In: Handbook of Properties of Textile and Technical Fibres, pp. 699–755. Elsevier (2018)

10. van der Horst, M., et al.: Improving inspection practices of offshore mooring systems for optimal integrity management. In: SNAME 25th Offshore Symposium. OnePetro (2020)

11. La Grotta, A., Harris, R.L., Da Costa, C.: Mooring sense project: a risk-based integrity management strategy for mooring system of floating offshore wind. In: Abu Dhabi International Petroleum Exhibition & Conference. OnePetro (2021)

12. Vidmar, P., Perković, M., Gucma, L., Łazuga, K.: Risk assessment of moored and passing ships. Appl. Sci. **10**, 6825 (2020)

13. MTN SHOP. https://shopmtn.com/blogs/mtn-shop-news/rope-inspection-when-you-need-to-replace-your-gear

14. Lian, Y., Liu, H., Li, L., Zhang, Y.: An experimental investigation on the bedding-in behavior of synthetic fiber ropes. Ocean Eng. **160**, 368–381 (2018)

15. Wang, S., Xu, S., Soares, C.G., Zhang, Y., Liu, H., Li, L.: Experimental study of nonlinear behavior of a nylon mooring rope at different scales. In: Developments in Renewable Energies Offshore, pp. 690–697. CRC Press (2020)

16. Spong, R., et al.: Mooring integrity issues and lessons learned database-DeepStar® project 20401. In: Offshore Technology Conference. OnePetro (2022)

17. Liagre, P.F., Ang, Z., Wibner, C.G., Aragh, S.H.: Appomattox mooring system lessons learned. In: Offshore Technology Conference. OnePetro (2020)

18. Li, W., Liu, X., Li, G., Lin, S., Li, H., Ge, Y.: Temperature and humidity effects on the dynamic stiffness of a polyester mooring rope. J. Mar. Sci. Eng. **11**, 91 (2023)

19. Zhang, D., Gao, X., Su, G., Du, L., Liu, Z., Hu, J.: Corrosion behavior of low-C medium-Mn steel in simulated marine immersion and splash zone environment. J. Mater. Eng. Perform. **26**, 2599–2607 (2017). https://doi.org/10.1007/s11665-017-2723-6

20. Shahzada, N.S.: Damage and failure of steel wire ropes. Politecnico di Torino (2022)

21. Yang, Y., Yuan, X., Li, Y., He, Z., Zhang, S., Zheng, S.: Effect of time-varying corrosion on the low-cycle fatigue mechanical properties of wire rope. Ocean Eng. **250**, 111027 (2022)

22. Hu, Z., Wang, E., Jia, F.: Study on bending fatigue failure behaviors of end-fixed wire ropes. Eng. Fail. Anal. **135**, 106172 (2022)

23. Mendoza, J., Haagensen, P.J., Köhler, J.: Analysis of fatigue test data of retrieved mooring chain links subject to pitting corrosion. Mar. Struct. **81**, 103119 (2022)

24. Lone, E.N., Sauder, T., Larsen, K., Leira, B.J.: Fatigue assessment of mooring chain considering the effects of mean load and corrosion. In: International Conference on Offshore Mechanics and Arctic Engineering, p. V002T002A020. American Society of Mechanical Engineers (2021)

25. Mackay, T., Ridge, I.M.: Abrasion testing of fibre rope on impermeable fabrics for wave energy converter systems. Renew. Energy **201**, 993–1009 (2022)

26. Zhao, C., Zhang, W., Chen, C., Yang, X., Yue, J., Han, B.: Recognition of unsafe onboard mooring and unmooring operation behavior based on improved YOLO-v4 algorithm. J. Mar. Sci. Eng. **11**, 291 (2023)

27. Necci, A., Tarantola, S., Vamanu, B., Krausmann, E., Ponte, L.: Lessons learned from offshore oil and gas incidents in the Arctic and other ice-prone seas. Ocean Eng. **185**, 12–26 (2019)

28. Nevshupa, R., Martínez, I., Ramos, S., Arredondo, A.: The effect of environmental variables on early corrosion of high–strength low–alloy mooring steel immersed in seawater. Mar. Struct. **60**, 226–240 (2018)

29. Ozguc, O.: Collision damage analysis of FPSO hull caisson protection structure. Trans. Marit. Sci. **9**, 130–149 (2020)

30. Vijayaraghavan, V.: Operational readiness and operational safety on FPSO project. In: SPE Asia Pacific Oil and Gas Conference and Exhibition. OnePetro (2018)

31. https://www.ntsb.gov/investigations/AccidentReports/Reports/MAR1401.pdf
32. freightwaves. https://www.freightwaves.com/news/oocl-vessel-blamed-for-crane-collapse-at-taiwan-port and https://www.taiwannews.com.tw/en/news/4843440
33. MarineLink. https://www.marinelink.com/news/tugboat-sinking-highlights-dangers-mooring-487044
34. safety4sea. https://safety4sea.com/cm-case-study-mooring-line-failure-onboard/
35. Vinnem, J.E.: FPSO Cidade de São Mateus gas explosion–lessons learned. Saf. Sci. **101**, 295–304 (2018)
36. International Ocean Energy Resources (OER). https://ocean-energyresources.com/2020/02/01/petrobras-p-70-floater-breaks-moorings-in-brazil-storm/

Data Analytics Modelling System for Short Courses at Seberang Jaya Community College

Zuriana Zamberi[1] and Nur Intan Raihana Ruhaiyem[2(✉)]

[1] Seberang Jaya Community College, 13700 Perai, Penang, Malaysia
`zuriana@kksbj.edu.my`
[2] School of Computer Sciences, Universiti Sains Malaysia, USM, 11800 George Town, Penang, Malaysia
`intanraihana@usm.my`

Abstract. Community College adhered to the Ministry of Higher Education is well known for its lifelong learning prospects and distinctively offers a short course about the community surrounding the institute. To date, the primary focus in the academic and industrial realms is on descriptive and predictive analytics. Nevertheless, prescriptive analytics, which seeks to find the best course of action for the future, has increasingly garnered research interest. Meanwhile, the analysis will be used to implement actionable plans to help in decision-making that can benefit the institution as well as the officers concerned. This paper investigates the problem arising by using analytical methods in elevating short course enrolment in Seberang Jaya Community College. Upon completion with the usage of Market Basket Analysis (MBA) techniques integrating the descriptive and predictive analysis, results obtained are established thoroughly with specific details that were to attain cluster insights based on the participant's interest that leads to non-mainstream courses related to the college credential-expertise program. Course modelling proposal for participants' enrolment through MBA that leads to output produced for Lift Parameter, uses specific rules that have higher lift and confidence that participants tend to join *Kursus Penyelenggaraan Komputer* (consequents) when they joined *Kursus Rangkaian Komputer* (Antecedents). In looking at the association rules, it seems that both these courses are highly considered to be enrolled.

Keywords: Community College · data analytics · lifelong learning · short courses

1 Introduction

1.1 Background

Community Colleges under the supervision of *Jabatan Pendidikan Politeknik* and *Kolej Komuniti* (JPPKK), Ministry of Higher Education (MOHE) was launched in 2001 and established as the peak body for the non-profit community that owned learning organizations across Malaysia. Community-based providers are committed to both employment and outcomes as well as the personal development of the learners.

In addition to providing accredited Technical and Vocational Education and Training (TVET), Community College offers various learning opportunities, including non-accredited training and lifelong learning. As stated by Jaafar [5], lifelong learning has resulted in the creation of skilled employees who are well-equipped to meet the demands of the industry and contribute to economic development. These educational activities help to build self-esteem, re-engage by upskilling and re-skilling the learners, and provide social networks for the community that lead to a high-income economy.

Despite all the expertise and professionals who exist in the TVET institutions, Community Colleges have a greater responsibility to spread their Educator expertise and skills related to the programs offered by the respective colleges amongst the local community and for their development that skillfully led them to the futuristic industrial revolution. Seberang Jaya Community College specifically offers programs ranging from Diploma to certificates that are Diploma in Electronics (Instrumentation) followed by certificate programs such as the Internet of Things, Electrical Technology along with General Studies as a completion of the programs offered. These programs are categorized by lifelong learning as technical courses that indicates the commonalities of the educator's expertise with the short courses offered. Subsequently, non-technical courses or non-related courses are offered to verify these elements of short courses in Seberang Jaya Community College to boost the community skills by offering a wide variety of choices.

According to the paper published by [14], the role of Community College is for Community Development. The mission of Community Colleges in Malaysia is to utilize Technical and Vocational Education and Training (TVET) and Lifelong Learning to empower local communities, creating a well-informed and skilled workforce. TVET education was seen as a pertinent part of economic evolution in Vision 2020, which was crafted by the Ministry. The outstanding feature identified in this Community College education is the short course that falls under the lifelong learning category. Not only allowed for the dropouts to take this as an alternative but endorsed the various classes of nonprofessional to professional, skillful employees to entrepreneurship.

1.2 Problem Statement

Short courses in brief can range from any field regardless of the institute chosen in the community. It has a wide range of duration, lasting from a few days to several months, and some of the courses have certain exams or training to pass. This training is well suited to several specific needs such as providing added skills to a cadre of workers at any level, upgrading knowledge and skills at low cost, and providing networking opportunities for the local community. This study focuses on the short courses variation offered and conducted in Seberang Jaya Community College which is in the Penang mainland. This part of the mainland state is surrounded by some manufacturing and industrial sectors. Hence, the short courses offered by this college are to fulfil the needs of the surrounding industries and communities.

Despite the community college courses providing essential skills development and practical-based learning, the differing durations of these courses have become a challenge to maximizing their benefits. While certain courses are offered annually, others are available only once, leading to disparities in opportunities for students. Courses that channel its educator's professional skills and in collaboration with agencies receive prominent applications from the community, but then again courses that are conducted once and don't have continuous progress to it, are proven to have limited participants. Thus, it contributes to lower enrolment annually and imparts low profit to institutions. Such limitation is seen as the biggest obstacle for the institute and its educators to attain one of the features specified in the Key Performance Index (KPI) as they are obliged to such attribution annually. Educators have trouble planning courses that can increase enrolment and benefit the college in terms of cost and attaining the KPI. Consequently, to such limitations, data analytics will be implemented to analyze the data record and to find patterns to accommodate the educators and officers in planning courses with maximum benefit in the future.

In alliance to benefit in the long term, educators must be equipped with the ability to predict the alignment of short courses in the future that will attract higher enrolment and profitability. One of the productive approaches will be enforcing data analysis for the institute's futuristic prediction with higher accuracy [9]. Through the analysis, institutes, and officers can effectively and precisely allocate resources for short courses. By utilizing the patterns derived from the analysis, they can improve enrolment productivity and cost management, resulting in increased contributions towards the personal development of both the institute and officers on an annual basis.

1.3 Objectives of Study

Community colleges have trained a large number of participants through short-term courses, and the number of participants and courses offered has increased year by year since its establishment. With the trust given by the community, the institution needs to continue providing good quality courses and services. Therefore, implementing data analytics towards the acquired data can help the institutions to predict effective courses to be run in the future.

The main purpose of this study is to gain cluster insights based on the participant's interest for five years, and adjacently proposing the course modelling for participants' enrolment through the Market Basket Analysis technique. Thus, this approach will function as a forward-thinking instrument, enabling decision-makers to evaluate the course's effectiveness in fulfilling JPPKK's annual requirements and aligning with the community's needs.

2 Related Works

2.1 Introduction

Key Performance Index, known as KPI is a measuring instrument in any private or public organization that is monitored by the superior administering the organization. This is used as one of the main instruments that adhere to the success of the program or business conducted annually. The short course is one of the community college's missions that registers "empower the community through lifelong learning" and each college is accounted for to achieve a certain number of KPIs that have been determined by the JPPKK based on the grades of Directors who administer the institution. The primary mission creation was to adapt lifelong learning and spread the knowledge to surrounding local communities by utilizing the respective College's expertise or professional technical-related skills.

2.2 Related Works

Across every industry, large data can bring new findings, and new conclusions, discover meaningful patterns, and predict future trends. Such predicament of database usage is related to Association Mining exploited in finding the correlation among the large data items that lead to the discovery of interesting relationships, especially in the business decision-making process. According to the researcher [12], in their article regarding Market Basket Analysis with Networks, typically trends in search of meaningful associations in customer data revolve in one of the oldest areas, known as Market Basket Analysis. About one of the data mining in higher education [4], stated that the association of rule mining can be used to analyze the performance of students in their examinations and predict the outcome of the incoming examination. This prediction allows students and teachers to identify the subjects that need extra attention even before the commencement of the semester. On top of that, the predictions are also helping students at the very beginning of the semester by identifying the subjects that they need to focus on.

To enhance the understanding of historical information, the approach employed in [12] can be implemented in this research to assess its relevance in current healthcare decisions and enable well-informed choices for the future. The descriptive model utilized in this context demonstrates the capacity to categorize, characterize, aggregate, and analyze data.

In this research scenario, unsupervised learning data were used where no examples or test outcomes were available. It can greatly benefit from the application of a novel algorithm based on association rule learning, as developed by [4]. The use of the algorithm is to achieve precise predictions for example in coronary illness examinations. This valuable capability makes it an essential tool for medical specialists and experts seeking accurate coronary illness prediction.

3 Methodology

3.1 Introduction

This project focuses on analyzing and querying large datasets for generating participants' analyses in short courses in KKSBJ by implementing two analytical techniques. Each analysis technique is performed to have a better understanding of the participant's behavior concurrently for the linear is to elevate enrolment of the participants in the institute. As a result, this analysis will predict the minimal and maximal short courses required according to the attainment of the Institute's KPI annually.

3.2 Dataset

The dataset employed in this project is obtained from the Lifelong Learning Unit in Seberang Jaya Community College with five years records attained from the year 2015 until 2020, however, in the year 2018 this data was excluded from the analysis due to technical problems that occurred while transferring related files. Table 1 shows the sample dataset with several attributes provided such as the name of the participants, their identification number, courses attended, the date of the courses conducted as well and the fee amount for each course. Implementing the analysis of the data can provide hidden information related to the participants to predict future business expansion to the institute.

Table 1. Attributes sample in the dataset.

Name	Course Name	Date	Fees
Ali	Bakery Course: Blueberry Cheesecake	24 January 2015	60
Shima	Bakery Course: Blueberry Cheesecake	24 January 2015	60

3.3 Data Preparation

The initial stage of the process before implementing the analysis is to unveil the error existence in the unrefined dataset, in particular the data duplicates, outliers, and incomplete and irrelevant data using Python. Each error displayed in the raw dataset consists of repetitive and identical data, irregularities of data, missing attributes, and value in the data set that is unrelated to the attributes from the foregoing errors as shown in Fig. 1.

The existing problem has been improved to achieve the objective of the study by improving the data record through the written records available in the possession of the Lifelong Learning Officer. Succeeding the data scrubbing, the total data obtained were 3264 rows consisting of a complete dataset as shown in Fig. 2. Despite the dataset acquired, new attributes were included such as gender and cluster. Course classifications, on the other hand, are predetermined according to the clusters.

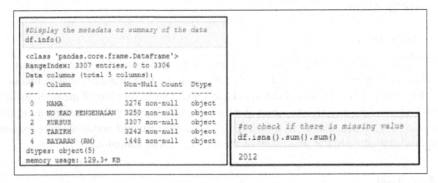

Fig. 1. Data summary with a total number of errors (before data cleaning).

```
<class 'pandas.core.frame.DataFrame'>
RangeIndex: 3264 entries, 0 to 3263
Data columns (total 8 columns):
 #   Column               Non-Null Count   Dtype
---  ------               --------------   -----
 0   BIL                  3264 non-null    int64
 1   NAMA                 3264 non-null    object
 2   KATEGORI JANTINA     3264 non-null    int64
 3   NO KAD PENGENALAN    3264 non-null    object
 4   KURSUS               3264 non-null    object
 5   KLUSTER              3264 non-null    int64
 6   TARIKH               3264 non-null    object
 7   BAYARAN (RM)         3264 non-null    int64
dtypes: int64(4), object(4)
memory usage: 204.1+ KB
```

```
#to check if there is missing value
df.isna().sum().sum()

0
```

Fig. 2. Data summary with zero number of errors (after data cleaning).

3.4 Data Exploration

Overall data after including additional attributes that will promote better analysis of the trend as portrayed in Fig. 3. The Python application for listed attributes will be queried further based on figures in terms of statistical value that will be conveyed in a visualization form such as histogram and many more in the list as depicted in Fig. 4. Complete exploitation of these datasets reveals a clear pattern/trend that will properly direct for pre-analysis based on the correlation created on the queries.

```
df.dtypes

BIL                  int64
NAMA                 object
KATEGORI JANTINA     int64
NO KAD PENGENALAN    object
KURSUS               object
KLUSTER              int64
TARIKH               object
BAYARAN (RM)         int64
dtype: object
```

Fig. 3. Data types for each attribute

Associations within the attributes by Fig. 5 indicated that a positive value that is near 1.000000 prevails strong correlation. These attributes such as number, and gender with fees show a debilitated relation due to the numerical obtained being less than 0.500000.

3.5 Data Analysis Using Predictive Analytics

Data processing at this stage is using Python and RapidMiner to transform data into Pivot Table. Data that were analyzed in the MBA containing 168 different types of courses. This technique is going to answer which course has the highest frequency or which course is to be promoted in the future.

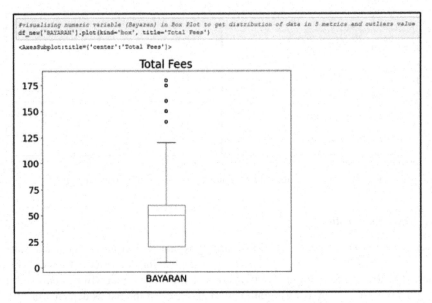

Fig. 4. An example of data distribution for fee information.

```
df.corr()
```

	BIL	KATEGORI JANTINA	KLUSTER	BAYARAN (RM)
BIL	1.000000	-0.326631	0.433824	0.053426
KATEGORI JANTINA	-0.326631	1.000000	-0.476971	-0.030802
KLUSTER	0.433824	-0.476971	1.000000	-0.194077
BAYARAN (RM)	0.053426	-0.030802	-0.194077	1.000000

Fig. 5. Correlation between attributes

4 Results and Discussion

4.1 General Statistics

The widening cluster disparity is represented by demographic trends such as age, gender, and race of the course participants which are represented in table forms. This general analysis plays a significant role in pre-determining the trend amongst the community based on specific standards and serves as a touchstone for courses incipient by their ecology. Thus, such analysis will lead further into the studies of community behavior that favors Lifelong Learning decision-making.

Primarily analysis performed starting from the data displayed in Table 2 indicates a very close number of enrolments in the short course programs offered in the Institute.

Overall, the respondent's profile indicates that the highest enrolment is amongst Malay with 92.40% whilst a trifling percentile recorded for non-Malay is 7.60% participants. This inclination serves as basic information due to the surrounding community racial population consists of Malay province in the majority. In parallel with this, gender segregation amongst the races also serves as another interesting trend for study As seen in Table 2 females from Malay race and males from non-Malay set up high percentile of enrolment is 54.19% and 61.29% respectively. This might appear as an interesting comparison but insignificant if compared with the figure attained between these races. Over and above that finding, there are many factors found that leads to participatory. Besides, these findings don't appear surprising due to the common ground of the non-technical courses towards the community surroundings are always overwhelmed by such genders. Among the profiles are gender basis that is attained between Malay and non-Malay respondents. Ensuing research analysis should be about the connection of interest amongst the race/religion with gender.

Table 2. Respondents Profile

Profile	Percent (%)
Malay	92.40
Non-Malay	7.60
Malay	**Percent (%)**
Male	45.81
Female	54.19
Non-Malay	**Percent (%)**
Male	61.29
Female	38.71

By the age basis in Table 3, it is collectively announced that the most active participation comes from the range of less than 50 years of age. Along with this data, male participants for age below 50 enrolments are 50.93% and more as compared to females which is 49.07%. Whilst results found for participants of age above 50 are shown on the contrary for the gender with female participants having the highest enrolment throughout five years with a female enrolment of 64.80% and male 35.20%. This pattern is proven that women of golden ages either retired persons, homemakers, or businesswomen, have a higher tendency to fulfil their time with short courses and thus, apply the skills attained to their daily life.

In conjunction with this, another element was triggered for a futuristic investigation of whether courses offered by the Institute caters to the need of the male participants in the surrounding community for this age category especially. Conveniently, female participants from such age groups utilize skills learned and applied at their homes such as the range of clusters such as Bakery, Sewing, Computer, and Entrepreneurship. All these clusters play a vital role in determining this gender decision-making, especially

Table 3. Demographic

Age >50	Percent (%)
Male	35.20
Female	64.80
Age <50	Percent (%)
Male	50.93
Female	49.07

as aforementioned amongst the freelancers, retirees, businesswomen, and homemakers. Hence, such demanding non-technical clusters do cater to the needs of the female participants in that age range.

Consequently, to this result, yet another investigation can be performed to find out why the non-technical courses offered are omitted by the male participants from the age above 50. Perhaps it sounded insignificant for this surrounding community that serves more as the industrial hub area, Having said that such data analysis would most probably be worthwhile to be researched in a dominant community of such ages, particularly in suburban and urban areas. In other words, they can develop systems that provide well-being for the present and future educational vision that values the Lifelong Learning across various generations.

4.2 Descriptive Analytics

The descriptive analysis technique is used to show the overall performance for short courses conducted at KKSBJ from 2015 to 2020. The main objective of the dashboard picture is to show the highest and lowest participant enrolments by the clusters during the course period. The visualization shown on the dashboard as in Fig. 6 gives a brief and compact overview of the entire data, where the highest and lowest number of participants, clusters, and courses can be identified quickly and accurately.

This technique makes it easier for the institution to understand the data and interpret it conclusively. A better decision in business is achievable through data analytics. The first approach in analyzing large-scale data is to implement data mining to have a better understanding of the historical and current business [8] besides it can summarize past data and generate some useful patterns from that data as stated by [2]. The data is summarized into meaningful charts and reports for a better understanding of overall business performance. A dashboard that consists of charts and reports is used to describe statistical data comprehensively that is related to the business.

In this project, the tools that will be used are Power BI software to find the summarization of courses to make the organization more understandable based on past and current data. This method will be used as summaries data that will be presented through various forms of visualizations such as charts to illustrate the number of annual courses that have been run, the number of annual fees, the age range of participants for high-demand courses, participants based on gender as well as cluster selection. This technique will help answer questions such as the opportunity to add courses equivalent to the course high in demand or the opportunity to produce course packages that assist participants in making more accurate choices. The analysis was made by the software used, Power BI, as shown in Fig. 6. With a complete descriptive such as the statistical and numerical data were formed in attractive visualization form. Hence, this dashboard serves as a predictive feeder providing a proper analysis and constant observation of an analyst. The dashboard display is well equipped with visualization that caters to valuable sets of information particularly the overall participation, total enrolment by clusters, and participants by courses found within the cluster every year. Each size and column of bars of the visualization represents information depending on the categories specified.

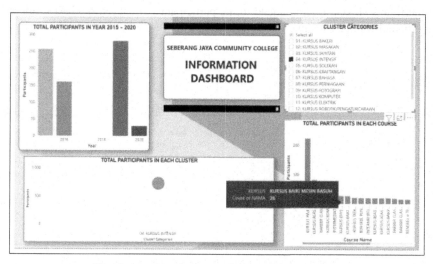

Fig. 6. Overall Analysis Report Findings Dashboard

4.3 Predictive Analytics

This method uses his Market Basket Analytics Technique where the entire course is analyzed using the appropriate algorithm. The second technique proposed by [4] is about uncovering hidden patterns of behavior of the participants using the Market Basket Analysis with Association Rules technique. This data is assumed to be in unsupervised learning as each of the participants comes to college to register, we and the participant usually do not know which course they can join. Hence, based on this, we cannot classify the participants to any of the courses listed in the record.

4.4 Parameters

In this analysis, the minimum support value that was chosen is 0.004. The reason to select the value is due to the output generated by the coding itself. We might want the result to be not too big or too small according to the total rows of overall data. Since the purpose of this technique is to find interesting rules, we may want to find an output with at least 2 courses in a row which 0.004 is the best support value to provide those outputs. The reason is to find the least course in the model to pair with any course that has been selected by participants. In this project, the length chosen is 2 since most of the participants rarely attend the other course. To attract their interest, we can suggest at least 1 course for them to take part in the future during registration. The next process is to generate frequent item sets with length value 2 with a support value of at least 0.004% as shown in Fig. 7. The Final phase is to filter the outcome based on lift parametric for at least a minimum value of 1. From the outcome, the result has 9 rows with 2 suggestions courses that consist of for instance *Kursus Rangkaian Komputer* followed by the second row that is *Kursus Penyelenggaraan Komputer.* Since the data is quite small, we can use all the results shown to recommend to the participants. However, the best result with high lift and confidence value will be referred to.

	antecedents	consequents	antecedent support	consequent support	support	confidence	lift	leverage	conviction
0	(KURSUS RANGKAIAN KOMPUTER)	(KURSUS PENYELENGGARAAN KOMPUTER)	0.005249	0.005249	0.005249	1.000000	190.500000	0.005222	inf
1	(KURSUS PENYELENGGARAAN KOMPUTER)	(KURSUS RANGKAIAN KOMPUTER)	0.005249	0.005249	0.005249	1.000000	190.500000	0.005222	inf
2	(BENGKEL e-TESTIMONI)	(BENGKEL PENYEDIAAN FRP PSH)	0.005624	0.006749	0.004874	0.866667	128.411111	0.004836	7.469381
3	(BENGKEL PENYEDIAAN FRP PSH)	(BENGKEL e-TESTIMONI)	0.006749	0.005624	0.004874	0.722222	128.411111	0.004836	3.579753
4	(KURSUS JAHITAN BAJU MELAYU SLIM FIT (SELUAR))	(KURSUS JAHITAN BAJU MELAYU SLIM FIT (BAJU))	0.007124	0.008249	0.006374	0.894737	108.466507	0.006315	9.421635
5	(KURSUS JAHITAN BAJU MELAYU SLIM FIT (BAJU))	(KURSUS JAHITAN BAJU MELAYU SLIM FIT (SELUAR))	0.008249	0.007124	0.006374	0.772727	108.466507	0.006315	4.368654
6	(BARBER CLASS VOL_THREE: ADVANCED BARBERING)	(INTERMIDIATE BARBER CLASS VOL_TWO)	0.005749	0.007124	0.004499	0.666667	93.578947	0.004451	2.978628
7	(INTERMIDIATE BARBER CLASS VOL_TWO)	(BARBER CLASS VOL_THREE: ADVANCED BARBERING)	0.007124	0.006749	0.004499	0.631579	93.578947	0.004451	2.695967
8	(BARBER CLASS : BASIC BARBERING)	(INTERMEDIATE BARBER CLASS VOL_TWO.1)	0.012373	0.009749	0.004124	0.333333	34.192308	0.004004	1.485377
9	(INTERMEDIATE BARBER CLASS VOL_TWO.1)	(BARBER CLASS : BASIC BARBERING)	0.009749	0.012373	0.004124	0.423077	34.192308	0.004004	1.711886

Fig. 7. Overall output after setting the parameters.

4.5 Outcome

From the output produced for the Lift Parameter, we can identify the specific rules that have higher lift and confidence that participants will tend to join *Kursus Penyelenggaraan Komputer* (consequents) when they join *Kursus Rangkaian Komputer* (Antecedents). Seemingly, both courses *Kursus Penyelenggaraan Komputer* and *Kursus Rangkaian Komputer* are highly considered to be enrolled together by participants.

4.6 Discussion

As aforementioned, the analysis results are based on the two objectives to attain cluster insights based on the participant's interest for five years, and a course modelling proposal for participants' enrolment through the Market Basket Analysis technique. Several principles are paramount in philosophy for Data Science Analytical research based upon the Computer Science principle. Pertinently this project's data analysis requires a series of data collection, transformation, and organization of data to conclude, make predictions, and hence drive informed decision-making. Whilst attaining the dataset from the Institute was convenient, however, some of the primary challenges faced were excessive missing values, inconsistent and duplicate data as well as missing records for one whole year's worth of dataset. Hence, the solution taken was painstakingly to allocate time for data cleaning and updating missing data by referring to written record that is kept by the officer and deleting unrelated information. Despite coping with all the data cleaning processes, in the end, attained a good dataset for analysis, though precious time went missing that could have been used for better decision-making and analysis. Likewise, insufficient data to learn or to process for analysis was another scrupulous point that arose. Though appears to be insignificant in the beginning, as the analysis of the datasets continued, the objective of this project was taken out. To elucidate that issue, the analysis proceeded with existing data and narrowed it down into certain categories. Succeeding from being able to cater to the needs of the problems faced, another foregoing barrier was faced though it is expected amongst commoners that lack of Data Science Analytical knowledge a practical place. The Institute's mentor is unable to relate the importance of using Data Science techniques to achieve the Institute's mission of Lifelong Learning. This leads to a series of show-and-tell sessions on how vital such data science analysis is and how data can help the Management Team with the Lifelong Learning team to manage their work. Likewise, proves, data analytical techniques and correlation of this project analysis were presented ahead of based on previous research and technique that related to the problem and objectives that was intended to be obtained from the research. It provides an opportunity for students to analyze data in real terms and face problems.

In the process of problem analysis, the student knows the best techniques for achieving the objectives of the project and knows the method of implementation based on the project experience made during the class. To achieve the proper objectives, the available data needs to support the work. Refers to KPI (original plan). The data available in the written record is not properly recorded in the Excel record. Demographic data exists in written records but is not recorded in Excel such as participant's information and background.

5 Conclusion

The facts discussed provide a clear picture of the real-world situation. This study is conducted to encourage and facilitate KKSBJ for the Lifelong Learning Unit. Currently, no systematic planning and analysis is carried out by this unit. With the increasing availability of large amounts of data within the institute, the outcome aims to contribute to the analytics field to enable the institute to gain meaningful insights about its performance and future. Despite that existing drawback, optimistically through the implementation of analytical data, it can unravel the vital hidden information for better course planning. This study will eradicate what formerly been practiced in the institute that applies the number of enrolments by participants. In conclusion, analytical data can boost the successful implementation of short courses in any Community College in Malaysia with higher reliability.

References

1. Ahmad, M.A.Z., Ahmad, A.A., Vasista, T.G., Sattam, A.A.: Enhancing customer loyalty with market basket analysis using innovative methods: a python implementation approach. Int. J. Innov. Creativity Change **14**(2), 1351–1368 (2020)
2. Aanchal, P.: Student Progression System Using Descriptive and Predictive Analytics. [Master in Thapar Institute of Engineering and Technology Patiala]. TIET Digital Repository. (2018). http://117.203.246.91:8080/jspui/handle/10266/5180
3. Cicekli, U.G., Kabasakal, I.: Market basket analysis of basket data with demographics: a case study in E-retailing. J. Oper. Res. Stat. Econometrics Manag. Inf. Syst. **9**(1), 1–12 (2021)
4. Gangurde, R., Kumar, B., Gore, S.D.: Building prediction model using market basket analysis. Int. J. Innov. Res. Comput. Commun. Eng. **5**(2), 1302–1309 (2017)
5. Jaafar, W.N.W., Maki, T.: Roles of community college for community development in malaysia: entrepreneurship education program. In: Raby, R.L., Valeau, E.J. (eds.) Handbook of Comparative Studies on Community Colleges and Global Counterparts. SIHE, pp. 619–635. Springer, Cham (2018). https://doi.org/10.1007/978-3-319-50911-2_10
6. Jain, A.K., Saxena, H., Bhardwaj, R.: Application of linear programming for profit maximization of a pharma company. J. Crit. Rev. **7**(2), 1118–1123 (2020)
7. Kurniawan, F., Hammad, J., Nugroho, S.M.S., Hariadi, M.: Market basket analysis to identify consumer behaviors by way of transaction data. Knowl. Eng. Data Sci. (KEDS). **1**(1), 20–25 (2018)
8. Lepenioti, K., Bousdekis, A., Apostolou, D., Mentzas, G.: Prescriptive analytics: literature review and research challenges. Int. J. Inf. Manage. **50**, 57–70 (2020)
9. Luan, J.: Data mining applications in higher education. SPSS Executive, p. 7 (2004)
10. Malaymail: Deputy Minister: Employability rate of community college (2021)
11. Polytechnic graduates in Malaysia at 98pc annually. https://www.malaymail.com/news/malaysia/2021/04/04/deputy-ministeremployability-rate-of-community-college-polytechnic-graduat/1963729
12. Raeder, T., Chawla, N.V.: Market-based analysis with networks. http://citeseerx.ist.psu.edu/viewdoc/download?doi=10.1.1.363.3730&rep=rep1&type=pdf. Accessed July 2021
13. Raghupathi, W., Raghupathi, V.: An overview of health analytics. J. Health Med. Inform. **4**(132), 2 (2013)
14. Jaafar, W.N.W., Maki, T.: Roles of Community College for Community Development in Malaysia: Entrepreneurship Education Program (2017). https://www.researchgate.net/publication/320953927

Examining the Software Developers' Perception in Open-Source Software of Blockchain Project Using Association Rules Mining

Alawiyah Abd Wahab[1]([⊠]), Huda Hj. Ibrahim[1] [iD], Shehu M. SarkinTudu[2] [iD], and Bilyaminu A. Romo[3] [iD]

[1] School of Computing, University Utara Malaysia, 06010 Sintok, Kedah, Malaysia
alawiyah@uum.edu.my
[2] Department of Computer and Information Technology, Sokoto State University, P.M.B 2134, Near Airport, Road, Sokoto, Sokoto State, Nigeria
[3] School of Architecture, Computing and Engineering, University of East London, London, UK
B.Auwal@uel.ac.uk

Abstract. Developers are vital in enhancing blockchain projects like Bitcoin through feature additions, bug fixes, and performance optimization. However, comprehending developers' perception of the growing amount of information regarding new features and bug fixes becomes challenging as blockchain projects gain popularity. Data mining, a technique that extracts valuable patterns and information from extensive data sets, assists in decision-making. The Apriori algorithm, widely used in data mining, uncovers association rules among sets of items. Despite its effectiveness, the Apriori algorithm remains relatively underutilized in the field of Open Source Software (OSS) developer turnover. Previous studies have employed approaches like mining software project repositories, social network analysis, quantitative data analysis, and surveys, which shed light on turnover but fail to reveal interesting relationships and patterns related to subjective factors and collaboration. To address this gap, this paper proposes combining survey data with association rule mining. This approach aims to identify co-occurrence patterns between specific personal and project-related variables (e.g., intention to learn or system integration). By analyzing these variables and their associations, the paper intends to provide valuable insights to project leaders, aiding decision-making in developer turnover management. Ultimately, this research contributes to enhancing the quality of blockchain projects.

Keywords: Developer's Turnover · Perception Patterns · Intention to Learn

1 Introduction

Open Source Software (OSS) project nowadays try to ensure the loyalty of their developers in various ways. However, instead of most project invest in precise research to understand developers' motivation to leave, or to stay, most project invest in additional benefits or measures to search for talent [1]. In blockchain project, the technological innovation and fundamental changes required in the design, development, and deployment of

N. H. Zakaria et al. (Eds.): ICOCI 2023, CCIS 2001, pp. 287–300, 2024.
https://doi.org/10.1007/978-981-99-9589-9_22

blockchain have also attracted tremendous interests from the software developer's community [2]. For example, prior studies found hundreds of thousands of blockchain software projects were hosted on GitHub [2–5]. Unlike traditional OSS projects, blockchain developers work in a decentralized and hostile environment, requiring caution against malicious actors. They must prioritize security and the establishment of an immutable distributed database. Furthermore, they need to design efficient and reliable software protocols, taking into account the scarcity of maintenance tools and resources since the existing tools are designed for traditional OSS development [6]. These differences posed significant challenges for software developers, and as a result, many may choose to leave the project for personal convenience [7]. However, as the popularity of blockchain projects continues to grow among software developers, their turnover perceptions regarding these projects remain highly uncertain and subject to rapid change. Such uncertainties in their perceptions pose challenges for project leaders in effectively managing developer turnover in a timely manner [7–9].

To enhance the success of blockchain projects, it is crucial for the community to gain a better understanding of software developer's perception regarding personal and project-related factors. However, in most blockchain projects that follow an OSS model, there is no centralized control over the operation of a blockchain itself [10]. The underlying philosophy is that project control is distributed among multiple developers or stakeholders [2]. This decentralized structure grants software developers a higher degree of autonomy, leading to increased uncertainty in their turnover rates [7]. Consequently, it becomes challenging to accurately gauge the perceptions of potential software developers, particularly those who show promise in adhering to technical contribution norms and remaining committed to the project [8].

In addition, as stated earlier, there is an estimated involvement of approximately a thousand software developers in contributing to blockchain-related innovations [11]. However, only a small fraction of these developers are actively engaged in the actual blockchain project developments [12]. At this point, it remains uncertain whether knowledge and understanding of the personal and project-related factors will spread widely enough to attract a sufficient number of developers reaching a critical mass for a stable mainstream ecosystem [13]. To prevent the loss of capable developers and attract new ones, project leaders must proactively identify potential developers as early as possible [3]. Unfortunately, project leaders lack knowledge into software developer perception patterns, which would enable them to determine whether a recommended developer is likely to adhere to the technical contribution norms that sustain long-term project involvement [14, 15]. Priors studies have employed approaches like mining software project repositories, social network analysis, quantitative survey data which shed light on developer turnover, but failed to reveal interesting relationships and patterns related to subjective factors and collaboration. Most scholars largely focused on traditional OSS projects using single approaches to provide valuable insights into developers' turnover [16, 17]. There has been limited published research on understanding developer perception in blockchain. To date, only a few studies have been identified that explore software developer turnover in the context of blockchain [2, 5, 10]. It is crucial to conduct further empirical work to gain a deeper understanding of software developer turnover perceptions regarding personal and project-related factors using hybrid analysis of PL-SEM and machine learning techniques. Therefore, the objective of this study is to investigate and analyze the software developer perception patterns within a sample of individuals involved in blockchain projects.

1.1 Related Works

Developer turnover is known to occur frequently in OSS projects and it is important to understand developers' perceptions regarding their turnover and its impact on the overall quality of such projects [8]. Gaining insights into the hidden or unexpected relationships between different variables influencing developer turnover can help identify hidden relationships among various variables in a dataset [17]. There are various studies on developer turnover in Open Source Software (OSS) projects, including blockchain [7, 8, 18, 19]. For instance, [8] proposed a method to identify developer inactivity, achieving 94% agreement among surveyed developers. The study analyzed 18 GitHub projects to reveal common developer turnover, with 45% completely disengaging for a year or more. To address project abandonment and sustain OSS communities, policies and mechanisms are suggested. Iaffaldano et al. [20] analyzed active developers, using semi-structured interviews to understand reasons for transitions, identifying "sleeping" and "dead" states representing temporary and permanent breaks in contribution turnover. Constantino et al. [16] conducted an in-depth investigation to understand why highly involved developers adhere to project norms and sustain their contributions, benefiting project leaders in attracting new developers. Kaur et al. [7] explored OSS project turnover from a different perspective, analyzing personal and project characteristics, finding patterns in abandonment based on experience, role, and joining date, but no clear relationship with coding language, change profile, or sentiments. Bosu et al. [2] surveyed 156 active Blockchain software developers, highlighting their motivation to create a decentralized financial system while facing challenges like higher defect costs and technological complexity influencing turnover behavior. Garagol et al. [3] addressed the governance gap in public blockchain OSS communities, identifying and analyzing six governance mechanisms and exploring similarities and differences with traditional OSS community turnover. The study aimed to collectively determine turnover in the blockchain community and utilized association rule mining to complement survey analysis, potentially discovering hidden patterns and relationships among factors influencing developer turnover.

There is, however, no study conducted to using a hybrid SEM-Association Rule Mining (ARM) analysis approach for deeper understanding of software developer turnover perception in OSS blockchain project which this paper proposes to address.

2 Apriori Algorithm

The Apriori algorithm is a well-known approach for association rule mining. It aims to identify all frequent item sets and generate strong association rules from them [21]. While the basic version of the algorithm requires categorical variables, numeric variables can be discretized to accommodate them. However, more sophisticated variants of the Apriori do not have such a restriction [22]. The algorithm derives its name from the Apriori property, which refers to its utilization of prior knowledge about itemset properties.

The analysis of frequently occurring factors combinations does not imply causality or suggest any theories about software developers view [23]. Rather, these relationships are discovered by examining the co-occurrences of factors in the transaction database [21]. These relationships are known as association rules and can be defined as an implication of the form A → B, where A (the antecedent) and B (the consequent) are conjunctions of variable-value pairs. An association rule may be interpreted as when the variables represented by A are present in a database, the variables represented by B also tend to occur. For example, the rule "intention to learn ∧ financial gain → technical contribution norm" suggests that when intention to learn and financial gain are present technical contribution norm is likely to be observed as well.

An issue with ARM is that there is an exponential growth in the number of association rules as the number of variables used increases [23]. In ARM, two measures are commonly used to help a researcher decide the usefulness of an association rule: support and confidence. The support of an association rule A → B is the percentage of transactions that contain A∪B. The confidence of an association rule A → B is the ratio of the number of transactions that contain A∪B to the number of transactions that contain A. Support measures how frequently an association rule occurs in the entire set of transactions, whereas confidence measures the strength/reliability of a rule. In ARM, rules are selected only if they satisfy both a minimum support and a minimum confidence threshold.

3   Methodology

The data were collected through a web-based survey (173 respondents working in bitcoin projects). All participating software developers were asked to complete a questionnaire consisting of demographic questions, such as gender, age and geographical location, and questions relating to factors influencing developers project abandonment. Table 1 shows the operational definitions of the variables selected for this study. Additionally, developers were given the opportunity to provide any additional comments they wished to share. The collected data underwent descriptive analysis and was analyzed using both the SPSS software and Partial Least Squares approach (PLS-SEM).

This study employs a combination of Partial Least Squares Structural Equation Modeling (PLS-SEM) and Association Rule Mining (ARM) to identify co-occurrence patterns between specific personal and project-related characteristics that are relevant to developers' perceptions of blockchain technology. Each feature is assessed using items on a 7-point scale, as presented in Table 1. The number of items for each feature varies, but all features exhibit high internal validity, with Cronbach's alpha values above 0.8, indicating that the items accurately represent each feature. The dataset comprises 173 participants who completed the survey in its entirety. PLS-SEM facilitates simultaneous measurement and analysis of the structural model, exploring relationships between features. Additionally, ARM is utilized to uncover association rules and patterns that may not be apparent from the survey alone, providing a more accurate understanding of the underlying causes. Subsequently, the data was transformed into Boolean and discrete formats to make it suitable for ARM.

Table 1. Operational Definitions of variables Used to Analyze Association Rules

Variables	Operational Definitions	Items	Sources
Intention to learn	The degree to which an individual intends to learn from a project that may benefit future work opportunities	3	[24]
Financial gain intention	The degree to which an individual intends to profit financially in the future by participating in a blockchain project	5	[25]
Expertise heterogeneity	The diversity in the expertise possessed by the members of a blockchain project team	3	[26]
Technical contribution norm	The degree to which a developer adheres to community-defined standards and procedures in order to contribute to the blockchain project	6	[27]
System integration	Developer effort required to manage contributed code dependencies with the blockchain project	4	[28]
Code testing task	The level of developer factual knowledge and technical expertise in the code testing domain	8	[29]
Contributed code decoupling	The degree to which modifications in source code do not affect its interoperability with the blockchain project	6	[28]
Developer involvement	The degree to which psychological belief on the project in which he/she was participating as personally relevant	5	[30]
Decision right delegation	The degree to which the developer has authority over certain design and development decisions	5	[28]
Project desertion	The developer's decision to discontinue further contributions to the specified project	3	[26]
Developer experience	Is the degree of the developer's interactions and experiences with the tools, frameworks, platforms, and APIs use in the blockchain project	4	[31]

3.1 Data Preparation

Data preparation involves cleaning, sampling, splitting, integrating and transforming raw data into a suitable format for analysis. Ensuring the accuracy and reliability of the data used is vital as the quality of the analysis heavily relies on the quality of the data.

3.2 Data Conversion

Since the developer perception data consists of continuous numeric data, it is necessary to convert it into Boolean and discrete data to facilitate mining as recommended by [21]. This requires grouping the original dataset and discretizing it into a Boolean format. The following variables were included: intention to learn, financial gain, expertise heterogeneity, technical contribution norm, system integration, code testing task, contributed code decoupling, developer involvement, decision right delegation, project desertion and developer experience.

This study categorized the variables as follows: intention to learn was classified as ['poor_intention', 'avg_intention', 'good_intention', 'excelent_intention'], financial gain was divided into: ['low_gain', 'mid_gain', 'high_gain'], expertise heterogeneity was grouped as ['low', 'mid', 'high'], technical contribution norm was assigned as ['low', 'mid', 'high'], system integration was categorized into ['low', 'mid', 'high'], code testing task was classified as ['low', 'mid', 'high'], contributed code decoupling was divided into ['low', 'mid', 'high'], developer involvement was categorized as ['low', 'mid', 'high'], decision right delegation was group as ['low', 'mid', 'high'], project desertion was classified as ['low_desertion', 'mid_desertion', 'high_desertion'], and developer experience was categorized as ['low', 'mid', 'high']. Detailed information can be found in Table 2 and Table 3.

Table 2. Developer and project description

Variables	Description
Gender	Gender
Age	Developer age
Development status	Refers to the progress of a software project, which is often measured by milestones or the completion of specific tasks
Project age	Refers to the length of time that has passed since the start of a Project

Table 3. Preparing Data for ARM

	itl	fgi	eh	tcn	si	ctt	ccd	drd	di	pd	de
0	excellent intention'	mid_gain	low	high	high	high	mid	high	mid	high	low
1	excellent intention'	mid_gain	low	high	mid	high	mid	mid	high	low	high
2	excellent intention'	high	low	high	high	high	high	mid	high	mid	low
3	excellent intention'	high	low	high	high	mid	low	low	high	low	low
4	good intention	high	low	high	mid	mid	mid	high	mid	mid	low
...	...	...	...	...	...	...	...	...	...	...	...
168	good intention	mid_gain	low	high	mid	mid	mid	mid	mid	mid	mid
169	Avg intention	mid_gain	mid	high	mid	mid	mid	mid	high	high	low
170	excellent_intention'	mid_gain	mid	high	high	mid	high	mid	high	mid	low
171	good intention	mid_gain	low	high	high	high	mid	mid	mid	high	low
172	Avg intention	mid_gain	mid	high	mid	high	mid	mid	mid	high	low

intention to learn = itl, financial gain intention = fgi, experts' heterogeneity = eh technical contribution norm = tcn, system integration = si, code testing task = ctt, contributed code decoupling = ccd, decision right delegation = drd, developer involvement = di, project desertion = pd, developer involvement = di

4 Findings

4.1 Respondents Demographic

The sample consists of 124 males, accounting for the majority (71.7%), while the remaining 49 individuals are female. In terms of age distribution, the majority of respondents (67.6%) are between 20 and 29 years old, followed by a group of 41 individuals (23.6%) in the 30–39 age range. There are 14 respondents (8.1%) in the remaining age category, and a small fraction (0.6%) of individuals above 50 years old. The majority of respondents, 62 individuals (35.0%) were located in North America, followed by 58 individuals (32.8%) from Europe, and 39 individuals (22.0%) from Asia. The remaining respondents were distributed as follows: 6 (3.4%) from Central America, 4 (2.3%) from Africa, 2 (1.1%) from Oceania, 1 (0.6%) from the Caribbean and 1 (0.6%) South America.

With regard to the project age, the highest number of developers, 44 individuals (25.4%), contributed to projects that were 2–3 years old. This was followed by 36 individuals (20.8%) contributing to projects less than 1 year old, 32 individuals (18.5%) contributing to projects that were 1–2 years old, 28 individuals (16.2%) contributing to projects that were 3–4 years old, 18 individuals (10.8%) contributing to projects older than 5 years, and 15 individuals (8.7%) contributing to projects that were 4–5 years old. With regards to development status of the projects, various responses were collected. The majority of developers, 59 individuals (34.1%) contribute to blockchain project at the planning stage. This is followed by 31 individuals (17.9%) who contribute to projects at the beta stage, 18 individuals (10.4%) at the pre-alpha stage, 16 individuals (9.2%) at the stable maturity stage, and 15 individuals (8.7%) at the maturity stage. Please refer to Table 4 for more details.

Table 4. Demographic Characteristics of the Respondents

Variable	Frequency	Percentage
Gender		
Female	49	28.3
Male	124	71.7
Total	**173**	**100.0**
Age		
20–29	117	67.6
30–39	41	23.7
40–49	14	8.1
>50	1	0.6
Total	**173**	**100.0**
Project Age		
<1 year	36	20.8
1–2 years	32	18.5
2–3 years	44	25.4
3–4 years	28	16.2
4–5 years	15	8.7
>5 years	18	10.4
Total	**173**	**100.0**

5   Generating an Association Rules Using Unsupervised Apriori

In data mining and machine learning, association rule mining algorithms are commonly employed to discover patterns or relationships among variables in a dataset [21]. Two crucial parameters, namely minimum support and minimum confidence, are used to govern the behavior of these algorithms and assess the quality of the generated association rules [32]. In order to apply Apriori algorithm for association rules mining, the developer perceptions dataset must satisfy a minimum threshold of 80 rules.

Table 5 shows the initial association rule derived from the dataset, which can be interpreted as follows: When a developer's involvement and effort to integrate their contribution to the blockchain project are both high, it is expected that their technical contribution norm will also be high, given that the decision right delegation is at a medium level. Similarly, another rule suggests that if the code testing group has a high level and the decision-making ability of the group is low, it is anticipated that the technical contribution norm group will be high, accompanied by a higher intention to learn.

However, it is important to note that association rules do not necessarily imply causality. The presence of an association rule does not necessarily imply that one variable causes or influences another. Instead, association rules are based on statistical correlations and can be used to identify potential patterns or relationships within the data. Therefore, it is important to exercise caution when interpreting association rules and to conduct further analysis to explore the underlying data and context in order to assess the validity and usefulness of the rule. In this study, a parameter was set for the algorithm, specifically a minimum support of 0.2 and a minimum confidence of 0.5. These parameter settings help filter out noise and improve the efficiency of the algorithm by considering only item sets that occur frequently in the data. In this case, the minimum support of 0.2 means that the algorithm considered only item sets that appear in at least 20% of the records.

Table 5. Rules generated as set minimum support of 0.2, and the minimum confidence of 0.5

Antecedents	Consequents	Support (%)	Confidence (%)	Lift
di = high, si = higher	tcn_group = high, drd_group = med	0.202312	0.500000	1.351562
prject_age_group = low_project_age, gender = m	tcn_ group = high, si_group = high	0.202312	0.700000	2.752273
tcn_group = high, project age...	si_group = high, gender = m, devel...	0.202312	0.625000	3.003472
si_group = high, developments...	tcn_ group = high, project_ag	0.202312	0.777778	3.003472
gender = m, development_status_group = p	Tcn_group = high, project_ag...	0.202312	0.700000	2.752273
tcn_group = high, development...	prject_age_group = low_project_age, sytem_inte...	0.202312	0.625000	3.003472
gender = m, pd_group = mid	si_group = high	0.202312	0.972222	1.39003
ctt_group = high, drd_group = high	tcn_group = high, intention_...	0.202312	0.686275	1.484069
tcn_group = high, code_testi...	drd_group = high, age_group = low_age	0.202312	0.538462	1.312026
tcn_group = high, intention_...	ctt_group = high, drd_group = low	0.202312	0.625000	1.368671
tcn_group = high, code_testi...	drd_group = high, fgi_gro...	0.202312	0.714286	1.625940

(*continued*)

Table 5. (*continued*)

Antecedents	Consequents	Support (%)	Confidence (%)	Lift
ctt_group = high, age_group = low_age, f...	tcn_group = high, drd_group	0.202312	0.777778	1.446834
tcn_group = high, code_testi...	itl_group = eh_group, drd_group =	0.202312	0.686275	1.648965
pd_group = mid_drd_group =, si_group = high_...	di _group = high	0.202312	0.777778	1.359147
di_group = high, si_group	pd_group = mid	0.202312	0.530303	1.054511
pd_group = mid	si_group = high, gender = m	0.202312	0.636364	1.158852

Then, the parameters were adjusted for another iteration of the model. The minimum support was set to 0.5, along with the minimum confidence of 0.5, resulting in the extraction of the top 10 rules. Additionally, to explore more robust associations, the authors re-ran the model with an increased confidence threshold of 0.8, resulting in ten rules which can be observed in Table 6.

Table 6. Rules generated with min_support is set to 0.5 and the min_confidence is set to 0.8

Antecedents	Consequents	Support (%)	Confidence (%)	Lift
eh_group = low	tcn_ group = high	0.687861	0.915385	1.077289
tcn_group = high	eh_group = low	0.687861	0.809524	1.077289
si_group = high	tcn_group = high	0.676301	0.966942	1.137966
gender = m	tcn_group = high	0.635838	0.887097	1.043998
eh_group = low	si_group = high	0.624277	0.830769	1.187794
si_group = high,	eh_group = low	0.624277	0.892562	1.187794
tcn_group = high, eh_group = low...	si_group = high	0.601156	0.873950	1.249531
tcn_group = high, si_group = low	eh_group = low	0.601156	0.888889	1.182906
eh_group = low, si_group = high	tcn_group = high	0.601156	0.962963	1.133284
si_group = high	tcn_group = high, eh_group	0.601156	0.859504	1.249531

5.1 Tuning Again with Higher Support of 0.6 and Confident of 0.9

The model was further fine-tuned by increasing the support and confidence thresholds. The unsupervised Apriori algorithm was utilized with a minimum support of 0.6 and a minimum confidence of 0.9. The resulting association rules were examined, including the first rule presented in Table 7. This rule exhibited a support of 0.601156%, indicating it occurrences in a relatively small percentage of transactions within the dataset. However, the rule displayed a high confidence of 0.962963%, implying that the consequent is almost always present when the antecedent is present. The lift value of 1.133284 suggests a slight positive correlation between the antecedent (eh_group = low, si_group = high) and the consequent (tcn_group = high). This implies that when the expertise group is low, the presence of the si_group slightly increases the likelihood of the tcn_group occurring in a transaction. Understanding the practical implications of association rules is vital for the development and management of blockchain projects. Identifying patterns related to personal features can help recruit developers with specific beliefs and skills to improve decision-making and project success. The rationale for the choice of minimum support threshold (e.g., 0.5 or 0.6) affects the relevance and selectivity of association rules based on their frequency of occurrence.

Table 7. min_support = 0.6, and min_confidence = 0.9, rule generated

Antecedents	Consequents	Support (%)	Confidence (%)	Lift
eh_group = low, si_group = high	tcn_group = high	0.601156	0.962963	1.133283
si_group = high, eh_group = low	tcn_ group = high	0.676301	0.966942	1.137966
eh_group = low	tcn_ group = high	0.687861	0.915385	1.077289

6 Relationship Between Confidence and Lift

The study explores the relationship between confidence and lift in association rules, emphasizing their significance in decision-making for blockchain projects. Lift and lift for unsupervised rules calculate association based on observed joint probabilities without assumptions. The study visually presents confidence, support, and lift measures, revealing strong associations among itemset variables. This insight is valuable for prioritizing variables in blockchain project management, aiding in the identification of key factors to enhance decision-making and success. Lower thresholds (0.5) create more rules with diverse confidence and lift, showing no significant additional association. Higher thresholds (0.6, 0.9) contrastingly. Using more stringent criteria (minimum support and confidence) selects fewer but stronger association rules, emphasizing no significant additional association beyond chance (lift = 1). Graphs with lower thresholds (0.5) generate a larger set of rules with moderate confidence, while higher thresholds (0.6 and 0.9) produce a smaller, more reliable set with higher confidence levels and stronger dependencies (Fig. 1). Both approaches focus on lift equal to 1.

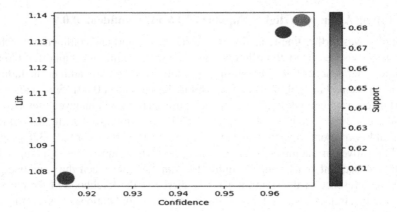

Fig. 1. The relationship between confidence at 0.9 and lift for Unsupervised rules

7 Conclusion

This paper introduces association rule mining (ARM) and its application in developer turnover, with a focus on OSS projects like blockchain. It covers ARM's key concepts and the Apriori algorithm for generating rules. Past ARM applications are mentioned, along with a counseling example. However, the paper stresses the need for caution in interpreting ARM's discovered rules, as they serve as exploratory findings requiring validation by domain experts. Its primary objective is to demonstrate ARM's value as a potent data analysis tool for researchers in various fields.

References

1. Foucault, M., Palyart, M., Blanc, X., Murphy, G.C., Falléri, J.R.: Impact of developer turnover on quality in open-source software. In: 2015 10th Joint Meeting of the European Software Engineering Conference and the ACM SIGSOFT Symposium on the Foundations of Software Engineering, ESEC/FSE 2015 – Proceedings, pp. 829–841 (2018)
2. Bosu, A., Iqbal, A., Shahriyar, R., Chakraborty, P.: Understanding the motivations, challenges and needs of blockchain software developers: a survey. Empir. Softw. Eng. **24**, 2636–2673 (2019). https://doi.org/10.1007/s10664-019-09708-7
3. Garagol, D., Nilsson, O.: Public blockchain communities A study on how governance mechanisms are expressed within blockchain communities (2018)
4. Lindman, J.: What open source software research can teach us about public blockchain (s)?— lessons for practitioners and future research. Front. Hum. Dyn. **3**, 1–7 (2021). https://doi.org/10.3389/fhumd.2021.642556
5. Chakraborty, P., Shahriyar, R., Iqbal, A., Bosu, A.: Understanding the software development practices of blockchain projects. In: Proceedings of the 12th ACM/IEEE International Symposium on Empirical Software Engineering and Measurement, 11 October 2018, pp. 1–10. ACM, New York (2018)
6. Almogahed, A., Omar, M.: Refactoring techniques for improving software quality: practitioners ' perspectives. J. Inf. Commun. Technol. **4**, 511–539 (2021)
7. Kaur, R., Chahal, K.K.: Exploring factors affecting developer abandonment of open source software projects. J. Softw. Evol. Process. **4**, 1–21 (2022). https://doi.org/10.1002/smr.2484

8. Calefato, F., Gerosa, M.A., Iaffaldano, G., Lanubile, F., Steinmacher, I.: Will you come back to contribute? Investigating the inactivity of OSS core developers in GitHub. Empir. Softw. Eng. **27**, 1–41 (2022). https://doi.org/10.1007/s10664-021-10012-6
9. Rashid, M., Clarke, P.M., O'Connor, R.V.: Exploring knowledge loss in open source software (OSS) projects. In: Mas, A., Mesquida, A., O'Connor, R.V., Rout, T., Dorling, A. (eds.) SPICE 2017. CCIS, vol. 770, pp. 481–495. Springer, Cham (2017). https://doi.org/10.1007/978-3-319-67383-7_35
10. Dirose, S., Mansouri, M.: Comparison and analysis of governance mechanisms employed by blockchain-based distributed autonomous organizations. In: 2018 13th System of Systems Engineering Conference, SoSE 2018, pp. 195–202 (2018). https://doi.org/10.1109/SYSOSE.2018.8428782
11. Mattila, J.: The blockchain phenomenon: the disruptive potential of distributed consensus architectures. Notes Rec. R. Soc. J. Hist. Sci. **70**, 393–395 (2016). https://doi.org/10.1098/rsnr.2016.0036
12. De Filippi, P., Loveluck, B.: The invisible politics of bitcoin: governance crisis of a decentralized infrastructure. Internet Policy Rev. **5**, 1–32 (2016). https://doi.org/10.14763/2016.3.427
13. Arruñada, B., Garicano, L.: Blockchain: the birth of decentralized governance (2018)
14. Balali, S., Steinmacher, I., Annamalai, U., Sarma, A., Gerosa, M.A.: Newcomers' barriers… is that all? An analysis of mentors' and newcomers' barriers in OSS projects. Comput. Support. Coop. Work **27**, 679–714 (2018). https://doi.org/10.1007/s10606-018-9310-8
15. Nyman, L., Lindman, J.: Code forking, governance, and sustainability in open source software. Technol. Innov. Manag. Rev. **3**, 7–12 (2018). https://doi.org/10.22215/timreview/644
16. Constantino, K., Zhou, S., Souza, M., Figueiredo, E., Kästner, C.: Understanding collaborative software development: an interview study. In: Proceedings - 2020 ACM/IEEE 15th International Conference on Global Software Engineering, ICGSE 2020, pp. 55–65 (2020). https://doi.org/10.1145/3372787.3390442
17. Khan, B., et al.: Evolution of influential developer's communities in OSS and its impact on quality. Intell. Autom. Soft Comput. **28**, 337–352 (2021). https://doi.org/10.32604/iasc.2021.015034
18. Walton, R.: What do the consequences of environmental, social and governance failures tell us about the motivations for corporate social responsibility? Int. J. Financ. Stud. **10**, 1–19 (2022). https://doi.org/10.3390/ijfs10010017
19. Shahzad, A., Malik, R.K.: Workplace violence: an extensive issue for nurses in Pakistan: a qualitative investigation. J. Interpers. Violence **29**, 2021–2034 (2014). https://doi.org/10.1177/0886260513516005
20. Iaffaldano, G., Steinmacher, I., Calefato, F., Gerosa, M., Lanubile, F.: Why do developers take breaks from contributing to OSS projects? A preliminary analysis. In: Proceedings - 2019 IEEE/ACM 2nd International Workshop on Software Health, SoHeal 2019, pp. 9–16 (2019)
21. Ugur, O., Arisoy, A.A., Can Ganiz, M., Bolac, B.: Descriptive and prescriptive analysis of construction site incidents using decision tree classification and association rule mining. In: 2021 International Conference on INnovations in Intelligent SysTems and Applications, INISTA 2021 - Proceedings (2021). https://doi.org/10.1109/INISTA52262.2021.9548427
22. Pawlicka, A., Tomaszewska, R., Krause, E., Jaroszewska-Choraś, D., Pawlicki, M., Choraś, M.: Has the pandemic made us more digitally literate? Innovative association rule mining study of the relationships between shifts in digital skills and cybersecurity awareness occurring whilst working remotely during the COVID-19 pandemic. J. Ambient Intell. Humaniz. Comput. (2022). https://doi.org/10.1007/s12652-022-04371-1
23. Ayhan, B.U., Doğan, N.B., Tokdemir, O.B.: An association rule mining model for the assessment of the correlations between the attributes of severe accidents. J. Civ. Eng. Manag. **26**, 315–330 (2020). https://doi.org/10.3846/jcem.2020.12316

24. Xu, B., Jones, D.R., Shao, B.: Volunteers' involvement in online community based software development. Inf. Manag. **46**, 151–158 (2009). https://doi.org/10.1016/j.im.2008.12.005

25. Hars, A., Ou, S.: Working for free? Motivations for participating in open-source projects. Int. J. Electron. Commer. **6**, 25–39 (2002). https://doi.org/10.1080/10864415.2002.11044241

26. Tiwana, A., McLean, E.: Expertise integration and creativity in information systems development. J. Manag. Inf. Syst. **22**, 13–43 (2018)

27. Stewart, K.J., Gosain, S.: The impact of ideology on effectiveness in open source software development teams. MIS Q. **30**, 291–314 (2006)

28. Tiwana, A.: Platform desertion by app developers. J. Manag. Inf. Syst. **32**, 40–77 (2015). https://doi.org/10.1080/07421222.2015.1138365

29. Green, P., Robb, A., Rohde, F.H.: A model for assessing information systems success and its application to e-logistics tracking systems. Pac. Asia J. Assoc. Inf. Syst. **6**(4), 39–68 (2014)

30. Barki, H., Hartwick, J.: Measuring user participation, user involvement, and user attitude. MIS Q. **18**, 59 (2006). https://doi.org/10.2307/249610

31. Vadlamani, S.L., Baysal, O.: Studying software developer expertise and contributions in stack overflow and GitHub. In: Proceedings - 2020 IEEE International Conference on Software Maintenance and Evolution, pp. 312–323 (2020)

32. Gupta, P.R., Mane, P., Mirji, H.: Application of data mining techniques for measuring and predicting employee performances in automotive industry. Am. J. Econ. Bus. Manag. **6**(1), 10–18 (2023)

Support Vector Machine for Satellite Images Classification Using Radial Basis Function Kernel Method

Nur Suhaili Mansor[1]([✉]) [ID], Hapini Awang[1] [ID], Sarkin Tudu Shehu Malami[2] [ID], Amirulikhsan Zolkafli[1], Mohammed Ahmed Taiye[3] [ID], and Hanhan Maulana[4] [ID]

[1] Institute for Advanced and Smart Digital Opportunities, School of Computing, Universiti Utara Malaysia, 06010 Sintok, Kedah, Malaysia
nursuhaili@uum.edu.my

[2] Department of Computer Science and Information Technology, Faculty of Science, Sokoto State University Sokoto, Sokoto 852101, Nigeria

[3] Department of Cultural Sciences, Faculty of Arts and Humanities, Linnaeus University, 351 95 Vaxjo, Sweden

[4] Department of Informatics Engineering and Computer Science, Universitas Komputer Indonesia, Bandung 40134, Indonesia

Abstract. Machine learning, particularly Support Vector Machines (SVM), has gained popularity in geospatial data processing and image classification. Geospatial data from various sources may contain errors, impacting image classification accuracy. Traditional pixel-based and object-based methods struggle to classify complex land cover classes accurately. Previous studies explored machine learning algorithms like Random Forests, K-Nearest Neighbors, and Neural Networks. Still, they faced challenges capturing intricate relationships within images and required substantial labeled training data, leading to computational expenses. SVM with polynomial kernels was attempted in some studies, but it suffered from potential overfitting and inefficiency for large datasets. To overcome these issues, this study employed SVM with RBF and Linear kernels to classify multispectral satellite images from the SPOT-6 Satellite Imagery dataset in Sungai Kelang, Malaysia. Previous research evaluated each kernel's performance accuracy compared using a test dataset, utilizing open-source tools like Jupyter Notebooks and Python libraries to explore SVM's potential as a high-performance satellite image classification technique. The findings revealed that SVM with RBF kernel outperformed SVM with polynomial or linear kernels in classifying satellite images. The RBF kernel's robustness allowed SVM to model intricate decision boundaries and capture complex patterns in the image data, making it suitable for tasks with non-linearly separable data. The study introduces a new methodology and theoretical contribution to image classification-related literature, shedding light on the efficacy of SVM-RBF for geospatial data processing. It provides an alternative to traditional approaches for complex image classification tasks. Moreover, the research assists in selecting the optimal algorithm for remote sensing and satellite imagery applications.

Keywords: Support Vector Machine · Geospatial · Image Classification · Radial basis function (RBF) Kernel · Linear Kernel

N. H. Zakaria et al. (Eds.): ICOCI 2023, CCIS 2001, pp. 301–312, 2024.
https://doi.org/10.1007/978-981-99-9589-9_23

1 Introduction

Geospatial technologies is a field of study in which multispectral refers to using multiple electromagnetic radiation wavelengths or spectral bands for analysis and mapping [1]. Satellite image classification is a technique that involves grouping pixels with similar radiance or digital number values across various image bands or data channels [2]. In addition, applying different statistical learning techniques has become instrumental in extracting valuable information from remote sensing data [3]. Multispectral data in geospatial typically involves the integration of remote sensing imagery with spatial data layers, allowing for a more comprehensive understanding of geographic phenomena [4]. Multispectral remote sensing images are crucial in various fields, including environmental monitoring, agriculture, forestry, urban planning, disaster assessment, and resource exploration [5]. They enable researchers, scientists, and decision-makers to gain insights into the Earth's features, changes over time, and environmental conditions by leveraging different materials' distinct spectral signatures and interactions of other materials with electromagnetic radiation. Prior studies used traditional methods of handling multispectral remote sensing images, such as pixel-based methods [6] and object-based methods [7].

However, the conventional method faces challenges in complex applications due to distributional assumptions and the nature of the input data image [8]. Older approaches also have limitations in accurately classifying and interpreting multispectral data due to difficulties extracting complex characteristics [9]. Recent studies have shown that intelligent computing systems, such as machine learning (ML) tools like the Random Forests, K-Nearest Neighbors, and Neural Networks, offer interesting classification task results but face challenges capturing intricate relationships within images and requiring substantial training data, leading to higher computational cost [10, 11]. Support vector machine (SVM) with polynomial kernels can effectively replace conventional statistical methods in handling multispectral remote sensing image classification problems [2]. Although this method requires more processing resources, it has been found to have potential overfitting and inefficiency for large datasets.

This study aims to improve the existing methods in handling multispectral remote sensing image classification problems; perhaps a new approach is needed, one that requires less computing power and provides more accurate results. This study utilizes Python libraries and data science tools such as Jupyter Notebook to perform SVM classification with a radial basis function kernel approach, addressing a gap in the existing literature. Figures 1 and 2 depict satellite images of the study area, while Figs. 3 and 4 illustrate the ground truth data for training samples and compare them with the data. Generating supervised training sample datasets necessitates carefully collecting ground truth data through surveys using georeferenced satellite image data.

1.1 Support Vector Machine (SVM)

Support Vector Machine (SVM) is a learning theory developed to address the challenge of pattern recognition and construct classification and regression methods across various technological disciplines, including remote sensing [2]. The concept of decision surfaces forms the foundation of SVM [12]. In addition, multi-class classification using SVM has also been studied [13]. SVM divides classes using a decision surface that maximizes the margin between them, often called the "optimal hyperplane." To create training sample sets, support vectors of the data points close to this hyperplane are essential [14].

2 Related Studies

Multispectral remote sensing images have emerged as a vital tool across diverse fields, including agriculture [15], forestry [10], environmental monitoring [16], urban planning [17], and disaster management [18]. These images' extensive research and utilization have paved the way for significant advancements. For instance, a study by [18] in the Caraga Region of Mindanao, Philippines, focused on mapping Falcata plantations using ML classifiers and Sentinel-2 satellite imagery. The ML classifier achieved an impressive overall accuracy of 90.90% with a 10-m resolution image, while Linear SVM classifiers attained 92.05% accuracy with a 20-m resolution image. Based on these findings, the study recommended using ML for Falcata mapping at a 10-m resolution and Linear or RBF SVM at a 20-m resolution. The researchers also emphasized the potential of parameter optimization to enhance classification accuracy further.

Another noteworthy exploration in multispectral remote sensing is the study conducted by [16], which utilized ML algorithms to map inselbergs in Brazil. Inselbergs are rocky outcrops with high biodiversity that require conservation. The researchers employed image classification techniques and geospatial modeling to address these areas' anthropogenic and climate change threats. The models achieved remarkable accuracy and kappa values, with algorithms such as Gradient Boosting Machine, Support Vector Machines with Radial Basis Function Kernel, C5.0, and Random Forest outperforming others. This methodology holds promise for selecting and managing Inselberg landscapes worldwide.

In a different context, [2] focused on classifying multispectral satellite images using SVM and compared its accuracy against conventional methods. The study utilized data from LISS-3 and AWIFS sensors on the Resourcesat-1 satellite. Open-source tools were leveraged to explore the potential of SVM for high-performance satellite image classification. The findings demonstrated the efficacy of SVM in achieving accurate classification results. While these studies have significantly contributed to multispectral remote sensing, it is crucial to acknowledge that they often demand substantial computing power and processing resources to achieve higher accuracy. Consequently, future research should explore alternative approaches that mitigate the computational requirements while delivering more precise results. This avenue of inquiry involves investigating techniques to optimize computational efficiency, developing novel algorithms that demand fewer resources, and capitalizing on advancements in hardware and software technologies.

Thus, the extensive research and utilization of multispectral remote-sensing images have revolutionized various domains. The examples cited above demonstrate the potential of ML classifiers, SVM, and other algorithms in achieving accurate results for tasks such as mapping Falcata plantations, identifying critical areas for conservation, and classifying multispectral satellite images. However, achieving enhanced accuracy is imperative to address the need for higher computing power and processing resources. Future research should strive to develop alternative approaches that balance computational requirements and improved precision, ensuring the wider accessibility and practical implementation of multispectral remote sensing technologies. By doing so, researchers can unlock the full potential of these images and pave the way for groundbreaking advancements in various applications.

3   Methodology

The SVM classification technique was employed in the study's analysis to classify satellite images and determine accuracy. The maximum likelihood estimator selects statistical model parameters to generate a distribution that closely matches the observed data. However, this approach encounters challenges when dealing with complex scenarios involving distributional assumptions and the nature of the input data. Recent research has shown that intelligent computing systems, such as SVM, can effectively address multispectral remote sensing image classification issues and be a viable alternative to conventional statistical techniques. SVM uses the "one against one approach" for multiclass classification, wherein n $(n-1)/2$ classifier models are built, with n representing the number of classes [12].

Although the method requires more processing time, it has been shown to achieve higher accuracy. Open-source Python libraries such as matplotlib, NumPy, image, and sci-kit-learn were utilized in this study for image classification and for creating training sample data [11, 19–21]. In addition, Jupyter Notebook and other data science tools were employed for SVM classification. Figure 1 and 2 display the study area's satellite image and the training samples' ground truth data. Generating supervised training sample datasets involves meticulously collecting ground truth data through surveys using georeferenced satellite image data.

Fig. 1. Training Sample 1

Fig. 2. Training Sample 2

Overall, the methods used SVM-RBF to optimize the model's performance, improve generalization, and accurately classify images into their respective categories. The data was collected from Sungai, Kelang is known as the Kelang River; it is a significant river in Malaysia that flows through the state of Selangor, which include the capital city, Kuala Lumpur, and eventually discharges into the Malacca Strait. The kelang river is one of the major rivers in the Klang Valley region and plays a crucial role in water supply, transportation, and recreational activities for the local communities. To achieve the aim and objectives of the research, the researchers resorted to choosing the appropriate software for accessing and processing the SPOT-6 satellite imagery. This study used popular remote sensing software like ENVI and Erdas Imagine and open-source tools like GDAL and RSGISLib for data collection.

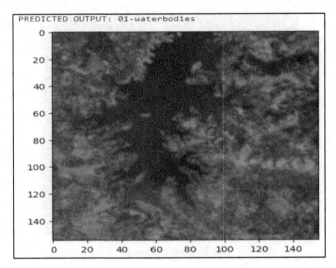

Fig. 3. Normalization of Images Output

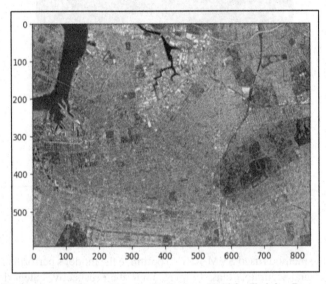

Fig. 4. Sample Sites within the Study Area Used for Training Purpose

3.1 Classification Workflow

Before conducting the actual image classification using two different approaches, analyzing multispectral remote sensing data involves several steps. These include georeferencing, image registration to a reference image, and sub-setting selected image regions from the scene [22]. In a workflow configuration (see Fig. 5), these geographic procedures were performed sequentially, one after the other. The input dataset and image data format in this workflow are JPG files. In addition, georeferencing satellite images requires assigning geographic coordinates (latitude and longitude) to each image pixel.

This georeferenced data is crucial for subsequent geospatial operations. Georeferencing can enhance the model's accuracy by improving the certainty of the geographic location for each image pixel when the input image is registered to a reference image. Select a region of interest by performing image subsetting to classify the images. Next, the SVM classifier is trained using the provided training sample set. The model is trained after importing the vector data as an image shape. The SVM was then configured to perform supervised classification, assess overall accuracy by validating the classified image, and display more accurate classification results.

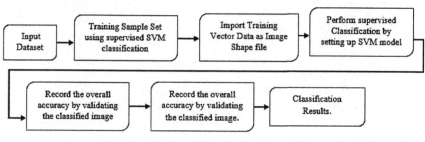

Fig. 5. Workflow

4 Result and Discussion

4.1 Classification Results

The classification accuracy analysis considered five classes, including built-up areas, vegetation, forests, and bodies of water. The selection of training samples for crop classification was determined through ground surveys (Fig. 4). Creating the training sample dataset can be done using a straightforward method since the class of each sample pixel is already known. An experienced remote sensing analyst, who can distinguish between water bodies and land objects based on color combinations, can choose the training samples for other classes based on the spectral properties of the multispectral dataset. Figure 6, designed for this exercise, illustrates the number of training pixels chosen for each class. Additionally, SVM was utilized to classify the images in Fig. 3 and Fig. 4.

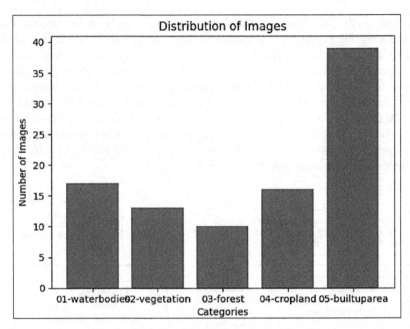

Fig. 6. Statistics of the Pixels in the Training Set

Support Vector Machines (SVM) can transform data using various kernel functions, enabling the creation of non-linear decision boundaries. Figure 7 illustrates the overall accuracy of the classified images using the maximum likelihood method and two different SVM kernel functions. This investigation utilized two common SVM kernel types: the linear kernel and the radial basis function (RBF). The overall accuracy refers to the proportion of correctly identified observations to all observations made during the formation of the training sample set. The effect of the accuracy must be evaluated to hyperparameters on the model's precision. Grid or randomized search over a predefined range to understand the relationship between the accuracy of a machine learning model and the values assigned to its hyperparameters, hyperparameter values have successfully found the optimal combination of hyperparameter values that maximizes the model's accuracy on the validation or test set.

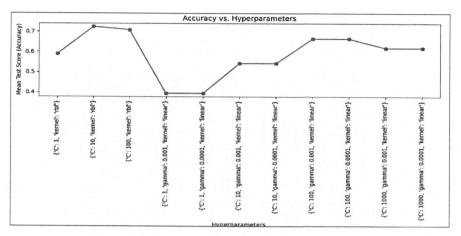

Fig. 7. Accuracy versus Hyperparameter

As this is the standard general practice, the training sample data set used for learning was once more used to compute the accuracy. Additionally, this experiment was used to compare SVM performance across several kernel types and to establish the process for SVM classification of satellite photos. The same classifier SVM was applied to the same training sample data set to estimate accuracy using a different kernel to define decision boundaries. This study allows us to investigate various data representations and enhance the model's performance by comparing the model performance.

To learn how the model performs across several classes and to make conclusions about its advantages and disadvantages for a given class. In Fig. 8, an analysis of the bar chart shows that precision, recall, and F1-score predictions show higher precision, recall, and F1-scores for all classes. Still, trade-offs may exist depending on the problem and the importance of different evaluation metrics.

To gain insights into the model's confidence in its predictions and the trade-off between precision and recall. This paper examines the precision-recall graph and analyzes the probabilities for each class. These insights can help understand the model's behavior, optimize classification thresholds, and help agriculture, land administrators and disaster management, and policymakers to make an informed decision based on the desired precision-recall trade-off. Figure 9 below shows the probability of each class, accuracy, and confidence of the model. Classes 4 and 5 have the highest chance, with 93% each. Class 3 has 82%, class 1 has achieved 81%, and finally, cropland class 2 has a probability of 57%.

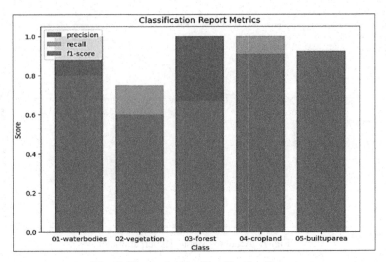

Fig. 8. Generating the Classification Report

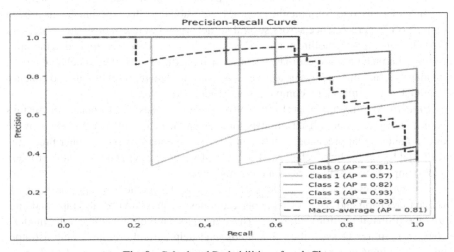

Fig. 9. Calculated Probabilities of each Class

5 Conclusion

The results demonstrate that the SVM algorithm with Radial Basis Function (RBF) outperforms the SVM with Polynomial Kernel or Linear Kernel approaches in classifying satellite images using the linear kernel and Radial Basis Function (RBF). The overall average accuracy for SVM Radial Basis Function (RBF) and the previous polynomial model is greater than 80%. Several classification experiments were conducted to validate the assertion that the accuracy of the SVM model can be enhanced for the region with less than 89% accuracy. Further improvements can be achieved by employing alternative kernel types, such as the sigmoid function, and refining parameters like the degree of bias in the kernel function. These parameters can be evaluated in terms of performance with different kernel types, potentially leading to improved accuracy in future studies focused on the segmentation of multispectral satellite images.

Acknowledgment. This research is supported by the Universiti Utara Malaysia (UUM)-Universitas Komputer Indonesia (UNIKOM) Matching Grant: S/O Code: 21529.

References

1. Fahad, S., Tariq, A., Mousa, B.G., Mumtaz, F., Aslam, M.: Spatiotemporal variation in land use land cover in the response to local climate change using multispectral remote sensing data. Landsc. Urban Plan. **4**, 1–24 (2022)
2. Manthira Moorthi, S., Misra, I., Kaur, R., Darji, N.P., Ramakrishnan, R.: Kernel-based learning approach for satellite image classification using support vector machine. In: 2011 IEEE Recent Advances in Intelligent Computational Systems, RAICS 2011, pp. 107–110 (2021). https://doi.org/10.1109/RAICS.2011.6069282
3. Tien Bui, D., Tuan, T.A., Klempe, H., Pradhan, B., Revhaug, I.: Spatial prediction models for shallow landslide hazards: a comparative assessment of the efficacy of support vector machines, artificial neural networks, kernel logistic regression, and logistic model tree. Landslides **13**, 361–378 (2016). https://doi.org/10.1007/s10346-015-0557-6
4. Lü, G., et al.: Reflections and speculations on the progress in Geographic Information Systems (GIS): a geographic perspective. Int. J. Geogr. Inf. Sci. **33**, 346–367 (2019). https://doi.org/10.1080/13658816.2018.1533136
5. Fan, K., Su, W.: Applications of fluorescence spectroscopy, RGB- and multispectral imaging for quality determinations of white meat: a review. MDPI **2**, 1–30 (2022)
6. Yan, Z., Ma, L., He, W., Zhou, L., Lu, H., Liu, G.: Comparing object-based and pixel-based methods for local climate zones mapping with multi-source data. MDPI **3**, 1–30 (2022)
7. Ghorbanzadeh, O., Shahabi, H., Crivellari, A.: Landslide detection using deep learning and object - based image analysis. Landslides **2**, 929–939 (2022). https://doi.org/10.1007/s10346-021-01843-x
8. Hu, X., et al.: Hyperspectral anomaly detection using deep learning: a review. MDPI **4**, 1–30 (2022)
9. Jiang, J., Feng, F., Lian, X., Zhang, L.: Long-term active integrator prediction in the evaluation of code contributions. In: Proceedings of the International Conference on Software Engineering and Knowledge Engineering, SEKE, January 2016, pp. 177–182 (2016). https://doi.org/10.18293/SEKE2016-030
10. Jackson, C.M., Adam, E.: Machine learning classification of endangered tree species in a tropical submontane forest using worldview-2 multispectral satellite imagery and imbalanced dataset. Remote Sens. **13**, 1–10 (2021). https://doi.org/10.3390/rs13244970
11. Muzumdar, P., Basyal, G.P., Vyas, P.: An empirical comparison of machine learning models for student's mental health illness assessment. Asian J. Comput. Inf. Syst. **10**(1), 1–10 (2022). https://doi.org/10.24203/ajcis.v10i1.6882
12. Georgoula, I., Pournarakis, D., Bilanakos, C., Sotiropoulos, D.N., Giaglis, G.M.: Using time-series and sentiment analysis to detect the determinants of bitcoin prices. SSRN Electron. J. (2015).https://doi.org/10.2139/ssrn.2607167
13. Khalil, U., Imtiaz, I., Aslam, B., Ullah, I., Tariq, A., Qin, S.: Comparative analysis of machine learning and multi-criteria decision making techniques for landslide susceptibility mapping of Muzaffarabad district. Front. Environ. Sci. **10** (2022). https://doi.org/10.3389/fenvs.2022.1028373

14. Can, A., Dagdelenler, G., Ercanoglu, M., Sonmez, H.: Landslide susceptibility mapping at Ovacık-Karabük (Turkey) using different artificial neural network models: comparison of training algorithms. Bull. Eng. Geol. Environ. **78**, 89–102 (2019). https://doi.org/10.1007/s10064-017-1034-3

15. Subba Reddy, T., Harikiran, J.: Hyperspectral image classification using support vector machines. IAES Int. J. Artif. Intell. **9**, 684–690 (2020). https://doi.org/10.11591/ijai.v9.i4.pp684-690

16. da Silveira, V.A., et al.: Modeling and mapping of Inselberg habitats for environmental conservation in the Atlantic Forest and Caatinga domains. Brazil. Environ. Adv. **8**, 1–18 (2022). https://doi.org/10.1016/j.envadv.2022.100209

17. Hekmatmanesh, A., Huapeng, Wu., Jamaloo, F., Li, M., Handroos, H.: A combination of CSP-based method with soft margin SVM classifier and generalized RBF kernel for imagery-based brain computer interface applications. Multimedia Tools Appl. **79**(25–26), 17521–17549 (2020). https://doi.org/10.1007/s11042-020-08675-2

18. Santillan, J.R., Gesta, J.L.E.: Evaluation of machine learning classifiers for mapping Falcata plantations in Sentinel-2 image. Int. Arch. Photogramm. Remote. Sens. Spat. Inf. Sci. **XLIII-B3-2021**, 103–108 (2021). https://doi.org/10.5194/isprs-archives-XLIII-B3-2021-103-2021

19. Pham, B.T., Khosravi, K., Prakash, I.: Application and comparison of decision tree-based machine learning methods in landside susceptibility assessment at Pauri Garhwal Area, Uttarakhand, India. Environ. Process. **4**(3), 711–730 (2017). https://doi.org/10.1007/s40710-017-0248-5

20. Yusof, Y., Fajila, F.: Artificial intelligence and machine learning in education, chap. 7. In: Digital Transformation for the University of the Future, pp. 121–141. World Scientific Publishing Co. Pte. Ltd. (2022). https://doi.org/10.1142/9789811254154_0007

21. Lee, H.S., Gweon, G.H., Lord, T., Paessel, N., Pallant, A., Pryputniewicz, S.: Machine learning-enabled automated feedback: supporting students' revision of scientific arguments based on data drawn from simulation. J. Sci. Educ. Technol. **30**, 168–192 (2021). https://doi.org/10.1007/s10956-020-09889-7

22. Sharma, G., Kumar, K.: Acceleration of images via software and hardware using proprietary tools & open sources for healthcare industry. Int. J. Image Graph. Sig. Process. **9**, 10–22 (2017). https://doi.org/10.5815/ijigsp.2017.07.02

Harnessing Technology for Sustainable Development

A Regression Test Case Prioritization Framework for Software Sustainability

Bakr Ba-Quttayyan[1] ⓘ, Haslina Mohd[1,2(✉)] ⓘ, and Yuhanis Yusof[1] ⓘ

[1] School of Computing, College of Arts and Sciences, University Utara Malaysia, 06010 Sintok, Kedah, Malaysia
haslina@uum.edu.my

[2] Data Management and Software Solution (DMSS), School of Computing, College of Arts and Sciences, University Utara Malaysia, 06010 Sintok, Kedah, Malaysia

Abstract. In software development, test cases are stored for later use, such as retesting or regression testing. Optimization is one of the approaches used in regression testing, particularly test case prioritization (TCP). TCP aims to rapidly uncover defects during software development. Existing TCP methods lack reliability and suffer from efficiency and effectiveness due to insufficient evaluation, reproducibility, and benchmarking. Currently, no existing TCP framework is integrated with the hybrid PSO-ABC optimization method. This paper aims to introduce a TCP framework that includes five factors, namely fault detection and severity, test case dependency, clustered test cases, and test input, which are used to prioritize test cases. The process starts by determining three factors from the literature (i.e., fault detection and severity, as well as clustered test cases) and contributing the other two (i.e., test case dependency and test input) to seek better optimization. Historical data from previous runs regarding these TCP factors were extracted and stored for analysis. The proposed TCP framework was verified by ten experts, and it was learned that this framework received positive feedback. TCP is closely related to the longevity of software since it can ensure that systems remain reliable, dependable, and maintainable over time. By identifying and prioritizing essential test cases, developers can focus their testing efforts on the areas of the system that are most likely to be affected by changes.

Keywords: Test Case Prioritization · Swarm Intelligence · Multi-objective optimization

1 Introduction

Computer software continuously undergoes multiple modifications to cope with the changing needs of stakeholders. Such modifications may lead to a potential risk of errors. Because humans are fallible, there is a need to correct mistakes, especially in the software systems domain. Testing software is needed first to ensure its quality and acceptability and, secondly, to discover software problems [1]. Hence, testing and retesting functionalities and non-functionalities of the system after source code modification is conducted to ensure that the modifications do not adversely affect the system by

© The Author(s), under exclusive license to Springer Nature Singapore Pte Ltd. 2024
N. H. Zakaria et al. (Eds.): ICOCI 2023, CCIS 2001, pp. 315–329, 2024.
https://doi.org/10.1007/978-981-99-9589-9_24

bringing up bugs when executing the source code. This software testing technique is called *regression testing* [2, 3]. Regression testing is an unavoidable and significantly integral activity in software development performed once an alteration occurs in the software under development [4]. Since it consumes time and budget, software system development without regression testing is hazardous [1, 5]. Such an important step is time-consuming compared to other steps in the whole process of development. Regression testing can be carried out in various ways, in which test case prioritization is one of the most effective ways [4].

Test case prioritization (TCP) is the process of optimizing test cases by effectively rearranging them to attain a performance goal, such as early fault detection [6]. The aim of regression testing, i.e., TCP as well, is to increase the fault detection rate. Hence, researchers proposed code-based, fault-based, requirement-based, multi-objective, and other methods to enhance testing performance, as depicted in Table 1.

Table 1. Existing TCP Methods

TCP method	Aim	Studies
Code-based	To expose faults by attaining code coverage based on code aspects such as statements, branches, methods, loops, etc.	[6–8]
Fault-based	To detect errors by achieving coverage of fault-prone areas using fault history or probability	[9, 10]
Requirement-based	To reveal defects by reaching the requirements coverage	[11–13]
Multi-objective	To uncover software bugs by incorporating coverage of multiple factors	[14, 15]
Other methods	To find faults by gaining coverage of other aspects related to software criteria	[16–18]

Table 1 summarizes the current TCP methods in the literature, their aims, and related studies. The code-based TCP methods are broadly popular, in which their focus is concentrated on achieving maximum code coverage for revealing defects. Fault-based TCP methods mainly focus on fault-proneness, where fault history, impacts, and probability are utilized. Requirement-based TCP techniques attain coverage of stakeholder requirements to build confidence in software functionality. On the contrary, employing multiple factors in optimizing test cases is gaining popularity due to their performance. Finally, several TCP methods apply different aspects of the information related to software development for test optimization.

With the increasing use of multi-objective optimization to solve NP-hard problems, TCP has been treated as a multi-factor problem in the research community [19, 20]. On the contrary, using a single factor for optimizing test cases restricts the ability of the optimized test cases to locate faults and minimizes the flexibility of the technique against the increased complexity of regression testing and other practical considerations [2, 22]. So, multi-objective optimization methods in TCP received wide acceptance and popularity in the research society because they surpassed single optimization methods in several aspects, such as their capability to cope with the increasing complexity of test case optimization and tackle two or more objectives for optimization [22–25]. Also, their capability to accelerate fault detection ability, maximize coverage criteria, minimize cost, provide better performance in industrial case studies, and provide better distributions of the weighted average percent of faults detected (APFD) metric values makes them widely acceptable [22, 26, 27]. This paper aims to contribute four aspects to the body of knowledge, as follows:

- A new method for optimizing test cases through multiple factors mainly focuses on testware without considering the source code in optimizing test cases.
- New optimizing factors were introduced to the literature in the prioritization activity.
- A new implementation of the hybrid swarm algorithm in TCP coped with tackling the optimization process.
- A new weighted objective (fitness) function was formulated to handle these factors for the optimization process.

This paper proposes a new TCP framework in which five factors, namely fault detection and severity, test case dependency, clustered test cases, and test input, are considered for optimizing test cases. The framework uses a hybrid swarm algorithm to tackle the multi-objective optimization process. This proposed framework aims to enhance the efficiency and effectiveness of the testing process by involving different factors and focusing on the testware artifacts and their historical data. The rest of this paper is organized as follows: Sect. 2 discusses the related works of literature. Section 3 elaborates on the proposed work, and Sect. 5 concludes this paper and highlights directions for future research.

2 Related Work

Increasing demand for optimization-based solutions to real-world problems prompted the application of computational intelligence to these issues. In the meantime, artificial intelligence (AI) techniques and algorithms have become extremely popular with their application in several software engineering and testing fields. AI techniques have been frequently implemented in regression testing for optimizing test cases, particularly in the TCP [28]. The literature survey revealed several studies that involve the application of nature-inspired algorithms in the TCP domain.

A close look at the research community shows several works published in the TCP field since its first appearance in the literature in 1997. For example, Kim and Porter [29], Aggrawal et al. [30], Srikanth et al. [31], and Korel et al. [32] proposed works on TCP. However, these are traditional works with several issues compared to other search-based techniques, i.e., AI [33, 34]. Mirarab and Tahvildari [35] introduced the first TCP framework based on Bayesian Networks (BN), which rely on probability theory. However, BN is challenging to build and use, as well as time-consuming during execution [22, 36].

Swarm intelligence algorithms are recently gaining increasing usage among researchers for solving challenging optimization problems due to their powerful performance and flexibility [37, 38]. Concerning TCP, swarm intelligence algorithms were widely used due to their effectiveness in solving NP-hard problems, ease of implementation, and shorter computation time, among other AI techniques [37–39]. There are several swarm intelligence studies based on TCP, such as Lu and Zhong [40], Manaswini and Rama Mohan Reddy [41], Su et al. [42], Pathik et al. [43], and Singhal et al. [44]. Hence, researchers argued that hybrid swarm algorithms outperform single swarm algorithms in optimizing test cases [39, 45]. It was also reported that multi-factor (multi-objective) TCP outperforms single-factor TCP for several reasons, such as their capability to cope with the increasing complexity of test case optimization and to tackle two or more objectives for optimization [22–25, 46].

Likewise, TCP, as a maintenance activity, can favorably affect the production of sustainable software towards reliable functionality in the long term. Currently, the term *"sustainability"* is frequently used in requests for research proposals and conference sessions, as well as in ICOCI proceedings. In the software engineering domain, sustainability comprises five pillars: environmental, social, economic, technical, and individual (i.e., human), in which sustainability is treated as a quality objective [47, 48]. As stated by [48], testing activities can directly affect technical and economic sustainability, as well as the three other dimensions indirectly. Thus, TCP contributes to producing sustainable software by reducing the overall cost, time, and effort required, as well as producing reliable software functionalities that last longer for long-term use.

In summary, existing TCP techniques lack reliability and suffer from efficiency and effectiveness issues for several reasons, such as evaluation issues, results reproducibility issues, comparison issues, more hybridization among swarm algorithms that needed to be involved, and more practical factors that needed to be incorporated in optimizing test cases [4, 36, 49, 50]. This leads to introducing more TCP methods and trying more new TCP factors to enhance testing efficiency and effectiveness. Therefore, the following section describes the proposed TCP framework of the study and details the process involved for each component in the framework.

3 Proposed Work

The TCP strategy is one of the means to improve the efficiency and effectiveness of software testing, particularly regression testing. This section explains the development of the proposed TCP framework in detail, where the framework focuses mainly on the available testware for exposing faults, as the absence of source code cannot affect the process of optimization. Basically, this TCP framework consists of three main components: inputs, processes, and outputs. The inputs to the system are unit test cases (test suites) and historical data (i.e., data related to previous test runs, such as a fault matrix). The process consists of two stages. First, extract data related to the five TCP factors (indicators) and store those indicators in a file. The indicators that are extracted are emphasized as numbers. For the fault detection factor, the indicator is the number of faults detected by a test case and the fault severity indicated by the fault impact level. Test case dependency is indicated by the number of test cases that a specific test case depends on or must run before. Although test cases were classified dissimilarly, no two similar test cases are in the same group. The risk is high when the user keys in data to the system, so responsible test cases for that part are given higher priority than others.

All these indicators are stored in a spreadsheet file. Next, the spreadsheet file is passed to the optimization part for the preparation of the suitable artifact. Lastly, the intended outputs of the framework are the optimized test cases. Further details are in the following subsections. The proposed TCP framework is presented in Fig. 1.

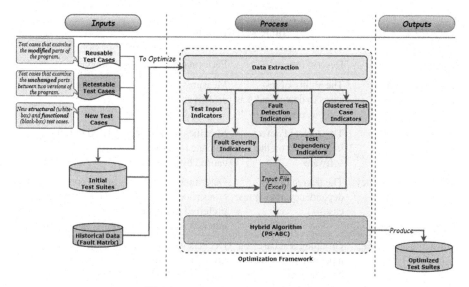

Fig. 1. The proposed TCP framework

The development of the proposed TCP framework consists of four distinct steps. These steps include selecting TCP factors, designing a weighted fitness function that represents the five TCP factors in the optimization process, the identification of a hybrid swarm algorithm for managing the optimization process, and the evaluation of the developed framework. The following subsections provide a comprehensive breakdown of each of these steps.

3.1 Determination of Test Case Prioritization Factors

Regarding TCP factors, the most deployed factors are fault detection, code coverage (statement, branch, loop, decision, function, and comments), fault coverage, and requirements [7, 49, 51, 52]. Nevertheless, this study utilized five TCP factors, in which three were selected from the literature, while the remaining two were new. Determining fault detection and severity as parts of this framework are based on two aspects; the first one is related to the theory of fault-based testing, and the second is the judgment of Hao et al. [53], as the main aim of regression testing is fault detection and most efforts surround this aim. Clustering test cases in a certain way also adds benefits to the optimization, where classifying test cases based on dissimilarity outperforms similarity techniques and gains popularity due to its effectiveness and performance [54–56]. Furtherly, the test case dependency is recommended to be utilized in optimizing test cases by Harman

[24] and Onoma [57] due to practice needs. Finally, user inputs are risky due to the nature of human beings as fallible beings. As guided by fault-based testing theory and the aim of regression testing, risk needs to be managed and reduced by covering the risk area using test cases with the aim of exposing faults [1, 58, 59]. Hence, these factors are described in Table 2 below.

Table 2. TCP Factors

Factor	Description	Performance	Source
Fault detection	The ability of test cases to detect faults as early as possible	Measures test effectiveness	Used in [9, 10]
Fault severity	The detected defect impact level on the software	Identifies the possible damage to software caused by an error	Used in [60–62]
Test case dependency	The degree of dependency among test cases	Determines which test cases should be or are preferred to run before others	As reported in [24], the Contribution
Clustered test cases	Grouping test cases on a pattern basis, such as similarity or dissimilarity	Decides which pattern group of test cases run first	Used in [54, 63–65]
Test Input	The risk of user input to the software	Gives a privileged for risky tests based on user input to be run first	Contribution

Table 2 elaborates on the selected TCP factors with a brief description, performance, and studies related to these factors. The development of the framework is based on the theory of fault-based testing by Morell [66, 67]. This theory assumes that there is a relationship between a program, its specifications, and test sets. Due to this theory, the focus of the design of the TCP framework is concentrated on testware and test sets with the goal of exposing faults. In terms of the fault detection factor, Hao et al. [53] reported that TCP has one primary objective (i.e., fault detection) and several secondary objectives (e.g., structural coverage or risk coverage), in which fault detection is a measure of regression testing effectiveness, and enhancing early fault detection is the aim of this study. In this paper, fault detection is identified as the test case's ability to detect faults, i.e., the number of faults detected by the test case. Fault severity has been used in TCP since 2001 by Elbaum et al. [60], in which the impact of faults on software is not equal, and the more severe faults are the first to be detected and fixed. Fault severity cannot be treated as an independent factor for optimization, so it is usually incorporated with other factors such as fault detection, fault coverage, and the cost of test cases [60–62].

For clustering techniques, they have been used in optimizing test cases. Studies [54, 63–65] considered this technique in TCP. Clustering test cases based on the similarity of faults detected [63], clustering test cases based on their similarity [64], and dissimilarity clustering of test cases using historical data analysis [54]. To the best of our knowledge, test case dependency and test input factors have not been used in the regression testing domain before. Harman [24] reported that this soft constraint can be treated as a factor for optimizing test cases (i.e., some test cases must be executed before others to establish a system state or provide better performance in some way). Onoma [57] stated that ignoring test case dependency during the testing process could introduce additional problems. Accordingly, this study exploits test case dependency as one of the TCP factors for seeking a better prioritization process.

Testing the input of the software systems can be potentially faulty and delay any system process when users have keyed in (i.e., inserting data manually into the system) rather than generated by systems. Besides, such features in any system are more important to stakeholders and should be precisely tested due to their documented requisition and risky nature related to human fallibility. In other words, test cases with user input are given higher priority than those with input generated by the system.

3.2 Designing Weighted Fitness Function

In this TCP framework, each test case under optimization will have five values matched to the factors represented in the fitness function; below is a brief description of each factor.

Fault Detection (Maximizing). It represents the ability of a test case to detect a fault, ranging from 0 to 100%. In other words, it means the test case that captures a higher number of faults has higher priority than others, i.e., the range can be from 0 (no fault detected) up to the possible number of faults that the test case can capture [68].

Fault Severity (Maximizing). It indicates the impact level/scale of the detected fault (i.e., possible damage caused by this fault) on the software. According to several researchers [69–71], faults can be categorized into five levels based on their impact (severity), as shown in Table 3 below.

Table 3. Fault Severity Categorization

Severity	Level	Description
Critical	5	Crashes, data loss, severe memory leak
Major	4	Major loss of functionality
Normal	3	Some loss of functionality, regular issues
Minor	2	Minor loss of functionality
Trivial	1	Cosmetic issue

Test Case Dependency (Minimizing Dependency). It denotes the dependability of test cases, whether a test case depends on other test cases or is independent. Hence, there are test cases that should be run before other test cases in which subsequent test cases become possible. For instance, some test cases cannot be appropriately run before others because such test cases establish a system state. Values of dependency ranged from 0 for independent test cases up to several dependent test cases (test cases that must execute before). In other words, a test case with no or less dependency is given higher priority than others.

Clustered Test Cases (Minimizing Similarity). It implies the test cases will be classified into several groups based on dissimilarity, so there will not be any two similar test cases in a cluster. Each test case is given a number for its cluster (group number). Any test case located in the first group is given a higher priority than later groups. The start value of the clustered test cases is (1), and no (0) value is accepted.

Test Input (Maximize). It presents the input type, i.e., to the system under test (SUT), based on whether input data is keyed in by users or generated by the system. Test input was considered to improve robustness and minimize the SUT's input risk. The value is represented as a Boolean (0 or 1). If the input to the system were keyed in by the user, the value would be (1), which means the input risk is high. Otherwise, it takes the value 0, which indicates a low-risk test case.

In this study, the proposed TCP framework consists of five optimization factors reflected in the fitness function for multi-objective optimization. These factors vary for maximization and minimization and need to be weighted. This study will adapt the analytic hierarchy process (AHP) method for defining the weights of each factor in the TCP framework for further steps. AHP is a popular multi-criteria decision-making (MCDM) method introduced in 1980 by Saaty [72]. To assign importance level to the TCP factors, seven experts were involved in scaling the TCP factors, while factors were ranked based on importance degree (i.e., extreme, strong, moderate, low, or least importance).

Table 4. Experts' feedback on scaling the importance of TCP factors

Participant	Fault Detection	Fault Severity	Test Case Clustering	Test Case Dependency	Test Input
1	Strong Importance	Extreme Importance	Low Importance	Least Importance	Moderate Importance
2	Moderate Importance	Least Importance	Strong Importance	Extreme Importance	Low Importance
3	Strong Importance	Extreme Importance	Moderate Importance	Least Importance	Low Importance
4	Extreme Importance	Strong Importance	Least Importance	Low Importance	Moderate Importance

(continued)

Table 4. (*continued*)

Participant	Fault Detection	Fault Severity	Test Case Clustering	Test Case Dependency	Test Input
5	Moderate Importance	Extreme Importance	Least Importance	Low Importance	Strong Importance
6	Extreme Importance	Strong Importance	Moderate Importance	Low Importance	Least Importance
7	Extreme Importance	Strong Importance	Moderate Importance	Low Importance	Least Importance

The experts' feedback reveals the importance of each factor in the TCP process from the expert's perspective, as presented in Table 4. To analyze the above ordinal data, steps of descriptive analysis by Kumar [73] were utilized. Accordingly, the TCP factors were ranked based on their importance as fault detection, fault severity, test case clustering, test case dependency, and then test input. After obtaining the importance degree for each TCP factor, AHP was conducted to acquire the weights for each TCP factor. Based on the aforementioned, the fitness function in the first form is designed as follows:

$$f(x) = (min(TCD), max(FD), max(FS), min(CTC), max(TI)) \qquad (1)$$

where:

- *TCD* denotes test cases dependency,
- *FD* represents fault detection,
- *FS* indicates fault severity,
- *CTC* implies clustered test case (the cluster of a test case),
- *TI* presents test input.

By adding the weight for each TCP factor, the fitness function is represented mathematically as:

$$f(x) = (TDC \times w_1) + (FD \times w_2) + (FS \times w_3) + (CTC \times w_4) + (TI \times w_5) \qquad (2)$$

where:

- w_i conveys the weight of each factor.

Mathematically, the fitness function can be represented in a short form if we unify the weights symbol and TCP factors:

Let

$$T = [TCD\ FD\ FS\ CTC\ TI], \text{ and } w = [w_1\ w_2\ w_3\ w_4\ w_5]$$

Then

$$f(x) = \sum_{i=1}^{5} T(i)w(i) \qquad (3)$$

where T represents the five TCP factors, and w represents the weights for every factor. Given the equation above, the test case with the highest score is given the highest priority among others during the optimization process.

3.3 Hybrid Swarm Algorithm for Test Case Prioritization

After extracting the data for the five TCP factors regarding each test case and storing them in a file, the test cases are now ready for optimization against the weighted fitness function stated earlier. A hybrid swarm intelligence algorithm was selected to handle the extracted data regarding the five TCP factors. This study utilizes the hybrid swarm algorithm named the *"PS–ABC"* algorithm, which was proposed by Li et al. [74], to optimize test cases based on the five factors mentioned earlier. This hybrid PS–ABC algorithm is deployed due to the strengths of PSO and ABC in producing global and optimized solutions. Furthermore, it has yet to be reported in any studies concerning the integration of PSO and ABC algorithms in facilitating the TCP.

4 The Framework Evaluation

This proposed TCP framework is evaluated through two processes: verification and validation. For the verification process, a total of ten software testing and quality assurance experts participated in an *expert review* activity consisting of five, each from academia and industry. The expert review was designed to evaluate this TCP framework based on five evaluation criteria through a five-point Likert scale instrument. The evaluation criteria are understandability, relevancy, consistency, organization, and completeness, which have been used in previous studies such as [75] and [76]. Based on such criteria, 125 invitations were sent through e-mails and social media to potential experts world-wide, where ten experts were chosen for this evaluation activity for feedback analysis due to the completeness of the expert review form. Their feedback was analyzed through descriptive statistics and was significantly positive, which will be discussed and detailed later in future work. Based on the findings of the verification stage, the proposed TCP framework is reliable and practical to be implemented in a real-world environment. The validation process will be carried out after programming this TCP framework, and generally accepted metrics, public benchmarking, and measurements in the regression testing domain will be used.

Additionally, the TCP framework will be subjected to controlled experiments utilizing open-source programs sourced from public repositories designated for research purposes in the software testing field. The examination will involve the APFD metric and a comparative analysis with existing TCP studies. It is anticipated that forthcoming reports will detail the outcomes of these delicately conducted experiments.

5 Conclusion

Test cases in software development are reusable as a testing artifact that can be optimized through diverse ways, such as prioritization, reduction, generation, augmentation, as well as automation. Test case prioritization is the process of rescheduling test cases to attain a performance goal. It can effectively reduce time, cost, and effort in testing and maintenance activities. This study introduces a new TCP framework in which the components and development process are elaborated in detail. The framework takes inputs, extracts indicators for five TCP factors, passes them to an optimization algorithm, and then provides a prioritized test artifact, i.e., optimized test cases. One of the aims of this framework is to provide sustainable software through a testing process that ensures the longevity of software functions over an extended period. The proposed framework is currently under development. In the future, the implemented framework will be empirically evaluated.

Acknowledgments. This research was supported by the Ministry of Higher Education (MoHE) under the Consultation Project Grant Scheme (Reference Code: P-58/614). The content of this article is solely the responsibility of the authors and does not necessarily represent the official views of MoHE, Malaysia. The authors would also like to extend their gratitude to the Data Management & Software Solution Research Lab, School of Computing, Universiti Utara Malaysia for their generous support in sponsoring the publication of this article.

References

1. Jorgensen, P.C., De Vries, B.: Software Testing: A Craftsman's Approach. CRC Press (2021)
2. Vaidyanathan, S., Lakshmi Priya, B.: Challenges in developing software in today's scenario: an analysis at developmental stage level. In: Misra, S., et al. (eds.) Confluence of AI, Machine, and Deep Learning in Cyber Forensics, pp. 199–222. IGI Global (2021)
3. Cao, H., Cui, Z., Deng, M., Chu, Y., Meng, Y.: Automatic repair of Java programs with mixed granularity and variable mapping. Inf. Technol. Control. **52**, 68–84 (2023). https://doi.org/10.5755/j01.itc.52.1.30715
4. Ba-Quttayyan, B., Mohd, H., Yusof, Y.: A critical analysis of swarm intelligence for regression test case prioritization. J. Theor. Appl. Inf. Technol. **100**, 3997–4025 (2022)
5. Liu, Z., Chen, Q., Jiang, X.: A maintainability spreadsheet-driven regression test automation framework. In: 2013 IEEE 16th International Conference on Computational Science and Engineering, pp. 1181–1184. IEEE (2013)
6. Rothermel, G., Untch, R.H., Chengyun Chu, Harrold, M.J.: Prioritizing test cases for regression testing. IEEE Trans. Softw. Eng. **27**, 929–948 (2001). https://doi.org/10.1109/32.962562
7. Lu, C., Zhong, J., Xue, Y., Feng, L., Zhang, J.: Ant Colony System with sorting-based local search for coverage-based test case prioritization. IEEE Trans. Reliab. **69**, 1004–1020 (2020). https://doi.org/10.1109/TR.2019.2930358
8. Zhu, Y., Liu, F.: Test case prioritization algorithm based on improved code coverage. IAENG Int. J. Comput. Sci. **50**, 785 (2023)
9. Yadav, D.K., Dutta, S.: A new cluster-based test case prioritization using cat swarm optimization technique. In: Nath, V., Mandal, J.K. (eds.) Proceedings of the Third International Conference on Microelectronics, Computing and Communication Systems. LNEE, vol. 556, pp. 441–450. Springer, Singapore (2019). https://doi.org/10.1007/978-981-13-7091-5_36
10. Samad, A., Mahdin, H.B., Kazmi, R., Ibrahim, R., Baharum, Z.: Multiobjective test case prioritization using test case effectiveness: multicriteria scoring method. Sci. Program. **2021**, 1–13 (2021). https://doi.org/10.1155/2021/9988987

11. Abbas, M., Inayat, I., Saadatmand, M., Jan, N.: Requirements dependencies-based test case prioritization for extra-functional properties. In: 2019 IEEE International Conference on Software Testing, Verification and Validation Workshops (ICSTW), pp. 159–163. IEEE (2019)

12. Dahiya, O., Solanki, K.: An efficient requirement-based test case prioritization technique using optimized TFC-SVM approach. Int. J. Eng. Trends Technol. **69**, 5–16 (2021). https://doi.org/10.14445/22315381/IJETT-V69I1P202

13. Abd Halim, S., Abang Jawawi, D.N., Sahak, M.: Similarity distance measure and prioritization algorithm for test case prioritization in software product line testing. J. Inf. Commun. Technol. **18**, 57–75 (2018). https://doi.org/10.32890/jict2019.18.1.8281

14. Vescan, A., Pintea, C.-M., Pop, P.C.: Solving the test case prioritization problem with secure features using Ant Colony System. In: Martínez Álvarez, F., Troncoso Lora, A., Sáez Muñoz, J.A., Quintián, H., Corchado, E. (eds.) CISIS/ICEUTE -2019. AISC, vol. 951, pp. 67–76. Springer, Cham (2020). https://doi.org/10.1007/978-3-030-20005-3_7

15. Sun, J., Chen, J., Wang, G.: Multi-objective test case prioritization based on epistatic particle swarm optimization. Int. J. Perform. Eng. **14**, 2441–2448 (2018). https://doi.org/10.23940/ijpe.18.10.p20.24412448

16. Zhang, L., Hou, S.-S., Guo, C., Xie, T., Mei, H.: Time-aware test-case prioritization using integer linear programming. In: Proceedings of the Eighteenth International Symposium on Software Testing and Analysis, ISSTA 2009, p. 213. ACM Press, New York (2009)

17. Khatibsyarbini, M., Isa, M.A., Jawawi, D.N.A., Abang, D.N.: A hybrid weight-based and string distances using particle swarm optimization for prioritizing test cases. J. Theor. Appl. Inf. Technol. **95**, 2723–2732 (2017)

18. Chen, Z., et al.: Exploring better black-box test case prioritization via log analysis. ACM Trans. Softw. Eng. Methodol. **32**, 1–32 (2023). https://doi.org/10.1145/3569932

19. Lu, Y., et al.: How does regression test prioritization perform in real-world software evolution? In: Proceedings of the 38th International Conference on Software Engineering, ICSE 2016, pp. 535–546. ACM Press, New York (2016)

20. Nayak, S., Kumar, C., Tripathi, S., Mohanty, N., Baral, V.: Regression test optimization and prioritization using honeybee optimization algorithm with fuzzy rule base. Soft. Comput. **25**, 9925–9942 (2021). https://doi.org/10.1007/s00500-020-05428-z

21. Bian, Y., Li, Z., Zhao, R., Gong, D.: Epistasis based ACO for regression test case prioritization. IEEE Trans. Emerg. Top. Comput. Intell. **1**, 213–223 (2017). https://doi.org/10.1109/TETCI.2017.2699228

22. Khatibsyarbini, M., Isa, M.A., Jawawi, D.N.A., Tumeng, R.: Test case prioritization approaches in regression testing: a systematic literature review. Inf. Softw. Technol. **93**, 74–93 (2018). https://doi.org/10.1016/j.infsof.2017.08.014

23. Harman, M., Jia, Y., Zhang, Y.: Achievements, open problems and challenges for search-based software testing. In: 2015 IEEE 8th International Conference on Software Testing, Verification and Validation (ICST), Graz, Austria, pp. 1–12. IEEE (2015)

24. Harman, M.: Making the case for MORTO: multi-objective regression test optimization. In: 2011 IEEE Fourth International Conference on Software Testing, Verification and Validation Workshops, Berlin, Germany, pp. 111–114. IEEE (2011)

25. De Castro-Cabrera, M.D.C., García-Dominguez, A., Medina-Bulo, I.: Trends in prioritization of test cases: 2017–2019. In: Proceedings of the 35th Annual ACM Symposium on Applied Computing, SAC 2020, Brno, Czech Republic, pp. 2005–2011. Association for Computing Machinery, New York (2020)

26. Parejo, J.A., Sánchez, A.B., Segura, S., Ruiz-Cortés, A., Lopez-Herrejon, R.E., Egyed, A.: Multi-objective test case prioritization in highly configurable systems: a case study. J. Syst. Softw. **122**, 287–310 (2016). https://doi.org/10.1016/j.jss.2016.09.045

27. Ricken, K., Dyck, A.: A survey on multi-objective regression test optimization. In: Full-scale Software Engineering/The Art of Software Testing, pp. 32–37 (2017)

28. Ramírez, A., Feldt, R., Romero, J.R.: A taxonomy of information attributes for test case prioritisation: applicability, machine learning. ACM Trans. Softw. Eng. Methodol. **32**, 1–42 (2023). https://doi.org/10.1145/3511805

29. Kim, J.-M., Porter, A.: A history-based test prioritization technique for regression testing in resource-constrained environments. In: Proceedings of the 24th International Conference on Software Engineering, ICSE 2002, New York, USA, p. 119. ACM Press, New York (2002)

30. Aggrawal, K.K., Singh, Y., Kaur, A.: Code coverage-based technique for prioritizing test cases for regression testing. ACM SIGSOFT Softw. Eng. Notes. **29**, 1–4 (2004). https://doi.org/10.1145/1022494.1022511

31. Srikanth, H., Williams, L., Osborne, J.: System test case prioritization of new and regression test cases. In: 2005 International Symposium on Empirical Software Engineering. pp. 62–71. IEEE (2005)

32. Korel, B., Koutsogiannakis, G., Tahat, L.H.: Application of system models in regression test suite prioritization. In: 2008 IEEE International Conference on Software Maintenance, pp. 247–256. IEEE (2008)

33. Do, H., Mirarab, S., Tahvildari, L., Rothermel, G.: The effects of time constraints on test case prioritization: a series of controlled experiments. IEEE Trans. Softw. Eng. **36**, 593–617 (2010). https://doi.org/10.1109/TSE.2010.58

34. Yoo, S., Harman, M.: Regression testing minimization, selection and prioritization: a survey. Softw. Test. Verification Reliab. **22**(2), 67–120 (2013). https://doi.org/10.1002/stvr.430

35. Mirarab, S., Tahvildari, L.: A prioritization approach for software test cases based on Bayesian Networks. In: Dwyer, M.B., Lopes, A. (eds.) FASE 2007. LNCS, vol. 4422, pp. 276–290. Springer, Heidelberg (2007). https://doi.org/10.1007/978-3-540-71289-3_22

36. Ba-Quttayyan, B., Mohd, H., Yusof, Y.: Regression test case prioritization frameworks: challenges and future directions. Int. J. Recent Technol. Eng. **8**, 8457–8462 (2019). https://doi.org/10.35940/ijrte.D9735.118419

37. Chakraborty, A., Kar, A.K.: Swarm intelligence: a review of algorithms. In: Patnaik, S., Yang, X.-S., Nakamatsu, K. (eds.) Nature-Inspired Computing and Optimization. MOST, vol. 10, pp. 475–494. Springer, Cham (2017). https://doi.org/10.1007/978-3-319-50920-4_19

38. Karaboga, D., Akay, B., Karaboga, N.: A survey on the studies employing machine learning (ML) for enhancing artificial bee colony (ABC) optimization algorithm. Cogent. Eng. **7**, 1855741 (2020). https://doi.org/10.1080/23311916.2020.1855741

39. Bajaj, A., Sangwan, O.P.: A survey on regression testing using nature-inspired approaches. In: 2018 4th International Conference on Computing Communication and Automation (ICCCA), Greater Noida, India, pp. 1–5. IEEE (2018)

40. Lu, C., Zhong, J.: An efficient ant colony system for coverage-based test case prioritization. In: Proceedings of the Genetic and Evolutionary Computation Conference Companion, Kyoto, Japan, pp. 91–92. ACM (2018)

41. Manaswini, B., Rama Mohan Reddy, A.: A shuffled frog leap algorithm-based test case prioritization technique to perform regression testing. Int. J. Eng. Adv. Technol. **8**, 671–674 (2019)

42. Su, W., Li, Z., Wang, Z., Yang, D.: A meta-heuristic test case prioritization method based on hybrid model. In: 2020 International Conference on Computer Engineering and Application (ICCEA), Guangzhou, China, pp. 430–435. IEEE (2020)

43. Pathik, B., Pathik, N., Sharma, M.: Test case prioritization for changed code using nature-inspired optimizer. J. Intell. Fuzzy Syst. **44**, 5711–5718 (2023). https://doi.org/10.3233/JIFS-222433

44. Singhal, S., Jatana, N., Subahi, A.F., Gupta, C., Khalaf, O.I., Alotaibi, Y.: Fault coverage-based test case prioritization and selection using African Buffalo Optimization. Comput. Mater. Contin. **74**, 6755–6774 (2023). https://doi.org/10.32604/cmc.2023.032308

45. Hassanien, A.E., Emary, E.E.: Swarm Intelligence: Principles, Advances, and Applications. CRC Press (2016)

46. Birchler, C., Khatiri, S., Derakhshanfar, P., Panichella, S., Panichella, A.: Single and multi-objective test cases prioritization for self-driving cars in virtual environments. ACM Trans. Softw. Eng. Methodol. **32**, 1–30 (2023). https://doi.org/10.1145/3533818

47. Noman, H., Mahoto, N.A., Bhatti, S., Abosaq, H.A., Al Reshan, M.S., Shaikh, A.: An exploratory study of software sustainability at early stages of software development. Sustainability **14**, 8596 (2022). https://doi.org/10.3390/su14148596

48. Lago, P., Koçak, S.A., Crnkovic, I., Penzenstadler, B.: Framing sustainability as a property of software quality. Commun. ACM **58**, 70–78 (2015). https://doi.org/10.1145/2714560

49. Bajaj, A., Sangwan, O.P.: A systematic literature review of test case prioritization using genetic algorithms. IEEE Access **7**, 126355–126375 (2019). https://doi.org/10.1109/ACCESS.2019.2938260

50. Brunetto, M., Denaro, G., Mariani, L., Pezzè, M.: On introducing automatic test case generation in practice: a success story and lessons learned. J. Syst. Softw. **176**, 110933 (2021). https://doi.org/10.1016/j.jss.2021.110933

51. Vats, R., Kumar, A.: Test case prioritization using cat swarm optimization. Int. J. Adv. Trends Comput. Sci. Eng. **9**, 8142–8148 (2020). https://doi.org/10.30534/ijatcse/2020/175952020

52. Zhang, W., Qi, Y., Zhang, X., Wei, B., Zhang, M., Dou, Z.: On test case prioritization using ant colony optimization algorithm. In: 2019 IEEE 21st International Conference on High-Performance Computing and Communications; IEEE 17th International Conference on Smart City; IEEE 5th International Conference on Data Science and Systems (HPCC/SmartCity/DSS), Zhangjiajie, China, pp. 2767–2773. IEEE (2019)

53. Hao, D., Zhang, L., Mei, H.: Test-case prioritization: achievements and challenges. Front. Comput. Sci. **10**, 769–777 (2016). https://doi.org/10.1007/s11704-016-6112-3

54. Abu Hasan, Md., Abdur Rahman, Md., Saeed Siddik, Md.: Test case prioritization based on dissimilarity clustering using historical data analysis. In: Kaushik, S., Gupta, D., Kharb, L., Chahal, D. (eds.) ICICCT 2017. CCIS, vol. 750, pp. 269–281. Springer, Singapore (2017). https://doi.org/10.1007/978-981-10-6544-6_25

55. Abdur, M., Abu, M., Saeed, M.: Prioritizing dissimilar test cases in regression testing using historical failure data. Int. J. Comput. Appl. **180**, 1–8 (2018). https://doi.org/10.5120/ijca2018916258

56. Sulaiman, R.A., Jawawi, D.N.A., Halim, S.A.: A dissimilarity with Dice-Jaro-Winkler test case prioritization approach for model-based testing in software product line. KSII Trans. Internet Inf. Syst. **15**, 932–951 (2021). https://doi.org/10.3837/tiis.2021.03.007

57. Onoma, A.K., Tsai, W.-T., Poonawala, M., Suganuma, H.: Regression testing in an industrial environment. Commun. ACM **41**, 81–86 (1998). https://doi.org/10.1145/274946.274960

58. Lou, Y., Chen, J., Zhang, L., Hao, D.: A survey on regression test-case prioritization. In: Advances in Computers, pp. 1–46. Elsevier Inc. (2019)

59. Chauhan, N.: Software Testing: Principles and Practices. Oxford University Press, Oxford (2010)

60. Elbaum, S., Malishevsky, A., Rothermel, G.: Incorporating varying test costs and fault severities into test case prioritization. In: Proceedings of the 23rd International Conference on Software Engineering, ICSE 2001, pp. 329–338. IEEE Computer Society (2001)

61. Gao, D., Guo, X., Zhao, L.: Test case prioritization for regression testing based on ant colony optimization. In: 2015 6th IEEE International Conference on Software Engineering and Service Science (ICSESS), Beijing, China, pp. 275–279. IEEE (2015)

62. Vescan, A., Pintea, C.-M., Pop, P.C.: Solving the test case prioritization problem with secure features using Ant Colony System. In: Álvarez, F.M., Lora, A.T., Muñoz, J.A.S., Quintián, H., Corchado, E. (eds.) CISIS/ICEUTE -2019. AISC, vol. 951, pp. 67–76. Springer, Cham (2020). https://doi.org/10.1007/978-3-030-20005-3_7

63. Yoo, S., Harman, M., Tonella, P., Susi, A.: Clustering test cases to achieve effective and scalable prioritisation incorporating expert knowledge. In: Proceedings of the Eighteenth International Symposium on Software Testing and Analysis, ISSTA 2009, New York, USA, p. 201. ACM Press, New York (2009)

64. Zhao, X., Wang, Z., Fan, X., Wang, Z.: A clustering-Bayesian network based approach for test case prioritization. In: 2015 IEEE 39th Annual Computer Software and Applications Conference, pp. 542–547. IEEE (2015)

65. Siddik, M.S., Sakib, K.: RDCC: an effective test case prioritization framework using software requirements, design, and source code collaboration. In: 2014 17th International Conference on Computer and Information Technology, ICCIT 2014, pp. 75–80. IEEE (2003)

66. Morell, L.J.: A theory of error-based testing (1984). http://www.dtic.mil/dtic/tr/fulltext/u2/a143533.pdf

67. Morell, L.J.: A theory of fault-based testing. IEEE Trans. Softw. Eng. **16**, 844–857 (1990). https://doi.org/10.1109/32.57623

68. Rothermel, G., Untch, R.H., Chu, C., Harrold, M.J.: Test case prioritization: an empirical study. In: Proceedings IEEE International Conference on Software Maintenance - 1999 (ICSM 1999). "Software Maintenance for Business Change" (Cat. No. 99CB36360), pp. 179–188. IEEE (1999)

69. Doğan, S., Betin-Can, A., Garousi, V.: Web application testing: a systematic literature review. J. Syst. Softw. **91**, 174–201 (2014). https://doi.org/10.1016/j.jss.2014.01.010

70. Mirshokraie, S., Mesbah, A., Pattabiraman, K.: Efficient JavaScript mutation testing. In: 2013 IEEE Sixth International Conference on Software Testing, Verification and Validation, pp. 74–83. IEEE (2013)

71. Mistrik, I., Soley, R.M., Ali, N., Grundy, J., Tekinerdogan, B.: Software Quality Assurance: In Large Scale and Complex Software-Intensive Systems (2016)

72. Saaty, T.L.: The Analytic Hierarchy Process: Planning, Priority Setting, Resource Allocation. McGraw-Hill, Inc. (1980)

73. Kumar, P.: Ranking scale questions for survey questionnaires. https://edifo.in/ranking-scale-for-survey-questionnaires/

74. Li, Z.Z., Wang, W., Yan, Y., Li, Z.Z.: PS–ABC: a hybrid algorithm based on particle swarm and artificial bee colony for high-dimensional optimization problems. Exp. Syst. Appl. **42**, 8881–8895 (2015). https://doi.org/10.1016/j.eswa.2015.07.043

75. Alaidaros, H., Omar, M., Romli, R.: An improved model of Agile Kanban method: verification process through experts' review. Int. J. Agil. Syst. Manag. **13**, 390 (2020). https://doi.org/10.1504/IJASM.2020.112337

76. Barraood, S.O., Mohd, H., Baharom, F.: An initial investigation of the effect of quality factors on Agile test case quality through experts' review. Cogent Eng. **9** (2022). https://doi.org/10.1080/23311916.2022.2082121

Towards a Sustainable Digital Society: Supporting Producer Mobility in Named Data Networking Through Immobile Anchor-Based Mechanism

Ahmad Abrar⬤, Khuzairi Mohd Zaini⬤, Ahmad Suki Che Mohamed Arif[(✉)] ⬤,
and Mohd Hasbullah Omar⬤

InterNetWorks Research Laboratory, School of Computing, Universiti Utara Malaysia, UUM
Sintok, 06010 Sintok, Kedah, Malaysia
abrar_ahmad@ahsgs.uum.edu.my, ahmadabrar2011@yahoo.com,
{khuzairi,suki1207,mhomar}@uum.edu.my

Abstract. The increasing proliferation of intelligent mobile devices and the subsequent surge in data traffic have placed a burden on the current Internet infrastructure. To address this challenge, Named Data Networking (NDN) has emerged as a
promising future Internet architecture. NDN aims to address the evolving patterns
of Internet traffic by providing inherent support for consumer mobility through in-
network caching. This approach enhances content availability while minimizing
delays. However, producer mobility in NDN raises numerous challenges, including
Interest packet loss, Interest retransmission, high signalling costs, and unnecessary bandwidth consumption. This research explores and critically analyses the
most widely used approaches for managing producer mobility in NDN. This paper
introduces an innovative immobile anchor-based mobility mechanism designed to
address the challenges associated with producer mobility in NDN. The immobile refers to the fixed nature of the anchor router, which is strategically placed
within the network topology to facilitate the management of producer mobility.
This immobile anchor router serves as a centralized control point for caching and
redirecting Interest packets during producer handoff processes, thereby mitigating
packet loss and optimizing bandwidth usage. The focal point of this novel approach is to reduce the repercussions of producer mobility on network performance.
Its aim is to minimize factors like packet loss, signalling overhead, and bandwidth
usage, with the ultimate goal of enhancing the overall efficiency of NDN-based
networks.

Keywords: Handoff · Mobility Management · Producer Mobility ·
Information-centric networking · Named data networking

1 Introduction

The widespread adoption of smart mobile devices and applications in our digital society has greatly increased the use of the current Internet paradigm. This paradigm
places a strong emphasis on accessing data and services, leading to new demands for

improved content distribution, seamless support for mobility, and security [1]. Conversely, advanced technologies like Internet of Everything (IoE), Internet of Things (IoT), and Internet of Medical Things (IoMT) are currently some of the most popular trends in the digital society. A digital society is a term that refers to a community or nation where the majority of citizens have access to and regularly use digital technologies such as the Internet, computers, smartphones, and other digital devices to communicate, access information, conduct business, and participate in social and civic activities. All of these contemporary technologies have a big impact on the medical field (e-health system), building smart homes, making smart cars (autonomous vehicles), and many other IoT applications [2, 3]. Furthermore, existing Internet data connection services are primarily reliant on these cutting-edge technologies. In addition, the communication of these game-changing innovations is controlled by a particular application on the smart mobile device of the end user. In effect, this has led to a sharp rise in both Internet users and applications [4]. Yet, the current Internet paradigm is not fully capable of adapting to these new technological eras. A new Internet infrastructure is required in addition to the growth of intelligent mobile devices and applications. In the realm of Information-Centric Networking (ICN), the Named Data Networking (NDN) architecture has emerged as a promising effort to satisfy these needs [3].

2 Information-Centric Networking (ICN)

The idea of ICN was first proposed by Cheriton et al. in 1999 as a replacement for the host-centric Internet Protocol/Transmission Control Protocol architecture that now governs the Internet [5]. ICN's core concept is to switch from a host-centric to a content-centric paradigm of network communication, where content is identified by unique names rather than IP addresses [6]. To retrieve content, the user sends a request packet (Content Name: ILab.my/video) that specifies the particular content source ("ILab.my") and the type of information required "video" [1]. While ICN has several projects, the Named Data Networking (NDN) architecture stands out due to its innovative and efficient design [7].

3 Named Data Networking (NDN)

The NDN paradigm is ICN's foremost initiative towards enhancing network performance. Its primary objective is to transition from an IP-based system to a content-based communication system, where content is identified by its unique name. Therefore, in the NDN paradigm, content is the main focus of communication [8]. In the NDN paradigm, device-to-device content exchange is facilitated using Interest and Data packets. The Interest packet contains the specific content name in its field to access the content, which is also used in the Data packet's field. The consumer, who requests the content, uses the Interest packet, while the producer, who fulfills the consumer's content needs, uses the Data packet. The NDN data structure plays a vital role in controlling the packet exchanges between the consumer and producer, including packet forwarding and path optimization. This data structure comprises three components: Content Store (CS), Pending Interest Table (PIT), and Forwarding Information Base (FIB) [9]. The CS component of the NDN data structure is responsible for caching incoming content on the router. The PIT maintains the incoming interface associated with the requested content name, while the FIB maintains the outgoing interfaces associated with the name prefix of the content provider [1]. According to Fig 1, a content request (IRL.my/ahmad.jpg) is generated to retrieve content (ahmad.jpg).

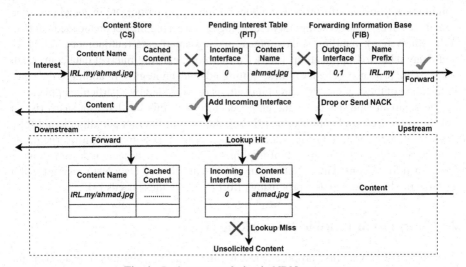

Fig. 1. Packets transmission in NDN structure.

When a request is made in the NDN paradigm, the CS is the first component to look for a match with the requested content name. If a match is found, the content is promptly sent back to the content requester. However, if the requested content is not found in the router CS, the content request is directed to the PIT phase. The PIT initiate examines for duplication of the same request and records any duplicates to avoid forwarding them. If the request is not a duplicate, the PIT saves the request's entry with the incoming interface of request and passes it on toward the FIB phase. The FIB explores its list of all name prefixes in order to find the most appropriate content source. If no prefix found, the request is discarded, or a Negative Acknowledgement (NACK) is sent. Otherwise, the request is routed to the matching content source (e.g., IRL.my). When a respective content arrives, if the corresponding PIT record is found (known as a lookup hit), the immediately content is delivered to the content requester, cached in the CS, and the related PIT entry of the delivered content is declined [10]. If there is no matching PIT entry found for the content, it is discarded as unsolicited content.

Consequently, NDN paradigm has an innovative architectural design that provides network management, authenticity, and self-sufficiency. Its unique features include in-router content caching, proficient content distribution, named content, smart named-based routing, best path forwarding and improved bandwidth utilization. Additionally, it grants protection for every piece of content, guarantees content privacy, and supports mobility, which refers to the physical movement of devices within and between networks. In NDN, there are two types of mobility: consumer mobility and producer mobility [11].

4 Consumer Mobility Assistance

The consumer is referred to as a content requester or content user in NDN. It sends an Interest packet with the name of the required content to request content. Consumer mobility refers to the movements of consumers to different access points or Content Routers (CR). In Fig 2, the consumer transmits Interest from the connected router CR3, and the Interest moves from junctional router CR2 to CR1 until it reaches the producer.

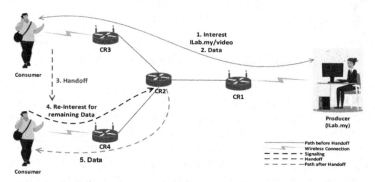

Fig. 2. Assistance of consumer mobility in NDN.

The producer sends the requested content in the form of data packets to the consumer via the Interest reverse path. The consumer disconnects from CR3 and connects to CR4 during the packet exchange, which is known as handoff. The consumer handoff process disrupts ongoing communication. Surprisingly, due to the in-router caching ability the remaining contents already caches at the junctional router CR2. When a consumer relocates to a new location CR4, it sends the Interest for remaining content to the junctional router CR2 and retrieves it. As a result of the in-router caching feature, the NDN inherently supports consumer mobility and improves the content availability [12].

5 Producer Mobility Assistance

In NDN paradigm, a producer implies to a content source that supplies content in response to consumer data demand. Every producer has its a unique name prefix to distinguishes it from others, and the FIB in the NDN data structure maintains the list of these different name prefixes. The FIB also determines the best path to access content with the least amount of effort. Typically, a consumer generates an Interest packet as of CR1 to the producer's location at CR3 to retrieve content. However, if the producer physically relocates from CR3 to CR4 router, the consumer's new incoming Interest packets continue to follow the producer's CR3 old location router. This can result in lost Interest packets at CR3 router due to producer inaccessibility and inadequate stored contents, as presented in Fig 3.

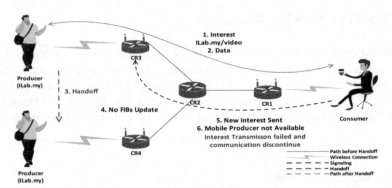

Fig. 3. Assistance of Producer mobility in NDN.

In NDN paradigm, when a producer relocates, the consumer constantly forwards the Interest packet in an attempt to locate the required content. However, this approach results in excessive loss of Interest packets, higher Interest retransmission rate, unnecessary bandwidth utilization, and extensive handoff latency. As a result, producer is not capable of fully supporting the mobility in NDN environment [5, 17]. Additionally, the current router-level protocol, Listen First Broadcast Later (LFBL), is not entirely capable of addressing the issues of losing Interest packets and constant Interest retransmission [13].

6   Classification of Producer Diverse Mobility Approaches

Various solutions have been proposed by researchers to address the issues related to producer mobility in the NDN paradigm. These solutions have been categorized into specific approaches based on their characteristics and advantages.

6.1   Indirection-Based Mobility Approach (IMA)

To enable support for producer mobility in the NDN paradigm, the Indirection-based Mobility Approach (IMA) introduces a Home Agent (HA) router in the network. The HA is responsible for maintaining information regarding the content prefix and its location. The content prefix identifies the producer, while the location indicates its physical position. During the handoff process, the HA redirects packets towards the producer's new location [14]. As illustrated in Fig 4, When a producer moves from CR3 to CR4, it sends binding information to update its new location and name prefix to the HA router, which acknowledges the information. Consequently, when an incoming Interest packet reaches CR3, it is redirected to the HA, which in turn forwards it to the producer at CR4 using a triangular routing path.

Triangular communication uses encapsulation and decapsulation in order to exchange Interest and data packet. However, during the handoff process Interest packets experiences loss and excessive Interest transmissions. Further, it uses the triangular routing after the handoff process which may result in high signalling and extra overhead for each packet.

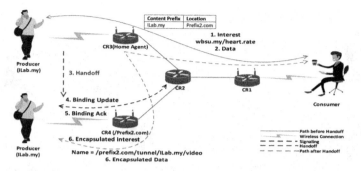

Fig. 4. Indirection-based mobility approach in NDN.

6.2 Mapping-Based Mobility Approach (MMA)

To support producer mobility in the NDN paradigm, the Mapping-based Mobility Approach (MMA) proposes a server within the network called the mapping/DNS/rendezvous server. This server manages the movement and location information of producers by mapping their content prefix with their location [15]. When a producer relocates from CR3 to CR4, it sends mapping updates and acknowledgement messages to the mapping server from its new location at CR4 to update the routing path towards the new location. However, when the producer handoffs from CR3 to CR4, consumer Interest packets are unable to reach the content producer at CR3, as the producer has relocated to CR4, as shown in Fig. 5.

In MMA, when a producer relocates from one location to another, the consumer sends a query to the mapping server to obtain the producer's new location. The mapping server then forwards the producer's new location information to the consumer, who can directly send Interest packets to the producer's new location at CR4 using this information to retrieve data packets. However, during the producer's long handoff process, consumer Interest packets are subject to major losses. Additionally, the approach is unable to control Interest packet loss during mapping information updates towards the server. Moreover, frequent producer movements and additional consumer queries to the mapping server can cause high signalling and Interest transmission in the network.

6.3 Locator/Identifier Split-Based Mobility Approach (LISMA)

The Locator/Identifier Split-based Mobility Approach (LISMA) introduces a Home Agent (HA) router in its network to facilitate producer mobility. The HA is responsible for maintaining the locator and identifier information of the producer, where the locator indicates the location, and the identifier refers to the content prefix of the producer [16]. As reflected in Fig. 6, when a producer handoff from CR3 to CR4, it exchanges location update and acknowledgement packets with the HA to update its new location.

In LISMA, when a consumer sends an Interest packet to the HA, the HA modifies the Interest packet by adding the producer's location information and redirects it towards the producer. The producer then sends the data packet to the HA, which in turn forwards it to the consumer. This exchange of Interest and data packets between the consumer and

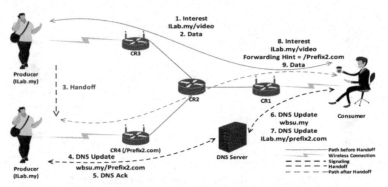

Fig. 5. Mapping-based mobility approach in NDN.

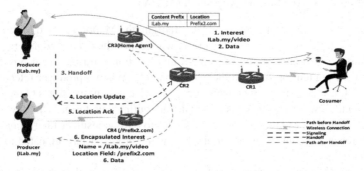

Fig. 6. Locator/Identifier split-based mobility approach in NDN.

producer involves triangular routing and uses encapsulation and decapsulation methods, which can cause high signalling and complexity in large networks. Additionally, the unavailability of the producer during the handoff process can lead to excessive loss of consumer Interest packets and increase the need for retransmission of lost Interest packets.

6.4 Control Data Plane Split-Based Mobility Approach (CDPSMA)

The Control Data Plane Split-based Mobility Approach (CDPSMA) is another approach that supports producer mobility by introducing the Rendezvous Point (RP) and Resource Handler (RH) in the network. The RP is created by modifying a regular router to provide the routing path for Interest and data packets. RH is established by modifying a server to monitor the producer's movement behaviour [12]. When a producer decides to handoff from CR3, it sends a deregistered query to the RH to initiate the handoff process, as shown in Fig. 7.

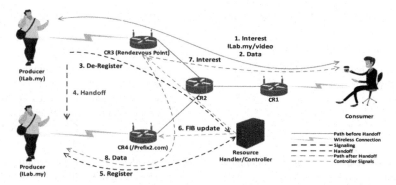

Fig. 7. Control data plane split-based mobility approach in NDN.

In CDPSMA, when a producer initiates a handoff process from CR3, it sends a deregistered query to the RH to remove its location information. At the same time, upcoming consumer Interest packets are cached at the RP. When the producer handoffs to CR4, it sends a register query to the RH to inform it of its new location information. The RH then forwards the producer's new location information to the RP, which redirects the consumer Interest packets to the producer's new location at CR4. However, this approach can result in high signalling to manage producer mobility. Additionally, frequent producer movements towards different CRs may cause redirection of consumer Interest packets towards an outdated route, leading to Interest packet loss and retransmission.

An analysis of different mechanisms for supporting producer mobility, such as IMA, MMA, LISMA, and CDPSMA, shows that each approach has its strengths and weaknesses. IMA supports mobility through the use of a Home Agent (HA), but it may suffer from high signalling issues and packet encapsulation challenges in large networks. MMA avoids packet encapsulation but experience problems with Interest packet loss, high latency, and signalling overhead. LISMA addresses packet loss but may not be suitable for large networks and may not provide support in certain network scenarios. CDPSMA reduces the negative impact of mobility through monitoring but can also experience high overhead and signalling. Despite these approaches' potential benefits, there is still a need for a feasible solution that addresses their limitations. This research proposes a new mechanism for controlling producer mobility that overcomes the challenges presented by existing approaches. Table 1 summarizes the analysis of the various producer mobility support mechanisms, including their benefits and drawbacks, and lists unresolved issues.

7 Proposed Producer Mobility Management Mechanism

By critical analysis of previous approaches some notable factors have been identified such as packet loss, high signalling, extra bandwidth usage and excessive Interest retransmission. In order to overcome the impact of the identified factors, this research proposed a mechanism that will be able to control the associated issues due to producer handoff mobility. The proposed mechanism design consists of mobility packet and immobile

Table 1. A review and comparative analysis between different producer mobility approaches.

Approach	Method	Merits	Demerits
Indirection-based Mobility Approach (IMA)	Home Agent/Router	Provides forwarding path for Interest and Data packets	High signaling cost Interest packet loss Uses encapsulation and decapsulation for Interest and Data packets
Mapping-based Mobility Approach (MMA)	DNS/Mapping/Rendezvous Server	Provides forwarding link and tracks the producer location	High signaling cost Interest packets loss Interest retransmission Consume extra bandwidth
Locator/Identifier Split-based Mobility Approach (LISMA)	Home Agent/Router	Forwards the Interest packets towards the producer location	Interest packet loss Interest retransmission Uses complex encapsulation and decapsulation
Control Data Plane Split-based Mobility Approach (CDPSMA)	The control plane and data plane points	Reduce the Interest packet loss	High overhead Long Handoff latency Intence handoff singnaling Consume extra bandwidth

anchor router. The mobility packet is responsible for updating the producer's location information in the network, while the immobile anchor router manages the flow of Interest packets during the producer's handoff mobility process, ensuring minimal packet loss. Moreover, the proposed design modifies the normal NDN forwarding plane. By modifying the normal NDN forwarding plane, the proposed mechanism effectively distinguishes between mobility packets and Interest data packets. This differentiation enables the network to prioritize mobility updates and maintain efficient routing during the handoff process, thus minimizing disruptions to ongoing data exchanges. By referring to Fig. 8, when producer moves from CR3 to CR4, the consumer Interest is unable to retrieve content from producer due to handoff process.

During the handoff process, the consumer Interest redirected to CR2 which work as an immobile anchor. The immobile anchor buffers the redirected Interest packets. Meanwhile, when producer relocate and connects to CR4, it sends Mobility Notification (MN) packet to immobile anchor to broadcast its location in the network. The broadcast of MN packet updates the FIBs in the network router to inform about the producer new location. When the location updated, the immobile anchor redirects the cached

Interest packets towards the producer location. The producer sends the data packets by following the Interest revers path towards the consumer. The new incoming Interest from consumer follows the optimal path due to update in the FIB. The consumer Interest moves from CR1 to CR2 and further moves to producer router CR4. In response, the producer forwards the data packets towards the consumer but in the reverse manner. As a result, the proposed mechanism effectively reduces Interest packet loss, signalling overhead, bandwidth usage, and excessive Interest retransmissions.

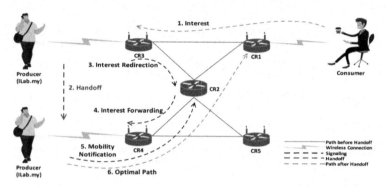

Fig. 8. Proposed producer mobility management mechanism.

The new incoming consumer Interest packets follow the optimal path, due to update in the FIB. The consumer Interest packets move from CR1 to CR2 and further moves to producer router CR4. In response, the producer forwards the data packets towards the consumer by following the Interest packets path in reverse manner. In this way, the proposed mechanism reduces the Interest packet loss, high signalling, extra bandwidth usage, and excessive Interest retransmission.

8   Message Flow

Figure 9 illustrates the message exchange between a consumer and a producer under the proposed mechanism. It is assumed that the consumer and producer are already in communication with each other. To retrieve data packets, the consumer at CR1 sends an Interest packet (/pic.jpg) to the producer's (IRL.my) router at CR3. The producer responds to the Interest packet with a data packet, which is divided into versions and several segments corresponding to the requested Interest packets (IRL.my/pic.jpg/v1/sn, where n = 1, 2, 3, 4......). The Interest path from the consumer location towards the producer is (Consumer/CR1/CR3/Producer), while the data path follows the Interest packet path in a reverse way (Producer/CR3/CR1/Consumer). During the communication, the producer decides to move and subsequently disconnects from CR3. While the producer is in the process of handoff, the consumer sends another Interest packet direct towards the producer's router at CR3, following the path (Consumer/CR1/CR3). Since the producer is not available at CR3, the consumer's Interest packet is redirected to the immobile anchor router, CR2, following the path (Consumer/CR1/CR3/CR2).

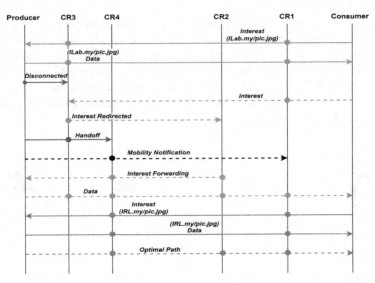

Fig. 9. The interest data stream in proposed mobility management mechanism.

The CR2 caches the redirected Interest packets. Meanwhile, the producer completes its handoff process by connecting to CR4 and sends the Mobility Notification (MN) packet to CR2. The MN packets updates the producer location towards the network and provides the new route towards producer location. Once the producer updates its location in the network, the cached Interest packets at CR2 are forwarded to producer router CR4 with path Consumer/CR1/CR3/CR2/CR4/Producer). In response, the producer sends the data packets to consumer by following the Interest reverse path (Producer/CR4/CR2/CR3/CR1/Consumer).

Furthermore, after the producer's location update, new incoming consumer Interest packets follow the updated optimal path (Consumer/CR1/CR2/CR4/Producer) and the data path (Producer/CR4/CR2/CR1/Consumer), ensuring efficient routing and minimizing latency. As a result, the associated concerns during the producer mobility are handled by the proposed mechanism. Additionally, the proposed mechanism provides an effective solution that can control excessive Interest packet loss, high signalling, Interest retransmission, and extra bandwidth consumption compared to existing approaches such as IMA, MMA, LISMA, and CDPSMA.

9 Conclusion

The most interesting NDN producer mobility approaches have been addressed in this study. All of these approaches offer various ways to control producer mobility, that each have fundamental design and unique properties. However, following a rigorous examination of each approach, we draw attention to a number of problems, including losing of Interest packet, constant Interest retransmission, prolonged handover latency, and an inefficient routing path. To address these challenges, we propose a producer mobility management mechanism, which is expected to effectively resolve the identified issues and enhance the overall performance of NDN-based networks. A performance evaluation of the proposed producer mobility management mechanism is currently underway. Future research could investigate the integration of the proposed mechanism with other NDN features such as caching strategies and security measures. Additionally, studying the applicability of the mechanism in various real-world scenarios, such as vehicular networks and the Internet of Things, could provide valuable insights and further validate the effectiveness of the proposed approach.

Acknowledgements. This research is sponsored by the Ministry of Higher Education (MoHE) of Malaysia through Fundamental Research Grant Scheme with reference (FRGS/1/2021/ICT11/UUM/02/1).

References

1. Abrar, A., Arif, A.S.C.M., Zaini, K.M.: A mobility mechanism to manage producer mobility in named data networking. In: Region 10 Symposium (TENSYMP), pp. 1–6 (2022)
2. da Costa, V.C.F., Oliveira, L., de Souza, J.: Internet of everything (IoE) taxonomies: a survey and a novel knowledge-based taxonomy. Sensors (Switzerland). **21**, 1–35 (2021). https://doi.org/10.3390/s21020568
3. Duan, Y., Ni, H., Zhu, X., Wang, X.: A single-rate multicast congestion control (SRMCC) mechanism in information-centric networking. Futur. Internet. **14**(2), 38 (2022). https://doi.org/10.3390/fi14020038
4. Karim, F.A., Aman, A.H.M., Hassan, R., Nisar, K., Uddin, M.: Named data networking: a survey on routing strategies. IEEE Access **10**, 90254–90270 (2022). https://doi.org/10.1109/ACCESS.2022.3201083
5. Fang, C., Yu, F.R., Huang, T., Liu, J., Liu, Y.: A survey of energy-efficient caching in information-centric networking. IEEE Commun. Mag. **52**, 122–129 (2014)
6. Ali, I., Lim, H.: NameCent: name centrality-based data broadcast mitigation in vehicular named data networks. IEEE Access **9**, 162438–162447 (2021). https://doi.org/10.1109/ACCESS.2021.3133016
7. Pereira, J.F., Nicolau, M.J., Costa, A.D.: VAL - vehicular adaptation layer, for NDN. IEEE Access **11**, 50064–50074 (2023). https://doi.org/10.1109/ACCESS.2023.3275763
8. Zhiyi, Z., et al.: An overview of security support in named data networking. IEEE Commun. Mag. **56**, 62–68 (2018)
9. Fayyaz, S., Rehman, M.A.U., Din, M.S. ud, Biswas, M.I., Bashir, A.K., Kim, B.S.: Information-centric mobile networks: a survey, discussion, and future research directions. IEEE Access **11**, 40328–40372 (2023). https://doi.org/10.1109/ACCESS.2023.3268775
10. Low, X.W., Leau, Y.-B., Yan, Z., Park, Y.-J., Anbar, M.: Performance evaluation of route optimization management of producer mobility in information-centric networking. Int. J. Electr. Comput. Eng. **12**, 2088–8708 (2022)
11. Abrar, A., Mohamed Arif, A.S., Mohad Zaini, K.: A systematic analysis and review on producer mobility management in named data networks: research background and challenges. Alexandria Eng. J. **69**, 785–808 (2023). https://doi.org/10.1016/j.aej.2023.02.022
12. Feng, B., Zhou, H., Xu, Q.: Mobility support in Named Data Networking: a survey. Eurasip J. Wirel. Commun. Netw. **2016**, 220 (2016). https://doi.org/10.1186/s13638-016-0715-0
13. Abrar, A., Arif, A.S.C.M., Zaini, K.M.: Producer mobility support in information-centric networks: research background and open issues. Int. J. Commun. Networks Distrib. Syst. **28**, 312–336 (2022)

14. Kim, D., Ko, Y.-B.: On-demand anchor-based mobility support method for named data networking. In: 19th International Conference on Advanced Communication Technology (ICACT), pp. 19–23 (2017)

15. Gohar, M., Khan, N., Ahmad, A., Najam-Ul-Islam, M., Sarwar, S., Koh, S.J.: Cluster-based device mobility management in named data networking for vehicular networks. Mob. Inf. Syst. **2018**(11), 1–7 (2018). https://doi.org/10.1155/2018/1710591

16. Zhiwei, Y., Park, Y.-J., Leau, Y.-B., Ren-Ting, L., Hassan, R.: Hybrid network mobility support in named data networking. In: International Conference on Information Networking (ICOIN), pp. 16–19 (2020)

17. Abrar, A., Arif, A.S.C.M., Zaini, K.M.: Internet of things producer mobility management in named data networks: a survey, outlook, and open issues. Int. J. Commun. Netw. Distrib. Syst. **29**(5), 493–512 (2023). https://doi.org/10.1504/IJCNDS.2023.133166

Enabling a Sustainable and Inclusive Digital Future with Proactive Producer Mobility Management Mechanism in Named Data Networking

Nurul Hidayah Ahmad Zukri[1,2] ⓘ, Ahmad Suki Che Mohamed Arif[1(✉)] ⓘ,
Mohammed AlSamman[1] ⓘ, and Ahmad Abrar[1] ⓘ

[1] University Utara Malaysia, Sintok, 06010 Kedah, Malaysia
suki1207@uum.edu.my
[2] Universiti Teknologi MARA, Cawangan Perlis, Kampus Arau, 02600 Arau, Perlis, Malaysia

Abstract. Named Data Networking (NDN) is the most remarkable initiative of Information-Centric Network (ICN) to improve overall network performance. With its data-centric architecture and forwarding philosophy, NDN natively addressed consumer mobility. However, the producer mobility problem remains a challenging issue in NDN architecture. Among the critical issues of producer mobility are handover latency, Interest packet loss, and Interest retransmission. This paper classifies existing producer mobility solutions into rendezvous, anchor-based, and anchor-less approaches. Despite the efforts of many researchers poured into solving these issues, there is still room for improvement. This paper proposes a producer mobility management mechanism based on a proactive approach to managing producer mobility in NDN. The proposed mechanism proactively evaluates the handover time of the producer and sends the mobility notification packet to inform about the producer's movement. In the meantime, a new Interest packet for the moving producer will be buffered on the router. Thus, the proposed mechanism aims to reduce the handover latency and packet loss.

Keywords: Named Data Networking · Producer Mobility · Consumer Mobility

1 Introduction

The rapid advancements of mobile devices and applications increase Internet traffic demand. The current Internet paradigm places a heavy emphasis on accessing services and retrieving data, leading to new demands from society for things like improved security, effective content distribution, and mobility assistance. This is because the future Internet is seen as a tool for inclusion whereby technology is being catered to a diverse society [1]. Researchers have proposed various solutions to satisfy the requirements by integrating content-centric features in its protocols which work on top of the Internet Protocol (IP) network infrastructure [2, 3]. However, the current IP network based on the end-to-end communication model is not designed to support secure data distribution naturally, and inherently hard to meet the requirement of efficient data distribution and mobility.

N. H. Zakaria et al. (Eds.): ICOCI 2023, CCIS 2001, pp. 343–354, 2024.
https://doi.org/10.1007/978-981-99-9589-9_26

An emerging novel future Internet called the Information-Centric Network (ICN) is committed to the development of decentralized networks. With its new structure, ICN replaces IP addressing with the idea of addressing the content for network addressing. Respective research communities keep an eye on this subject matter. Thus, introducing some new architectures, namely Data-Oriented Network Architectural (DONA) [4], Content-Centric Networks (CCN) or Named Data Networks (NDN) [5], Publish-Subscribe Internet Technology (PURSUIT) [6], and Network of Information (NetInf) [7]. NDN receives immense attention from the ICN architectural research group among these architectures.

Future Internet architecture Named Data Networking (NDN) has caused a paradigm shift in network communication from point-to-point to name delivery. In addition, NDN depends on the stateful forwarding plane for datagram delivery. The adoption of the NDN forwarding plane indeed supports consumer mobility. If the consumer is relocated to a new attached content router (CR), no signaling from the network is required to handle consumer mobility. Instead, Interest retransmission is adequate for successful communication. However, producer mobility is a more complex problem that impacts overall communication. This is because the routers' Forwarding Information Base (FIB) needs to be updated once the producer reconnects with the new attached content router. Failure to update FIB will affect the search for the desired Data. Ultimately, it results in high-Interest packet loss, high-Interest retransmission, increased bandwidth demand, and high handoff latency [8, 9]. Further, the aforementioned issues will restrain the work for building a sustainable and more inclusive digital future.

Therefore, this paper introduces a producer mobility management mechanism design in NDN using a proactive approach. The proposed mechanism will handle the mobility of the producer by analyzing the producer's mobility status and informing the router and consumer to take necessary action, such as delaying the Interest transmission. Managing the producer mobility before the handover process based on a proactive approach would minimize the handover latency and interest retransmission. Also, it aims to alleviate other critical issues, such as high signaling and Interest packet loss issues.

The remainder of this paper is organized as follows. Section 2 presents the mobility in Named Data Networking. Section 3 discusses the producer mobility approaches. Section 4 shows the proposed design and the conclusion in Sect. 5.

2 Mobility in Named Data Networking

One of the auspicious Information-centric networking (ICN) approaches to address the challenges of the future Internet is NDN [10]. The NDN relies on named data, name-based routing, and in-network caching to distribute content efficiently and improve network bandwidth. Additionally, the NDN facilitates consumer mobility easily and has incorporated security for every piece of Data. The essence of NDN comes from CCN [11, 12]. This can be shown in NDN architectural and protocol operations. Besides that, NDN has a modular and extensible codebase.

As NDN architecture changes the Internet architecture model, the network communication changes to retrieve content. Any communication in NDN is based on two kinds of packets: Interest and Data. A Data packet is a named sequence of bytes. A name is a sequence of arbitrarily many components. As an example, a picture could be identified by the name /xyz/pics/tree.jpg, which contains three components: xyz, pics, and tree.jpg.

Network communication begins as soon as the consumer sends the producer an Interest to request a certain Data packet. After the router gets an Interest, three data structure tables would be involved, which are a Forwarding Information Base (FIB), a Pending Interest Table (PIT), and a Content Store (CS). FIB is the table that contains information on the publisher and interfaces. PIT caches all Interest yet received Data. In contrast, CS provides a provisional cache for storing acquired Data packets. The forwarding process would be performed until the name of Interest is a prefix of a Data packet's name.

In NDN, there are two types of mobility: consumer mobility and producer mobility. The following subsections present both types of mobility.

2.1 Consumer Mobility

Data retrieval begins when NDN consumers express Interest packet in the NDN network. Upon accepting the Interest, the NDN router searches for Data in the CS. If the prefix matches, the Data will be returned to the consumer. Or else, the router registers the Interest in the PIT. The Interest is sent using the stateful forwarding strategy, which utilizes the information of the following face from the FIB and Data (traffic measurements) planes. Each record in the PIT constructs an inverse path known as the breadcrumb trail, which will be used as the primary path between the provider of the content and the consumer. The breadcrumb trail function shows how consumer mobility is instinctively established in NDN.

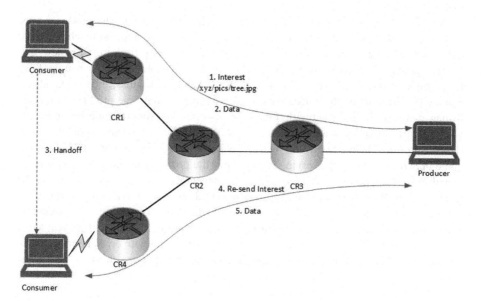

Fig. 1. Consumer Mobility in NDN

As shown in Fig. 1, the consumer can resubmit any outstanding or expired Interests if they relocate while the network gets the desired data. By doing so, the intermediate router can update the path to the consumer's current location. If the old and new paths cross, the consumer will retrieve the previously requested Data from a router's cache without propagating further. Given this NDN nature, the consumer effortlessly gets the remaining content from these routers to fulfill its content needs. For the next request, the consumer can efficiently get the remaining Data packets only by re-issuing Interest again for similar content [13, 14], and it can be done within the minimum delay. In conclusion, the consumer mobility issue is inherently solved through cached contents at router space or resending the Interest packet to the intermediate router after the completion of consumer mobility [15].

2.2 Producer Mobility

In NDN, consumer issue Interest messages carrying the name of the requested information object. Although the name of the content is separated from the location, the hierarchical name comprises the location of the content such as the example 'uum/edu/my/ahsgs/homepage.pic'. The NDN directly coupled the location with the content name, adding them to FIB in the routing protocol [15]. Consequently, whenever the consumer delivers an Interest packet, the connected router determines the path by looking up the FIB for a suitable producer (content source). Generally, FIB contains the entries of long prefixes address for the next-hop or content source. This allows it to determine the optimal path to access content and further the Interest. The producer satisfies the consumer's content needs by sending the desired content from its location to the consumer.

Whenever the producer shifts and connects with the other CR, the producer must update the FIB of all routers in the NDN network. Otherwise, Interest reaches the old CR to retrieve the content. Sometimes, it takes quite a long time to get a new CR. Due to the unavailability of the producer, no content is available for the consumer [16]. Furthermore, the network will suffer from high overhead, packet loss, and long handover latency [8]. Ultimately, the consumer lost communication until the producer informed its new name prefix in the network. Figure 2 illustrates the producer mobility in NDN.

To control mobility in ad-hoc networks, NDN uses the Listen First Broadcast Later (LFBL) protocol. LFBL floods the Interest packet to the serving routers and broadcasts name prefixes across all the serving routers after the producer handoff process is completed [17, 18]. The decisions for prefix announcements are made depending on the availability of the wireless channel. If no other node has sent a matching data packet, the router forwards the packet. However, the LFBL protocol generates high signaling and has no mechanism to recover the dropped and incoming Interest packets sent at the previous attached CR. Furthermore, producer mobility is not natively supported due to the unavailability of content locators and failures in content access through the routing system. The second NDN solution to minimize the producer mobility effect is caching content at the router.

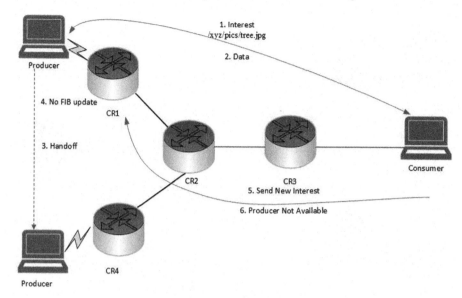

Fig. 2. The Producer Mobility in NDN

3 Producer Mobility Approaches

Many researchers associated producer mobility support systems with various titles and grouping to find a solution to the producer mobility challenges in NDN. The producer mobility approaches can be divided into the following categories:

3.1 Rendezvous Approach

In this study, rendezvous represents a general concept of "indirection" [19]. The rendezvous point maintains the binding between the source and target prefixes. The operation of a rendezvous point is presented in Fig. 3. As an indirection concept of approach, the rendezvous point is central to giving out mobility knowledge for each mobile node. All consumers' requests go through the rendezvous point first to obtain the producer's new location and are sent to it. Whenever the producer re-attaches to the newly attached Content Router (CR), it must inform its current location to the rendezvous point. Then, as in [20], the rendezvous node propagates the routing prefix to the forwarding planes. Dealing with the unique trace Interest and trace Data on the rendezvous node adds some extra costs. [21] Use the concept of rendezvous for the proxy implementation between the consumer and producer path.

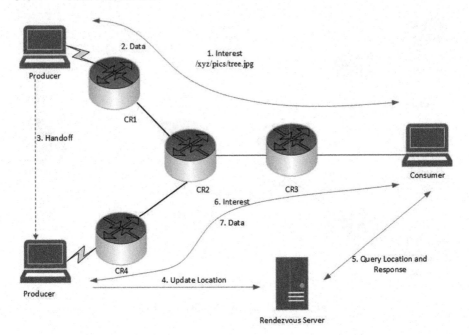

Fig. 3. Operation of a Rendezvous Approach [8].

3.2 Anchor-Based Approach

Similar to the idea of MobileIP in TCP/IP, the anchor-based solution made use of an anchor node called Home Agent (HA). HA keeps tracking the position information of relocated mobile nodes. Figure 4 shows a consumer resubmitting the Interest to HA and finding a new location for the producer. Then, HA transmits the Interest directly to the producer. Various schemes [16, 22] introduce the notification method about the producer's relocation to HA. Although these schemes are simple and reduce the handover latency, this approach is vulnerable because of heavily dependent on a single node (HA). One of the drawbacks is the transmission of all packets via the anchor node will lead to the bottleneck effect [23].

3.3 Anchor-Less Approach

The anchor-less approach allows a producer to update its new location information in the network without relying on third-party [24, 25], as shown in Fig. 5. Upon receiving the notification, routers update the FIB table with the latest location information. Since FIB is keeping up to date, the Interest can be submitted to the current location of the producer. Thus, no specific node like a rendezvous point or HA is required to forward the packet.

[26] apply this strategy and update FIBs of associated routers to facilitate forwarding the Interest to the node. However, the disadvantage of this scheme lies in a scenario in which the producers are relocating regularly, which frequently updating the FIB of the connected routers may trigger traffic [23].

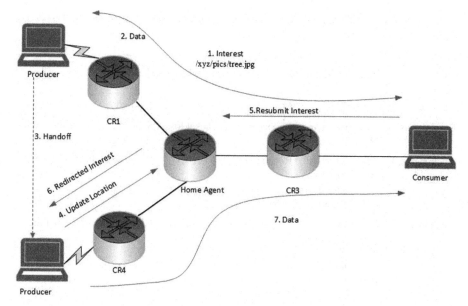

Fig. 4. Operation of the Anchor-based Approach.

In [27], the producer announces the leaving status of the network, including the previous attached CR. The producer's frequent movement hampered the propagation of the concurrent FIB updates. This scheme provides a fast and lightweight handover but incurs high signaling due to extra packets sent for the notification from the leaving producer.

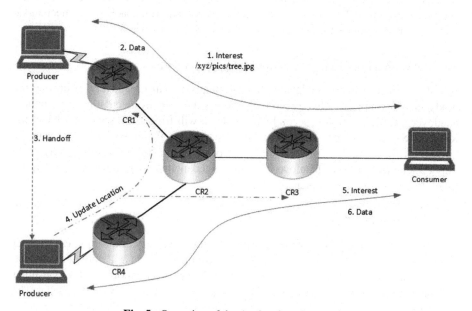

Fig. 5. Operation of the Anchor-less Approach.

Table 1 shows different producer mobility approaches and presents the respective solutions' type, merits, and demerits.

Table 1. Summary of producer mobility approaches in NDN

Approaches	Ref	Type	Merits	Demerits
Rendezvous	[20]	Reactive	Reduce Interest packet loss	Single points of failure, high signaling
	[21]	Proactive		
Anchor-based	[28]	Reactive	Reduce handover latency	Bottleneck effect
	[16]	Reactive		
	[22]	Reactive		
	[29]	Proactive		
Anchor-less	[24]	Reactive	Reduce Interest packet loss	High traffic, high signaling
	[25]	Reactive		
	[30]	Proactive		
	[26]	Reactive		
	[27]	Reactive		

4 Proposed Mechanism

In this section, we present the mechanism that describes the main ideas in addressing the issues of long handover latency, high-Interest packet loss, and Interest retransmission. Based on these issues, Fig. 6 illustrates the proposed proactive producer mobility management mechanism. Despite the exchange of Interest and Data packet, this mechanism proposed three schemes for normal communication in NDN which are:

4.1 Determine the Producer's Mobility Handover Time

In order to reduce handover latency, the mechanism shall proactively determine the producer's leaving time. This research overcomes the issue by calculating the minutes' handover begins. Every few seconds, the scheme will trigger the sensor to detect the Received Signal Strength (RSS) of the producer with CR1. If RSS is lower than the threshold (th), the scheme will calculate the producer's mobility handover time. It is important to determine the handover time so that the method to minimize the producer's mobility effect would be implemented sooner.

4.2 Send Mobility Packet

After determining the producer's handover time, it is necessary to inform the consumer that the producer is leaving the router. The mobility packet acts as a notification signal to the consumer that contains information about the producer's mobility. The consumer may delay the Interest transmission to the same producer upon receiving the packet. The Interest retransmission is delayed until the consumer receives further notice about the producer's new location.

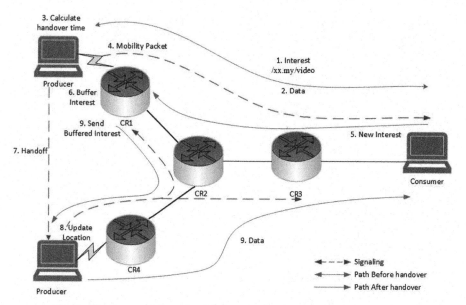

Fig. 6. The Proposed Proactive Producer Mobility Management Mechanism

4.3 Buffer Interest

Buffer Interest will be implemented on the router's side for a limited time based on the pre-determined handover time. Instead of dropping the Interest packet whose producer is moving away, the Interest is buffered at the router for a given time. So, the producer may immediately retrieve the unattended Interest after reconnecting with the new CR. By buffering Interest, the issue of the Interest packet loss will be diminished.

4.4 Message Flow

Figure 7 illustrates the real communications between producer and consumer using the proposed mechanism. In this example, the consumer watches a live-streaming video (/xx.my/video) from the producer. The communication between consumer and producer went smoothly, as in NDN normal communication, until the RSS of the producer was detected to be lower than the threshold (-77dBm). The first scheme calculates the handover time of the producer and sends the information encapsulated in the mobility packet. The purpose of sending the mobility packet is to inform the routers along the route, which are CR1, CR2, and CR3, and the consumer about the moving status of the producer.

While the packet is underway, CR1 may retrieve new Interest from the consumer (/xx.my/video). If that's the case, CR1 will buffer the Interest of the moving producer until it receives an update about the producer's new location. After the producer is connected to the new router at CR4, the producer updates its location on the network. When CR1 receives the location information, all Interest buffered is sent to the producer. Upon receiving the Interest, the producer sends Data (/xx.my/video/v2) to the consumer via a new path.

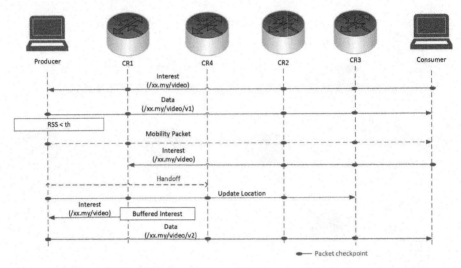

Fig.7. The Message Flow of The Proposed Mechanism

The proposed mechanism will be measured based on handoff latency, interest packet loss, data packet delivery, and throughput for the evaluation. The formula for each parameter will be studied. Results from the simulation will be accumulated and compared with the OPMSS [25] and MAP-Me [27].

5   Conclusion

The NDN architecture is key to building a more inclusive and sustainable future Internet. Nevertheless, the NDN does not provide enough assistance for mobile producers, particularly if they lose their connections. Given the severe effects of mobility towards communication in the network, much research has been done, and these research works are categorized into various approaches. However, after thoroughly investigating previous research, we have identified several problems, such as high signaling, high packet loss, and long handover latency. Thus, this paper proposed a proactive producer mobility management mechanism to solve such problems. The contribution of this paper is twofold. First, we look at mobility in NDN and producer mobility approaches. The approaches are categorized into rendezvous, anchor-based, and anchor-less approaches. All papers are being analyzed and criticized, respectively. By comparing both approaches, we can identify the best fit for designing the proactive mobility management mechanism. Second, we design the proactive producer mobility management mechanism by incorporating three strategies: determining the producer's mobility handover time, sending the mobility packet, and buffer Interest. The proposed mechanism is expected to provide the mobility solution to support producer mobility in NDN architecture by minimizing the Interest retransmission and handoff latency.

The future work includes: 1) further investigating the methods for developing the producer mobility mechanism; 2) implementing the mechanism in the simulation environment; 3) evaluating the sustainability for inclusive real-world deployment by comparing the performance between other popular mechanisms.

References

1. Sharma, S., et al.: In pursuit of inclusive and diverse digital futures: Exploring the potential of design fiction in education of children. Interact. Des. Archit. **51**, 219–248 (2021)
2. Ahmad, A., Hussaini, M., Awang Nor, S.: Overview of future internet: named data networking. In: Seminar Teknologi Multimedia & Komunikasi, pp. 313–319 (2019). e-Prosiding SMT-Comm'19, School of Multimedia Technology & Communication, Universiti Utara Malaysia (2019)
3. Ghodsi, A., Shenker, S., Koponen, T., Singla, A., Raghavan, B., Wilcox, J.: Information-centric networking: seeing the forest for the trees. In: Proceedings of the 10th ACM Workshop on Hot Topics in Networks (2011)
4. Koponen, T., et al.: A data-oriented (and beyond) network architecture. In: Proceedings of the 2007 Conference on Applications, Technologies, Architectures, and Protocols for Computer Communications (2007)
5. Jacobson, V., Smetters, D.K., Thornton, J.D., Plass, M.F., Briggs, N.H., Braynard, R.L.: Networking named content. In: Proceedings of the 5th international conference on Emerging networking experiments and technologies (2009)
6. Fotiou, N., Nikander, P., Trossen, D., Polyzos, G.C.: Developing information networking further: From PSIRP to pursuit. In: Lecture Notes of the Institute for Computer Sciences, Social Informatics and Telecommunications Engineering, pp. 1–13 (2012)
7. Dannewitz, C., Kutscher, D., Ohlman, B., Farrell, S., Ahlgren, B., Karl, H.: Network of Information (NetInf) – an information-centric networking architecture. Comput. Commun. **36**, 721–735 (2013)
8. Abrar, A., Che Mohamed Arif, A.S., Zaini, K.M.: A mobility mechanism to manage producer mobility in named Data Networking. In: 2022 IEEE Region 10 Symposium (TENSYMP). IEEE (2022)
9. Chen, Y.-S., Hsu, C.-S., Huang, D.-Y.: A pipe-assisted mobility management in named Data Networking Networks. In: The 16th Asia-Pacific Network Operations and Management Symposium (2014)
10. Liu, W.-X., Yu, S.-Z., Tan, G., Cai, J.: Information-centric networking with built-in network coding to achieve multisource transmission at network-layer. Comput. Netw. **115**, 110–128 (2017)
11. Chaabane, A., De Cristofaro, E., Kaafar, M.A., Uzun, E.: Privacy in content-oriented networking: threats and countermeasures. ACM SIGCOMM Comput. Commun. Rev. **43**, 25–33 (2013)
12. White, G., Rutz, G.: Content Delivery with Content-Centric Networking (2016)
13. Cha, J.-H., Choi, J.-H., Kim, J.-Y., Han, Y.-H., Min, S.-G.: A mobility link service for NDN Consumer Mobility. Wirel. Commun. Mob. Comput. **2018**, 1–8 (2018)
14. Mars, D., Mettali Gammar, S., Lahmadi, A., Azouz Saidane, L.: Using information centric networking in Internet of Things: a survey. Wirel. Pers. Commun. **105**, 87–103 (2019)
15. Feng, B., Zhou, H., Xu, Q.: Mobility support in named Data Networking: A Survey. Springer International Publishing, EURASIP Journal on Wireless Communications and Networking (2016)

16. Kim, D., Ko, Y.-B.: On-demand anchor-based mobility support method for named data networking. In: 2017 19th International Conference on Advanced Communication Technology (ICACT), pp. 19–23(2017)

17. Abrar, A., Arif, A.S., Zaini, K.M.: Producer mobility support in information-centric networks: research background and open issues. Int. J. Commun. Netw. Distrib. Syst. **28**(3), 312–316 (2022)

18. Xylomenos, G., et al.: A survey of information-centric networking research. IEEE Commun. Surv. Tutorials **16**, 1024–1049 (2014)

19. Zhang, Y., Afanasyev, A., Burke, J., Zhang, L.: A survey of mobility support in named Data Networking. In: 2016 IEEE Conference on Computer Communications Workshops (INFOCOM WKSHPS) (2016)

20. Zhang, Y., Xia, Z., Mastorakis, S., Zhang, L.: Kite: producer mobility support in named data networking. In: Proceedings of the 5th ACM Conference on Information-Centric Networking, pp. 125–136. Association for Computing Machinery (2018)

21. Rui, L., Dai, S., Gao, Z., Qiu, X., Chen, X.: Double-lead content search and producer location prediction scheme for producer mobility in named data networking. Comput. J. **66**(11), 2825–2843 (2022)

22. Hussaini, M., Nor, S.A., Ahmad, A.: PMSS: producer mobility support scheme optimization with RWP mobility model in named data networking. Int. J. Commun. Netw. Inf. Secur. (IJCNIS), **10**(2), 329–339 (2022)

23. Lee Chee Hang, L.C., Lee Chee Hang, Y.-B.L., Yu-Beng Leau, Y.J., Yong Jin Park, Z.Y., Zhiwei Yan, S.P.: Protocol and evaluation of network mobility with producer nodes in named Data Networking. J. Internet Technol. **23**, 459–466 (2022)

24. Korla, S., Chilukuri, S.: T-MOVE: a light-weight protocol for improved QoS in content-centric networks with producer Mobility. Future Internet **11**(2), 28 (2019). MDPI

25. Hussaini, M., Naeem, M.A., Kim, B.-S.: OPMSS: optimal producer mobility support solution for named data networking. Appl. Sci. **11**, 4064 (2021)

26. Do, T.X., Kim, Y.: Optimal provider mobility in large-scale named- data networking. In: KSII Transactions on Internet and Information Systems, vol. 9, no. 10, pp. 4054–4071 (2015)

27. Auge, J., Carofiglio, G., Grassi, G., Muscariello, L., Pau, G., Zeng, X.: MAP-me: managing anchor-less producer mobility in content-centric networks. IEEE Trans. Netw. Serv. Manage. **15**, 596–610 (2018)

28. Gohar, M., Khan, N., Ahmad, A., Najam-Ul-Islam, M., Sarwar, S., Koh, S.-J.: Cluster-based device mobility management in named data networking for Vehicular Networks. Mob. Inf. Syst. **2018**, 1–7 (2018)

29. Araújo, F.R., de Sousa, A.M., Sampaio, L.N.: SCaN-Mob: an opportunistic caching strategy to support producer mobility in named data wireless networking. Comput. Netw. **156**, 62–74 (2019)

30. Ali, I., Lim, H.: Anchor-less producer Mobility Management in named data networking for real-time multimedia. Mob. Inf. Syst. **2019**, 1–12 (2019)

The Recent Trends of Research on GitHub Copilot: A Systematic Review

Zhamri Che Ani[1(✉)], Zauridah Abdul Hamid[1], and Nur Nazifa Zhamri[2]

[1] School of Computing, University Utara Malaysia, 06010 Sintok, Kedah, Malaysia
zhamri@uum.edu.my
[2] Sime Darby Motors, 47301 Petaling Jaya, Malaysia

Abstract. GitHub Copilot is an AI-powered code generation tool developed by OpenAI and GitHub that has gained significant attention from the software engineering community. Despite the significant attention received from the software engineering community, there is a lack of comprehensive examination of its effectiveness, reliability, and ethical implications on GitHub Copilot. The absence of a systematic review of GitHub Copilot's recent research trends hinders a thorough understanding of its current state of development and potential impact on software development practices. Therefore, this systematic review aims to analyze the recent trends of research on GitHub Copilot to assess its current state of development, identify gaps in existing knowledge, and provide insights into potential future research directions. This study used PRISMA for searching the relevant databases, screening and selecting eligible studies based on inclusion and exclusion criteria, data extraction and synthesis, and critical appraisal of the quality and relevance of the studies included. The results show that the trend of the studies is focusing on four main areas: developer productivity, code quality, code security and education.

Keywords: GitHub Copilot · Code Generation · OpenAI

1 Introduction

GitHub Copilot, developed by OpenAI and GitHub in 2021 [1], is an AI-powered code generation tool that has garnered significant attention in the software engineering community. It aims to assist developers by automatically suggesting code snippets and completing lines of code based on natural language descriptions and context [2]. Leveraging machine learning techniques and a vast codebase, Copilot has the potential to enhance developer productivity and accelerate software development processes. Previous studies have explored the use of AI in code generation [15], the impact of automated coding tools on developer workflows [3], and the ethical considerations associated with AI-assisted coding [4]. However, there is a lack of comprehensive examination of its effectiveness, reliability, and ethical implications on GitHub Copilot. The absence of a systematic review of GitHub Copilot's recent research trends hinders a thorough understanding of its current state of development and potential impact on software development practices. A comprehensive review of recent research trends on GitHub Copilot is essential to assess its effectiveness, identify limitations, and uncover potential future directions.

N. H. Zakaria et al. (Eds.): ICOCI 2023, CCIS 2001, pp. 355–366, 2024.
https://doi.org/10.1007/978-981-99-9589-9_27

Therefore, the objective of this article is to analyze the recent trends of research on GitHub Copilot to assess its current state of development, identify gaps in existing knowledge, and provide insights into potential future research directions. This study used the PRISMA (Preferred Reporting Items for Systematic Reviews and Meta-Analyses) methodology to systematically search relevant databases, apply pre-determined inclusion and exclusion criteria, extract and synthesize data, and critically appraise the quality and relevance of included studies. These rigorous procedures ensure a comprehensive and reliable analysis of the literature on GitHub Copilot.

2   Methodology

This section describes the approach employed to retrieve articles relevant to GitHub Copilot. The PRISMA method, including the prominent databases Scopus, ACM Digital Library, and ScienceDirect, were used to conduct the systematic review. The review process encompassing identification, screening, and eligibility, as well as the data abstraction and analysis methods, are also presented.

2.1   PRISMA

PRISMA stands for Preferred Reporting Items for Systematic Reviews and Meta-Analyses. The PRISMA statement was first published in 2009 and has been updated several times. The most recent version, PRISMA 2020, was published in June 2021. It is a widely recognized tool for conducting systematic reviews and meta-analyses in healthcare research. PRISMA provides a checklist that researchers should consider when preparing their systematic review or meta-analysis, such as defining the research question, specifying the inclusion and exclusion criteria, and assessing the risk of bias in included studies. Its use is recommended for reporting systematic reviews and meta-analyses to enhance transparency, completeness, and reproducibility [5].

2.2   Resources

The review relied on three primary journal databases – Scopus, ACM Digital Library, and ScienceDirect. Scopus, recognized as one of the largest and most comprehensive bibliographic databases, encompasses various disciplines such as science, technology, medicine, social sciences, and humanities. It offers many indexed and abstracted articles from scholarly journals, conference proceedings, and books [6]. The ACM Digital Library is a vast repository of scholarly resources, encompassing articles, books, conference proceedings, and other computer science and information technology publications. Recognized as a valuable resource, it is a comprehensive platform for researchers, educators, and practitioners who aim to remain abreast of the latest advancements in their respective domains [7]. ScienceDirect is a robust database that offers access to an extensive collection of scientific, technical, and medical research articles from various journals and books. It is an invaluable resource for researchers, scholars, and students who strive to keep up with the latest developments in their respective fields [8].

2.3 Eligibility and Exclusion Criteria

Several eligibility and exclusion criteria are determined. The first criterion, Literature type, specifies that only research articles published in journals and proceedings will be eligible for inclusion. These articles are typically peer-reviewed and provide original research findings, making them more reliable and valuable for research purposes. The exclusion criteria under this criterion include systematic reviews, book series, books, chapters in books, and conference proceeding books. The second criterion, Language, specifies that only articles published in English will be considered. This criterion ensures that the selected articles can be easily understood and reduces the potential for language-related bias in the selection process. The final criterion is Timeline. Since the GitHub Copilot is a new tool, selecting articles is unlimited. All articles published in 2023 and the years before, have been selected. This criterion ensures that all articles related to the GitHub Copilot were chosen (see Table 1).

Table 1. The inclusion and exclusion criteria.

Criterion	Eligibility	Exclusion
Literature type	Journal (research articles), proceeding (research articles)	Journal (systematic review), proceeding (systematic review), book series, book, chapter in book, conference proceeding book
Language	English	Non-English
Timeline	Any time < 2023	None

2.4 Systematic Review Process

The systematic review was conducted in April 2023 and comprised four distinct stages. The first stage involved the identification of relevant keywords for the search process. Since GitHub Copilot is a unique keyword, "GitHub Copilot" was used. Following a meticulous process, 12 duplicated articles were eliminated. The second stage was the screening process, which excluded two articles due to their status as conference proceedings, leaving 26 eligible articles for review. In the third stage, the eligibility criteria were applied to the full articles, excluding nine articles that focused on topics other than GitHub Copilot. Finally, the review's last stage yielded 15 articles suitable for qualitative analysis, as presented in Fig. 1.

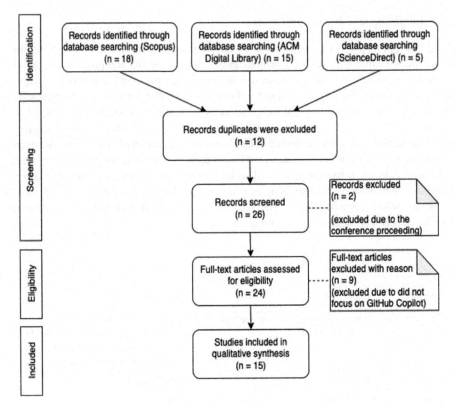

Fig. 1. The flow diagram of the study. (Adapted from [16]).

2.5   Data Abstraction and Analysis

The remaining articles were assessed and analyzed. Efforts were concentrated on studies that met the predetermined inclusion criteria, which ensured that the analysis focused on relevant sources of evidence. To extract relevant data, the team initially read through the article abstracts, followed by a more in-depth analysis of the full articles to identify significant trends related to GitHub Copilot. Qualitative analysis was performed using content analysis techniques, which allowed the team to identify relevant themes and patterns in the data. This rigorous and systematic approach to data analysis ensured that the study's findings were grounded in the available evidence and provided a robust synthesis of the research on GitHub Copilot.

3   Results

Table 2 shows the recent trends of GitHub Copilot research. There are four main areas studied by researchers in 2022 and 2023: developer productivity, code quality, code security and education.

Table 2. Recent Trends in GitHub Co-pilot Research.

Authors	Developer Productivity	Code Quality	Code Security	Education
Yetistiren et al. (2022) [24]		✓		
Sobania et al. (2022) [19]	✓			
Ziegler et al. (2022) [25]	✓			
Siddiq et al. (2022) [18]			✓	
Imai (2022) [10]	✓			
Puryear and Sprint (2022) [14]				✓
Sun et al. (2022) [20]			✓	
Vaithilingam et al. (2022) [22]	✓			
Nguyen and Nadi (2022) [11]		✓		
Al Madi (2022) [2]		✓		
Siddiq et al. (2022) [17]			✓	
Pearce et al. (2022) [13]			✓	
Finnie-Ansley et al. (2023) [6]				✓
Denny et al. (2023) [3]				✓
Wermelinger (2023) [23]				✓

3.1 Developer Productivity

The study [9] aimed to assess the performance of GitHub Copilot, an automatic program synthesis tool, and compare it with genetic programming approaches on common program synthesis benchmark problems. The results revealed that both approaches had similar performance on benchmark problems. However, genetic programming approaches still needed to be mature enough to support practical software development due to their reliance on expensive hand-labelled training cases, long execution times, and bloated and hard-to-understand generated code. The researchers suggested that future work on program synthesis with genetic programming should prioritize improving execution time, readability, and usability to overcome these challenges and enable more practical applications of this approach.

The study [10] aimed to assess the impact of GitHub Copilot on user productivity and identify measurable user data that reflects their perceptions. The researchers analyzed user behaviors and feedback to determine the factors influencing developers' productivity when using Copilot. The results showed that the rate of acceptance of suggestions was the primary driver of productivity, indicating that user satisfaction and acceptance of suggested code snippets were more critical to productivity than the longevity of the code snippets. The study underscores the importance of user-centered design in developing AI-powered programming tools that can enhance developer productivity.

The study [11] aims to investigate the effectiveness of GitHub Copilot in pair programming contexts compared to human pair programming. The researchers experimented with 21 participants, who were randomly assigned to one of three conditions: pair programming with Copilot, human pair programming as a driver, and human pair programming as a navigator. The results suggest that while Copilot can increase productivity in terms of lines of code added, the quality of the generated code is inferior, as indicated by a higher number of lines of code deleted in subsequent trials. The study highlights the importance of being cautious when relying solely on AI-based tools in pair programming contexts.

The study [12] investigates GitHub Copilot's usability and perceived usefulness, a large language model-based code generation tool, in the programming workflow. The study employs a within-subjects user study with 24 participants to examine how programmers use the tool. The results show that Copilot did not improve task completion time or success rate. Still, most participants preferred to use it in their daily programming tasks since it provided a useful starting point and saved them the effort of searching online. However, participants faced challenges in understanding, editing, and debugging code snippets that were generated by Copilot, which reduced their task-solving effectiveness. The study highlights the need to improve the design of Copilot based on the observed difficulties and participants' feedback.

3.2   Code Quality

The study [13] aimed to assess the quality of code generated by GitHub Copilot and to examine the impact of input parameters on its performance. The researchers utilized an experimental setup to evaluate the generated code's validity, correctness, and efficiency. The results showed that GitHub Copilot generated valid code with a success rate of 91.5%, and 28.7% of the problems were correctly generated, while 51.2% were partially correct and 20.1% were incorrect. The study indicates that GitHub Copilot holds significant promise as a programming tool, but further assessments and improvements are necessary to optimize its performance in generating entirely accurate code that meets all requirements.

The study [14] aims to evaluate the correctness and understandability of the code generated by Copilot, which assists programmers by generating code based on natural language descriptions of desired functionality. The study utilizes 33 LeetCode questions in four programming languages to create queries for Copilot. It assesses the corresponding 132 Copilot solutions for correctness using LeetCode's provided tests and for understandability using SonarQube's complexity metrics. The findings indicate that Copilot's Java suggestions have the highest correctness score (57%) while JavaScript has the lowest (27%). Overall, Copilot's recommendations have low complexity, with no significant differences between programming languages. The study also identifies some potential shortcomings of Copilot, such as generating code that could be further simplified and relying on undefined helper methods. The study concludes by highlighting the need for further research to address these issues and explore the potential of Copilot in supporting software development.

The study [15] examines the impact of code generated by machine learning models on code readability and visual attention. Specifically, focus on GitHub Copilot to compare the generated code with code written entirely by human programmers. The study conducted a human experiment with 21 participants, used static code analysis, and used eye tracking to evaluate the code's readability and visual inspection. The findings suggest that model-generated code is comparable in complexity and readability to code written by human pair programmers. However, the eye-tracking data indicates that programmers tend to pay less visual attention to model-generated code. Consequently, reading code remains essential, and programmers should be mindful of automation bias and avoid complacency when working with model-generated code.

3.3 Code Security

The study [16] introduces SecurityEval, an innovative dataset designed to evaluate machine learning-based code generation models' security. The dataset comprises 130 diverse samples, each corresponding to 75 different vulnerability types and mapped to the widely recognized Common Weakness Enumeration. By leveraging SecurityEval, the authors assess the security of two prominent code generation models, InCoder and GitHub Copilot, and unveil that both models are susceptible to generating vulnerable code in certain cases. With its robustness and comprehensiveness, the SecurityEval dataset can serve as a valuable benchmark for scrutinizing the security features of other code generation models in future research.

The study [17] delves into the ethical and security concerns surrounding GitHub Copilot and comparable products that harness deep learning models to learn from open-source code. To mitigate the potential exploitation of such code, the authors introduce a prototype named CoProtector, which employs data poisoning techniques. The primary aim of the CoProtector is to substantially decrease the performance of deep learning models similar to Copilot while simultaneously detecting covert watermark backdoors. The authors conducted extensive large-scale experiments to validate CoProtector's effectiveness in achieving its objectives. The results demonstrate that CoProtector can effectively safeguard open-source code from misuse and potential breaches.

The study [18] examines the presence of code smells and security vulnerabilities in datasets employed to train coding generation techniques and whether these issues are reflected in the output of such techniques. The study utilizes Pylint and Bandit to evaluate three training sets and analyze the output generated by an open-source transformer-based model and GitHub Copilot. The study results reveal that code smells and security vulnerabilities exist within the training sets, and these issues propagate into the output of the coding generation techniques. This underscores the need for further refinement to ensure the generated code is devoid of such issues. The findings also emphasize the significance of careful selection and scrutiny of the training data to minimize the risk of code smells and security vulnerabilities in the generated code.

The study [19] examines the security of GitHub Copilot, the pioneering AI pair programmer that automatically produces computer code. The concern arises from Copilot's exposure to a vast amount of unverified code, raising the possibility of generating insecure code. The study thoroughly analyses 1,689 programs generated by Copilot in scenarios relevant to high-risk cybersecurity weaknesses. The results reveal that approximately 40% of the generated programs are vulnerable, indicating a significant security risk. Moreover, the study demonstrates that Copilot's performance varies considerably based on the diversity of weaknesses, prompts, and domains. These findings emphasize the need for caution when employing AI-based code generation tools and underscore the importance of vetting generated code for security vulnerabilities to prevent potential security breaches.

3.4 Education

The study [20] examines the impact of GitHub Copilot on the learning process in introductory computer science and data science courses. The authors evaluate the correctness, style, skill level appropriateness, grade scores, and potential plagiarism of programming assignments generated by Copilot. The results demonstrate that Copilot produces original primary code that can effectively solve introductory assignments, with human-graded scores ranging from 68% to 95%. Based on these findings, the authors recommend that educators adjust their courses to integrate new AI-based programming workflows.

The research [21] investigates the effectiveness of OpenAI Codex, the underlying model for GitHub Copilot, in solving more advanced CS2 exam questions in comparison to the performance of students. The results indicate that Codex outperformed most students on these questions, generating accurate and comprehensive code. The study suggests that generative AI models like Codex have the potential to support students in completing programming assignments and exams and promote equitable access to high-quality programming education. The study emphasizes the significance of considering the ramifications of these tools for the future of undergraduate computing education.

The study [22] investigates the performance of GitHub Copilot on a diverse dataset of 166 programming problems, analyzing the types of problems that challenge Copilot and the natural language interactions between students and Copilot when resolving errors. The results demonstrate that Copilot solves approximately 50% of the problems on its initial attempt and can effectively solve 60% of the remaining problems using only natural language modifications to the problem description. The study suggests that the prompt engineering used to interact with Copilot when it initially fails can be a valuable learning activity that promotes the development of computational thinking skills and transforms the nature of code-writing skill acquisition.

The study [23] examines the use of OpenAI's Codex machine learning model in programming education, particularly its implementation as the GitHub Copilot plugin, and the implications it raises for educators. The study evaluates the model's performance and limitations in supporting programming instruction through qualitative analysis of the code suggestions generated by Copilot and student feedback. The goal is to provide insight into Copilot's potential for programming education and to highlight the need for instructors to adapt their teaching practices accordingly. The findings indicate that while Copilot can generate correct and understandable code, it cannot replace the process of learning programming. Therefore, educators must incorporate Copilot into their pedagogical strategies judiciously.

4 Discussion

GitHub Copilot is an AI-powered programming tool that has gained attention for its ability to generate code automatically. Several studies have explored Copilot's performance, productivity, and usability in different contexts. One study compared Copilot with genetic programming approaches on common program synthesis benchmark problems, concluding that both approaches had similar performance but that genetic programming approaches still needed to be mature enough for practical software development. Another study investigated the impact of Copilot on user productivity and found that the rate of acceptance of suggestions was the primary driver of productivity. The third study compared Copilot with human pair programming and found that while Copilot increased productivity, the quality of generated code was inferior. The fourth study revealed that Copilot provided a useful starting point for programmers but needed help understanding, editing, and debugging generated code snippets.

Several studies have recently assessed the code quality generated by GitHub Copilot, which assists programmers by generating code based on natural language descriptions of desired functionality. The studies have used various methods to evaluate the correctness and understandability of the generated code and have generally found that Copilot holds significant promise as a programming tool, generating valid code with high success rates. However, the studies also identify potential shortcomings, such as generating code that could be further simplified and relying on undefined helper methods. Further assessments and improvements are necessary to optimize Copilot's performance in generating entirely accurate code that meets all requirements.

Using machine learning-based code generation models, such as GitHub Copilot, raises ethical and security concerns. Several recent studies highlight the potential for such models to generate vulnerable code and the need for careful selection and scrutiny of training data to minimize risks. To address these concerns, researchers have introduced SecurityEval, a dataset for evaluating the security of code generation models, and CoProtector, a prototype aimed at safeguarding open-source code from misuse and breaches. While Copilot's performance varies considerably based on the diversity of weaknesses, prompts, and domains, the studies emphasize the importance of vetting generated code for security vulnerabilities to prevent potential breaches.

The studies explore using OpenAI's Codex machine learning model in programming education through its implementation as the GitHub Copilot plugin. They investigate Copilot's impact on the learning process, its ability to generate original code, and its performance on diverse programming problems. The studies show that Copilot has the potential to support students in completing programming assignments and exams and can promote equitable access to high-quality programming education. However, the studies also suggest that Copilot cannot replace the process of learning programming, and educators must adapt their teaching practices to integrate these AI-based programming workflows effectively.

5   Future Direction or Recommendation

Based on the above studies, the future direction of GitHub Copilot and similar AI-powered programming tools should focus on improving the accuracy and simplicity of generated code while addressing ethical and security concerns. This could involve further refinement of the training data and algorithms the tool uses to minimize the risk of generating vulnerable code. Additionally, developers could work on enhancing the tool's ability to understand and edit generated code snippets and improving its debugging capabilities.

In terms of programming education, the studies suggest that AI-powered programming tools like Copilot have the potential to support students in completing programming assignments and exams and promote equitable access to high-quality programming education. However, it is also essential for educators to adapt their teaching practices to integrate these tools effectively, emphasizing the importance of learning programming concepts and not relying solely on generated code. The future direction of programming education should thus explore ways to integrate these AI-based programming workflows into the classroom while ensuring that they complement and enhance traditional programming education rather than replace it.

The future direction of AI-powered programming tools should prioritize accuracy, simplicity, and security while promoting equitable access to high-quality programming education. This requires balancing the benefits and risks associated with these tools and continued research and development to optimize their performance and address any potential ethical and security concerns.

6   Conclusion

In conclusion, the recent trends of the studies are focusing on four main areas: developer productivity, code quality, code security and education. The research on GitHub Copilot has shown significant promise in generating valid code with high success rates and increasing user productivity. However, potential shortcomings need to be addressed, such as generating code that could be further simplified and vetting for security vulnerabilities. The studies also suggest that Copilot can support students in completing programming assignments and exams, but it cannot replace the process of learning programming entirely. As AI-based programming workflows become more prevalent, educators must effectively adapt their teaching practices to integrate them into programming education. Future research should address the ethical and security concerns raised by machine learning-based code generation models and optimize their performance to generate entirely accurate code that meets all requirements.

References

1. Gershgorn, D.: GitHub and OpenAI launch a new AI tool that generates its own code
2. Friedman, N.: Introducing GitHub Copilot: your AI pair programmer
3. Tu, C., H., Y., Lo, D.: Investigating the impact of AI-powered code completion on developer workflows. In: ACM 44th International Conference on Software Engineering (ICSE), pp. 1024–1035 (2022)
4. Hao, M., Zhou, Y., Yang, Y.: Ethical considerations of AI-assisted coding tools: a systematic review. J. Comput. Sci. Technol. **38**, 99–115 (2021)
5. Page, M.J., et al.: The PRISMA 2020 statement: an updated guideline for reporting systematic reviews. Int. J. Surg. **88** (2021). https://doi.org/10.1016/j.ijsu.2021.105906
6. Elsevier: Scopus
7. ACM: ACM Digital Library
8. Elsevier: ScienceDirect. https://www.sciencedirect.com/. Accessed 04 Nov 2023
9. Sobania, D., Briesch, M., Rothlauf, F.: Choose your programming copilot: a comparison of the program synthesis performance of GitHub copilot and genetic programming. In: Proceedings of 2022 Genetic and Evolutionary Computation Conference, GECCO 2022, pp. 1019–1027 (2022). https://doi.org/10.1145/3512290.3528700
10. Ziegler, A., et al.: Productivity assessment of neural code completion, 21–29 (2022). https://doi.org/10.1145/3520312.3534864
11. Imai, S.: Is GitHub copilot a substitute for human pair-programming? 319–321 (2022). https://doi.org/10.1145/3510454.3522684
12. Vaithilingam, P., Zhang, T., Glassman, E.L.: Expectation vs. experience: evaluating the usability of code generation tools powered by large language models. In: Proceedings of the Conference on Human Factors in Computing Systems (2022). https://doi.org/10.1145/3491101.3519665
13. Yetistiren, B., Ozsoy, I., Tuzun, E.: Assessing the quality of GitHub copilot's code generation. In: Proceedings of the 18th International Conference on Predictive Models and Data Analytics in Software Engineering, Co-located with ESEC/FSE 2022, pp. 62–71 (2022). https://doi.org/10.1145/3558489.3559072
14. Nguyen, N., Nadi, S.: An empirical evaluation of GitHub copilot's code suggestions. In: Proceedings of the 2022 Mining Software Repositories Conference, MSR 2022, pp. 1–5 (2022). https://doi.org/10.1145/3524842.3528470
15. Al Madi, N.: How readable is model-generated code? Examining readability and visual inspection of GitHub copilot. In: ACM International Conference Proceeding Series, pp. 2–6 (2022). https://doi.org/10.1145/3551349.3560438
16. Siddiq, M.L., Santos, J.C.S.: SecurityEval dataset: mining vulnerability examples to evaluate machine learning-based code generation techniques. Assoc. Comput. Mach. (2022). https://doi.org/10.1145/3549035.3561184
17. Sun, Z., Du, X., Song, F., Ni, M., Li, L.: CoProtector: protect open-source code against unauthorized training usage with data poisoning. In: Proceedings of the ACM Web Conference, WWW 2022, pp. 652–660 (2022). https://doi.org/10.1145/3485447.3512225
18. Siddiq, M.L., Majumder, S.H., Mim, M.R., Jajodia, S., Santos, J.C.: An empirical study of code smells in transformer-based code generation techniques. In: International Working Conference on Source Code Analysis and Manipulation, SCAM, pp. 71–82. Dagstuhl Publishing, Limassol (2022)
19. Pearce, H., Ahmad, B., Tan, B., Dolan-Gavitt, B.R.K.: Asleep at the keyboard? Assessing the security of GitHub copilot's code contributions. In: IEEE Symposium on Security and Privacy (SP), pp. 754–768. IEEE (2022)

20. Puryear, B., Sprint, G.: Github copilot in the classroom: learning to code with AI assistance. J. Comput. Sci. Coll. **3**, 37–125 (2022)

21. Finnie-Ansley, J., Denny, P., Luxton-Reilly, A., Santos, E.A., Prather, J., Becker, B.A.: My AI wants to know if this will be on the exam: testing OpenAI's codex on CS2 programming exercises. In: ACM International Conference Proceeding Series, pp. 97–104 (2023). https://doi.org/10.1145/3576123.3576134

22. Denny, P., Kumar, V., Giacaman, N.: Conversing with copilot: exploring prompt engineering for solving CS1 problems using natural language. In: Proceedings of the 54th ACM Technical Symposium on Computer Science Education, SIGCSE 2023, vol. 1, pp. 1136–1142 (2023). https://doi.org/10.1145/3545945.3569823

23. Wermelinger, M.: Using GitHub copilot to solve simple programming problems. In: Proceedings of the 54th ACM Technical Symposium on Computer Science Education, SIGCSE 2023, vol. 1, pp. 172–178 (2023). https://doi.org/10.1145/3545945.3569830

Blockchain Over Named Data Networking Architecture: A Review

Mohammed Alsamman[1]([✉]) [iD], Suhaidi Hassan[1] [iD], Fathey Mohammed[2] [iD], and Yousef Fazea[3] [iD]

[1] School of Computing, Universiti Utara Malaysia, Sintok, 06010 Bukit Kayu Hitam, Kedah, Malaysia
alsamman@uum.edu.my
[2] Sunway Business School, Sunway University, 47500 Subang Jaya, Selangor, Malaysia
[3] Computer and Information Technology, Marshall University, 1 John Marshall Drive, Huntington, WV 25755, USA

Abstract. With infinite apps and online services, future Internet architecture will face new challenges and consequences, such as scalability, dependability, suitable mobility, and security. Internet use has changed spectacularly from one-way communication to content distribution, as much content is generated every minute. Blockchain and Named Data Networking (NDN) are two cutting-edge technologies on the verge of revolutionizing how we use the Internet. Blockchain is a decentralized ledger technology allowing users to store and share data securely. On the other hand, NDN is a new way of networking that focuses on content instead of location. Combining blockchain and NDN can create a safer, more efficient, and more decentralized internet. Blockchain can provide tamper-proof data records, and NDN can deliver content to users efficiently and securely. This paper emphasizes the importance of research in the field of blockchain over Named Data networks. It highlights the advantages of combining blockchain with NDN and discusses the difficulties and open research questions related to the use of blockchain over NDN. Also, the potential impact of blockchain over NDN on the future of the Internet as it can create a safer, more efficient, and more decentralized Internet.

Keywords: Blockchain · Content Distribution · Content-Centric Network · Future Internet

1 Introduction

Blockchain technology is currently one of the most popular technologies [1], as seen in Fig. 1, which shows the market size of blockchain technology globally. The widespread recognition of blockchain technology as a technological revolution generates enormous attention and publicity. The history of all transactions is kept in the distributed digital ledger, which comprises blocks of encrypted, signed transactions [2]. By providing copies of documents to each participant, the Blockchain concept avoids the need for centralized authority. Unlike traditional transactions, data control stays in the hands of

© The Author(s), under exclusive license to Springer Nature Singapore Pte Ltd. 2024
N. H. Zakaria et al. (Eds.): ICOCI 2023, CCIS 2001, pp. 367–379, 2024.
https://doi.org/10.1007/978-981-99-9589-9_28

a central authority, which is also in charge of verifying the customers' credentials. The conventional source manages and administers data and ensures that it cannot be changed or erased. Contrarily, the blockchain concept employs. However, decentralized control eliminates the dangers present in the conventional paradigm.

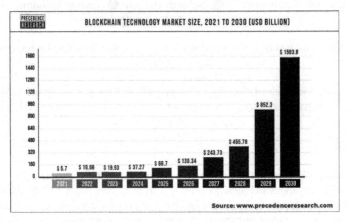

Fig. 1. Blockchain Technology Market [1].

Blockchain technology has several uses in various industries, including crypto currency, the Internet of Things, healthcare, and distributed cloud storage. Every transaction in a blockchain network generates a hash dependent on the current and the prior transaction. Even minor changes in the transaction generate a whole new hash. The P2P network of nodes receives the broadcast of the transaction after that. The network nodes examine the hash to confirm that the transactions have not been altered. This network uses well-known techniques to authenticate the transaction. After confirmation, the transaction is combined with other transactions to create a new ledger data block. Similar to how the Internet evolved, the blockchain paradigm's rapid expansion has become pivotal. While decentralized approaches eliminate the single point of failure problem by allowing each node to calculate ratings and share them with other nodes independently, this requires the trustworthiness of the individual nodes to perform the computations and provide reputation values that cannot be found in today's network architectural (TCP/IP) [2].

The Named Data Networking (NDN) architecture was developed to address the challenges of tracking and delivering the ever-increasing amount of content produced and delivered online. Unlike the current TCP/IP architecture, which focuses on the location of data, NDN focuses on the content itself. This allows for more efficient and scalable content delivery, and improved security and privacy. In NDN, data is named using a hierarchical naming scheme that makes it easy to find and retrieve. Data can be stored locally or in the cache of nearby nodes. The physical address of the host node is not required for communication in NDN, as the names of the data themselves are sufficient to identify the desired content. This eliminates the need for DNS, which is a major bottleneck in the current Internet architecture. The NDN architecture is designed to be backward-compatible with the existing Internet, making it a straightforward and scalable upgrade path [3].

The original Internet design is elegant and powerful due to its hourglass architecture. The narrow waist of the hourglass represents the core network layer, which implements the essential features necessary for global interconnectedness. This small size has been essential to the development of the Internet, as it has freed higher- and lower-layer technologies from unnecessary limitations. The NDN design also has a narrow waist, but it differs from the IP architecture in a fundamental way [3]. The use of data names in NDN allows for more efficient and scalable content delivery, as well as improved security and privacy. Data names are hierarchical, making finding and retrieving content easy. They are also self-describing, which means they contain information about the content, such as its type, size, and last modified date. Routers can use this information to make more informed decisions about how to route data packets [4].

Integrating blockchain technology with NDN has recently gained much attention in the research community. Scholars have highlighted the potential benefits of this integration, such as improved security, privacy, and scalability. NDN can also fulfill the needs of blockchain applications by providing a secure and efficient way to store and transfer data. This study focuses on integrating NDN and blockchain technology and discusses the potential benefits of this integration [5, 6].

The use of blockchain over NDN will be examined in this paper. The document layout is as follows: We'll present the Methodology in Sect. 2 and the Background review in Sect. 3. A review of the latest studies of blockchain over NDN will be covered in Sect. 4. The discussions on the value of blockchain over NDN will be covered in Sect. 5. Open challenges will be presented in Sect. 6 and Sect. 7 will conclude the paper.

2 Methodology

The narrative review method is used in this study to give readers enough background information to comprehend the research issue and emphasize the value of new knowledge. IEEE, ACM, Springer, and Elsevier are just a few of the research databases that the researchers use. Papers are initially chosen based on the broad keyword" Named Data Networks" and filtered to exclude duplicates and irrelevant ones. Additionally, particular keywords like" Blockchain over Named Data Network," Named Data Networks," and" Blockchain" are utilized to narrow down the articles that have been gathered. With 45% of the total publications from the IEEE database, the papers are mostly from 2021 to 2023. The remaining papers are sourced from various conferences and journals, with distribution percentages of 4%, 14%, 14%, 9%, and 14% for ACM, Springer, MDPI, Elsevier, and other conferences and journals, respectively. The study adopts a qualitative approach and conducts a narrative investigation. Qualitative research allows researchers to obtain comprehensive data in their natural settings, offering the opportunity for data interpretation given the interpretative nature of the study. Figure 2 illustrates the distribution of articles from different resources.

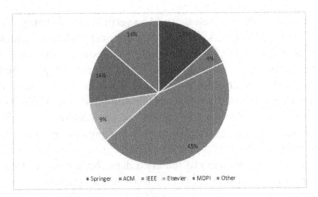

Fig. 2. Articles from different resources.

3   Background First Section

Blockchain and named data networking (NDN) are two emerging technologies that have the potential to revolutionize the way we interact with the Internet. Blockchain is a distributed ledger technology that can securely record and share data, while NDN is a new networking paradigm focusing on content rather than location. In this section, we will provide a background on blockchain and NDN. We will then discuss the potential benefits of combining these two technologies [6].

3.1   NDN Forwarding Plane

NDN architectural design proposes two packet types: interest packets and data packets. NDN users can access the data by subscribing to an Interest packet, which requests a content object and returns it as a Data packet; both packets contain the name of the content object. The Forwarding Information Base (FIB), the Pending Interest Table (PIT), and the Content Store are the three significant Data structures that an NDN router must maintain (CS) [3].

The FIB of an NDN router is often similar to the FIB of an IP router, with the architectural difference that it holds name prefixes rather than IP address prefixes. By doing this, the name prefixes may be sent to various interfaces. Each PIT section keeps a record of the Interest's name, arriving interface(s), and forwarding interface(s) that it has been passed to (like a history table), when a router receives an interest packet, it first checks the Content Store (CS) to see whether there is any matching Data. The CS provides short-term in-network storage (caching) of the incoming Data packet. The interface from which the Interest is coming receives the data immediately [7].

On the other hand, if the name matches, the interest will proceed to look up the PIT entries. Suppose the name already appears in the PIT. In that case, it may be a duplicate Interest that has to be discarded or a retransmitted Interest from the same customer sent via a different outgoing interface (or an Interest from an alternate consumer requesting the same Data). This causes the PIT to check the nonce of the Interest and update the existing PIT record with the number of incoming interfaces. This effectively creates a multicast tree for users requesting the same Data simultaneously. If the Interest name does not already exist in the PIT, it is added to the PIT and sent to the FIB, where the forwarding plane module will handle it.

When a Data packet comes at this stage, the PIT is checked using the packet's name. The router delivers the Data packet to the interface(s) from which the Interest arrived and deletes the PIT entrance if there is a match in the PIT entrance. Data packets then frequently follow the interests' backward routes. The Data packet is discarded or cached in the CS if no match is detected. Every Interest has an associated lifespan that the consumer determines; if an Interest is unsatisfied before its lifetime expires, a PIT item is removed. Nevertheless, an NDN router may keep a Data packet in the CS due to the signature's uniqueness and the dependability of the caching strategy. Even so, future interests can be satisfied using the data packets stored in the CS [8].

3.2 Blockchain Framework

Most modern blockchain systems use a common framework that was first established in Bitcoin and Ethereum and may be organized generally into four levels [9] as follow:

Application Layer: By utilizing smart contracts, the decentralized applications of blockchain technology, such as supply chain management, identity management, and notarial services, have grown to include the application layer, which is used for cryptocurrency transfers.

Data Layer: A blockchain framework's data layer contains structures for consensus, data transfer, and ledger maintenance. Blocks are connected via hash references; however, block architectures may vary.

Consensus Layer: The shared ledger is created via a process followed by the consensus layer in blockchain nodes, with copies on each node. Consistency requires agreement on how transactions should be executed in order. For quicker processing, transactions are organized into blocks, and the block sequence is chosen instead. The PoW consensus, used by many blockchain systems, is infamous for its lengthy transaction times and lack of transactional finality because of ledger forking. Researchers are looking into novel consensus methods to get over these restrictions and support a range of blockchain technology use cases.

Transport Layer: The blockchain network's transport layer defines how transactions are recorded to the ledger and how blockchain data is propagated. Public blockchains like Bitcoin and Ethereum use a P2P overlay to transfer data items to all nodes from a single source. The transport layer of the blockchain network controls how transactions are recorded and propagated.

4 Blockchain over Named Data Networks

Most research on Named Data Networks and Blockchain technology has been done independently. Table 1 shows recent years that adopted Blockchain over NDN in various fields, including security and privacy, networks, the Internet of Things, mobility, and others. TCP/IP was the primary platform for the blockchain's creation. When a node sends data over TCP/IP to several nodes, it must first package that data in a packet and send it to each node separately, which results in extra data transfer. NDN uses in-network caching, which can help to enhance the entire broadcast of a blockchain application.

NDN's data-centric methodology makes it possible to synchronize blocks on a blockchain effectively and distribute records. Data in NDN is gathered from the complete network rather than from a single node or location. Since there is no concept of a light node or a full node with blockchain technology via NDN, all nodes are treated equally. This resolves a critical security flaw in existing distributed ledger systems where the light node depends on the entire node to receive and deliver data, leaving it vulnerable to the full nodes' malevolent behavior [10].

The studies in [10–12] investigate how different blockchains, including public, private, and consortium blockchains, can distribute data across NDN. Anyone with internet connectivity can become a certified node on a public blockchain, which is open and unrestricted and welcomes new nodes. A new node relay pressure metric is used for routing decisions in a green global routing system (GGNRP) to reduce power consumption and forwarding time [11]. Using a blockchain-based key management system for safe key distribution and verification is also suggested. While several organizations run consortium blockchains, private blockchains are used only by particular enterprises or organizations.

With the potential to expand NDN application ecosystems, a new blockchain platform proposed in [12] uses named data networking (NDN) rather than the conventional internet protocol (IP) to build blockchain platforms. The suggested framework [13], which uses NDN and IPFS for data management and has three layers—the data layer, the blockchain layer, and the application layer—offers superior privacy protection, scalability, and efficiency than existing federated learning frameworks. The blockchain is used to store the aggregated data and to ensure its integrity. The framework has several advantages over traditional federated learning frameworks. First, it provides better privacy protection for the raw data. Second, it is more scalable and can support many edge devices. Third, it is more efficient, as it does not require transferring large amounts of data to the cloud server.

A new certificate ledger system called CLedger. CLedger is a distributed system that uses named data networking (NDN) to store and manage certificates [14]. As NDN is naming data instead of nodes, this makes it possible to store and manage certificates in a distributed manner without having to worry about the identity of the nodes that store the certificates [14].

In addition, researchers in [15] proposed an XRP-NDN Overlay as a solution for improving the communication efficiency of consensus-validation-based blockchains like the XRP Ledger. It does this by using a Named Data Networking (NDN) overlay network. This allows for more efficient routing, as data can be routed directly to the destination, without having to go through a central server. In [9] it is suggested to use blockchain technology and hierarchical identity-based cryptography (HIBC) to construct anonymous identities and independently verify the validity of data in named data networking (NDN).

Table 1. Blockchain over Named Data Network related works

Ref	Year	Area	Contribution
[11]	2021	Security	Present a routing scheme based on node relaying pressure and blockchain-based key management scheme
[12]	2023	Routing	Present new protocols for propagating blockchain data using NDN features
[13]	2022	Routing	Proposed framework consists of three layers and used NDN to name the aggregated data
[14]	2023	Security	Design of CLedger, a secure distributed certificate ledger
[15]	2023	Routing	Proposed an XRP-NDN Overlay to enhance the effectiveness of communication across consensus - validation-based blockchains
[9]	2022	Security	Presents hierarchical identity-based cryptography (HIBC) and blockchain-based security method for NDN
[16]	2023	Security	Proposed efficient and secure auditing of data transmission behavior for NDN IIoT networks
[17]	2023	Security	Proposed a NACDA approach for data verification in NDN, which improved the considerable delays brought on by the extremely dynamic nature of vehicle networks
[18]	2023	Security	Proposed a decentralized data authentication mechanism based on blockchain technology
[19]	2023	Trust	Build mechanics trust between vehicles using NDN to route data efficiently, and blockchain to record transactions securely
[20]	2022	Security	proposed a system called BIoVN, to secure IoV over NDN
[21]	2023	Routing	Present a new data dissemination protocol called A-C is based on the NDN forwarding
[6]	2022	Routing	Proposed a deployment of named data networking (NDN) at the network layer of the blockchain to provide differentiated QoS assurance
[22]	2023	Routing	Proposed a framework called AFFIRM for generating, validating, storing, and retrieving mobility data in Web3 applications
[23]	2022	Trust	Present a trust management system is to allow well-behaved peers to gain a good reputation
[24]	2021	Security	Proposes a novel encryption-based data access control scheme for Named Data Networking (NDN) using Role-Based Encryption (RBE)
[25]	2023	Trust	Proposes a proof-of-trust-based data authentication system for blockchains in NDN
[26]	2022	Routing	Proposed access control system based on NFT enables NDN routers to forward ciphertext data
[27]	2022	Routing	This paper proposes integrating blockchain and NDN to improve document content storage

(*continued*)

Table 1. (*continued*)

Ref	Year	Area	Contribution
[28]	2023	Security	Proposed a CCN-based secure content delivery scheme for V2G networks
[29]	2022	Security	Proposes a security architecture for NDN based on a consortium blockchain and bootstrapping procedures

The authors [16] In the Industrial Internet of Things (IIoT), the study provides a simple transmission behavior audit scheme for Named Data Networking (NDN). The blockchain-based system makes it possible to audit data transmission behavior in NDN networks safely and effectively. It consists of three basic parts: a lightweight auditor for gathering and submitting records to the blockchain, a blockchain-based audit system for managing records, and a data packet for carrying audit records. The findings show that NDN networks can effectively detect malicious activities and have high throughput and low latency.

IN [17] proposed Naming-Based Access Control and Decentralized Authorization (NACDA) system addresses challenges in data verification in dynamic vehicular net works by enabling secure and flexible data sharing on the Named Data Network (NDN) using Identity-Based Encryption with Wildcard Key Derivation (WKD-IBE) and blockchain. A new mechanism has been proposed in [18] to provide a decentralized data authentication mechanism based on blockchain technology that is both efficient and straightforward.

A new framework proposed in [19] uses VSNs to build trust between vehicles, NDN to route data efficiently, and blockchain to record transactions securely. The framework is designed to be P2P, meaning that vehicles can trade energy directly with each other without needing central authority. While in [20] the authors proposed another system called BIoVN, which is a combination of blockchain technology and named data networking (NDN) for the Internet of Vehicles (IoV). The purpose of this system is to improve the security of vehicular communications over NDN.

The authors in [21] introduce the Named Data Networking (NDN) and Erasure Coding (EC)-based A-C data distribution protocol. The protocol uses a two-layer NDN-based publication-subscription mechanism to maximize bandwidth efficiency and speed up data dissemination. It focuses on the prompt distribution of blocks and transactions in blockchain systems, which is crucial for consensus, effectiveness, and security. The A-C protocol improves data transmission efficiency and security in blockchain systems, reduces data redundancy, and addresses shortcomings of flooding-based gossip protocols.

A deployment of named data networking (NDN) at the network layer of the blockchain to provide differentiated QoS assurance is proposed in [6]. It discussed the use of window sliding and forwarding strategies to speed up packet processing and meet the delay requirements of delay-sensitive packets. Also, a blockchain framework called AFFIRM for generating, validating, storing, and retrieving mobility data in Web3 applications. This framework enables nearby devices to self-organize as a fog network and collaboratively train machine learning algorithms locally to securely generate, validate, store, and retrieve mobility data via consensus leveraging Information Centric Networking as the underlying architecture [22].

Author in [24] proposes a novel encryption-based data access control scheme for Named Data Networking (NDN) using Role-Based Encryption (RBE). The scheme ensures efficient data access control over hierarchical content, making it suitable for large-scale content-centric applications like Netflix. The study [25] proposes a proof-of-trust-based data authentication system for blockchains. The technique collects votes from a group of nodes to distribute and store items in the cache memory. The suggested system provides a fresh data authentication option for the upcoming Internet environment while attempting to address difficulties with tainted cache memory. In [26] smart contracts are used to distribute AttributeNFT and AccessNFT, a proposed access control system based on Non-Fungible Token (NFT) that enables NDN routers to forward ciphertext data packets only to authorized users, assuring data security and secure distribution. To increase document content distribution, security, and network speed, research in [27] suggests fusing blockchain technology with Named Data Networks (NDN).

Three key contributions are made in the paper's proposal for a CCN-based Three key contributions are made in the paper's proposal for a CCN-based secure content delivery scheme for V2G networks: in-network caching for quick content delivery; a contract theory-based incentive scheme to entice vehicle participation, and the proof of authority consensus algorithm for secure content delivery and network trust [28]. Authors in [29] Used a symmetric-key-based authenticated encryption technique and a one-way hash chain for source authentication, this article suggests a security architecture for NDN that is based on a consortium blockchain and bootstrapping procedures. In [30] proposed CPA detection and prevention mechanism includes a threshold-based content caching system, a blockchain system for privacy, and an extension of NDN to push-based content dissemination.

5 Discussion

With the goal of replacing TCP/IP at the network layer, adopting blockchain technology over NDN offers special benefits and applications that will benefit both the blockchain community and established online services. [5]. By focusing on network-level connectivity and adopting "data-driven authenticity" to assure the security of the data's source, blockchain over NDN prioritizes data over location and ensures real decentralization.

Researchers are interested in how specific technologies are emerging. Data retrieval is efficient using NDN, and data security is ensured via blockchain. Some scholars believe using blockchain technology for the current IP would be unwise. Instead, using blockchain technology over NDN may lead to more effective performance [6, 11]. NDN, a hypothetical future Internet architecture, can support blockchain technology, offering a dependable way to maintain databases without central authority. Blockchain over NDN fixes IP network problems and provides a decentralized system, making connecting nodes and synchronizing data simpler. Trust models can be centralized or decentralized; a prior method involved a central credit authority to collect and disseminate reputation values, but this method still entailed communication costs [15].

Decentralized approaches eliminate the single point of failure problem by allowing each node to calculate ratings and share them with other nodes independently, but this requires the trustworthiness of the individual nodes to perform the computations and provide reputation values. While Encryption is incorporated into NDN to provide data security and authentication, and trust management enables good peers to build up a positive reputation while identifying and excluding bad peers from transactions [13, 25].

The decentralized nature of P2P networks needs a dispersed strategy in contrast to online reputation models. Blockchain over NDN can provide a decentralized system that is more efficient and simpler to implement. By using blockchain technology over NDN, it is possible to reduce the transmission cost, eliminate redundant network traffic, clear up congestion, and boost network efficiency.

Blockchain over-Named Data Network (NDN) provides several advantages and addresses specific data networking needs. Here are some of the reasons why blockchain is seen as useful in conjunction with data networking [5, 6, 9, 11–30]:

Enhanced Security: Blockchain provides a decentralized, tamper-resistant framework to secure data transactions and data distribution. Integrating blockchain into NDN strengthens data integrity and authentication reducing the risk of unauthorized access and manipulation.

Data Ownership and Control: Blockchain's smart contracts allow for fine-grained data ownership and control. In NDN, where data is accessed based on the name, blockchain can help to secure and transparently manage data ownership, enabling content creators to take control of their intellectual property.

Trust and Transparency: Blockchain's distributed ledger provides an unalterable record of data exchanges and transactions. Integration into NDN increases trust and transparency by allowing for verifiable, auditable, and transparent delivery and sharing of data. This is especially important in supply chain management and decentralized applications, where participant trust is essential.

Resilience and Data Availability: NDN's in-network caching capability, combined with the blockchain's decentralized nature, can improve the availability and resilience of data. Blockchain over NDN can utilize distributed storage and caching capabilities, ensuring that content remains available even during network disruption or failure.

Better Consensus and Governance: Blockchain introduces consensus mechanisms allowing decentralized decision-making and governance. When integrated with NDN, blockchain can be used to implement consensus protocols to facilitate agreement on the content distribution policies, the allocation of network resources, and participation rules in the NDN ecosystem.

6 Open Research Challenges

The review highlights the possible advantages and drawbacks of employing blockchain technology in the context of Named Data Networking (NDN), emphasizing the need for additional research into security and content caching issues as well as unsolved privacy-related concerns [5, 25, 28]. It also highlights the need for real-time fairness among network miners, emphasizing the unfairness that results when the miner nearest to the producer receives a newly created block earlier than other miners and the need to foster network miner dynamics [5, 6].

Performance Optimization: Future research should concentrate on creating effective consensus mechanisms and algorithms to integrate blockchain with NDN, to reduce overhead and maintain security guarantees by investigating solutions like sharing off-chain transactions, and optimized consensus protocols to improve scalability and transaction throughput.

Privacy-Preserving Techniques: The highlighted text suggests that researching privacy-preserving methods in Blockchain over NDN can aid in creating mechanisms that safeguard data privacy while utilizing the blockchain's transparency. These methods include zero-knowledge proofs, secure multi-party computation, and differential privacy.

Interoperability and Standardization: Future research can concentrate on creating interoperability frameworks and standards to allow seamless integration with current network infrastructures and protocols as blockchain integration with NDN advances. This entails determining standardized data formats for blockchain-based NDN and looking into ways to connect various blockchain systems.

Security and Trust Model Design: By establishing new cryptographic methods and consensus mechanisms, more research is required to produce secure and reliable models for integrating blockchain with NDN, solving issues such as secure content naming, identity management, and combating Sybil attacks.

Real-World Use Cases and Applications: Future research should concentrate on identifying and examining real-world use cases and applications, such as IoT, content distribution networks, supply chain management, decentralized finance, and healthcare, where Blockchain over NDN can offer significant benefits to assess feasibility, performance, and impact.

7   Conclusion

Blockchain technology is a new concept in NDN that is quickly gaining footing. Blockchain technology over IP still has several significant issues, such as a lack of hierarchical access efficiency. These issues have been resolved by adopting blockchain technology over NDN, which provides a decentralized system and streamlines the design. This article outlined the research examining the application of blockchain technology in NDN. Over NDN, we discussed some of the difficulties with blockchain technology.

The investigation revealed that with an increased number of articles each year, blockchain technology in NDN is receiving increased attention. The survey report demonstrates that the search for Blockchain technology over NDN is still in its infancy, encouraging the NDN research community to devote serious attention to the issue. This study will clear the way for scholars interested in learning more about leveraging blockchain technology over NDN.

References

1. Precedence Research. Blockchain Technology Market Size to Hit USD, 593.8 Bn By 2030 (2021). https://www.precedenceresearch.com/blockchain-technology-market. Accessed 25 Oct 2022
2. Zheng, Z., Xie, S., Dai, H., Chen, X., Wang, H.: An overview of blockchain technology: architecture, consensus, and future trends. In: 2017 IEEE International Congress on Big Data (BigData Congress), pp. 557–564 (2017). https://doi.org/10.1109/BigDataCongress.2017.85
3. Jacobson, V., et al.: Named Data Networking (NDN) Project 2012–2013 Annual Report (2013)
4. Askar, N., et al.: Forwarding strategies for named data networking based IOT: requirements, taxonomy, and open research challenges. IEEE Access (2023)
5. Asaf, K., Rehman, R.A., Kim, B.-S.: Blockchain technology in named data networks: a detailed survey. J. Netw. Comput. Appl. **171**, 102840 (2020). https://doi.org/10.1016/j.jnca. 102840
6. Shang, J., Huo, R., Wang, S., Huang, T.: An NDN-enabled differentiated routing strategy for blockchain. In: 2022 IEEE 2nd International Conference on Computer Communication and Artificial Intelligence (CCAI), pp. 96–101 (2022). https://doi.org/10.1109/CCAI55564.2022. 9807743
7. Abrar, A., Arif, A.S.C.M., Zaini, K.M.: A systematic analysis and review on producer mobility management in named data networks: research background and challenges. Alex. Eng. J. **69**, 785–808 (2023)
8. Alsamman, M., Hassan, S., Arif, S.: Deficit weighted round robin shaping mechanism for transport control in named data networking. J. Adv. Res. Dyn. Control Syst. **11**(8 Special Issue), 1115–1125 (2019)
9. Thai, Q.T., Ko, N., Byun, S.H., Kim, S.-M.: Design and implementation of NDN-based Ethereum blockchain. J. Netw. Comput. Appl. **200**, 103329 (2022). https://doi.org/10.1016/ j.jnca.2021.103329
10. Yi, D., Huo, R., Wang, S., Huang, T.: An NDN-enabled data transfer strategy for blockchain network layer. In: Journal of Physics: Conference Series, vol. 2026, no. 1, p. 012001 (2021). https://doi.org/10.1088/1742-6596/2026/1/012001
11. Liu, H., Zhu, R., Wang, J., Xu, W.: Blockchain-based key management and green routing scheme for vehicular named data networking. Secur. Commun. Netw. **2021**, 1–13 (2021). https://doi.org/10.1155/2021/3717702
12. Li, B., Ma, M.: An advanced hierarchical identity-based security mechanism by blockchain in named data networking. J. Netw. Syst. Manag. **31**(1), 13 (2023)
13. Shen, T., Cui, Z., Tian, S., Bai, F., Zhang, C.A.: Network-elastic scalable blockchain for privacy-preserving federated learning in cloud-edge collaboration industrial internet of things. In: Proceedings of the 2022 7th International Conference on Cloud Computing and Internet of Things, pp. 17–25 (2022)
14. Yu, T., et al.: CLedger: a secure distributed certificate ledger via named data network. IEEE ICC (2023)
15. Trestioreanu, L., Shbair, W.M., de Cristo, F.S., State, R.: XRP-NDN overlay: improving the communication efficiency of consensus-validation based blockchains with an NDN overlay. In: 2023 IEEE/IFIP Network Operations and Management Symposium, NOMS 2023, pp. 1–5. IEEE (2023). arXiv:2301.10209
16. He, Y., Ma, Y., Hu, Q., Zhou, Z., Xiao, K., Wang, C.: Lightweight transmission behavior audit scheme for NDN industrial internet identity resolution and transmission based on blockchain. Electronics **12**(11), 2538 (2023)

17. Li, M., Xue, J., Wang, Y., Ma, R., Huo, W.: NACDA: naming-based access control and decentralized authorization for secure many-to-many data sharing. Electronics 12(7), 1651 (2023)
18. Benmoussa, A., Kerrache, C.A., Calafate, C.T., Lagraa, N.: NDN-BDA: a blockchain-based decentralized data authentication mechanism for vehicular named data networking. Future Internet 15(5), 167 (2023)
19. Komala, C.R., Dhanalakshmi, M., Gayathri, R., Aruna, R., GR, T.: VANET backbone in data networking and block-chain. J. Pharm. Negative Results 1539–1553 (2023)
20. Sabir, Z., Amine, A.: BIoVN: a novel blockchain-based system for securing internet of vehicles over NDN using bioinspired HoneyGuide. In: Maleh, Y., Tawalbeh, Lo.'ai, Motahhir, S., Hafid, A.S. (eds.) Advances in Blockchain Technology for Cyber Physical Systems. IT, pp. 177–192. Springer, Cham (2022). https://doi.org/10.1007/978-3-030-93646-4_8
21. Wang, R., Njilla, L., Yu, S.: AC: an NDN-based blockchain network with erasure coding. In: 2023 International Conference on Computing, Networking and Communications (ICNC), pp. 591–595. IEEE (2023)
22. Khan, J.A., Ozbay, K.: AFFIRM: privacy-by-design blockchain for mobility data in Web3 using information centric fog networks with collaborative learning. In: 2023 International Conference on Computing, Networking and Communications (ICNC), pp. 456–462. IEEE (2023)
23. Sun, Y., Chen, S., Fang, Y., Xu, W., Luo, Q., Rui, L.: A trusted IoT communication architecture based on blockchain and named data network. In: Journal of Physics: Conference Series, vol. 2224, no. 1, p. 012091 (2022). https://doi.org/10.1088/1742-6596/2224/1/012091
24. Sultan, N.H., Varadharajan, V., Kumar, C., Camtepe, S., Nepal, S.: A secure access and accountability framework for provisioning services in named data networks. In: 2021 40th International Symposium on Reliable Distributed Systems (SRDS), Chicago, IL, USA, pp. 164–175 (2021). https://doi.org/10.1109/SRDS53918.2021.00025
25. Rosli, A., Hassan, S., Omar, M.H.: Data authentication mechanism using blockchain's proof-of-trust mechanism in named data networking. In: AIP Conference Proceedings, vol. 2608, no. 1. AIP Publishing (2023)
26. Zhao, H., Zhang, X., Li, R.: NFT-based access control in named data networks, pp. 139–146 (2022). https://doi.org/10.1109/ISPA-BDCloud-SocialCom-SustainCom57177.2022.00025
27. Kang, P., Wenzhong, Y., Ding, T.: Blockchain document forwarding and proof method based on NDN network. IEEE Access 10, 75312–75322 (2022)
28. Miglani, A., Kumar, N.: Blockchain-based co-operative caching for secure content delivery in CCN-enabled V2G networks. IEEE Trans. Veh. Technol. 72(4), 5274–5289 (2023). https://doi.org/10.1109/TVT.2022.3227291
29. Park, C.-S., Park, W.S., Woo, S.: Security bootstrapping for securing data plane and control plane in named data networking. IEEE Trans. Netw. Serv. Manag. https://doi.org/10.1109/TNSM.(2022).3232359
30. Magsi, A.H., Yovita, L.V., Ghulam, A., Muhammad, G., Ali, Z.: A content poisoning attack detection and prevention system in vehicular named data networking. Sustainability 15(14), 10931 (2023)

A Review of Policy on Creative Industry for Sustainable Nation: A Malaysian Perspective

Syamsul Bahrin Zaibon[1]([✉]) [iD], Asmidah Alwi[1] [iD], Ahmad Hisham Zainal Abidin[1] [iD], Adzrool Idzwan Ismail[1] [iD], Nur Kareelawati Abd Karim[2] [iD], and Shamsul Arrieya Ariffin[3] [iD]

[1] Consortium on Creative Industry and Sustainable Culture, School of Creative Industry Management and Performing Arts, Universiti Utara Malaysia, Sintok, 06010 Bukit Kayu Hitam, Kedah, Malaysia
syamsulbahrin@uum.edu.my
[2] Faculty of Leadership and Management, Universiti Sains Islam Malaysia, 71800 Nilai, Negeri Sembilan, Malaysia
[3] Faculty of Computing and Meta-Technology, Universiti Pendidikan Sultan Idris, Tanjong Malim, Malaysia

Abstract. The Malaysian *Dasar Industri Kreatif Negara* (DIKN), or the Malaysian National Creative Industry Policies, was launched in 2010 and created a list of creative offerings broken down into three sectors: Creative Multimedia, Creative Cultural Arts, and Creative Cultural Heritage. Each of these sectors has its behaviors, problems and mechanisms and requires a tailored approach to its promotion. The policy's main objective is to promote creativity, ensuring both economic and social benefits sustainably. It has now been ten years since DIKN was launched. Although it has generally shown a positive effect, the vibrancy of the creative economy is still less than satisfactory compared to other Asian countries such as Indonesia and Thailand. Until now, no comprehensive study has been conducted on the effectiveness and impact of DIKN on the country. Therefore, this article discusses the existing problems and compares the policies of different countries regarding the development of the creative industries sector. To achieve the study's objectives, a three-stage approach was adopted, including a comparative analysis and synthesis of the literature on creative industries concepts and policies, a quantitative survey of 134 creative industries stakeholders in Malaysia on their views on the DIKN, and a generalization of the overall findings. Findings from this study show that there are big spaces for improvements in the current policy in line with new trends and technological advancements. The results of this study will be able to highlight the weaknesses of existing policies in Malaysia and suggest improvements in the scope of the field, as well as propose a strategic framework for the development of Malaysia's creative industries sector.

Keywords: Creative Industry Policy · Sustainable Nation · Gross Domestic Product

© The Author(s), under exclusive license to Springer Nature Singapore Pte Ltd. 2024
N. H. Zakaria et al. (Eds.): ICOCI 2023, CCIS 2001, pp. 380–394, 2024.
https://doi.org/10.1007/978-981-99-9589-9_29

1 Introduction

The creative industry in Malaysia is one of the positive contributors to the Gross Domestic Product (GDP). Accordingly, the National Creative Industry Policy (DIKN) was launched in 2010 as the main policy to set the basic principle of development in driving the country's creative activities to be more productive and economical. Three main scopes are classified: creative multimedia, cultural arts, and cultural heritage to meet the industry's needs and support each scope's development and progress. It has now been ten years since DIKN was launched. Although it has generally shown a positive effect, the vibrancy of the creative economy is still less than satisfactory compared to other Asian countries such as Indonesia and Thailand. Until now, no comprehensive study has been conducted on the effectiveness and impact of DIKN on the country. Furthermore, the scope of the creative industry needs to be updated according to the latest trends towards globalization and Industrial Revolution 4.0.

Therefore, this article discusses the existing problems and compares the policies of several countries regarding the classification of the creative industry sector. The results of this study will be able to identify the weaknesses of existing policies in Malaysia and suggest improvements in the scope of the field, as well as in the future research to propose a strategic framework for creative industry.

With this strategy, existing policies can be improved, becoming a specific guide for the government, practitioners, entrepreneurs, and entrepreneurs to produce higher quality creative content and gain a place in the local and international markets without neglecting the local cultural aspect.

Today's global development, especially in the era of Industrial Revolution 4.0, greatly impacts the creative industry's and related fields' development. This directly contributes greatly to social, economic, cultural, and technological development in all corners of the world, including Malaysia. This development is one of the drivers of global economic growth, especially involving developed and developing countries. For example, in the United States in 2015, the growth of the creative industry contributed as much as USD763.6 billion in addition to providing employment opportunities of 4.92 million, which contributed 4.2% of GDP [1]. The United States is also a big pioneer in developing this industry with the establishment of Hollywood, which produces films and famous actors that greatly impact the country's income.

Research highlights from [2] explain in South Korea is another example of creative industry development in Asia resulting from the Asian economic recession in 1997. South Korea has stopped all imports of entertainment materials from outside, especially from Japan. In addition, the South Korean Ministry of Culture has also launched several entertainment projects to strengthen local culture and produce new talents. This project involves nearly 300 higher education institutions throughout South Korea. It turns out that the results of this strategy have yielded high-impact results today. As a result of this innovative initiative, South Korea is now one of the most successful countries in producing creative industries in the world. Programs like K-POP, Running Man and many more have millions of fans all over the world. According to a report by the Korean Foundation, there are 35 million 'Hallyu' fans from 86 countries. Hallyu or Korean Wave is a term given to spread Korean pop culture (K-Pop and drama) globally and internationally.

382   S. B. Zaibon et al.

This phenomenon is at least enough to worry creative industry superpowers like the United States about the possibility of South Korea dethroning them as the world's main cultural exporter in the future. The average analyst believes that the US Music Industry model built for the 20th century consumer with limited distribution channels, a hyperfocus on music and a strong reliance on copyright is no longer relevant to current and future global consumer trends [3]. In addition, the landscape of Korean Popular Culture, better known as K-Pop, focuses more on 21st-century strategies. The model of Korean pop music that we face today, for example, is the result of systematic planning that began two decades ago, considering the development of digital technology. They focus on the "industrialization" of music production, with hit warehouses and star production academies. Candidate artists are selected among those who are bilingual and can sing, dance, and act. The K-pop music industry is all about building "multimedia" stars for the global stage, with diverse income streams that are not overly dependent on copyright to earn royalties. K-Pop focuses on the consumer's "multimedia" experience through TV channels that use Korean-made brands. The first appearance of a new artist is broadcast on TV along with a video and via YouTube. For entertainment companies, Korean culture is a commodity that can be exported and sold around the world.

Therefore, as a country rich in culture with diverse races, Malaysia can make South Korea a case study for developing the country's creative industry. Thus, a robust creative industry development strategy framework in Malaysia needs to be established to achieve the desire and vision to become a country that produces quality creative content from cultural value and creativity.

It has now been ten years since DIKN was launched, although generally showing positive effects. However, the vibrancy of the creative economy is still less than satisfactory compared to other Asian countries such as Indonesia and Thailand. There are reports regarding the DIKN grant that failed to drive the creative industry [4]. Furthermore, the scope of the creative industry needs to be updated in accordance with the latest trends towards globalization and IR4.0 as recommended by the Minister of Communications and Multimedia [5] and recommendations from the Malaysian Television Producers Association (PPTM) to see the diversity of platforms new such as "digital movie", "digital games" and so on [6]. Until now, there has been no comprehensive study on the effectiveness and impact of DIKN after ten years of being enacted. This study needs to be done for all sectors of the creative industry and related new sectors.

Furthermore, Thomas Barker from the University of Nottingham Malaysia has also researched and emphasized the issue of non-creative creative industry policy [7]. He explained that despite the various funds and initiatives allocated by the government for the creative industry, these efforts are only for the short term without considering the investment of long-term methods to increase sustainability, expand the number of viewers and improve the quality of content.

Management aspects in creative industry projects also need to be aligned with the latest technology, employee lifestyles, working patterns, flexible production management, financial management and so on in order to meet current trends that require fast and efficient production [8–10]. In addition, a study by [11] found that the creative content industry in Malaysia exists in a less encouraging ecosystem. Malaysia's creative media content industry faces various challenges from the aspects of policy, value system, work culture and human management. Indirectly, unsystematic human management has had a negative impact on the quality of published content. Media production focusing on the capitalist and post-liberal value system (neoliberalism) can damage Malaysian society's aesthetic value and artistic heritage.

The creative industry suffers from an imbalance between the initiative towards human development (in the creative industry) and the ambition to place Malaysia among the countries known as producers of quality content. The training provided by government and private agencies is more focused on developing skills related to media production, which is more technical. Aspects of human development and management are given less attention. Therefore, a framework that includes humanitarian elements, skills and content values is very relevant, especially in an era where the industry needs to prepare to face the era of Industrial Revolution 4.0 (IR 4.0) and Society 5.0 (Society 5.0) [12]. The development of Society 5.0 needs to go hand in hand with soft development in the creative industry and be more comprehensive to ensure a sustainable and balanced community environment.

2 Methodology

A three-stage approach was designed to achieve the objectives of the study. The first stage involves the theoretical approach, which contains the logical and comparative analysis and synthesis of scientific literature on concepts of creative industry and the policies developed for some countries with a special interest in influencing the economic development of countries. Secondly, this study employed a quantitative survey of the creative industry stakeholders in Malaysia on their opinion on the National Policy of the Creative Industry. The data were analyzed using descriptive analysis. In the third stage, based on the obtained theoretical results and the results of statistical data analysis, the generalization and final results visualization were carried out.

Findings of the analysis for the first stage are discussed in Sect. 3, where further discussion revolves around data related to the Malaysian GDP, the definition of creative industry terms, an introduction to DIKN, local content and Islamic culture in the creative industry, as well as an analysis of the latest technology applied to the creative industry. In addition, Sect. 4 presents a comparative analysis of the differences between 11 classifications of creative industry in a few countries. It was also referred to the World Intellectual Property Organization (WIPO), United Nations Conference on Trade and Development (UNCTAD), European (EU) Commission, and United Nations Educational, Scientific and Cultural Organization (UNESCO). In the second stage of this study, a survey was employed to the 134 respondents from the creative industry stakeholders in Malaysia on their opinion on the DIKN. Finally, the study is concluded and discussed.

3 Creative Industry for Sustainable Nation

Malaysia is among the ten main contributing countries among developing countries that activate the creative industry and generate as much as RM11 billion for the national economy by providing as many as 86,000 job opportunities [13]. According to the UNCTAD report, in 2018, MSC Malaysia companies under this cluster recorded a sales value of

RM7.69 billion with an export value of RM1.4 billion. In addition, this industry has provided 11,471 job opportunities [14]. The potential of the country's creative industry can continue to be developed to a higher level. However, the DIKN launched in 2010 is still under-applied, and its development is relatively slow compared to neighboring countries such as Thailand and Indonesia. Many studies have also been done, such as a search on Google about the development of the creative industry in both countries. However, there is still little or no in-depth study on the impact of DIKN on this issue. The following graph shows the contributions of the creative industry to Malaysian GDP from 2010 to 2020 (see Fig. 1).

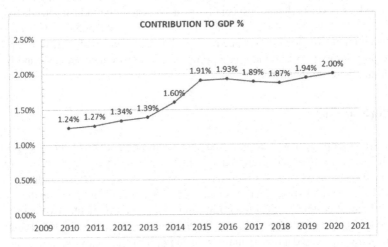

Fig. 1. Contribution of creative industry to GDP from 2010 to 2020 of Malaysia

3.1 Creative Industry Definition

Various definitions of the activities included in the creative industry have been proposed. The use of the term creative industry varies between countries. Major organizations such as UNESCO define creative industry as industries that combine the creation, production and commercialization of intangible and cultural products. These creative products are usually protected by copyright in the form of goods or services [15]. There is a view that says the focus should be on creativity rather than culture. The United Kingdom government, for example, defines the creative industry as an industry that has its origins in the creativity, skills and talents of individuals and that has the potential for wealth and creating employment opportunities through the generation and exploitation of intellectual property [16]. Although the United Kingdom government pioneered the concept and use of creative industry terminology, the definition above cannot escape criticism and debate. This is because this definition seems to place all creative products with potential economic generation as part of the creative industry. Does creating engineering products that start from creative ideas and have economic value also count as part of the creative industry?

The Malaysian government outlines the definition of the creative industry in the context of Malaysia as he consolidation and production of individual or group abilities and talents based on creativity, innovation and technology that lead to a source of economic success and high income for the country by emphasizing the aspect of works and intellectual copyright in accordance with the culture and the pure values of racial diversity in Malaysia [17]. This definition clearly shows that the Malaysian government gives a balanced focus between creativity and culture. In addition, the aspect of indigenous knowledge (IK) is also emphasized. This exploration and application of IK is very important and useful in finding uniqueness in producing creative products that can attract the interest of international consumers and the global market [18].

3.2   The National Creative Industry Policy (DIKN) in Malaysia

In Malaysia, the DIKN was formulated as a policy to set the basic principles of creative industry development. This policy was established to explain the direction and development of the country's creative industry and stimulate all creative activities to be more productive and economical through the synergy of the public and private sectors. Based on DIKN launched in 2010, the policy classification is divided into three main scopes of the creative industry: creative multimedia, cultural arts, and cultural heritage.

- Creative Multimedia. Creative Multimedia "consists of industries that apply the latest technological advances in producing creative products" [17], for example, film and TV, advertising, art design, animation, and digital content. The opportunities for the Creative Multimedia industry are vast to explore the latest trends towards film, video game development on multiple platforms, animated content on television or film, and even the latest mobile applications for mobile internet devices.
- Creative Art and Culture. Creative Art and Culture related to of producing artworks that are characteristic of Malaysian culture, music, performance art, visual art, crafts, creative writing, fashion, and textiles [17]. Among other things, the government has prepared the Palace of Culture, the National Gallery of Art and the National Craft Complex as an initiative to fuel these industries further. Apart from that, there is the City Hall, the City Theatre, and the Main Hall of the Malaysian Tourism Center, all located in Kuala Lumpur. In addition, various art and cultural activities are planned and organized, and most are concentrated around the Klang Valley only.
- Creative Cultural Heritage. This scope includes museums, archives, restoration, and conservation of local cultural heritage.

DIKN aims to provide a comprehensive creative industry development roadmap to achieve the following goals:

- Make the creative industry a dynamic sector that can increase its Contribution to the country's GDP and further contribute to a high-income economy;
- Support the development of a competitive, viable and resilient creative industry at the domestic and international levels;
- Provide facilities and infrastructure and improve a conducive environment to promote the growth of the local creative industry;
- Drive the growth and recognition of intellectual property in the creative industry through training and accreditation programs;

- Develop and utilize technology as a catalyst for creative industries and
- Proliferate information sources and highlight the symbolism of local culture and national identity to the global level.

The creative industry can generate the economy through financial returns generated from the industry's activities. A growing creative industry could increase investment in related aspects and supporting industries.

3.3 Local and Islamic Cultural Content from a Malaysian Perspective

Cultural heritage reflects a community's life among people inherited from generation to generation. According to UNESCO, cultural heritage consists of customs, practices, places, objects and artistic expressions. It can be produced in tangible and intangible forms [19]. For example, cultural heritage in the category of oral tradition (oral tradition) such as 'Awang Batil' (Awang Batil is a storyteller concept that can only be found in the state of Perlis) needs to be preserved in a documentary format so that it can be understood easily and clearly and attract the interest of the audience, especially among the younger generation.

Problems arise when there is a wide gap between the academic world and the creative industry, which is the main cause of failure to dignify Malay cultural heritage through documentary films. Many producers admit they lack time to research before publishing a documentary [20]. Scripts processed without being guided by research results will negatively affect the public's understanding of the Malay and Islamic cultural heritage that the media is trying to convey. This situation is very worrying after the study of [20] found that almost half of the screenwriters in this country think the research process is unimportant.

Screenwriters in this country are also found to be lacking in ideas and less creative, so much so that they are willing to take risks that can affect the quality and validity of a published documentary [21]. Therefore, documentaries based on research results are a suitable medium to educate the public about cultural heritage and human figures who are increasingly being forgotten, such as Awang Batil. It is the responsibility of scriptwriters, directors and producers of Muslim TV and films to produce media content with Islamic elements to spread good values through their works [11, 22].

Therefore, the effort to dignify cultural heritage is the responsibility of all parties, including the creative industry and policymakers. A comprehensive development strategy framework that includes working and religious life that applies good values in human management, education and content in the creative industry is very important. However, various local content can be produced through new guidelines for digital content, which also need to be established in parallel with IR4.0.

3.4 Technology Related to Creative Industry

Various elements based on the adaptation of Industrial Revolution 4.0, such as coding (QR-Code), 3D model making, simulation, animation, virtual reality, and various interactive applications, have been used now through the digitization of creative design and product development activities, education, marketing, and creative content development that relevant to the current situation. Examples are as follows:

- Advertising. The form of advertising is now not only through print media, radio, electronics, and websites but also using virtual technologies such as virtual reality (VR) and augmented reality (AR); for example, [23] uses advertising for housing and [24] discusses catalogs Ikea.

- Online Creative Services. Now, various platforms are available for creative entrepreneurs to get jobs through "freelancer" services worldwide for graphic design and video editing, such as Freelancer.com and Upwork.com [25].

- Crafts. Craft-making activities are also adapted with the use of creative technology, such as using 3 3-dimensional printers. In addition, this product is marketed through digital technology as has been carried out by Kraftangan Malaysia on National Craft Day 2019, which is to provide a Digital Park where visitors experience digital experiences through activities such as Virtual Assistant, Augmented Reality (AR), Digital Craft Book, Virtual Shop (e-Commerce), Chatbot, QR-Code AR, Interactive Wall and Virtual Reality [26].

- Video, Film and Photography. Creative activities related to video production, film and photography services, and video and film distribution include script writing, film shooting, cinematography, and film exhibition. This field is growing with the birth of various forms of digital media and audio-visual technology; the latest example is a film based on virtual reality [27].

- Interactive Games. Creative activities related to creating, producing, and distributing computer and video games are entertainment, dexterity, and educational. For example, online games that are now increasingly popular and have been recognized as e-sports are PUBG and Mobile Legend. This eSport has become a career that brings good results [28].

- Music. Creative activities related to creating, producing, distributing and retailing sound recordings, recording copyrights, music promotion, lyricists, composers of songs or music, musical performances, singers, and musical compositions. This creative work is produced digitally easily and marketed digitally on various platforms such as Spotify for global markets [29].

- Performing Arts. Show productions, ballet shows, traditional dance, contemporary dance, drama, traditional music, theater music, opera, and lighting art promise a fun audience experience such as the use of LED screens and can give interactive performances. For example, Encore in Melaka uses various elements of the latest technology (Encore-Melaka.com).

- Television and Radio. Creative activities related to the creation, production and packaging, broadcasting, and television and radio that combine high-resolution audio-visual quality (HD) with Internet technology such as IPTV supported by smart TV technology.

4 Classification of Creative Industry: Cross Country Comparison

A comparative analysis was conducted to find differences between the classification of the creative industry in a few countries. It was also referred to by the World Intellectual Property Organization (WIPO), United Nations Conference on Trade and Development (UNCTAD), European (EU) Commission, and United Nations Educational, Scientific and Cultural Organization (UNESCO). The countries include Malaysia, Thailand,

Indonesia, South Korea, Taiwan, China, and the United States of America (USA). Table 1 shows the classification of the creative industry among these countries.

The table indicates that different countries have different classifications and definitions of creative industry areas, which signifies the different calculation of GDP contributions for their economic indicators. Malaysia should revise its creative industry policy and include other areas that should be calculated for its GDP.

Table 1. Classification of the creative industry in different countries

Industries/Services	A	B	C	D	E	F	G	H	I	J	K
Advertising	/	/	/	/	/	/	/	/		/	/
Architectural and related	/	/	/	/		/	/		/		/
Design	/	/	/	/	/	/	/	/	/	/	/
Fashion	/			/	/	/	/	/			/
Film, video and sound	/	/	/	/	/	/	/	/	/	/	/
Hardware	/	/	/	/							
Music	/	/	/	/	/	/	/	/	/		/
Museum/gallery	/		/	/	/						/
Print media	/	/	/	/	/	/	/	/			
Software	/	/				/			/	/	
Sport		/									
Performing arts	/	/	/	/	/	/	/	/	/		/
Broadcasting/Production		/	/	/	/	/	/	/	/		/
Video games	/	/	/	/		/	/	/			
Visual arts and related	/	/		/	/	/	/	/	/	/	
Handicraft	/				/		/		/	/	
Innovative and lifestyle								/			
Tourism										/	
R & D							/				
Cultural exhibition							/		/	/	/
Publishing	/						/		/	/	/
Independent artist											/

Notes: A: WIPO, B: UNCTAD, C: EU Commission, D: UNESCO, E: Malaysia, F: Thailand, G: Indonesia, H: South Korea, I: Taiwan, J: China, K: United States of America

5   A Quantitative Survey of the Creative Industry Stakeholders in Malaysia

A quantitative survey was employed to the creative industry stakeholders in Malaysia on their opinion on the National Policy of Creative Industry. An online questionnaire was designed to collect data, and a five-point Likert Scale from 1 (Strongly Disagree) to 5 (Strongly Agree) was used to measure the agreement level of the respondents. Using convenience sampling, which was distributed online via social media, a short messaging system, and messaging services, the survey received 134 responses from various sectors (Table 2), education levels (Table 3) and monthly income (Table 4).

Table 2. Frequency distribution of respondent's employment sectors.

Sector	Frequency	Percentage
Government	63	47
Self-employed	25	18.7
Private	19	14.2
Statutory body	12	9
Government-linked Agency	2	1.5
Others	13	9.7
Total	134	100

Table 3. Frequency distribution of respondent's education levels.

Education Level	Frequency	Percentage
Undergraduate	55	41
Postgraduate	20	14.9
Diploma	20	14.9
Certificate of Malaysian Education (SPM)	20	14.9
Ph.D	2	1.5
Lower secondary Assessment (SRP/PMR)	1	0.7
Others	7	5.2
Total	134	100

The results of the respondent profiles indicate their demographics. The frequency distribution of respondent's employment sectors presented in Table 2 shows that the majority (63 out of 134, 47%) of the respondents were from Government sectors, followed by self-employed, 25 (18.7%). In terms of educational level, Table 3 presents the frequency distribution of the respondent's educational background. The analysis describes that 55 (41%) respondents were Undergraduate; 20 (14.9%) each were Post-graduate, Diploma and SPM. In addition, Table 4 shows that a majority (46.3%) of the respondents belonged to the monthly income group, RM2,500-RM5,000; 32 (23.9%) were from the monthly income group, RM5,000-RM10,000; 23 (17.2%) were from monthly income group RM1,000-RM2,500; and 7 (5.2%) were more than RM10,000.

Table 4. Frequency distribution of respondent's monthly income.

Monthly Income	Frequency	Percentage
Less than RM1,000	10	7.5
From RM1,000 to RM2,500	23	17.2
From RM2,500 to RM5,000	62	46.3
From RM5,000 to RM10,000	32	23.9
More than RM10,000	7	5.2
Total	134	100

5.1 Opinions on the Malaysian National Policy of Creative Industry

This section presents the descriptive analysis of the survey. Figure 2, 3, 4, 5, 6 and Fig. 7 and Table 5 show the survey results on the respondent's agreement on the Malaysian National Policy of Creative Industry. When they were asked about their understanding of the policy (see Fig. 2), the majority agreed that they understood the policy (mean 3.53, SD 1.09). However, in Fig. 3, they just reflected neutral opinions on referring to the policy to help them understand the scope of their work in the creative industry (mean 3.33, SD 1.12).

The results also show that respondents gave the opinion that the policy is still relevant today (mean 3.61, SD 1.06) (see Fig. 4), created a conducive environment by developing institutions, infrastructure and financial support (incentives/funds/investments) with mean 3.63, SD 0.99 (see Fig. 5), provided facilities, infrastructure and has improved a conducive environment to encourage the growth of the local creative industry (mean 3.62, SD 0.89) (see Fig. 6). In addition, the respondents satisfied with increasing in the diversity of assets provided for the creative industry in Malaysia (mean 3.52, SD 0.95) (see Fig. 7). In summary, based on the findings, the impact of the policy is not highly achieved for the economic growth of the country, and some improvements need to be implemented.

Table 5. Respondent's agreement on the Malaysian National Policy of Creative Industry.

No	Questions	Mean	SD	Result
1	I understand the National Creative Industry Policy (DIKN)	3.53	1.09	Agree
2	I referred to the National Creative Industries Policy (DIKN) to help me understand the scope of work	3.33	1.12	Neutral
3	DIKN is still relevant today	3.61	1.06	Agree
4	DIKN created a conducive environment by developing institutions, infrastructure, and financial support (incentives/funds/investments)	3.63	0.99	Agree
5	DIKN provides facilities, and infrastructure and has improved a conducive environment to encourage the growth of the local creative industry	3.62	0.89	Agree
6	The increase in the diversity of assets provided for the creative industry in this country is very satisfactory	3.52	0.95	Agree

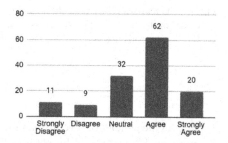

Fig. 2. I understand the National Creative Industry Policy (DIKN).

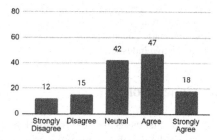

Fig. 3. I refer to the National Creative Industries Policy (DIKN) to help me understand the scope of work.

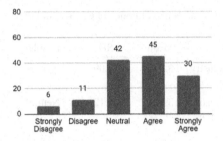

Fig. 4. DIKN is still relevant today.

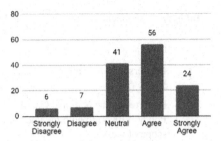

Fig. 5. DIKN created a conducive environment by developing institutions, infrastructure and financial support (incentives/funds/investments).

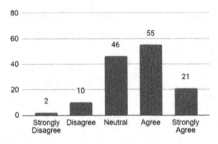

Fig. 6. DIKN provides facilities and infrastructure and improves a conducive environment to encourage the growth of the local creative industry.

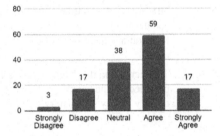

Fig. 7. The increase in the diversity of assets provided for the creative industry in this country is very satisfactory.

6 Conclusion

This study discusses the existing problems and compares the policies of several countries regarding the development of the creative industry sector. The results of this study will be able to identify the weaknesses of existing policies in Malaysia and suggest improvements in the scope of the field and propose a strategic framework to develop the country's creative industry sector. The survey results indicate that the policy has an average impact on the country's economic growth, and some improvements need to be implemented. The creative industry development can also increase and strengthen existing companies while opening space and career opportunities and further reducing the unemployment rate in Malaysia. Emphasis on the creative industry can help increase these industry players' number and level of expertise. Solid government and private support and a conducive environment can attract creative experts from outside to contribute their skills in this country. The creative industry offers more opportunities and job options regardless of background and educational level.

In conclusion, the findings from the three-stage approach relating to the creative industry policy and the survey indicate that some improvements are needed to the current policy in comparison with similar policies in other countries.

Acknowledgement. This research was supported by the Ministry of Higher Education (MoHE) of Malaysia through Consortium Research Excellence (KKP) Grant JP(BPKI)1000/016/018/25(63) under the Consortium on Creative Industry & Culture (CCIC), KKP.

References

1. ACPSA: Arts and culture grow for fourth straight year (2018). https://www.bea.gov/newsre leases/general/acpsa/2018/acpsa0318.htm
2. Ramsey, A.M.: Internasionalisasi budaya industri kreatif: studi komparasi cool Japan dan korean wave (Doctoral dissertation, Universitas Airlangga) (2018)
3. Throsby, D.: Cultural capital and sustainability concepts in the economics of cultural heritage. In: Economics of Cultural Heritage, pp. 101–117. Getty Conservation Institute (2002)
4. Harian, B.: Geran DIKN gagal pacu industri kreatif (2018). https://www.bharian.com.my/ber ita/nasional/2018/08/458672/geran-dikn-gagal-pacu-industri-kreatif
5. Bernama: Dasar industri kreatif negara perlu ditambah baik: Saifuddin (2020). https://www. bernama.com/bm/am/news.php?id=1845196
6. Abdul Rahman, R.: PTVM gesa kerajaan tambah baik dasar industri kreatif negara (2020). https://www.hmetro.com.my/rap/2020/05/584303/ptvm-gesa-kerajaan-tambah-baik-dasar-industri-kreatif-negara
7. Barker, T.: Dasar industri kreatif yang tidak kreatif (2020). https://www.projekmm.com/news/pendapat/2020/06/09/dasar-industri-kreatif-yang-tidak-kreatif-thomas-barker/1873809
8. Petrović, D., Milićević, V., Sofronijević, A.: Application of project management in creative industry. Eur. Project Manag. J. Udruženje za upravljanje projektima Srbije **7**(2), 59–66 (2017)
9. Maloney, N.: Understanding employability in the creative industries. In: Education for Employability, vol. 2, pp. 203–214. Brill Sense (2019)
10. Keinonen, A.: Managing for creativity and profit in creative industries: a case study in music industry (2020)
11. Sarji, A., Abdul Karim, N.K.: Kajian filem arahan pengarah muda sebagai saluran dakwah di malaysia. Representasi islam dalam media. Nilai: Universiti Sains Islam Malaysia (2011)
12. Ramdani, D., Hidayat, D.N., Sumarna, A., Santika, I.: Ideal character of Muslim generation of industrial revolution era 4.0 and society 5.0. Jurnal Iqra': Kajian Ilmu Pendidikan **5**(1), 171–182 (2020)
13. Negara, N.: Kepentingan industri kreatif pada negara (2019). http://www.nadinegara.com/uncategorized/kepentingan-industri-kreatif-pada-negara/
14. UNCTAD: Creative economy outlook: trends in international trade in creative industries (2019). https://unctad.org/en/pages/publications/Creative-Economy-Report-(Series).aspx
15. UNCTAD: Creative economy outlook: trends in international trade in creative industries (2010). https://unctad.org/en/pages/publications/Creative-Economy-Report-(Series).aspx
16. DCMS: Creative industries mapping document 1998 (2001). http://www.culture.gov.uk/ref erence_library/publications/4632.aspx
17. Kementerian Penerangan Komunikasi dan Kebudayaan (KPKK): Dasar industri kreatif negara (2010)
18. Shaari, N.: Indigenous knowledge creativity in batik cultural product based on Kansei. In: International Conference on Social Sciences and Humanities (ICSSH 2015), pp. 56–60. (2015). https://doi.org/10.15242/ICEHM.ED0515056
19. Ismail, N., Masron, T., Ahmad, A.: Cultural heritage tourism in Malaysia: issues and challenges. In: SHS Web of Conferences, pp. 01059-p.1–01059-p.8 (2014). https://doi.org/10.1051/shsconf/20141201059

20. Sarji, A., Ibrahim, F., Ramlee, S.: Industri dokumentari di Malaysia: Isu dan hala tuju. FINAS, Selangor (2009)

21. Ghazali, N., Md. Zain, A., Abdul Rahman, M.N.: Filem dokumentari jejak rasul pencetus inkuiri masyarakat malaysia dalam memahami sejarah Islam. Jurnal Sultan Alauddin Sulaiman Shah, Special Issue 2289–8042 (2018)

22. Sarji, A.: Perfileman dan kesannya terhadap masyarakat: Ke arah pengekalan dan penyuburan nilai-nilai murni masyarakat Malaysia. Jurnal Komunikasi **19**, 1–21 (2003)

23. Wirawan, R.: Aplikasi virtual iklan perumahan dengan sistem augmented reality. ILKOM Jurnal Ilmiah **10**(1), 11–16 (2018)

24. Ozturkcan, S.: Service innovation: using augmented reality in the IKEA Place app. J. Inf. Technol. Teach. Cases **11**(1), 8–13 (2020)

25. Roy, G., Shrivastava, A.K.: Future of gig economy: opportunities and challenges. IMI Konnect **9**(1), 14–27 (2020)

26. Metro, H.: Evolusi Teknologi Kraf (2019). https://www.hmetro.com.my/dekotaman/2019/02/426238/evolusi-teknologi-kraf-metrotv

27. Du, N., Yu, C.: Application and research of VR virtual technology in film and television art. In: 2020 International Conference on Computers, Information Processing and Advanced Education, pp. 108–114 (2020)

28. Bányai, F., Zsila, Á., Griffiths, M.D., Demetrovics, Z., Király, O.: Career as a professional gamer: gaming motives as predictors of career plans to become a professional esport player. Front. Psychol. **11**, 1866 (2020)

29. Al-Beitawi, Z., Salehan, M., Zhang, S.: What makes a song trend? Cluster analysis of musical attributes for spotify top trending songs. J. Mark. Dev. Competitiveness **14**(3), 79–91 (2020)

Author Index

N. H. Zakaria et al. (Eds.): ICOCI 2023, CCIS 2001, pp. 395–397, 2024.
https://doi.org/10.1007/978-981-99-9589-9